Population, Health and Development

PERSPECTIVES ON UTTARAKHAND

Editors

T.V. Sekher
Abhishek Singh
Sulabha Parasuraman

ACADEMIC FOUNDATION
NEW DELHI

www.academicfoundation.com

First published in 2013
by

ACADEMIC FOUNDATION
4772-73 / 23 Bharat Ram Road, (23 Ansari Road),
Darya Ganj, New Delhi - 110 002 (India).
Phones : 23245001 / 02 / 03 / 04.
Fax : +91-11-23245005.
E-mail : books@academicfoundation.com
www.academicfoundation.com

in association with

International Institute for Population Sciences

Cataloging in Publication Data--DK
Courtesy: D.K. Agencies (P) Ltd. <docinfo@dkagencies.com>

National Seminar on 'Population Environment and Development in Uttarakhand' (2008 : Dehradun, India)
Population, health and development : perspectives on Uttarakhand / editors, T.V. Sekher, Abhishek Singh, Sulabha Parasuraman.
p. cm.
ISBN 13: 9788171889464
ISBN 10: 8171889468

1. Uttarakhand (India)--Population policy--Congresses. 2. Medical policy--India--Uttarakhand--Congresses. 3. Women's health services--India--Uttarakhand--Congresses. 4. Sustainable development--India--Uttarakhand--Congresses. 5. Uttarakhand (India)--Social policy--Congresses. I. Sekher, T. V. II. Singh, Abhishek. III. Sulabha Parasuraman. IV. Title.

DDC 304.6095451 23

Typeset by Italics India, New Delhi.

Printed and bound by The Book Mint, New Delhi.
www.thebookmint.in

Contents

B. Fertility and Family Planning

C. Utilisation of Health Services

F. Urbanisation and Migration

G. Population and Development

List of Tables and Figures

Tables

Figures

Editors / Contributors

Editors:

T.V. Sekher, Associate Professor, International Institute for Population Sciences (IIPS), Mumbai.

Abhishek Singh, Assistant Professor, International Institute for Population Sciences (IIPS), Mumbai.

Sulabha Parasuraman, Former Professor, International Institute for Population Sciences (IIPS), Mumbai.

Contributors:

N. Audinarayana, Professor, Department of Sociology and Population Studies, Bharathiar University, Coimbatore.

Anup Badola, Consultant & Executive Director, Development & Research Institute for Social & Technical Education (DRISTE), Dehradun, Uttarakhand.

Suyash Badola, Research Scholar, Hemwati Nandan Bahuguna Garhwal (HNBG) University, Garhwal, Uttarakhand.

Dhananjay Bansod, Assistant Professor, Population Research Centre, Institute for Social and Economic Change (ISEC), Bangalore.

R.B. Bhagat, Professor, International Institute for Population Sciences (IIPS), Mumbai.

Anita Bhargava, Research Scholar, Jawaharlal Nehru University (JNU), New Delhi.

Bhagwan S. Bisht, Professor, Department of Sociology, Kumaun University, Nainital, Uttarakhand.

Jayanta Kumar Bora, Advanced Analytics, TNS Pvt. Ltd, Mumbai.

Chayan Roy Choudhury, Technical Coordinator (Monitoring), Urban Health Initiative, Lucknow.

Puspita Datta, Assistant Manager (Research), Population Services International, New Delhi.

Sujata Ganguly, Research Scholar, International Institute for Population Sciences (IIPS), Mumbai.

Nilabja Ghosh, Associate Professor, Institute of Economic Growth (IEG), Delhi.

Avishek Hazra, Assistant Programme Officer, Population Council, New Delhi.

D.C. Jain, Research Assistant, Regional Medical Research Centre for Tribals, Indian Council for Medical Research (ICMR), Jabalpur, Madhya Pradesh.

Sabyasachi Kar, Associate Professor, Institute of Economic Growth (IEG), Delhi.

Archana Kujur, Research Scholar, International Institute for Population Sciences (IIPS), Mumbai.

Subrata Lahiri, Former Professor, International Institute for Population Sciences (IIPS), Mumbai.

Hemkhothang Lhungdim, Associate Professor, International Institute for Population Sciences (IIPS), Mumbai.

R. Lusome, Assistant Professor, Department of Economics, Pondicherry University, Puducherry.

Sandhya Rani Mahapatro, Research Scholar, Population Research Centre, Institute for Social and Economic Change (ISEC), Bangalore.

Soumya Mohanty, Consultant, RCH-DC Division, Ministry of Health and Family Welfare, New Delhi.

Tilak Mukherji, Chief Mentor, Sigma Research and Consulting, New Delhi.

Dewaram A. Nagdeve, Associate Professor, International Institute for Population Sciences (IIPS), Mumbai.

Benoy Peter, National Manager, Knowledge Management, Population Services International, Bangalore.

Jalandhar Pradhan, Assistant Professor, Department of Humanities and Social Sciences, National Institute of Technology (NIT), Rourkela, Orissa.

C.P. Prakasam, Former Professor, International Institute for Population Sciences (IIPS), Mumbai.

Ravi Prakash, Manager (M&E), Karnataka Health Promotion Trust (KHPT), Bangalore.

C.V.S. Prasad, Senior Advisor, South Asia, ORG Center for Social Research, The Nielsen Company, New Delhi.

F. Ram, Director and Senior Professor, International Institute for Population Sciences (IIPS), Mumbai.

Manju Rani, Lecturer, Department of Economics, Government Degree College, Uttar Pradesh.

Manoj Kumar Raut, Consultant, United Nations Fund Population (UNFPA), Jaipur, Rajasthan.

Sanjay Rode, Assistant Professor, S.K. Somaiya College, Mumbai.

Satyaban Sahu, Project Officer (M&S), Pathfinder International, New Delhi.

Nandita Saikia, Assistant Professor, Population Research Centre, Institute of Economic Growth (IEG), Delhi.

Daliya Sebastian, Programme Officer (M&E), Technical Support Unit, Rajasthan State AIDS Control Society (RSACS), Jaipur.

Ravendra K. Sharma, Scientist 'B', Regional Medical Research Centre for Tribals, Indian Council for Medical Research (ICMR), Jabalpur.

Sandeep Kumar Sharma, Statistical Officer, Sir Sunderlal Hospital, Institute of Medical Science, Banaras Hindu University, Varanasi.

Suresh Sharma, Assistant Professor, Population Research Center, Institute of Economic Growth (IEG), Delhi.

U.V. Somayajulu, CEO, Sigma Research and Consulting, New Delhi.

H.C. Srivastava, Former Professor, International Institute for Population Sciences (IIPS), Mumbai.

Niharika Tripathi, Research Scholar, International Institute for Population Sciences (IIPS), Mumbai.

Sayeed Unisa, Professor, International Institute for Population Sciences (IIPS), Mumbai.

Narayan Prasad Uniyal, Department of Education, Hemwati Nandan Bahuguna Garhwal (HNBG) University, Garhwal, Uttarakhand.

Foreword

The International Institute for Population Sciences (IIPS) is a premier institution to impart education and training in Population Studies and to conduct programme oriented research in population, health and development. Over the years, IIPS has helped in building highly qualified professionals in the field of population and health in various countries. Many of the important studies undertaken by the Institute, like the National Family Health Surveys and District Level Household and Facility Surveys, have provided very valuable inputs for policy making in our country, apart from contributing significantly to the demographic and health research.

Every year IIPS organises a National Seminar focusing on certain states and themes. In 2008, we focused on the young state of Uttarakhand to address the developmental challenges, particularly population and health issues. The seminar organised by the Institute at Dehradun received an overwhelming response from researchers, policy makers and NGOs. The seminar was fully funded by the Ministry of Health and Family Welfare, Government of India. The Governor of Uttarakhand, Shri B.L. Joshi inaugurated the National Seminar and highlighted the need for collaborative and interdisciplinary research to understand multi-faceted dimensions of growth and development. The senior government officials also took active interest in the proceedings of the seminar. This book is a collection of 27 selected papers presented at the National Seminar. The papers addresses wide ranging issues in the context of Uttarakhand and have been grouped into seven broad categories : a) education, employment and income inequalities, b) fertility and family planning, c) utilisation of health services, d) gender issues, e) HIV/AIDS, f) urbanisation and migration and g) population and development. These papers provide excellent multidisciplinary analysis by making use of available data from various sources. I am sure, this volume will be of immense use to those interested in the developmental issues of Uttarakhand in general, and demographic and health aspects in particular.

I appreciate the efforts of the seminar coordinators, Dr. T.V. Sekher, Dr. Abhishek Singh and Prof. Sulabha Parasuraman for successfully organising the seminar as well as bringing out this edited book. I hope this book will provide helpful insights into the changes that are taking place in the state of Uttarakhand and also facilitate in better understanding of the complex relationships between population, health and development.

— Dr. F. Ram

Director and Senior Professor,
International Institute for Population Sciences, Mumbai

Message

The development of the state is closely linked with the physical and mental well-being of the people. The sustainable development and prosperity depends mainly on human well-being, literacy and environment. I am happy to note that the International Institute for Population Sciences have very well chosen the theme of 'Population, Environment, and Development of Uttarakhand' for this National Seminar. Though population and health indicators of Uttarakhand are better than many other states of this country, we have a long way to go and many things to achieve to ensure the desired standard of life for our growing population.

According to the National Family Health Survey-3 (NFHS-3) conducted in 2005-06 by the IIPS, shows that this state has achieved considerable progress with regard to many population and health indicators such as reduction in fertility, contraceptive use, maternal and child care, and nutrition status of women. According to this survey, the total fertility rate (TFR) has come down to 2.55 in the state as a whole and in urban areas it is 2.21, very close to the replacement level of fertility. The contraceptive prevalence rate in the state is nearly 60 per cent out of which overwhelming majority use modern methods of family planning. The unmet need for family planning has come down significantly from 21 per cent in 1998-99 to 11 per cent in 2005-06. Sixty per cent of the children are fully immunised and 45 per cent of the mothers received at least three antenatal care (ANC) visits during their last pregnancy. NFHS-3 also indicated that nearly 83 per cent of the men and 73 per cent of the women surveyed had regular exposure to media. However, the institutional deliveries are 36 per cent in the state as a whole and only 28 per cent in rural areas. Nearly 47 per cent of women in the reproductive age are anaemic. Making health service accessible to people living in small-sized villages in different terrain is a challenging task. Given its unique geographical features and topography, Uttarakhand has been witness to natural disasters like earthquakes, landslides, floods and forest fires. This necessitates the strong need to strengthen the capability of health system to provide immediate and effective response during disaster situations and natural calamities. The health system in the state faces several challenges including lack of sufficient human and financial resources, inadequate health infrastructure, and lack of transport and communication facilities.

I am happy to mention here that Uttarakhand is one among the few states that came out with a Health and Population Policy as early as 2002. The formulation of Health and Population Policy was a major step towards providing clear direction to the programmes and initiatives for improving health and family welfare services. State adopted a holistic approach while formulating its integrated Health and Population Policy. One of the objectives of the policy is to reduce the TFR to 2.1 by 2010. It also aims to reduce the crude birth rate (CBR) to 19.9 by 2010. We are well aware that population stabilisation cannot be achieved without the improvement in health status of people, particularly that of women and children. So the policy places special emphasis on integrated approaches to reach out to women, children, elderly and other disadvantaged sections of the society. To achieve the policy objectives, the government has been emphasising the need to strengthen the primary health care facilities, building partnerships with private and voluntary sectors, motivation and commitment of service providers at all levels, and an increased investment in social sector.

Every effort has been made to encourage people's participation in health and family welfare activities. In recent years, the government has been focusing on Panchayati Raj Institutions (PRIs) for the supervision and monitoring of essential services including primary health care and primary education.

The Uttarakhand government is fully committed to improve the health and quality of life of its people. We are very much aware of the regional disparities within the state and every effort will be made to provide quality health care services to the needy. Under the National Rural Health Mission (NRHM), the government has initiated various programmes. A state-level advisory board has been constituted under the chairmanship of the Chief Minister to periodically review and monitor the progress under

NRHM. District-level health advisory committees have been constituted at the *zilla panchayat* level with representation of all the stakeholders. In order to give maximum autonomy to district and community-level institutions, large number of Chikitsa Prabhandhak Samitis (hospital management committees) have been established and are fully functional. This has resulted in higher utilisation of health care services, better hygienic condition, and above all, greater satisfaction among the public. Sustained efforts are required over a period of time to educate people about their health rights, to improve the quality of services, and to influence direct and indirect determinants of health. This issue of health, population, environment and development are closely and integrally related. Needless to mention the higher quality of health status, we need to invest considerably on the provision of safe drinking water and adequate sanitation facilities, both in rural and urban areas.

I am sure, this seminar will address the existing health problems of the state as well as deliberate on the emerging health issues. I congratulate the IIPS, Mumbai for providing valuable data and information about population and health status of the state and its districts through the National Family Health Surveys (NFHSs) and District Level Household and Facility Surveys (DLHSs) under Reproductive and Child Health (RCH) project. We also expect that this seminar, focusing on Uttarakhand, will provide very useful analysis and inputs for addressing population and health concerns with specific suggestions for programme implementation. I eagerly look forward to fruitful discussions and deliberations which will be helpful for the policy makers and programme managers in the health and social sector.

— Shri B.L. Joshi,
Governor of Uttarakhand

Preface and Acknowledgements

The International Institute for Population Sciences (IIPS) organised a three-day National Seminar on 'Population, Environment and Development in Uttarakhand' during March 17th to 19th, 2008 at Dehradun. The issues of population, health and development are closely and integrally related. The purpose of the seminar was to examine these issues in detail with supportive evidence and to identify thrust areas for future investigation and action. The seminar also tried to sensitise the researchers and policy makers about the priority areas from the perspectives of people's changing aspirations and needs. About 200 delegates from various parts of the country attended the seminar and participated in the deliberations. This included policy makers, demographers, health specialists, social scientists and NGOs. This volume contains 27 selected papers from the seminar dealing with various issues of education, employment, income, population growth, fertility and family planning, maternal and child health, utilisation of health services, urbanisation and migration, population and development, HIV/AIDS and gender issues of Uttarakhand state. Most of these papers provide very detailed analysis at the state and district levels using available data from official statistics, National Family Health Surveys, District level Household and Facility Surveys, National Sample Surveys and Census of India. The volume also contains an overview paper on the emerging issues and challenges in population, health and development of Uttarakhand by incorporating recent evidences from the official statistics, sample surveys and the 2011 Census. We believe this edited book will serve as a ready reference material for those who are interested in health and developmental aspects of the Himalayan state.

We would like to acknowledge our sincere thanks to many institutions and individuals who have contributed to the organisation of the seminar as well as bringing out this edited volume. The Ministry of Health and Family Welfare, Government of India, generously financed the seminar. Prof. F. Ram, Director of IIPS, took active interest in the publication of this volume and extended all possible support. He also wrote the foreword for this book. Our sincere thanks to him. We are grateful to then Governor of Uttarakhand, Shri B.L. Joshi who inaugurated the National Seminar on 17th March 2008. The inaugural address of the Governor is also included in this volume. Senior government officials of Government of India and Government of Uttarakhand actively participated in the deliberations. Prof. S. Lahiri, then Officiating Director of IIPS took keen interest and extended necessary guidance and support in the organisation of the seminar. We are thankful to the paper contributors, chairpersons, discussants and media persons for their enthusiastic cooperation. The selected papers were reviewed by three experts: Prof. P.C. Saxena, Prof. S. Sivaraju and Prof. H.C. Srivastava, who offered valuable comments and suggestions. The research support and secretarial assistance were provided by Ms. Chaitra Todur and Ms. Archana Basu. We express our gratitude to all of them.

The publication of this edited volume is financially supported by the International Institute for Population Sciences and we are thankful to Prof. F. Ram, Director. Finally a word of special thanks to the Academic Foundation, New Delhi, the publisher of this volume. We hope the readers will find this book useful for the purpose of research, advocacy, policy formulation and programme implementation.

— T.V. Sekher
— Abhishek Singh
— Sulabha Parasuraman

Population, Health and Development in Uttarakhand

Issues and Challenges

T.V. Sekher and Niharika Tripathi

Introduction

Uttarakhand became the 27th state of Indian Union in 2000. It was carved out of the northwestern hilly region of the erstwhile state of Uttar Pradesh. It is divided into two broad regions—Garhwal and Kumaon. The state has 13 districts. Uttarakhand is primarily a mountainous state, as the plains constitute only 10 per cent of its total geographic area. The state is the part of the central Himalayas and most of the northern area comprises high ranges and glaciers and the lower ranges are covered by dense forests. This state spread over an area of 53,483 square kilometres, is the 18th largest state in India in terms of geographical area. But it has highly diversified topography and land use pattern. Seventy per cent of the population still lives in rural areas.

Since its formation, in terms of economic development, Uttarakhand is one of the fastest growing states. The Economic Survey of 2005 indicates that state has performed better than the all-India average in terms of growth of employment as well as growth of enterprises. Though the performance in recent years has helped in narrowing the gap with national average, poverty remains a serious concern particularly in rural areas. State is also threatened by considerable regional disparities. This has adversely affected the per capita income and social imbalance in Uttarakhand. The geographical divide between hills and plains, concentration of education, health and other infrastructure in the districts of plains are affecting the overall development of the state. Though the state is considered as economically fast growing among north Indian states, in reality, life remains largely rooted in villages. Vast majority of rural population lives on agriculture and related activities.

Based on the findings of the recent 2011 Census as well as other official statistics and sample surveys, we are presenting the socio-economic and demographic profile of the state here to provide a discussion on emerging scenarios and the way forward.

Population Growth and Distribution

According to the 2011 Census, the total population of Uttarakhand is 10 million among which 5.1 million are males and 4.9 million are females (Table 1). The most populated district in the state is Haridwar with a population of 19,27,029. The least populous district is Rudraprayag having 2,36,857 persons. Comparatively, the proportion of females is more in Almora, Bageshwar, Garhwal, Rudraprayag and Tehri Garhwal districts. In absolute terms, the population of the state has increased by about 1.6 million during the last decade. Uttarakhand contributes about one per cent (0.84) of India's total population in 2011 and holds 20th position in terms of population size among Indian states.

Table 1

Population Distribution in Uttarakhand: 2011

Districts	*Population*		
	Persons	*Males*	*Females*
Almora	621927	290414	331513
Bageshwar	259840	124121	135719
Chamoli	391114	193572	197542
Champawat	259315	130881	128434
Dehradun	1698560	893222	805338
Garhwal	686527	326406	360121
Haridwar	1927029	1025428	901601
Nainital	955128	494115	461013
Pithoragarh	485993	240427	245566
Rudraprayag	236857	111747	125110
Tehri Garhwal	616409	296604	319805
Udham Singh Nagar	1648367	858906	789461
Uttarkashi	329686	168335	161351
Uttarakhand	10116752	5154178	4962574

Source: *Census of India 2011*, Uttarakhand.

Table 2 presents a comparative picture of decadal growth rate and density of population in the districts of Uttarakhand for the years 2001 and 2011. It is significant to note that the percentage of decadal growth during 2001 to 2011 has recorded a decline from 20.41 to 19.17. The average annual growth rate of Uttarakhand was 1.77 per cent as against an all-India growth rate of 1.64 during the same period. Interestingly, there was negative growth recorded in Almora and Garhwal districts—-1.73 and -1.51 respectively. The growth rate has shown a decline in almost all the districts except in Dehradun and Haridwar. The population density has increased from 159 in 2001 to 189 in 2011. The all-India population density is 382 per sq km in 2011. The density of population influences the environment and ultimately the quality of life of people. There was considerable increase in the population density in some districts—Champawat, Dehradun, Haridwar, Nainital and Udham Singh Nagar. However, it decreased in Almora from 201 to 198 and in Garhwal from 131 to 129 during 2001 to 2011.

Table 2

Population Growth and Density in Uttarakhand: 2001 to 2011

Districts	*Decadal Growth Rate*		*Population Density (Per sq km)*	
	1991-2001	*2001-2011*	*2001*	*2011*
Almora	3.67	-1.73	201	198
Bageshwar	9.28	5.13	110	116
Chamoli	13.87	5.60	46	49
Champawat	17.60	15.49	127	147
Dehradun	25.00	32.48	415	550
Garhwal	3.91	-1.51	131	129
Haridwar	28.70	33.16	613	817
Nainital	32.72	25.20	179	225
Pithoragarh	10.95	5.13	65	69
Rudraprayag	13.43	4.14	115	119
Tehri Garhwal	16.24	1.93	166	169
Udham Singh Nagar	33.60	33.40	486	648
Uttarkashi	23.07	11.75	37	41
Uttarakhand	20.41	19.17	159	189

Source: *Census of India 2011* and *2001*, Uttarakhand.

Sex Ratio Scenario

Uttarakhand is one of the few states registering an upward trend in population sex ratio during the last decade. Interestingly most districts in the state have more number of females than males and also recorded a marginal increase (Table 3) over the years from 962 in 2001 to 963 in 2011. The districts of Chamoli, Dehradun, Haridwar, Nainital, Rudraprayag, Tehri Garhwal, Udham Singh Nagar and Uttarkashi show an increase over time. There was a decline in sex ratio in districts of Bageshwar, Champawat and Pithoragarh over time. However, the drastic decline in child sex ratio (0-6 years) in the state during the last decade is an extremely distressing trend. Though the overall sex ratio registered a marginal increase, child sex ratio declined to 885 from 908 during the same period. A huge decline in child sex ratio was found in the districts of Pithoragarh (902 to 812), Champawat (934 to 870), Rudraprayag (953 to 899) and Chamoli (935 to 889) during the last decade. However, the scenario is slightly better in rural areas (894) compared to urban areas of the state.

It is important to examine why female children are still at risk despite progress in education, increasing participation of women in economic and

Table 3

Sex Ratios in Uttarakhand (2001 to 2011)

Districts	*Population Sex Ratio*		*Child Sex Ratio (0-6 Years)*	
	2001	*2011*	*2001*	*2011*
Almora	1146	1142	933	921
Bageshwar	1105	1093	930	900
Chamoli	1016	1021	935	889
Champawat	1021	981	934	870
Dehradun	887	902	894	890
Garhwal	1106	1103	930	899
Haridwar	865	879	862	868
Nainital	906	933	910	891
Pithoragarh	1031	1021	902	812
Rudraprayag	1115	1120	953	899
Tehri Garhwal	1049	1078	927	888
Udham Singh Nagar	902	919	913	896
Uttarkashi	941	959	942	915
Uttarakhand	962	963	908	885

Source: Census of India 2011 and *2001*, Uttarakhand.

political activities and an overall improvement in the status of women? India is experiencing a significant shift from 'son preference' to 'daughter discrimination' during the last two decades (Sekher and Hatti, 2009). Girls have been aborted on a massive scale in recent decades simply because they are girls and this 'social epidemic' is spreading fast even to remote rural areas (Sekher, 2012). Uttarakhand is also no exception to this alarming trend (Figure 1).

Figure 1

Missing Girls? Changing Child Sex Ratio (0-6 Years) of Uttarakhand

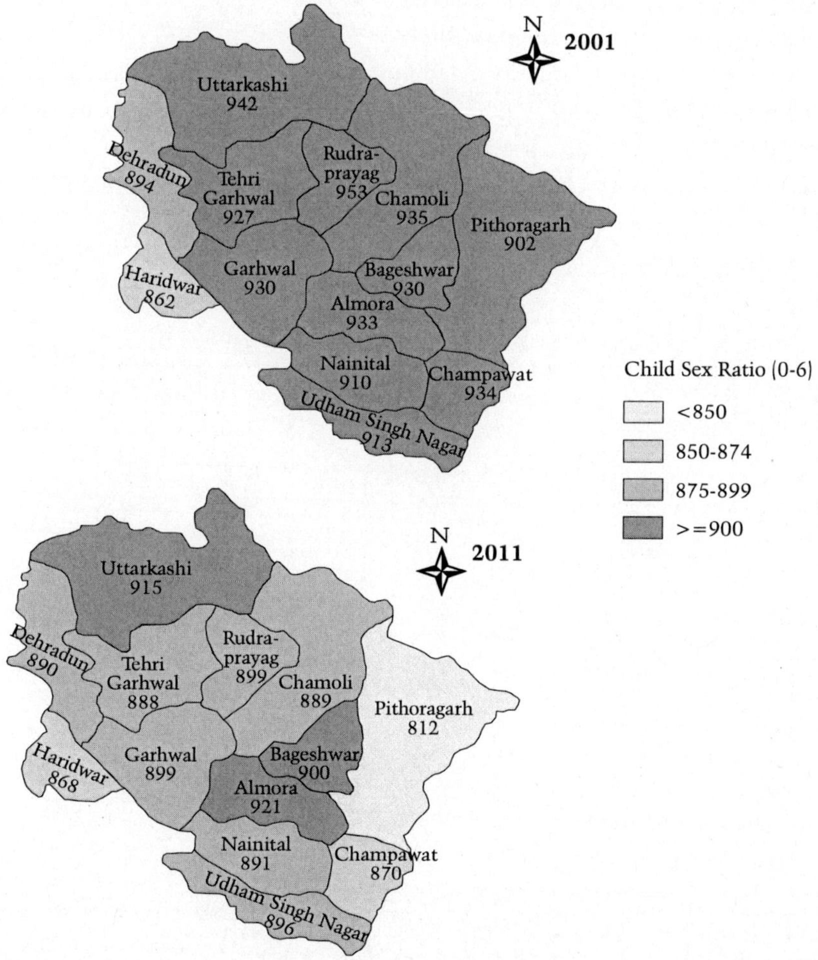

Literacy and Urbanisation

Literacy level is generally considered as a vital indicator of development in any society. The literacy rate of the state is close to 80 per cent, which is much higher than the national average of 74 per cent. However, it ranks only 17th among the states and union territories of India. These figures are much better than of Uttar Pradesh from which the state was formed. The overall literacy rate for the state has increased from 71.6 in 2001 to 79.6 in 2011. Interestingly, there was a considerable increase in female literacy from 59.6 in 2001 to 70.7 in 2011. Literacy rate is below 80 per cent in four districts—Haridwar, Tehri Garhwal, Udham Singh Nagar and Uttarkashi districts in 2011. Dehradun is the better performing district both in male literacy (90 per cent) and female literacy (80 per cent) in 2011 (Table 4). Udham Singh Nagar recorded the lowest literacy level in the state (74 per cent). The male-female gap in literacy level is 17.63 in the state, a considerable decline from 23.65 in 2001. Both Uttarkashi and Tehri Garhwal registered lowest figures in female literacy

Table 4

Literacy Rate: Uttarakhand—2001 to 2011

Districts	*Literacy Rate: 2001*			*Literacy Rate: 2011*		
	Total	*Male*	*Female*	*Total*	*Male*	*Female*
Almora	73.6	89.2	60.6	81.0	93.6	70.4
Bageshwar	71.3	87.7	57.0	80.7	93.2	69.6
Chamoli	75.4	89.7	61.6	83.4	94.2	73.2
Champawat	70.4	87.3	54.2	80.7	92.7	68.8
Dehradun	79.0	85.9	71.2	85.2	90.3	79.6
Garhwal	77.5	90.9	65.7	2.6	93.2	73.3
Haridwar	63.7	73.8	52.1	74.6	82.3	66.0
Nainital	78.4	86.3	69.6	84.8	91.0	78.2
Pithoragarh	75.9	90.1	62.6	82.9	93.4	73.0
Rudraprayag	73.6	89.8	59.6	82.0	94.9	70.9
Tehri Garhwal	66.7	85.3	49.4	75.1	90.0	61.8
Udham Singh Nagar	64.9	75.2	53.4	74.4	82.5	65.7
Uttarkashi	65.7	83.6	46.7	76.0	89.2	62.2
Uttarakhand	71.6	83.3	59.6	79.6	88.3	70.7

Source: *Census of India 2011* and *2001*, Uttarakhand.

(about 62 per cent). Though 2011 Census presents a highly encouraging picture, much needs to be done to improve the levels of literacy and educational attainment in the state, particularly in narrowing down the considerable gender gap.

According to the Census of 2011, 31 per cent of the state population resides in urban areas (Table 5). The least urbanised districts are Bageshwar (3.5), Rudraprayag (4.19) and Uttarkashi (7.35). Dehradun records the highest level of urbanisation (56 per cent) (Figure 2). However, the alarming increase in slum population is a matter of concern. Nineteen per cent of the urban population lived in slums in 2001. This also indicates the occurrence of considerable rural to urban migration in the state.

Table 5

Percentage Distribution of Rural/Urban Population: 2001-2011

Districts	*2011*		*2001*	
	Rural	*Urban*	*Rural*	*Urban*
Almora	89.98	10.02	91.35	8.64
Bageshwar	96.50	3.50	96.87	3.12
Chamoli	84.89	15.11	86.30	13.69
Champawat	85.21	14.79	84.95	15.04
Dehradun	44.10	55.90	47.06	52.93
Garhwal	83.59	16.41	87.10	12.89
Haridwar	62.23	37.77	69.16	30.83
Nainital	61.06	38.94	64.73	35.26
Pithoragarh	85.69	14.31	87.05	12.94
Rudraprayag	95.81	4.19	98.79	1.20
Tehri Garhwal	88.63	11.37	90.10	9.89
Udham Singh Nagar	64.42	35.58	67.38	32.61
Uttarkashi	92.65	7.35	92.23	7.76
Uttarakhand	69.45	30.55	74.33	25.66

Source: *Census of India 2011* and *2001*, Uttarakhand.

Figure 2

Levels of Urbanisation in Uttarakhand: 2011

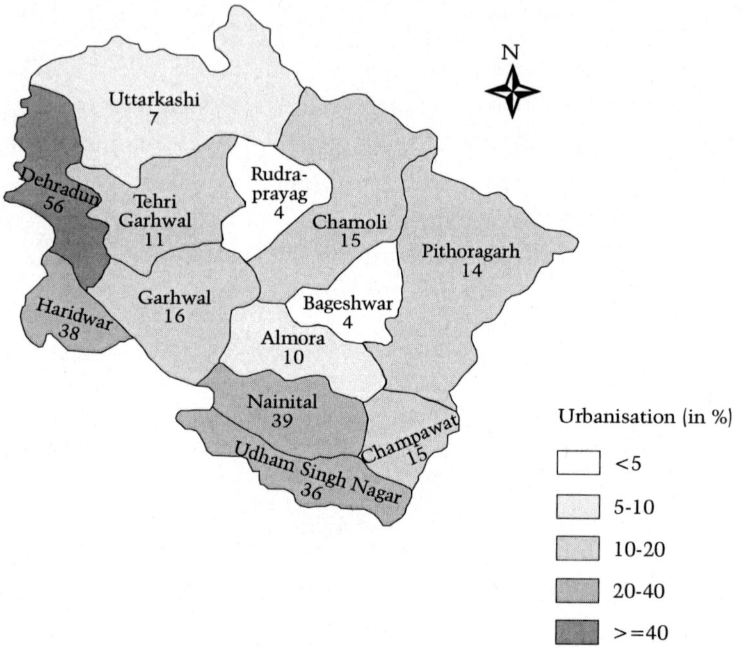

Household Assets and Characteristics

Table 6 depicts the housing characteristics by districts, based on District Level Household and Facility Survey (DLHS) conducted in 2007-2008. Nearly 83.4 per cent of the households in Uttarakhand has electricity connection. The situation is far better in districts of Dehradun, Haridwar and Udham Singh Nagar. Improved source of drinking water is accessible to 88 per cent of households in the state. In Haridwar, almost all the households are having the facility to avail drinking water. Toilet facility was available to only 53.2 per cent of households in the state. About 24 per cent of households used LPG for cooking in Uttarakhand. The use of LPG was more in districts of Dehradun (55 per cent), Nainital (42.5 per cent) and Udham Singh Nagar (31 per cent). According to DLHS-3, 56 per cent of households in Uttarakhand are living in *pucca* houses. The proportion was maximum in Pithoragarh (74.3 per cent) followed by Rudraprayag (71.4 per cent) and Dehradun (70.2 per cent). Approximately half of the households in Uttarkashi, Champawat and Pithoragarh districts are having BPL card. Nearly 34 per cent of households in the state reported as having BPL cards.

Table 6

Housing Characteristics by Districts: 2007-08

District	*With Electricity*	*With Drinking Water*[1]	*With Toilet Facility*[2]	*Using Liquefied Petroleum Gas*	*Living in Pucca House*	*Having BPL Card*
Almora	71.3	81.3	50.4	15.5	37.9	33.3
Bageshwar	80.2	77.4	51.0	14.6	51.6	39.2
Chamoli	82.0	85.2	45.4	18.3	64.1	34.7
Champawat	65.1	79.3	41.7	18.0	31.1	47.6
Dehradun	95.9	94.9	74.7	55.0	70.2	21.0
Garhwal	89.5	89.1	52.6	18.6	47.9	28.2
Haridwar	91.9	99.8	56.4	25.6	62.0	22.2
Nainital	88.2	90.5	77.5	42.5	61.0	22.5
Pithoragarh	74.8	86.3	48.2	26.3	74.3	45.6
Rudraprayag	89.7	91.0	52.1	14.7	71.4	37.7
Tehri Garhwal	83.5	81.7	54.3	22.2	54.7	38.6
Udham Singh Nagar	91.1	99.8	68.1	31.0	57.1	20.1
Uttarkashi	79.2	81.9	34.3	12.9	45.1	47.9
Uttarakhand	83.4	87.7	53.2	23.8	55.7	34.1

Note: 1 Includes piped into dwelling, piped to yard/plot, public tap/stand pipe/hand pump/tube well/ bore well/well covered/spring, tanker, cart with small tank and bottled water.

2 Households having access to toilet facility = improved source of sanitation + flush not to sewer/septic/pit/twin pit + pit without slab + dry toilet.

Source: IIPS (2010). *DLHS-3*.

The socio-economic status of the households can be indirectly assessed in terms of possession of consumer durables. More than 50 per cent of households in the state owned a television (47 per cent in rural and 83.5 per cent in urban areas); telephone (40.4 per cent of rural and 75 per cent of urban households); sewing machine (25.1 per cent of rural and 51.8 per cent of urban households), radio/transistor (27.1 per cent of rural and

23.8 per cent of urban households) and bicycle (12.7 per cent of rural and 28.6 per cent of urban households) (Table 7).

Table 7

Household Assets: 2007-08

Household Assets	*Ownership*	*Ownership (Percentage of Households)*	
		Rural	*Urban*
Radio/transistor	26.5	27.1	23.8
Sewing machine	30.1	25.1	51.8
Television	53.8	47.0	83.5
Telephone	46.9	40.4	75.0
Bicycle	15.7	12.7	28.6
Motor cycle/scooter	11.5	6.9	31.3
Car/jeep	3.0	1.3	10.1

Source: IIPS (2010). *DLHS-3*.

Availability of Basic Infrastructure

According to DLHS-3, almost all the villages in Uttarakhand were having either primary or middle school which provides a better scope for the schooling of children. Nearly 98 per cent of villages in the state have primary schools. About 52 per cent of the villages have middle schools and 29 per cent have secondary schools. Twenty-nine per cent of villages in Uttarakhand were having sub-centres and only 3.4 per cent of villages were having primary health centres (PHCs). The average population served by a sub-centre is 4801. Almost all the sub-centres have auxiliary nurse/midwife (ANM) in position. The percentage of villages having any government health facility is about 30 in the state. In three-fourth of the villages, accredited social health activists (ASHAs) are in position. The spread of *anganwadi* centres: Integrated Child Health Services (ICDS) is impressive. Eighty-four per cent of villages have *anganwadi* centres. However, the village health and sanitation committee (VHSC) is constituted only in 12 per cent of villages (Table 8).

Table 8

Availability of Facility and Health Personnel in Villages: 2007-08

District	Percentage of Villages with**							
	Primary/ Middle School	Sub-Centre	PHC	Any Government Health Facility[1]	Doctor	ASHA	Anganwadi Worker	VHSC
Almora	97.8	34.8	8.7	34.8	4.3	63.0	78.3	6.5
Bageshwar	100.0	16.7	0.0	16.7	2.1	81.3	72.9	29.2
Chamoli	93.0	37.2	0.0	37.2	7.0	69.8	76.7	18.6
Champawat	100.0	19.0	0.0	19.0	11.9	69.0	81.0	2.4
Dehradun	100.0	33.3	4.2	33.3	29.2	75.0	83.3	8.3
Garhwal	100.0	15.9	4.5	15.9	2.3	75.0	88.6	0.0
Haridwar	97.1	42.9	0.0	42.9	60.0	77.1	94.3	20.0
Nainital	100.0	37.5	3.1	37.5	18.8	87.5	87.5	9.4
Pithoragarh	97.7	34.1	4.5	34.1	4.5	77.3	77.3	9.1
Rudraprayag	91.8	40.8	6.1	40.8	18.4	71.4	89.8	18.4
Tehri Garhwal	100.0	22.2	2.2	22.2	8.9	60.0	80.0	8.9
Udham Singh Nagar	100.0	38.2	5.9	38.2	38.2	85.3	91.2	8.8
Uttarkashi	97.8	19.6	4.3	19.6	10.9	93.5	91.3	13.0
Uttarakhand	97.9	29.5	3.4	29.5	14.8	75.4	83.6	12.0

Note: ** Facilities are reported by village *pradhan/up-pradhan/panchayat* member/teacher/*gram sevak/ anganwadi* worker, etc.

1 Includes sub-centre, primary health centre (including block PHC), community health centre or referral hospital, government hospital and government dispensary within the village.

ASHA- Accredited Social Health Activist.

VHSC- Village Health and Sanitation Committee.

Source: IIPS (2010). *DLHS-3*.

Table 9 shows the rural health infrastructure (both facilities and personnel) of Uttarakhand as on March 2010. Overall, the state comprises of 1765 sub-centres, 239 PHCs and 55 CHCs. The average population served by these health facilities are 3575, 26403 and 114732 respectively. However, considerable shortage of male health worker (MHW), lady health visitor (LHV) and laboratory technician is reported from the state. Appointment of these health personnel will go a long way in improving the health facilities to rural population.

Table 9

Rural Health Statistics: Uttarakhand—2010

Health Facility	*Number*	*Average Population Served*
Sub-centre	1765	3575
PHC	239	26403
CHC	55	114732
Number of personnel	Required number	Staff in position
Auxiliary nurse midwife (ANM)	1765	1859
Male health worker (MHW)	1765	304
Medical officer (MO) (PHC)	239	234
Lady health visitor (LHV) (PHC)	239	137
Pharmacist (at PHCs and CHCs)*	294	267
Lab. technician (PHCs and CHCs)*	294	87

Note: * One each for PHCs and CHCs.

Source: Government of India (2010).

Social and Health Indicators for Women

An early age at marriage is an indicator of the low status of women in society. It curtails women's access to education, cuts short the time needed to develop and mature; it also has many negative health consequences. In India, the legally prescribed minimum age at marriage is 18 years for girls and 21 years for boys. According to DLHS-3 (2007-08), around six per cent of women in Uttarakhand get married before attaining 18 years. This is around 11 per cent in Haridwar and Pithoragarh districts. More than two-thirds of the births in Uttarakhand take place at home. Only 30 per cent of births are reported in any health facility (Table 10). This is one important aspect which needs immediate attention. Around 55 per cent of deliveries in Dehradun are institutional. The women's awareness regarding methods of family planning is almost universal in Uttarakhand. However, the contraceptive prevalence rate (CPR) is about 61 per cent. CPR is highest in Chamoli district (71.6 per cent) followed by Uttarkashi (70.3 per cent), Rudraprayag (69.3 per cent), Pithoragarh (68.6 per cent) and Nainital (66.8 per cent). In some districts, only half of the women are protected against unwanted pregnancy. Female sterilisation accounts for two-thirds of contraceptive use in the state. Condoms are the most commonly used spacing method. Traditional methods (rhythm and withdrawal) were used by only 2.3 per cent of couples (Figure 3). The unmet need for family planning (spacing and limiting) is 20 per cent in Uttarakhand. It was lowest in Uttarkashi (12.4 per cent) and highest in Champawat (28.9 per cent).

At current fertility levels, a woman in Uttarakhand will have an average of 2.6 children in her life time (IIPS and Macro International, 2008). Fertility in Uttarakhand is close to national average. However, significant differentials were observed in the fertility levels of women by education and economic status.

Table 10

Percentage Distribution of Women by Social and Health Indicators: 2007-08

Districts	*Marriage Below 18 Years*	*Institutional Delivery*	*Aware of Any Family Planning Method*	*CPR by Any Method*	*Unmet Need for Family Planning*
Almora	3.0	24.4	100.0	61.7	19.9
Bageshwar	5.7	17.0	98.8	53.6	26.2
Chamoli	0.1	31.7	99.9	71.6	13.9
Champawat	9.7	23.2	98.6	50.8	28.9
Dehradun	6.0	54.7	98.6	61.4	22.8
Garhwal	3.2	29.5	100.0	61.2	17.3
Haridwar	11.1	36.9	98.5	49.3	28.4
Nainital	2.2	31.9	99.1	66.8	15.3
Pithoragarh	10.7	24.3	99.4	68.6	15.2
Rudraprayag	5.6	20.9	99.8	69.3	14.9
Tehri Garhwal	5.6	25.1	99.7	57.2	21.8
Udham Singh Nagar	4.9	38.8	98.6	58.4	22.9
Uttarkashi	1.8	24.3	99.6	70.3	12.4
Uttarakhand	5.7	30.0	99.2	61.2	20.1

Note: CPR- Contraceptive Prevalence Rate.

Source: IIPS (2010). *DLHS-3*.

Figure 3

What Contraceptive Methods do Couples Use?

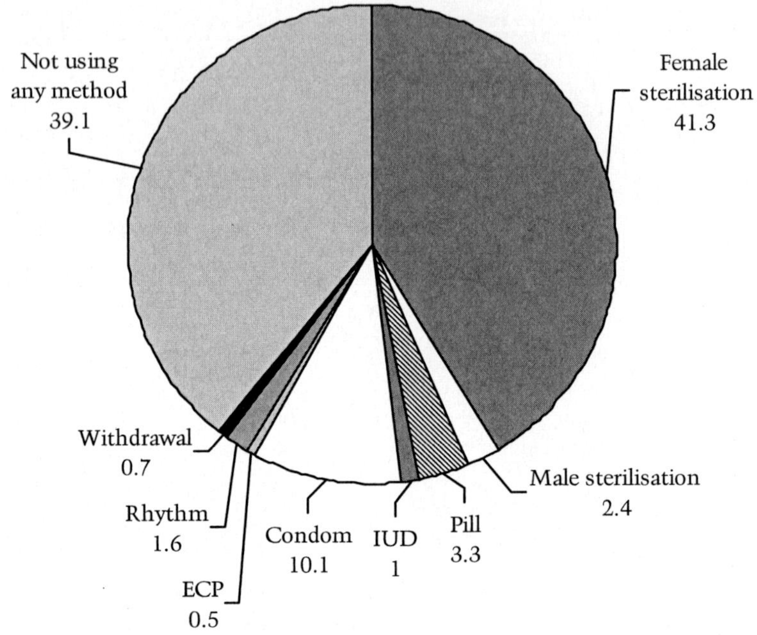

Note: IUD-Intra Uterine Device, ECP-Emergency Contraceptive Pill.
Source: IIPS (2010). *DLHS-3*.

Child Health Status

Around 63 per cent of children in Uttarakhand are fully protected against six major childhood illnesses: tuberculosis, diphtheria, pertussis, tetanus, polio and measles. However, seven per cent of children in the state never received any recommended vaccine. In Bageshwar, Garhwal, Haridwar and Nainital districts, more than 10 per cent of children did not receive any vaccine at all (Table 11). Vaccination coverage varies considerably across the districts (Figure 4). Undernutrition is a major problem in Uttarakhand. According to National Family Health Survey, 44 per cent of children under age five years were stunted, or too short for their age, which indicates that they have been undernourished for some time.

Thirty-eight per cent of children are underweight, which takes into account both chronic and acute under-nutrition. Adults of Uttarakhand also suffer from a dual burden of malnutrition. Thirty per cent of women and 28 per cent of men are too thin, and 13 per cent of women and 8 per cent of men are overweight or obese (IIPS and Macro International, 2008). The survey also indicates that more than half of the women in the state have anaemia. Among men, it is only 29 per cent. Undernutrition is particularly serious in rural areas.

Table 11

Child Health Indicators: 2007-08

Districts	*Vaccination*		*Children Received Colostrum*[a]	*Breastfeeding within One Hour of Birth*
	Full[1]	*No*[2]		
Almora	67.7	1.0	87.8	78.7
Bageshwar	53.5	10.0	62.0	50.5
Chamoli	59.6	3.9	91.7	75.6
Champawat	57.4	7.7	79.2	57.9
Dehradun	70.1	4.5	88.5	49.3
Garhwal	72.5	10.5	91.6	75.5
Haridwar	52.4	12.2	76.5	37.4
Nainital	61.5	11.0	90.6	66.4
Pithoragarh	58.8	2.2	88.3	73.1
Rudraprayag	69.5	2.3	86.8	80.5
Tehri Garhwal	73.4	5.1	86.5	73.1
Udham Singh Nagar	70.9	6.6	85.3	58.6
Uttarkashi	63.8	8.9	93.3	79.8
Uttarakhand	62.9	7.1	85.2	63.5

Note: Table based on youngest living child born since 01.01.2004.

a Yellowish thick milk secretion during the first few days after child birth.

1 Full vaccination includes BCG, three injections of DPT, three doses of Polio (excluding polio 'o') and Measles vaccine.

2 Children never received a single recommended vaccine.

Source: IIPS (2010). *DLHS-3.*

Figure 4

Level of Immunisation by Districts

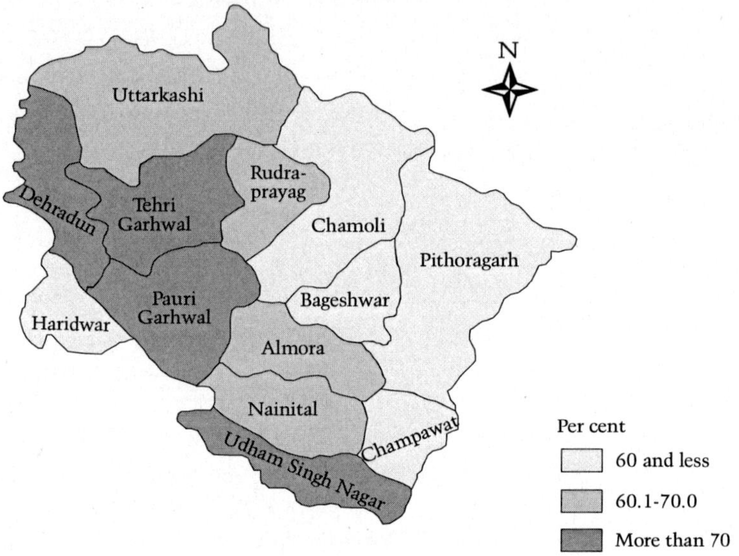

Source: IIPS (2010). *DLHS-3*.

State Health and Population Policy

In December 2002, Uttarakhand became the first state to formulate an integrated Health and Population Policy, which provided policy directions to initiate health reforms in the state. The processes followed to formulate the policy were open and participatory and involved different stakeholders. The overall mission of the policy includes efforts to improve the health status and quality of life of the population, alleviate inequalities in access to health care, address emerging health concerns and, eventually stabilise the population growth. The policy's key health and population objectives are listed in Table 12.

Table 12

Objectives of the Health and Population Policy 2002

Health objectives	• Eradicate polio by 2005. • Reduce the leprosy level per 10,000 population by 2004. • Reduce mortality on account of tuberculosis and vector-borne diseases by 50 per cent by 2010. • Reduce prevalence of blindness from 1 to 0.3 per cent by 2010. • Reduce the iodine deficiency disorder by 50 per cent by 2010. • Reduce reproductive tract infections by 50 per cent in men and women by the end of 2007. • Increase awareness of HIV and AIDS from the present 36 per cent to 70 per cent by the end of 2005. • Achieve zero level of growth in HIV infection by 2007 and launch curative care for those living with HIV. • Establish an integrated system of surveillance for health by 2007. • Increase state health spending to 8 per cent by 2010.
Population objectives	• Reduce the total fertility rate from the current estimated level of 3.3 to 2.6 by 2006 and further to 2.1 by 2010. • Reduce the crude birth rate from 26.0 in 2001 to 22.6 in 2006 and further to 19.9 by 2010. • Increase the contraceptive prevalence rate from 40 per cent to 49 per cent by 2006 to 55 per cent by 2010. • Reduce infant mortality rate of 50 per 1,000 live births to 40 by 2006 to 28 by 2010. • Reduce the child mortality rate of 19 per 1,000 live births to 17 by 2006 and further to 15 by 2010. • Reduce the maternal mortality ratio to 250 per 100,000 live births by 2006 and further to below 100 by 2010. • Increase life expectancy at birth from 63 years in 2001 to 67 years in 2006 to 70 years in 2010.

Source: Government of Uttarakhand (2002).

The Health and Population Policy outlines 28 policy interventions that address organisational issues, planning, finance, training, service delivery and quality, women's empowerment, equity, and other concerns. The ultimate purpose of the policy is to make people understand their health needs and rights so that they follow risk-free behaviour and seek quality health care whenever required. The thrust of the policy is to improve access to and quality of health services with the help of strategic planning and innovative approaches.

The Way Forward

The population and health indicators of the people of Uttarakhand are better than many Indian states. However, the health system in the state faces several challenges in providing sufficient, appropriate and quality health service delivery. This includes a scattered population widely dispersed over difficult terrain, inadequate infrastructural facilities and lack of both human and financial resources. Making education and health services accessible to people living in small-sized villages in a mountainous terrain is a daunting task. Though considerable improvements were observed during the last one decade after the formation of the state, the persisting regional disparities particularly between hills and plains is a matter of great concern. The integrated Health and Population Policy of the state (2002) was a major milestone and provided goals, strategies and guidelines for necessary action. Some of these goals were achieved through innovative approaches undertaken by the state by addressing infrastructure deficiencies, increasing accessibility and availability of health care services and enhancing the quality of health care. However, more can be achievable through strengthening decentralised planning and implementation, convergence of services, appropriate institutional arrangements and better partnerships with private providers.

References

Government of India (2009). *Uttarakhand Development Report*. New Delhi: Planning Commission and Academic Foundation.

———. (2010). *Rural Health Statistics in India*. New Delhi: Ministry of Health and Family Welfare.

Government of Uttarakhand (2002). *Health and Population Policy of Uttarakhand*. Dehradun: Department of Medical Health and Family Welfare.

International Institute for Population Sciences (IIPS) (2010). *District Level Household and Facility Survey (DLHS-3), 2007-08: India: Uttarakhand*. Mumbai: IIPS.

International Institute for Population Sciences (IIPS) and Macro International (2008). *National Family Health Survey (NFHS-3), India, 2005-06: Uttarakhand*. Mumbai: IIPS.

Mehta, G.S. (1996). *Uttarakhand: Prospects of Development*. New Delhi: Indus Publishing Company.

Office of the Registrar General of India (2011). *Provisional Population Totals of Uttarakhand*. New Delhi: Government of India. Available at: *http://censusindia.gov.in/2011-prov-results/paper2/prov_results_paper2_uttrakhand.html*

———. (2001). *Census of India*. New Delhi: Government of India. Available at: *http://www.censusindia.gov.in/Census_Data_2001/Census_Data_Online/Area_Profile/District_Profile.aspx?cki=M9YHf7vSKXj*

Sekher, T.V. and Neelambar Hatti (eds.) (2009). *Unwanted Daughters: Gender Discrimination in Modern India*. Jaipur: Rawat Publications.

Sekher, T.V. (2012). "Rural Demography of India", in L.J. Kuksar and K.J. Curtis (eds.), *International Handbook of Rural Demography*. New York: Springer.

USAID, Health Policy Initiative, Task Order 1 (2009). *The Health and Population Policy of Uttarakhand: A Review-Aplication of the Policy Implementation Assessment Tool*. New Delhi: Futures Group, U.S. Agency for International Development (USAID).

Appendix

Table A-1

Literacy Rates: Rural-Urban Differentials

Districts	*2011*		*2001*	
	Rural	*Urban*	*Rural*	*Urban*
Almora	79.46	94.78	71.81	91.67
Bageshwar	80.30	91.37	70.79	86.68
Chamoli	81.72	93.10	73.41	87.58
Champawat	80.23	83.51	68.62	80.05
Dehradun	80.01	89.24	70.51	86.19
Garhwal	81.21	89.57	75.91	87.79
Haridwar	69.66	82.45	57.15	77.38
Nainital	84.02	86.13	76.26	82.10
Pithoragarh	81.30	92.51	73.74	90.19
Rudraprayag	81.73	89.88	73.53	82.38
Tehri Garhwal	73.40	88.00	64.48	86.07
Udham Singh Nagar	72.97	77.08	61.82	71.00
Uttarkashi	74.90	89.12	63.84	86.61
Uttarakhand	77.11	85.20	68.07	81.44

Source: *Census of India 2011* and *2001*, Uttarakhand.

Table A-2

Population Sex Ratio: Rural-Urban Differentials

Districts	*2011*		*2001*	
	Rural	*Urban*	*Rural*	*Urban*
Almora	1180	848	1189	774
Bageshwar	1100	926	1116	810
Chamoli	1073	771	1073	715
Champawat	997	895	1055	849
Dehradun	924	884	913	863
Garhwal	1145	915	1155	820
Haridwar	886	867	874	844
Nainital	947	911	921	877
Pithoragarh	1040	916	1065	823
Rudraprayag	1143	697	1127	443
Tehri Garhwal	1117	816	1108	627
Udham Singh Nagar	930	901	915	875
Uttarkashi	969	838	961	725
Uttarakhand	1000	883	1006	844

Source: *Census of India 2011* and *2001*, Uttarakhand.

Table A-3

Child Sex Ratio (0-6 Years): Rural-Urban Differentials

Districts	*2011*		*2001*	
	Rural	*Urban*	*Rural*	*Urban*
Almora	926	859	936	880
Bageshwar	903	823	932	837
Chamoli	898	833	944	857
Champawat	878	821	945	856
Dehradun	915	866	918	865
Garhwal	906	862	940	844
Haridwar	873	859	861	865
Nainital	896	881	919	890
Pithoragarh	825	731	911	824
Rudraprayag	903	789	953	865
Tehri Garhwal	894	830	932	865
Udham Singh Nagar	900	888	923	891
Uttarkashi	922	801	952	783
Uttarakhand	894	864	917	871

Source: *Census of India 2011* and *2001*, Uttarakhand.

A. Education, Employment and Income Inequalities

1 Education for All in Rural Himalayas

A Study of Uttarakhand

Suresh Sharma and Nilabja Ghosh

Introduction

The decade of the 1990s is noted for some landmark initiatives with regard to the economy and society in India and in many developing countries. Not least among them is the goal of extending primary, elementary or other school education to the common people, especially in the vast lagging rural regions. The emphasis laid on school education is a policy initiative with radical implications. Many imbalances that arise at higher levels of education and employment and are further reflected in consequences such as poverty, lawlessness, class prejudices and poor levels of living, can be corrected by promoting universal quality education at the school level. Also, desirable attitudes towards society, gender and environment can be infused in society only by the exposure of the citizens to a well-planned and balanced curriculum from an early and formative stage. It is now increasingly being recognised that education is a 'capability' (Sen, 1999; 2003) and that 'investment in man' may be considered even more important than physical and tangible capital formation (Myrdal, 1957; 1968). The sources of modern economic growth may be found more in the changing quality of labour and capital than in the accumulation of conventional units of physical capital and in increased application of hours of labour (Kuznets, 1966).

The National Education Policy and the UNDP's inclusion of education as an important component of human development provided an impetus to this important aspect of development in India. The 1990s, often described as Education For All decade or the EFA decade, witnessed unprecedented dynamism in the spread of school education. As in all development programmes, the inequalities that are found imbedded in Indian society were kept in focus while drawing up suitable policies and designing programmes. It is pertinent for the nation at this point to examine how this important indicator of development has performed in terms of progress and inclusiveness.

This paper contributes to the literature by assessing the performance of the country in terms of educational diffusion and identifying the lingering areas of unevenness in the achievement so far attained even after the EFA decade using the data available for the state of Uttarakhand in North India. This state is mountainous and has areas that are difficult to access but it is a relatively progressive Indian state in terms of education and literacy. The study makes special reference to females especially among backward classes. After sketching the background to the topic under question, the paper presents a brief overview of the progress of literacy and infrastructural development achieved by the state in a comparative perspective. Based on primary data collected from three districts in the state, the spread of school education is further examined across generations, gender and sections. Both school entry (enrolled) and completion (retention) are considered as indicators of the success of school education. The complexities of unevenness are further exposed with spatially disaggregated analyses for identifying policy focus.

Background

The Indian Constitution mandated free and compulsory education for all children up to the age of 14. At that point of time, the literacy rate was just 18 per cent. The gross school enrolment ratio of only 43 per cent at the primary stage held little promise for the future of literacy. More appalling were the corresponding figures for literacy and enrolment specific to females, reported respectively at 9 per cent and 25 per cent. The gender bias against the female sex was not just by itself an indicator of social inequality but was also a further prophesy of the slow progress that the country was to make in the field of education in the coming years.

Yet, the goal of universal primary education was not pursued with the vigour it demanded. The 1991 Census of India brought out the shameful reality after nearly four decades that half of the 'population', above 7 years of age, still remained illiterate. Half of the 6-14 years old children were either not enrolled in schools or were dropouts there from. The failure of the state to educate the country's children was more glaring among the poor and the backward castes, among women, and in regions that were geographically disadvantaged or difficult to access. Needless to say that as the state dragged its feet; the rural people bore the major brunt of this negligence. The backward castes, the women and the people in remote areas continued to be among the most deprived. It is tragic that basic education remained the right of only the privileged sections.

The 1990s was a watershed decade for education in India. First, the Supreme Court of India (Unnikrishnan case, 1993) declared basic education as a fundamental right of the citizen. Second, after having been shackled to bureaucracy for years, education especially in rural and remote regions saw new light with the decentralisation process ushered by the 73rd and 74th Amendments of the Constitution. Finally, primary education gained importance the world over especially when the urgency of targeted social welfare measures found recognition in the structural adjustment programmes with a so-called 'human face'. The decade followed the announcement of a National Education Policy in India. The policy, declared in 1986, outlined the strategies to be pursued to achieve universal elementary education (UEE). External assistance for primary education following the Jomtien Conference further enhanced the motivation. 'Operation Blackboard' and the 'Sarva Shiksha Abhiyan' are state-sponsored movements that popularised the notion of education as the emergent need of the hour.

Women's education, health and empowerment in general have gained emphasis in recent decades. Further, the gender issue is increasingly being viewed as a part of sound economics rather than simply as a moral commitment in Indian planning. It is widely believed that female literacy is negatively related to fertility, population growth, infant and child mortality and is positively related with the marriage age and life expectancy of women, female participation in the modern sectors of the economy and also the future female enrolment in school (Govinda, 2002). It is inextricably linked to the status of women in rural India and with the overall empowerment of women (National Policy of Education 1986, 1992). Following the United Nations Decade for Women, Indian plans had begun to address women more as human resources and participants in development and less as targets of welfare since 1975. Taking advantage of the constitutional empowerment to practice protective discrimination in favour of women, the states have been drawing up several schemes and incentives to encourage education of the girl child.

Infrastructure, institutions and innovative schemes are all part of the effort to spread education. Attention has been directed to the access to school especially in rural and remote areas by building schools within a reasonable distance of habitation and by providing at least 2 classrooms in each primary school with separate toilets for boys and girls. Primary education cannot be denied due to physical distance. Recruitment of teachers is promoted where necessary. The whole focus of the development is on backward areas and classes while girls are encouraged for enrolment and discouraged from dropping out. Democratisation, transparency and efficiency of operations are attempted through initiatives like provision of elected management, decentralisation of management and involvement of *panchayats* and local bodies. Measures are taken to provide incentives not only for school enrolment but also for attendance and retention. The *panchayat* sometimes provides scholarships for attendance. The mid-day meal, a scheme modelled after a constituent state's (Tamil Nadu) successful School Lunch Programme, is meant to encourage school attendance while also improving food security. A minimum reservation in public and unaided schools for the weaker sections and free education for the single girl child are other schemes under active consideration.

Literacy

The literacy rate is a single minimum measure of the educational achievement of a community. Uttarakhand itself was part of the large state of Uttar Pradesh that had a poor standard in social development. Uttar Pradesh had a literacy rate of only 12 per cent against India's 18 per cent in 1951 measured by the definition used by Census 2001. In the EFA decade, literacy rate in India has improved from 52.2 per cent in 1991 to 65.4 per cent in 2001. Despite its daunting topography, disadvantages and its historical links to Uttar Pradesh, Uttarakhand largely a mountainous state cradled in the Himalayas ranks high among the most literate states in the country with a literacy rate at 72 per cent reported in 2001. Literacy in Uttarakhand, is reported to have been at 57.75 per cent even in 1991,[1] more than the all-India level. The new state of Uttarakhand now has a trifold strategy of achieving 100 per cent enrolment rate and 100 per cent retention and has a continuous education programme. The people of the state have been credited for their progressive attitude (Joshi, 1995) and awareness of a better life, environment and autonomy. Uttarakhand ranks third in India in 'education development and achievement at the elementary level' (*India Today* survey, 2005).

Figure 1.1

Literacy in Uttarakhand: 2001

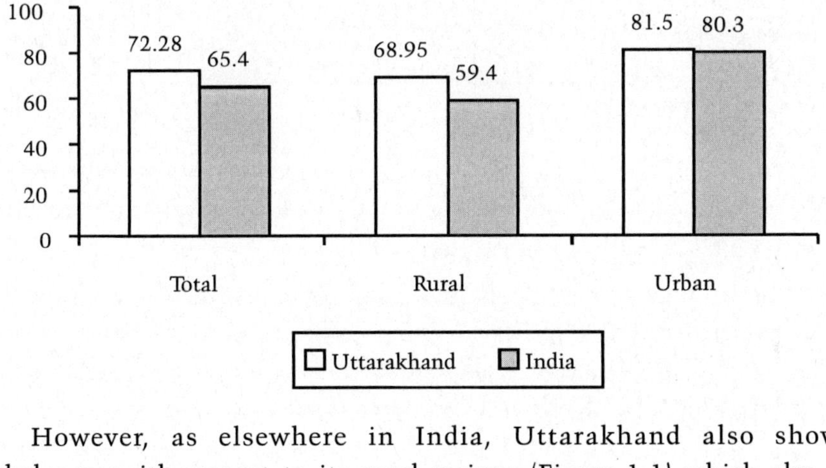

However, as elsewhere in India, Uttarakhand also shows imbalances with respect to its rural regions (Figure 1.1) which also in

1. Literacy rate of the newly formed state of Uttarakhand is estimated separately at 19 per cent for 1951 (*Economic Survey 2004-05*), even then above the national average.

general coincide with the hilly segments of the state. Table 1.1 further brings out the progress of literacy in Uttarakhand calculated by using the Census data along with the gender imbalance. The female literacy rate inched upwards in the decade 1951 to 1961 from 4.8 per cent to 7.8 per cent but 1971 showed more significant improvement and in 2001, the female literacy rate stood at 60 per cent. During the same period, from 1951 to 2001, the male literacy rate improved from 32 per cent to a relatively impressive 84 per cent. However, due to a change in the definition of literacy rate itself, the universal literacy goal also shifted upwards.

Table 1.1

Progress in Literacy in Uttarakhand

Year	*Total*	*Male*	*Female*
1951	18.93	32.15	04.78
1961	18.05	28.17	07.78
1971	33.26	46.95	18.61
1981	46.06	63.35	25.00
1991	57.75	72.79	41.63
2001	72.28	84.01	60.26

Source: Government of Uttarakhand.

With the gender gap still wide, the male literacy rate being 1.4 times that for females, the importance of encouraging girls for education cannot be over-emphasised.

The literacy rate, though important as a minimum measure has only a limited capacity to capture school education in its entirety or at various stages of education. Different levels of education through school can be associated with various dimensions of awareness and capability and the success of the school system will be largely reflected not just by the enrolment but also by its ability to retain students till completion. Such detailed information are not reported by the Census. The National Family Health Survey (NFHS-2), an alternative and smaller (sample) survey conducted by the International Institute of Population Sciences in 1998-99 also found (Table 1.2) similar gender and sectoral (rural-urban) dimensions at various levels. At the lower stages of education, the rural sector is ahead of the urban sector. The urban sector has a higher share of its population educated in the higher brackets, middle school onwards for male and high school onwards for females. The gender gap is glaring in the rural sector. For males, the share of high school completed members is about double that for females. The gap in the case of middle school completed members is nearly as wide.

Table 1.2

Percentage Distribution of the Household Population by Education Level: Uttarakhand

Background Characteristics	*Urban*	*Rural*	*Total*
Female Education			
Illiterate	18.8	44.8	38.9
Literate, incomplete primary school	13.1	19.0	17.7
Primary school complete	14.9	16.6	16.2
Middle school complete	11.1	9.0	9.4
High school complete	10.1	5.9	6.8
Higher secondary complete and above	32	4.8	10.9
Male Education			
Illiterate	9.6	13.5	12.6
Literate, incomplete primary school	19.5	23.1	22.3
Primary school complete	11.4	21.3	19
Middle school complete	8.9	16.9	15
High school complete	13.4	12.9	13
Higher secondary complete and above	37.4	12.1	18

Source: NFHS-2, 1998-99.

Infrastructure and Facilities

The All India Education Survey conducted by the National Council of Educational Research and Training (NCERT) makes it possible to examine the progress in school education, especially in primary education through its information on infrastructure, access and adoption. In Uttarakhand, the hilly landscape of the state and the scattered nature of the village population are an obstacle to the creation of any social infrastructure. Nevertheless, with the expansion of schools, in rural areas, Uttarakhand now has a primary school covering every 506 persons and school coverage (including higher schools) is 375. The pupil to teacher ratio is also favourable at 28. Table 1.3 shows that Uttarakhand compares well with all India and neighbouring states in having a higher (more than 100 per cent) enrolment ratio, lower pupil-teacher ratio, better gender balance in schooling and higher growth rate of schools at the primary level.

Table 1.3

Comparative Statistics on School Education (Primary)

	Enrolment Ratio		*Pupil/ Teacher*		*% Increase Over 1993*		*Girls % Enrolment*	
	Rural	*Total*	*Rural*	*Urban*	*Rural*	*Urban*	*Rural*	*Urban*
Uttarakhand	105	104	29	27	37	62	49	46
UP	88	88	61	36	48	49	36	45
Himachal	111	112	22	23	42	1	48	44
India	92	93	44	36	13	24	47	47

Source: NCERT, 2002.

The provision of schools within the habitations or at least within a short distance helps to improve the access available to rural children. Although the access is significant, more than 80 per cent of habitations having a primary school within a 1km radius, a large number of households still lack this basic education infrastructure in easy reach for the young children (Figure 1.2).

With the lack of transport, the distance poses a problem for education, especially for girls whose safety is a concern for the families. At the upper primary stage, the access is not as good and the largest section (71 per cent) have schools outside the habitations but within 3 km. More than 70 per cent of all schools are primary schools in the rural areas. Girls account for more than 40 per cent share of enrolment.

Figure 1.2

Access to Primary Schools (% Habitation)

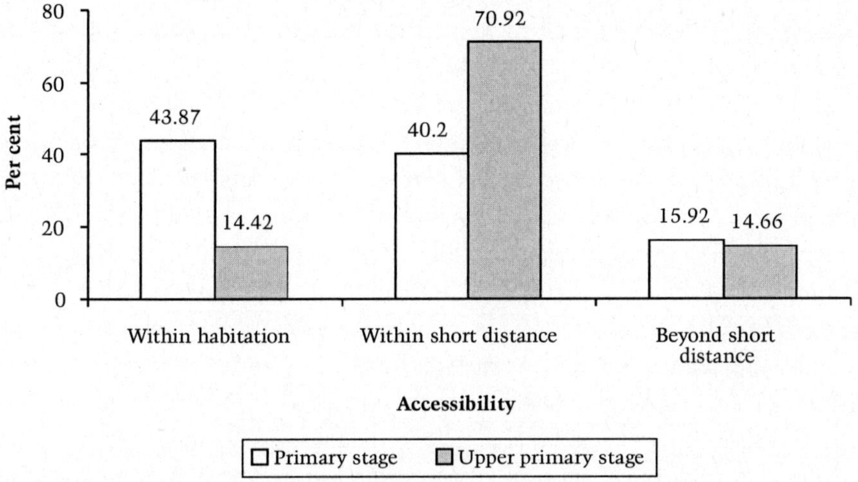

Note: Short distance measures 1 km at primary stage and 3 km at upper primary stage.

Table 1.4

Enrolment and Infrastructure in Schools in Three Districts

Performance	*Level*	*Uttarkashi*	*Nainital*	*Dehradun*
Net enrolment ratio	Primary	84.8	35.2	51.5
	Upper primary	37.5	20.0	21.3
% Schools with single classroom	Primary only	2.4	5.5	5.3
	Upper primary + Secondary	0.0	0.0	0.0
% Schools with girls toilet	Primary only	11.1	59.7	29.2
	Upper primary + Secondary	37.8	42.1	74.5
% Schools with drinking water	Primary only	76.8	73.2	78.5
	Upper primary + Secondary	86.5	68.4	98.0
% Schools without blackboard	Primary only	4.6	2.3	1.2
	Upper primary + Secondary	5.4	21.1	3.9

Source: NCERT, 2002.

Table 1.4 presents certain indicators of school infrastructure in the three districts Uttarkashi, Nainital and Dehradun along with the net enrolment ratios. Enrolment is found to be highest in the higher altitude, hilly and rural district of Uttarkashi followed by Dehradun, the most urbanised district that includes the capital city, while Nainital comes last. Considering the different physical and social infrastructural indicators of schooling facilities, diversity exists in performance. Nainital falls short with respect to measures such as the proportion of schools with 'only one classroom', with available 'supply of drinking water' and with 'blackboards'. In general, primary schools without blackbroad are low in share in all cases. Uttarkashi comes first with respect to the absence of 'girls' toilet' (only 11 per cent) and Dehradun performs better than at least one other district in all indicators and in fact leads in 'supply of drinking water', 'possession of blackboard' and of 'girls' toilet' at upper levels. The proportion of schools with 'girls' toilet' are not impressive; the highest shares recorded are at only 60 per cent at the primary level and over 74 per cent at the higher level. Comparing the varying ranks across indicators, infrastructure problem seems to be most acute in Nainital followed by Uttarkashi and are least present in Dehradun. Incidentally, Nainital lags behind both in infrastructure and in enrolment and that may be reflective of a nexus between the two measures.

Sampling Method and Result of Regression Analysis

A survey was conducted in June-July 2004[2] to study the socio-economic status of the state of Uttarakhand (Ghosh *et al.*, 2006). Census data from 1991 giving details of the districts is used as a frame. Three leading districts are chosen purposively avoiding contiguity. These are Dehradun from the west, Nainital from the east and Uttarkashi from the northeast, Uttarakhand being roughly a triangular shaped state. All these districts include both hill and plain regions but higher altitudes abound in Uttarkashi followed by Nainital. The districts also present a relatively balanced picture of occupational pattern spread over agriculture, manufacturing, trade and services. Census data of 1991 on industrial classification was consulted in making the choice and none of the chosen districts has been newly created or reorganised[3] in recent years.

2. The survey was done by the authors as part of a nation-wide study on rural development sponsored by the National Institute of Rural Development, Hyderabad.
3. Rudraprayag, Bageshwar, Champawat and Udham Singh Nagar are thé new districts carved out of pre-existing districts in recent times and information on these specific areas are obviously not found in earlier censuses.

To select the villages in the rural sector, the first step was to select one urban centre (UC) from each district and then choose six villages clustered around each of them. Since the proposal was to survey 30 households in each village, a cut-off number of 45 households was considered desirable. In order to give due consideration to the importance of urban influence that may vary across villages, they are chosen at increasing distances from the UC in the following way. The Village and Town Directory, 1981 (latest available) is used in this regard. All the villages within a radius of about 45 km of the UC are grouped as following remoteness categories: (1) least remote –1 to 10 km from the UC, (2) remote – 11 to 20 km from the UC, and (3) most remote – 21 or more[4] from the UC. Two villages are then chosen from each remoteness category. All villages considered feasible on the above counts are compared in terms of their shares of population engaged in the non-primary sectors, namely manufacturing, trade and services and in the agricultural sector. One village representing a high share in the non-primary sectors and one representing a low share in the same but reasonably high share in agriculture is chosen in each case.

The village population is then stratified by occupation of the household.[5] A random sample of 30 households is drawn from a village giving a total of 180 households surrounding each UC and 540 households for the rural sector. Questions regarding educational status are then canvassed from members of all ages in the households.

Findings from the Sample Survey

The first hand overall picture that emerged during the household survey was fairly positive for school education, especially elementary education. Nearly all households had access to primary schools in the villages. The availability however, weakened at higher stages and some households complained about the remoteness of a high school from the

---

4. Usually this category ranges from 31 to 40 km. In the case of a large district Uttarkashi with little urbanisation, there appear to be villages inhabited but remote from the nearest UC. The range has therefore crossed the 40 km mark.

5. Medium and big farmers, small and marginal farmers, artisans, agricultural and non-farm labourers, self-employed in business, services, household industries, etc., government employees, workers in rural unorganised sector, others.

village. This problem was accentuated by the transport difficulty in the hilly regions and the complaint was more pronounced in the case of girl students. In particular, girl students were found keen to seek higher education and future employment prospects and no significant attitudinal bias was fortunately apparent against female education that might have characterised past generations. Other information on social attributes is also collected including age, sex and social class.

In analysing the data, the population covered is classified into age groups with 10-year intervals. For the purpose of the study, only members aged between 10 years and 70 years are considered for the present analysis. The successive age groups are often referred to as generations. Second, the level of schooling is considered to represent educational status. For this purpose, various levels of attainment of schooling are considered and a particular emphasis is given to the status 'non-schooled' for members who have not been to school at all. This status is however viewed in the analysis as a particular stage. Similarly, the members who have gone for higher education beyond school level are assumed to constitute another stage. The typically school educated members are further divided into the following intervals-primary, class 8 and school passed (higher secondary). It may be noted that the school stage for children need not imply the maximum education attained but may simply imply the current engagement. In any case as mentioned, the very young children, mostly children not yet going to school or those in the primary school stage are excluded from the sample for simplicity.

The proportion of the population who have never been to school is first considered as an indicator of progress in school education. While the indicator conveys little information about the extent of achievement or quality and dimension of education, yet it gives some idea of the success of the state in motivating and drawing children to school. Figure 1.3 tells us that each generation of age group in the sample has shown improved performance over its previous counterpart, tracing a gradual process of diffusion of schooling practice.

Figure 1.3

Gender Gap in Schooling over Time

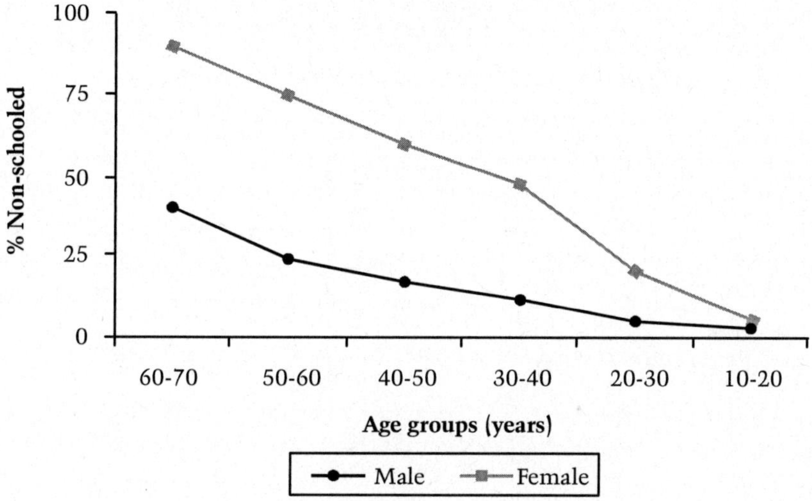

The figure also displays a wide historical gender gap. In fact, in the highest age group considered i.e., 60 to 70 years, nearly 90 per cent of the women in the sample did not even make a beginning in schooling, while about 40 per cent of the men had not been to school. As the social order gradually changed along with state intervention in infrastructure creation, female schooling did show improvement. A female belonging to any age group was more likely to have been in school at least sometime in her life than another female in the higher age group. However, among females in the higher age brackets, those who spent the early childhood in pre-independent or newly independent India, show relatively little improvement in respect of schooling compared to males in whose case the dynamism was obvious. The most visible break in the curves appears to be for females between the age groups 30-40 and 20-30. The latter group constitutes members who are most likely to have been in the more relevant age in EFA decade. Males too showed improvement in this range but the change was not that significant. The gender gap showed signs of convergence. Starting from the age group 30-40, it narrowed considerably in the group 20-30 and has nearly vanished in group 10-20. The gender gap was a shadow cast on an otherwise progressive state and its eradication would certainly mean a remarkable achievement.

Table 1.5

Schooling Level Completed by Age Groups

Age (years)	*60-70*	*50-60*	*40-50*	*30-40*	*20-30*	*10-20*
Females						
No school	89.7	74.7	59.5	47.4	20.9	5.5
Primary	9.2	11.6	22.8	16.2	13.9	13.7
8th class	0	6.8	7.9	15.4	12.0	33.2
School pass	1.1	5.5	7.0	14.6	33.0	41.6
Higher education	0	1.4	2.8	6.4	20.2	6.0
Males						
No school	39.6	24.2	17.1	11.9	4.9	3.0
Primary	27.7	27.5	17.1	15.6	7.9	20.4
8th class	18.8	15.7	18.1	16.3	16.7	34.3
School pass	10.9	25.5	33.7	39.0	47.9	39.0
Higher education	3.0	7.1	14.0	17.2	22.6	3.3

Source: Based on author's calculation.

For many decades, while schooling remained far from universal in society in general, the women mostly stayed away from schools. From Table 1.5, it seems that the 90s decade seems to have ended this exclusion. Whereas taking the girl child to the school precinct itself appears as a commendable accomplishment for the state, a more challenging and meaningful task is that of retaining the student through the various stages till completion or further into higher education. The focus has been on encouraging and motivating the girl student to carry on despite the difficulty of coping and managing the intellectual pursuit against the backdrop of a deprived family history, call for domestic commitments even marriage at early ages, safety concerns and a general discriminatory attitude arising mostly from a male-dominated traditional employment environment. Figure 1.4 again depicts an inter-generational picture of the progress of females.

Figure 1.4

Level of School Education among Age Groups in Females

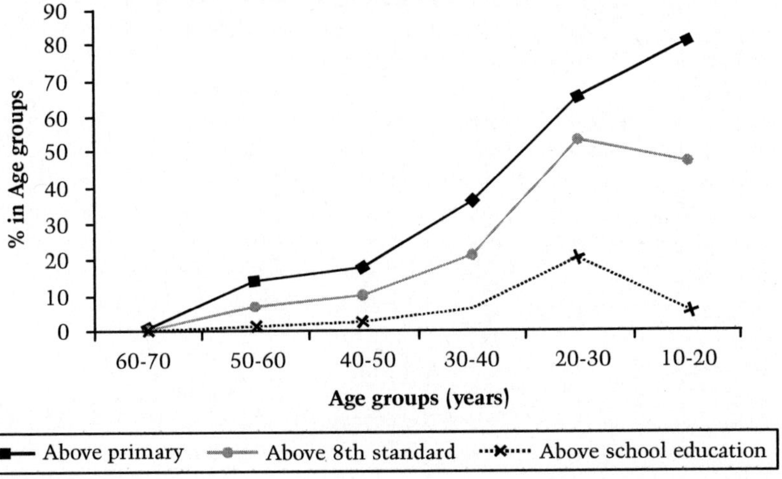

More women have crossed the primary stage of schooling in the youngest generation than others and the achievements of successive groups indicate the progress in diffusion of primary education. A similar progress is noted in higher education though not more than 20 per cent of the 20-30 years age generation has completed school. The downswing in the 10-20 year age group is probably due to the dominance of younger children in the set. The fall in the percentage attaining at least up to class 8 observed in the 10-20 years group compared to the earlier 20-30 years group may be, though less confidently said, explained by the same reason. What comes out is that till the age group 20-30 years, progress is observed at all stages of school education.

Having observed the achievement in female school education, Figure 1.5 examines how inclusive this education has been by comparing the proportion of the non-schooled among minority group females called the Scheduled Caste[6] (SC) with that of all females in the sample.

6. The other minority group, the Scheduled Tribe (ST) population is negligible in the state.

Figure 1.5

Non-Schooling among Females by Social Castes: All and Scheduled Caste (SC)

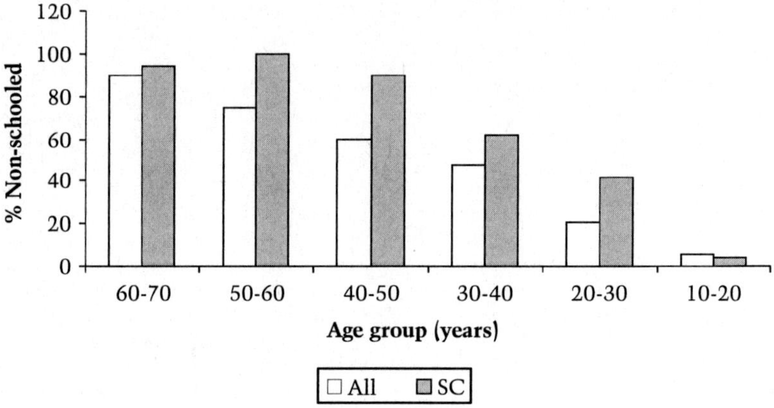

The gap is relatively low in the highest age group in which both categories record an above 80 per cent incidence reminiscent of an age when girls cutting across all castes avoided school. The gap emerged between the classes with the 50-60 years age group and persisted all along. Only in the lowest age group 10-20 portraying the current school goers is there convergence. Even in the 20-30 years age group, the proportion of non-school goers among SC is twice as large as that for all classes together. The effort to expand school education cannot stop at targeting females but a further focus on backward castes within females must continue to receive priority.

Statistical Testing

The caste and gender based disparities in accessing a minimum level of schooling, as measured from the sample proportions, can be subjected to statistical testing of the differences between the unknown population proportions. The null hypothesis that the proportions of members who are not schooled are same between the genders is tested against the alternative that the proportion is higher in case of females. The Z value is computed as below:

$Z_{ij}=d/\sigma_D$ where $d= p_i - p_j$

It can be mathematically represented as

$H_0 : P_i = P_j$

and $H_1 : P_i > P_j$

where i stands for female and j for male in the test of gender disparity and in test of caste-based disparity, i stands for SC females and j for General caste females.

Where p_i and p_j are the sample proportions, σ_D is the standard deviation of the population difference in proportions. This again is estimated using the weighted average of the sample proportions as an estimate for the unknown population proportion. The process is repeated for each age group. The same test is used to examine if the proportion is higher among SC communities than other women.

Given the large samples, we test for the significance of the Z values (standard normal variables) at 5 per cent and 10 per cent levels in Table 1.6. Since the Z values are less than 2.33 only for select age groups, the null hypothesis is rejected in other cases. The differences are found highly significant except for the lowest age group in case of gender and for the lowest as well as the highest age groups in case of SC women.

Table 1.6

Statistical Test for Education Disparity between Gender and Caste by Age Groups

	Gender Disparity		*Caste Disparity (Female)*	
Age Group (Years)	$p_i - p_j$	Z_{ij}	$p_i - p_j$	Z_{ij}
10-20	.025	1.95*	.016	0.86
20-30	.16	7.29**	.295	6.77**
30-40	.355	9.16**	.298	4.01**
40-50	.424	8.83**	.422	5.04**
50-60	.505	8.73**	.337	3.64**
60-70	.501	7.09**	.070	0.87

Note: ** significant at 1 per cent level, * significant at 5 per cent level.

Explaining the Attainments

To examine the unevenness in the diffusion of school education in rural Uttarakhand, a modeling exercise involving qualitative data has been attempted. In this case, information that is collected about the members belonging to rural households of the three districts is pooled and are categorised to reflect the educational achievement. The regression model considers certain social attributes and will bring out the specific role of each such attribute considering that the other attribute as given.

Variations in the school educational attainment are explained empirically using simple logistic models that incorporate dummy dependent variables used for qualitative data. School enrolment and retention are both addressed; first by considering the event of non-schooling examined against the composite event of schooling as a base in Model 1 and then considering the event of school completion against the event of incomplete schooling in Model 2. The binary logistic models used in the two cases are as follows:

Model 1
Y = 1, if an individual is non-schooled
Y = 0, otherwise.

Model 2
Y = 1, if an individual has completed schooling (class X)
Y = 0, otherwise.

The probability of the event $P_1 = P(Y=1)$ is as usual described by a logistic function and the odds are defined by,

$P_1/P_0 = \exp(\beta' X)$....1,

Where X is a vector of attribute variables describing the individual and β is a vector of parameters b_j, showing the direction of relation. The value of β itself being hard to interpret, exp (b) is presented in Table 1.7 indicative of the factor of change of the odds due to a unit changes in explanatory variables. Thus, $\exp(b_j) = 1$ signifies that the odds that an individual is non-schooled (relative to being schooled) in model 1 or school completed in model 2 is not affected by a change in variable X_i.

Explanatory Variables and Results

The explanatory variables denoted by vector X characterise the individuals by their relevant social attributes. To capture the generational dimension of the variations, age of the member was considered as a continuous variable. A quadratic term with age was also initially considered but omitted as it expectedly failed to show any relevant impact. The residential location of the individual can be important as backwardness as well as government efforts to mitigate the same are usually not uniformly dispersed. The distance from the nearest UC represents the location and can have an effect on school education through government effort as also spontaneous influence of urban life on society. The 'distance' is also taken as a continuous variable. A quadratic term of distance is retained allowing for the possibility that the most remote areas ideally enjoy priority in public efforts. Another locational variable is the specific district of residence as there can be wide spatial disparity of development even within the state. The 'district' is treated as a categorical variable with Dehradun as the base so that the effects of the other two districts come out only as a comparison to the base. Uttarkashi located at a higher altitude than others, has an undulated and hilly terrain and faces natural hazards. Nainital is a more accessible district with a railway station and major parts in the plains, while Dehradun in which the capital city of the state is located, is known for its industries and institutions of repute. Thus, the districts differ by their geographical, political and economic attributes.

The 'sex of the member' is a binary categorical variable with female as the base. Society in India is highly segregated with considerable overlapping of 'caste' and 'religion' based demarcations with levels of economic affluence. To explore the impact of the social status on education, 'caste' and 'religion' are taken to be categorical variables. Based on the composition of the sample, three castes namely, general, SC and other backward classes (OBC) are considered, with SC as the base. The groups SC and OBC are backward castes though only the SC enjoyed reservation so far. For 'religion', similarly, Hindu, Muslim and Sikh are taken and the last category is the base. Muslims and Sikhs belong to the minority in India. The estimated parameters and other statistics relating to the two models are presented in the Tables 1.7 and

1.8. Appendix Table A-2 provides the estimated odds ratios as exponents of the coefficients.

With 'gender' as a primary interest in this study, the significant and large negative value corresponding to the sex variable is noted as a sign of stark gender unevenness lingering in the system. A male is found merely 0.11 times (9 times) as likely to be not schooled (schooled) as a female is in the entire sample given all the other attributes. To the extent this draws from the neglects of past years, the unfortunate outcome is yet an unavoidable shadow captured in the present sample of pooled generations. To understand if the pooling and the past realities are entirely responsible for the result, the same model is estimated over varying and progressively younger samples. The results only corresponding to the gender variable of interest are reported in Appendix Table A-3, which discovers that the negative sign fails to disappear. However, the coefficient magnitude has come down from 2.169 for the entire sample covering age group from 10 to 70 years progressively as the sample becomes smaller to -0.590 for the sample age group 10 to 20 years, indicating a slow but certain improvement in the gender disparity that yet lingers. The coefficient is significant in each case though in the youngest sample group the male is less likely (.55 times) to be unschooled than the female but the coefficient is significant at 10 per cent rather than 0.1 per cent as in higher-age samples. Thus, the gender gap in schooling has the tendency to narrow down but iniquity is not removed even in a very young sample.

The binary model affirms that chances that a member is not schooled as against being schooled increases with age representing the generational gap due to historical reasons. The same chance is considerably less for males than females capturing the persisting gender gap. Despite the commendable progress observed, the inter-generational result represents the societal deprivation of earlier age groups that happily have got corrected through time and possibly draws attention towards adult education while the result pertaining to the gender disparity sadly captures the effect of a bias against female education that lingered through time.

'Religion' and 'caste' are also societal dividers in which Muslims appear as less privileged than Sikhs; even Hindus and general and OBC

Table 1.7

Explaining Variations in School Education among Members: Logistic Model

	No Schooling				*Schooling Completed*			
	Age Group—10 Years to 70 Years		*Age Group—10 Years to 20 Years*		*Age Group—10 Years to 70 Years*		*Age Group—20 Years to 30 Years*	
	Coefficient (b)	*Exp (b)*	*Coefficient (b)*	*Exp (b)*	*Coefficient (b)*	*Exp (b)*	*Coefficient (b)*	*Exp (b)*
Age	0.95	1.10	.185	1.20	-0.38	.962	-.127	.881
Distance from Nearest Urban Centre								
Distance	.079	1.08	.029	1.03	-.047	.954	-.072	.931
Distance^2	-.002	.998	.000	1.00	.001	1.00	.002	1.00
Sex (Female as Base)								
Male	-2.17	.114	-.590	.554	.769	2.156	.937	2.55
District (Dehradun as Base District)								
Uttarkashi	.406	1.50	-.318	.727	-.470	.625	-.352	.704
Nainital	.037##	1.04	.389	1.48	-.319	.727	-.221##	.802
Religion (Sikhs as Base)								
Hindu	.022##	1.02	-1.67	.188	-.361	.697	-.370##	.691
Muslim	2.001	7.40	1.17	3.215	-2.210	.110	-2.759	.063
Caste (SC as Base)								
General	-1.44	.238	-1.127	.324	1.119	3.062	1.579	4.850
OBC	-.397	.672	-.828	.437	.267	1.306	.833	2.300
% Correct	85.6		95.7		67.7		71.9	
Prediction	R2=.50		R2=.24		R2=.22		R2=.27	

Note: ## not significant at 1 per cent level but significant at 10 per cent level; Others coefficients are significant.

caste appear to be more likely to be schooled than SC. 'Location' is also found important. The influence of 'urban' life is evident since persons in remote villages appear deprived though the relation shows a quadratic pattern with the effect of distance from nearest town slowing down. The districts also vary in performance, Uttarkashi the hillier district being the most backward and Dehradun, the capital city leading.

Mere enrolment in a school may be an achievement as a beginning but retention says more about the success of the system in educating people. Considering completion of schooling as the dependent variable, the results are consistent and move in line with the earlier result on minimum schooling.

To focus on development in recent years and for recent generations, the regression analysis is conducted in Table 1.7 for a narrower range of age group, 10 to 20 years for the no-schooling case and 20-30 years for the schooling completed case. In the case of no schooling, the changes in coefficient signs are few in number while in the schooling completed case, there are none. The magnitudes have however changed. In the case of age, the impact of generation has come down for both indicators. The gender effect is impressively lower for no schooling though such improvement is not noticed in the case of schooling completion. Among the districts, the order itself changed and Uttarkashi performs better than base Dehradun in schooling and Nainital's position deteriorated with the coefficient becoming significant. Muslims continue to lag but Hindus gained in schooling.

The empirical analysis based on sample age group between 10 to 70, however is based on a presumption that no migration takes place after schooling age so that the sample capture the facilities of the sampled region. This is mostly true for men as our survey experience showed that households in the patriarchal society of the area are long-term residents but in the case of women this may not be true. Women above certain ages may have moved in due to marriage. This possibility is largely avoided in the second regression equation for no schooling (though not completely ruled out as the average marriage age is below 20). In the case of schooling completion, this limitation could not be avoided and we go by the presumption that the sample districts represent the state and (as supported by our general experience during survey) that the majority of the married women in villages hail from other villages, mostly neighbouring, of the state.

District Level Results

The policy directions indicated by the study of the pooled data from three districts related to the usual disadvantaged sections based on gender, caste, religion and distance. Traditional areas of unevenness persist and need to be addressed even in the new century. To examine finer variations over space, the regression analysis is conducted separately at the district level. This is also mandated by the known geographical heterogeneity among the districts in Uttarakhand. Table 1.8, which presents only the exponents of the coefficients of the equations estimated show little variety in the results. The equations and signs given in Appendix Table A-4 however illuminate a few subtle differences.

The distances or remoteness factor based on the proximate UC does not have the same impact on schooling. In Nainital and Dehradun, the effects of distance on education are all statistically insignificant. Distance from UC appears as a significant variable in Uttarkashi. Sikh population is present mainly in Nainital (11.03 per cent of rural population as per Census 2001) so for the other two districts, Muslim is taken as the base. In Nainital, differences among religious groups do not appear significant but in Dehradun, Muslims lag in education. In Uttarkashi, the Hindu population is dominant and the minority Muslims do not appear left behind educationally. Among the castes, 'general caste' and the OBC community also seem to be less 'unschooled' and more 'school completed' with aberrations only in the case of Nainital, but the differences between OBC and SC are normally insignificant. Age, as expected, is a significant variable for both non-schooling and school completion. The gender variable however remains significant in the usual direction in all cases. In Uttarkashi, a male is only 0.04 times likely as a female to be non-schooled. In other districts, the probability is higher at 0.16. Similarly, the male in Uttarkashi is nearly thrice as likely as a female to have completed school. The ratio is fairly high in Nainital and Dehradun at 1.9.

Table 1.8

Explaining Variations in School Education among Members District-wise (10-70 Years): Exp (β)

	No Schooling			Schooling Completed		
	Uttarkashi	*Nainital*	*Dehradun*	*Uttarkashi*	*Nainital*	*Dehradun*
Age	1.110	1.105	1.10	.957	.965	.963
	Distance from Nearest Urban Centre					
Distance	1.102	1.010	.930	.953	.905	1.031
Distance^2	.998	1.001	1.001	1.001	1.003	.999
	Sex (Female as Base)					
Male	.037	.166	.161	2.95	1.909	1.890
	Religion (Sikhs as Base Religion for Nainital and Muslims for Uttarkashi and Dehradun)					
Hindu	16.032	1.260	.047	.401	.516	23.191
Muslim		1.534			.286	
	Caste (SC as Base)					
General	.359	.213	.130	2.95	2.279	5.07
OBC	.402	1.671	.435	3.32	.420	1.72
Constant	.001	.019	2.25	2.22	3.268	.024

Source: Based on authors' calculation.

Conclusion

Education is a social good that confers multiple benefits on the subjects along with external and inter-generational dividends. In India in recent decades, commendable infrastructure is created for providing school education in the districts. However, as with many social goods, the diffusion of school education is far from uniform and has marked generational, gender, class and locational disparities. This analysis based on secondary and primary data from the hilly state of Uttarakhand reveals that even in a relatively advanced state in India where commendable recent development initiatives in infrastructure, institutions and innovative schemes have been observed with respect to school education, there is yet considerable unevenness among various sections of people. In particular, there is yet significant disparity in schooling attainments between male and female and between social castes among the females in various age groups. However, on a positive front, the analysis also affirms that recent endeavours have helped to narrow down gender disparities in a reversal to past tendencies. However, the task is hardly accomplished.

The regression analysis using the qualitative data indicates that traditional lags and disadvantages are still glaring with respect to location, gender and social class. Females are found trailing behind conspicuously in respect of schooling and fall behind males in schooling up to various stages. Uttarkashi, the hilly and remote district, has the lowest level of schooling while the capital district, Dehradun emerges as the most privileged one exposing a familiar geography-based inequality. The proximity to an urban centre improves schooling reflecting adversely on the balanced development aims of the country. Minority religion Muslim and SC population are disadvantaged in conformity with traditional concerns while the general or the majority caste leads for all schooling levels. The generational gap is an unavoidable truth bearing testimony to past neglects. Analysing the data separately for the three districts, we found subtle distinctions that need to qualify any policy focus. Nainital calls for a spatial attention in schooling development and Dehradun for an attention to religious communities. SC communities are underprivileged in all cases and OBC community is not significantly better-off.

Since education at the school level is a social good with potentials for both private and social benefits, it is the duty of the governments and particularly the newly instituted local level governments to emphasise inclusiveness in school education if the objective of 'Education for all' is to be pursued. That minority religions, backward castes, remote villages and less accessible and relatively underdeveloped districts deserve extra attention is a well-known dictum that is again salvaged from the data even at this stage. Above all, the gender dimension possibly remains the most glaring and draws attention towards the disadvantaged female class who embodies the other attributes of weakness also. The age dimension can be addressed to some extent through the adult or non-formal educational route but mostly by drawing the population to school with 'softer' age boundaries for different stages of schooling as conventionally defined by social norms. In conclusion, the recent achievements leave no place for complacency in view of the familiar areas of unevenness found lingering even after the elapse of the EFA decade.

References

Ghosh, Nilabja, Suresh Sharma and Sabyasachi Kar (2006). *Growing Rural Urban Disparity: Himalayan State of Uttarakhand.* New Delhi: National Institute of Rural Development and Institute of Economic Growth.

Govinda, R. (2002). *India Education Report. A Profile of Basic Education*. NIEPA: Oxford.

International Institution for Population Sciences (IIPS) and ORC Macro (2000). *National Family Health Survey 1998-1999 (NFHS-II)*, Mumbai.

Joshi, P.C. (1995). *Uttarakhand: Issues and Challenges*. New Delhi: Har-Anand Publications.

Kuznets, S. (1966). *Modern Economic Growth: Rate, Structure and Spread*. New Haven CT: Yale University Press.

Metha, Arun C. (2006). *Elementary Education in India*, District Report Cards 2005: Volume II. New Delhi: National Institute of Educational Planning and Administration.

Myrdal, Gunnar (1957). *Economic Theory and Under-developed Regions*. Gerald Duckworth & Co Ltd.

———. (1968). *Asian Drama: Inquiry into the Poverty of the Nations*. London: Allen Lane, The Penguin press.

Government of India (2002). National Council for Educational Research and Training (various), 7th *All India Education Survey.*

PRC 2002-04. *Uttarakhand, Reproductive and Child Health, District Level Household Survey*. New Delhi: Institute of Economic Growth.

Census of India (1981). *Town Directory Part X-A (ii)*, Office of the Registrar General and Census Commissioner, India.

———. (1991a). *Final Population Total Paper-1 of 1992 Vol. II*, Office of the Registrar General and Census Commissioner, India.

———. (1991b). *India-Vol.1, Part III, Union Primary Census Abstract*, Office of the Registrar General and Census Commissioner, India.

———. (2001). *Uttarakhand Provisional Population Totals, Series-6, Paper*1, Office of the Registrar General and Census Commissioner, India.

Sen, Amartya (2003). *India Development and Participation*. Oxford.

———. (1999). *Development as Freedom*. Oxford.

Schultz, T.P. (1990). "Education Investments and Return," Chapter 13, Yale University (*mimeo*).

Government of Uttarakhand, *www.gov.ua.nic.in/schooleducation/litracy-rate.htm*

Workshop Proceedings, Reproductive and Child Health, Population Policy Issue in Uttarakhand, Dehradun, 2-3-May 2002, The Policy Project The Futures Group International, New Delhi.

Appendix A-1.1

Table A-1

Schooling Level Achieved by Age Groups of Females: Scheduled Caste (% of population)

Level	*60-70*	*50-60*	*40-50*	*30-40*	*20-30*	*10-20*
No school	94.4	100	89.7	61.5	41.4	4.4
Primary	5.6		10.3	17.3	18.2	14.0
8th class			0	11.5	12.1	37.7
School pass				5.8	21.2	43.0

Table A-2

Explaining School Education: Results with Binary Logistic Model

Dependent is Non-Schooled	*Coefficient*	*Std. Error*	*Exp.*
Age	0.096	0.004	1.100
Distance from Nearest Urban Centre			
Distance	0.079	0.022	1.080
Distance2	-0.002	0.000	0.989
Sex (Female as Base)			
Male	-2.170	0.124	0.110
District (Dehradun as Base)			
Uttarkashi	0.406	0.141	1.500
Nainital	0.037	0.139	1.038
Religion (Sikhs as Base)			
Hindu	0.022	0.505	1.023
Muslim	2.001	0.558	7.398
Caste (SC as Base)			
General	-1.436	0.127	0.238
OBC	-0.397	0.237	0.672
Constant	-3.860	0.600	

Note: Significance levels are less than 0.001 except for religion = Hindu (insignificant at 1 per cent), district = Uttarkashi (insignificant at 1 per cent) and caste = OBC.

Number of observations = 3349.

R-square (Nagelkerke) = 0.49.

Percentage correctly predicted = 85.6 per cent.

Table A-3

Coefficient of Sex Variable (Male with Female as Base) with Varying Samples for Age Groups

Sample Age Group	*Sample Size*	*% Prediction Correct*	*R-sq Pseudo*	*Coefficient B*	*Exp(B)*	*Std. Error*	*Significance*
10-70	3349	85.6	.49	-2.169	0.114	0.124	0.000
10-60	3161	86.0	.45	-2.071	0.126	0.129	0.000
10-50	2862	86.8	.42	-1.929	0.145	0.140	0.000
10-40	2448	88.8	.38	-1.824	0.161	0.164	0.000
10-30	1906	92.0	.31	-1.518	0.219	0.212	0.000
10-20	978	95.7	.24	-0.590	0.554	0.356	0.097

Note: Estimation of Model 1 over varying samples.

Table A-4

Explaining Variations in School Education among Members District-wise (10-70 Years)

	Uttarkashi				*Nainital*				*Dehradun*			
	No Schooling		*Schooling Completed*		*No Schooling*		*Schooling Completed*		*No Schooling*		*Schooling Completed*	
	(β)	*S.E.*	*(β)*	*S.E.*	*(β)*	*S.E.*	*(β)*	*S.E.*	*t (β)*	*S.E.*	*(β)*	*S.E.*
Age	.104	.008	-.044	.005	.099	.007	-.036	.005	.095	.007	-.037	.005
Distance from Nearest Urban Centre												
Distance	.098	.033	-.049#	.024	.010##	.082	-.100#	.055	-.073##	.073	.031##	.051
Distance[2]	-.002	.001	.001#	.000	.001##	.002	.003#	.002	.001##	.002	-.001##	.001
Sex (Female as Base)												
Male	-3.29	.267	1.08	.139	-1.79	.210	.647	.130	.095	.007	.637	.136
Religion (Sikhs as Base Religion for Nainital and Muslim for Uttarkashi and Dehradun)												
Hindu	2.776##	1.452	-.913##	.738	.231##	.554	-.661#	.362	-3.05	.392	3.144	.546
Muslim					.428##	.817	-1.251##	.931				
Caste (SC as Base)												
General	-1.026	.216	1.081	.170	-1.55	.220	.824	.152	-2.04	.249	1.62	.184
OBC	-.912#	.749	1.20#	.483	.514##	.545	-.867#	.547	-.832#	.311	.541#	.246
Constant	-6.570	1.52	.798##	.782	-3.95	.879	1.18	.583	.810##	.866	-3.71	.79
% Correct Prediction	85.4 (.55)		69.3 (.24)		86.7 (.59)		63.1 (.17)		85.8 (.51)		73.2 (.30)	

Note: ## Not significant 1 per cent level; # Not significant even at 10 per cent; Others are significant.

2 Elementary Education in Uttarakhand State

Sandeep Kumar Sharma, Manju Rani and Ravendra K. Sharma

Introduction

The UN Millennium Development Goals (MDGs) spelt out to achieve universal primary education by ensuring that all boys and girls complete a full course of primary schooling; and to promote gender equality and empower women by eliminating gender disparity in primary and secondary education preferably by 2005 and at all levels by 2015 (MDG Report, 2008-09). The Government of India laid down similar goals much earlier to MDGs goals and had made various momentous efforts to achieve these educational goals. Article 45 of the Indian Constitution has provision of free and compulsory education for all children upto age 14 years. After independence of the country, various systematic and planned efforts were made to fulfil the national commitment mentioned under the Constitution.

Efforts were made through successive five year plans to achieve the target of 100 per cent literacy through compulsory and free education for all children aged 6-14 years. The National Policy on Education, 1986 and 1992 has given top priority for the achievement of goals of universal elementary education (UEE). Various programmes and incentives were initiated for universalising and improving the quality of elementary education in India. Major programmes in the direction of meeting above-mentioned objectives have been as: (1) Operation Blackboard Scheme (OBB), started in 1987 to improve enrolment of children in schools, enhancing retention and learning achievement levels of children by providing minimum essential facilities in primary schools; (2) Basic

Education Project (BEP) was launched in some selected districts during 1993 to 2000. BEP aimed at: (i) improving access, (ii) improving quality, (iii) building institutional capacity to manage elementary education, (iv) community mobilisation and to get community support; (3) Cooked Mid-Day Meal Programme—Mid-day meal programme was initiated in 1996 with an intention of providing nutritious food in addition to education facility to children in primary schools. This included provision of dry rations to children. Programme of "cooked" mid-day meal began in the State in 2001; (4) District Primary Education Programme (DPEP)—the programme commenced in the year 1994 with the objective of ensuring primary education facilities at primary level (class 1-5). It was a World Bank-aided programme and state governments contributed 15 per cent of funding support in the programme (USKLSP, 2007a).

After the DPEP of 1994, the Government of India launched Sarva Shiksha Abhiyan or SSA in the year 2001-02 in partnership with the state governments and local self-governments. It is a comprehensive and integrated flagship programme of Government of India to attain universal elementary education covering the entire country in a mission mode. The following are the main objectives of the scheme: i) Enrolment of all children in schools, education guarantee centre, alternate schools, back-to-school camps by 2003; ii) All children complete five years of primary schooling by 2007; iii) All children complete eight years of elementary schooling by 2010; iv) Focus on elementary education of satisfactory quality with emphasis on education for life; v) Bridge all gender and social category gaps at primary stage by 2007 and at elementary education level by 2010; vi) Universal retention by 2010 (MoHRD, 2001). Besides this, Government of India launched many other incentive schemes to retain the children in the school. Some of them are: i) Free textbooks; ii) Free uniforms, stationary, school bags etc; iii) Mid-day meal scheme; iv) Attendance scholarship for girls, etc.

However, even after 55 years of India's independence, the goal of universal elementary education has not been achieved so far. About 10 million children of school-going age are not attending elementary schools due to various reasons (Jain and Sharma, 2007). Moreover, a vast disparity exists in terms of literacy rate within the country. Where states like Kerala and Goa have almost reached 100 per cent literacy, states like Uttar Pradesh and Bihar are lagging far behind. According to Census 2001, the overall literacy rate varies from 91 per cent in Kerala state to as low as 47.5 per cent in Bihar state.

Thus, various state governments have recently initiated different prgrammes and committed towards universalising elementary education and to achieve the goals set in MDGs and 10th Five Year Plan. The Government of Uttarakhand has taken various such remarkable measures. It has entrusted the responsibility of overall implementation of SSA on an independent society –*Uttarakhand Sabhi Ke Liye Shiksha Parishad* (USKLSP). At the same time at its end, the state government has ensured steps to meet the goals of SSA in targeted time. Some of the important steps taken by Uttarakhand government are: (1) Sufficient budgetary support for all the programmes is ensured in state plans and budget; (2) Large scale recruitment of teachers and para teachers taken up on priority; (3) Distribution of free textbooks to the schools ensured in time; (4) Rajeev Gandhi Navodaya Vidyalaya in each district as a centre of excellence offering forward linkage for students passing out from junior high schools; (5) Him Jyoti School, a state-of-art residential school for meritorious girls passing from government and government-aided primary schools; (6) establishing Kasturba Gandhi Balika Vidyalaya (KGBV); (7) Special incentives for SC and ST children and children with special need (USKLSP, 2007; 2007b).

Thus, an attempt is made here to assess the scenario of elementary education in Uttarakhand state, keeping in view the government efforts for universalising elementary education. This paper will provide information on schooling facilities in habitations, school infrastructure in term of buildings, enrolment of children at primary and upper primary stages and teachers' availability, etc. Primary and upper primary stage education i.e., elementary education situation have been critically analysed.

Data and Methodology

Census is the primary source of information about the literacy status in the country. Information on literacy rates have been complied from various publications of Population Census, 2001. However, information about infrastructure in term of buildings, teacher availability and enrolment of children are complied from the publications of All India Education Survey. All India Education Survey conducted by NCERT have been useful sources of data in educational planning and formulation of policies (NCERT, 2002). Information from recently NCERT released report of 7th All India School Education Survey has been exploited for the present analyses (NCERT, 2007). The survey data are processed and analysed by simple statistical approach to provide an analytical overview on primary and upper primary school education in the state of Uttarakhand.

Results

Literacy in Uttarakhand State

The state of Uttarakhand is one of the newly constituted states of the Indian Union. The state was carved out from merging the hilly districts of the state of Uttar Pradesh on 9th November 2000, becoming the 27th state of India. Uttarakhand is located in the foothills of the Himalayas and it has international boundaries with Tibet in the north and Nepal in the east. On its northeast lies Himachal Pradesh while on the south is Uttar Pradesh. According to Census 2001, the state has 13 districts with a total geographical area of 53,483 square kilometres and have a total population of 84,89,349 (Govt. of Uttarakhand, 2009; USKLSP, 2007b).

Literacy, which is the first and foremost factor contributing directly to human resource development and quality of life, Uttarakhand has the 14th position in the country. Literacy percentage of the state is 72.28 against all-India average of 65.38. Male and female literacy rates are 84.01 per cent and 60.26 per cent against the all-India figures of 75.85 per cent and 54.16 per cent respectively (Table 2.1).

The overall literacy rate in the state has jumped from 19 per cent in 1951 to 72.28 per cent in 2001 census, i.e., about 3.85 times. The male literacy rate increased to 84.01 per cent in 2001 from 32.15 per cent in 1951, i.e., about 2.61 times, on the other hand during the same period female literacy jumped up to 60.26 per cent from a mere 4.78 per cent respectively, i.e., about 12.61 times (Figure 2.1). The literacy rates

Table 2.1

Literacy Rates in Some Selected Major Indian States (% of Literates: Aged 7 Years and Above)

States	*Literacy Rates*		
	Total	*Male*	*Female*
Kerala	90.92	94.20	87.86
Maharashtra	77.27	86.27	67.51
Karnataka	67.04	76.29	57.45
Madhya Pradesh	64.11	76.80	50.28
Uttar Pradesh	57.36	70.23	42.98
Bihar	47.53	60.32	33.57
Uttarakhand	72.28	84.01	60.26
India	65.38	75.85	54.16

Source: Census of India, 2001.

Figure 2.1

Decadal Growth in Literacy Rates in Uttarakhand (in Per cent)

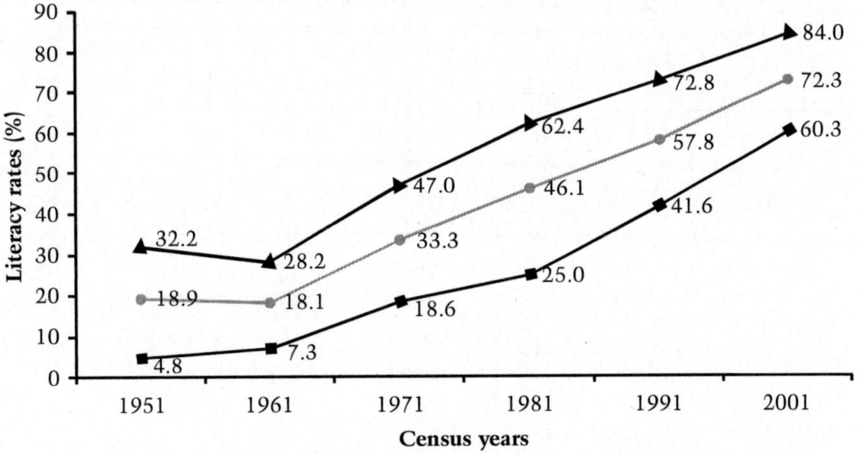

Note: Literacy rate for 1951, 1961 and 1971 relate to population aged five years and above; the years 1981 to 2001 relate to the population aged seven years and above.

Source: Census of India, 2001; USKLSP (2007a).

within the state vary among by place of residence (rural-urban), gender and regional disparity. The Census data reveals that literacy rates were relatively much higher among urban population dominated districts such as Dehradun and Nainital districts and hilly districts like Chamoli, Pauri, Rudraprayag and it was relatively poor in plain districts like Udham Singh Nagar and Haridwar. Female literacy rates were also lower in these plain districts. However, female literacy was substantially lower among some hilly districts like Uttarkashi, Tehri Garhwal and Chamawat where comparatively male literacy was higher. The gender gap in literacy varies from as low as 14.65 points in Dehradun and 16.41 points in Nainital to as high as 37.04 points in Uttarkashi and 35.66 points in Tehri Garhwal district (Table 2.2). Out of 13 districts, the gender gap was more than 30 points in 5 districts. Census data of 2001 shows that the gender gap is still an issue to be addressed in Uttarakhand, wherein focused interventions are required especially in the cities and farthest habitations.

Table 2.2

District-wise Population and Literacy Rates by Sex: 2001

S. No.	*State/District*	*Population*			*Literacy Rate*			*Gender Gap*
		Persons	*Male*	*Female*	*Persons*	*Male*	*Female*	
1.	Uttarkashi	294179	151599	142580	66.58	84.52	47.48	37.04
2.	Chamoli	369198	183033	186165	76.23	89.89	63.00	26.89
3.	Rudraprayag	227461	107425	120036	74.23	90.73	59.98	30.75
4.	Tehri Garhwal	604608	294842	309766	67.04	85.62	49.96	35.66
5.	Dehradun	1279083	675549	603534	78.96	85.87	71.22	14.65
6.	Pauri	696851	331138	365713	77.99	91.47	66.14	25.33
7.	Pithoragarh	462149	227592	234557	76.48	90.57	63.14	27.43
8.	Champawat	224461	110916	113545	71.11	88.13	54.75	33.38
9.	Almora	630446	293576	336870	74.53	90.15	61.43	28.72
10.	Bageshwar	249453	118202	131251	71.94	88.56	57.45	31.11
11.	Nainital	762912	400336	362576	79.60	87.39	70.98	16.41
12.	U.S. Nagar	1234548	649020	585528	65.76	76.20	54.16	22.04
13.	Haridwar	1444213	773173	671040	64.60	75.06	52.60	22.46
	Uttarakhand	8479562	4316401	4163161	72.28	84.01	60.26	23.75

Source: Census of India, 2001.

With the help of various government interventions, there has been significant progress in the field of education in Uttarakhand state. Now the state government is resolved to concentrate on putting intensive efforts for addressing the "quality" aspect of education. However, to assess the 'elementary education' status in a state, one needs to appraise the information in terms of availability of schooling facilities in habitations, school infrastructure in term of buildings, enrolment of children at primary and upper primary stages and teachers' availability, etc.

Schooling Facilities in Habitations of the State

As per SSA norms, there should be primary education facilities within 1 km and upper primary within 3 km of every habitation. In Uttarakhand, there are 25,495 habitations in 15768 villages with a rural population of about 64 lakh, i.e., 1.62 habitations per village. In 7th educational survey, 81.44 per cent habitations had primary stage education facilities within 1 km and 85.96 per cent upper primary facilities within 3 km. This shows that 18.56 per cent and 14.04 per cent habitations did not have primary and upper primary stage education facilities respectively (Table 2.3). The proportion of habitations without any primary stage facilities within 1 km was higher in hilly districts like Champawat (25.86 per cent), Pithoragarh (21.49 per cent), Tehri Garhwal (19.46 per cent), Uttarkashi (18.20 per cent), Chamoli (19.21 per cent) and Almora (18.95 per cent). On the other hand, only 6.31 per cent habitations in Haridwar district did not have primary school within 1 km. Similarly, the proportion of habitations without any upper primary school within 3 km was highest in Champawat district (26.24 per cent) and least in Rudraprayag district (8.57 per cent).

Number of Primary and Upper Primary Recognised Schools

As per 7th AISES, there were 13,902 primary schools and 3,471 upper primary schools in Uttarakhand. It is important to notice that about 90 per cent primary schools and 85 per cent upper primary schools were in rural areas. Most of the schools, both primary and upper primary in the state were government schools (Table 2.4). More than 80 per cent primary and 70 per cent upper primary schools were purely government schools and less than 1 per cent schools were administered by local bodies. Almost all (99 per cent) primary and 80 per cent upper primary schools were co-education schools. Though most of the primary and upper primary schools in the state were in rural areas, about one-third primary schools were in urban areas in Dehradun district, followed by 25.12 per cent in Haridwar, 21.83 per cent in Udham Singh Nagar and 15.05 per cent in Nanital district. Similarly, about 38, 34, 26 and 18 per cent upper primary schools were in urban areas of these districts respectively (Table 2.5). As needed, urbanised districts have more schools in urban areas, whereas rural dominated have most of the schools in rural areas.

Table 2.3

Percentage of Habitations not having Primary and Upper Primary Schools as per SSA Norms

S. No.	*Districts*	*Percentage of Habitation do not have*		*No. of Habitations*
		Primary School within 1 km	*Upper Primary within 3 km*	
1.	Almora	18.95	13.47	3378
2.	Bageshwar	17.66	16.58	1478
3.	Chamoli	19.21	14.54	2056
4.	Champawat	25.86	26.24	1311
5.	Dehradun	18.48	19.90	1412
6.	Garhwal	18.11	8.25	3877
7.	Haridwar	6.31	21.26	602
8.	Nainital	15.39	9.44	1897
9.	Pithoragarh	21.49	17.26	3383
10.	Rudraprayag	15.96	8.57	1178
11.	Tehri Garhwal	19.46	12.02	2729
12.	Udham Singh Nagar	14.30	9.96	1084
13.	Uttarkashi	18.20	18.65	1110
	Uttarakhand	18.56	14.04	25495

Source: 7th All India School Education Survey (AISES).

Table 2.4

Numbers of Schools by Type of Management

Management	*Primary*			*Upper Primary*		
	Rural	*Urban*	*Total*	*Rural*	*Urban*	*Total*
Government	10759	511	11270	2334	108	2442
Local body	84	21	105	31	8	39
Private aided	65	29	94	125	53	178
Private unaided	1558	875	2433	462	350	812
Total	12466	1436	13902	2952	519	3471
Boys	73	16	89	257	47	304
Girls	25	17	42	348	66	414
Co-ed.	12368	1403	13771	2347	406	2753

Source: 7th All India School Education Survey (AISES).

Table 2.5

Primary and Upper Primary Schools in Rural and Urban Areas

Sl. No.	*District*	*Primary*			*Upper Primary*		
		Rural (%)	*Urban (%)*	*Total*	*Rural (%)*	*Urban (%)*	*Total*
1.	Almora	96.79	3.21	1466	95.59	4.41	227
2.	Bageshwar	98.50	1.50	600	97.94	2.06	97
3.	Chamoli	93.39	6.61	1013	90.17	9.83	234
4.	Champawat	95.77	4.23	497	91.96	8.04	112
5.	Dehradun	68.12	31.88	1396	62.19	37.81	447
6.	Garhwal	96.37	3.63	1792	93.72	6.28	478
7.	Haridwar	74.88	25.12	1031	65.87	34.13	252
8.	Nainital	84.95	15.05	1116	81.87	18.13	342
9.	Pithoragarh	95.82	4.18	1197	93.03	6.97	244
10.	Rudraprayag	98.76	1.24	565	97.93	2.07	145
11.	Tehri Garhwal	96.19	3.81	1468	94.67	5.33	394
12.	Udham Singh Nagar	78.17	21.83	985	74.23	25.77	291
13.	Uttarkashi	96.52	3.48	776	94.23	5.77	208
	Uttarakhand	89.67	10.33	13902	85.05	14.95	3471

Source: 7th All India School Education Survey (AISES).

School Infrastructure

In the 7th AISES survey, information was also collected on school infrastructure, such as type of school building, etc. Out of 13,902 primary schools in the state, 788 primary schools (5.7 per cent) were running in non-*pucca* building (partly *pucca*, *kuchcha*, in tents and open space) in year 2002. The remaining 13,114 schools (94.3 per cent) were functioning in *pucca* building. Similarly, out of 3,471 upper primary schools, 3,200 (92.2 per cent) were running in *pucca* building and 7.8 per cent in non-*pucca* building. Relatively more primary schools in Pithoragarh (9.0 per cent), Dehradun (9.0 per cent), Rudraprayag (8.0 per cent) and Tehri Garhwal (7.8 per cent) were running in non-*pucca* buildings. But more than one-fourth upper primary schools in Tehri Garhwal district and more than 10 per cent in Rudraprayag, Uttarkashi, and Chamoli districts were running in non-*pucca* buildings (Table 2.6). This shows the lack of basic educational infrastructure in the state and particularly in hilly districts.

Table 2.6

Type of School Buildings of Primary and Upper Primary Schools

Sl. No.	*District*	*Primary Schools (%)*			*Upper Primary (%)*		
		Pucca	*Others*	*Total*	*Pucca*	*Others*	*Total*
1.	Almora	97.8	2.2	1466	96.5	3.5	227
2.	Bageshwar	99.0	1.0	600	94.8	5.2	97
3.	Chamoli	94.6	5.4	1013	89.7	10.3	234
4.	Champawat	94.8	5.2	497	91.1	8.9	112
5.	Dehradun	91.0	9.0	1396	91.1	8.9	447
6.	Garhwal	93.2	6.8	1792	96.0	4.0	478
7.	Haridwar	96.4	3.6	1031	97.6	2.4	252
8.	Nainital	98.6	1.4	1116	98.2	1.8	342
9.	Pithoragarh	91.0	9.0	1197	97.1	2.9	244
10.	Rudraprayag	92.0	8.0	565	89.0	11.0	145
11.	Tehri Garhwal	92.2	7.8	1468	73.4	26.6	394
12.	Udham Singh Nagar	95.5	4.5	985	98.6	1.4	291
13.	Uttarkashi	92.5	7.5	776	89.9	10.1	208
	Uttarakhand	94.3	5.7	13902	92.2	7.8	3471

Note: Others include partly *pucca*, *kuchcha*, tents, open space.

Source: 7th All India School Education Survey (AISES).

Availability of Teachers in Schools

Teachers (including para teachers) are defined as persons whose professional activity involves the transmitting of knowledge, attitudes and skill that are stipulated in a formal curriculum programme to students enrolled in the formal educational institutions. Of the total 79,722 teachers in Uttarakhand state in year 2002, 46.50, 19.22, 7.97 and 6.31 per cent teachers were respectively working in primary, upper primary, secondary and higher secondary schools. Teacher-school ratio (TSR), i.e., number of full-time teachers per school can be considered a good measure of quality of education. In Uttarakhand state, on an average 2.5 teachers were teaching in a primary school and 4.4 teachers in an upper primary school. It is interesting to observe that on an average, urban schools (both primary and upper primary) have more teachers irrespective of type of managements. On an average, 5 teachers in primary and 5.9 in upper primary schools were posted in urban areas as compared to 2.2 and 4.1 teachers respectively in rural areas. TSR was appreciably higher in private aided and unaided schools as compared to government schools (Table 2.7).

Table 2.7

Average Number of Full-Time Teachers (TSR) in Primary and Upper Primary Schools by Type of Management of Schools

Management	*Primary Schools*			*Upper Primary Schools*		
	Rural	*Urban*	*Total*	*Rural*	*Urban*	*Total*
Government	1.9	3.6	2.0	3.9	5.4	4.0
Local body	1.9	4.1	2.3	4.3	6.5	4.8
Private aided	3.6	7.5	4.8	5.1	6.8	5.6
Private unaided	4.6	5.8	5.0	4.8	5.9	5.3
Total	2.2	5.0	2.5	4.1	5.9	4.4

Source: 7th All India School Education Survey (AISES).

Teacher-school ratio in primary schools was highest in Haridwar district (3.9 teachers per school), followed by Udham Singh Nagar (3.7) and Dehradun (3.5) and it was just about two teachers per primary school in Almora, Bageshwar, Chamoli, Garhwal and Pithoragarh districts. In case of upper primary school, the availability of teachers per school was less than 4 teachers in Pithoragrh (3.9) and Tehri Garhwal (3.6) districts, whereas it was about five teachers per school in Haridwar (5.1) and Nainital (4.9) districts (Table 2.8).

Table 2.8

Average Number of Full-Time Teachers (TSR) in Primary and Upper Primary Schools by Districts

Sl. No.	*Districts*	*Teachers per School*	
		Primary	*Upper Primary*
1.	Almora	2.1	4.3
2.	Bageshwar	1.9	4.3
3.	Chamoli	2.0	4.5
4.	Champawat	1.8	4.0
5.	Dehradun	3.5	4.7
6.	Garhwal	2.0	4.4
7.	Haridwar	3.9	5.1
8.	Nainital	2.6	4.9
9.	Pithoragarh	2.1	3.9
10.	Rudraprayag	2.3	4.2
11.	Tehri Garhwal	2.3	3.6
12.	Udham Singh Nagar	3.7	4.5
13.	Uttarkashi	2.2	4.1
	Uttarakhand	2.5	4.4

Source: 7th All India School Education Survey (AISES).

Out of 13,902 total primary schools, 18 per cent were having only one teacher, and another 153 (1.1 per cent) schools were not having any teacher at all. About half schools (48.32 per cent) were having two teachers. In rural areas, out of 12,466 primary schools 150 (1.2 per cent) were not having any teacher and about 72 per cent were having two or less teachers in rural schools. In urban areas all 1,436 schools were having more than one teacher, and 3.4 per cent had one teacher only. More than 60 per cent urban primary schools had 5 or more teachers (Figure 2.2). This shows the enormous rural-urban areas variation in availability of teachers, and strong preference of teachers for urban postings.

Figure 2.2

Primary Schools with Number of Full-Time Teachers

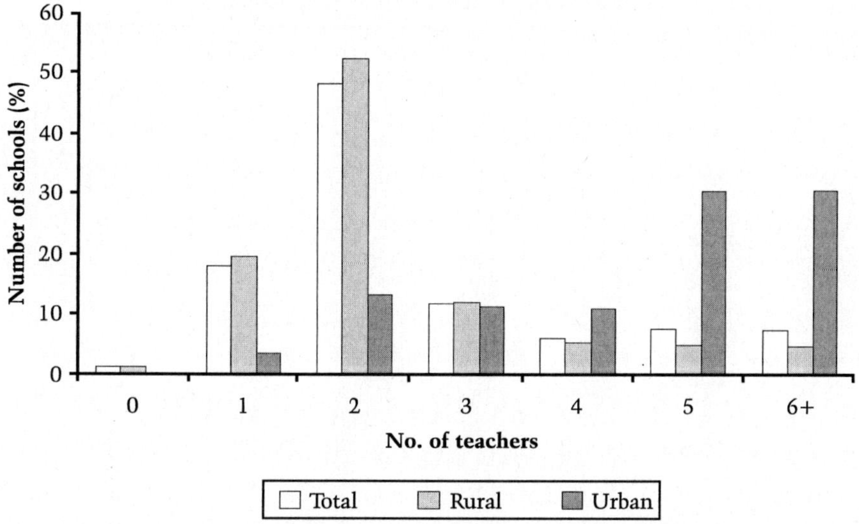

According to 7th educational survey, in Uttarakhand state, more than half (55.63 per cent) primary teachers were female. The ratio of primary female teachers to total primary teachers was much higher in urban areas as compared to rural areas. This ratio was highest in Dehradun district (80.03 per cent), followed by Nainital district (70.63 per cent). However, out of 13 districts, 7 districts namely Almora, Bageshwar, Champawat, Rudraprayag, Tehri Garhwal, Udham Singh Nagar and Uttarkashi have less than 50 per cent female teachers (Table 2.9). But in case of upper primary schools, the proportion of female teacher was much lower and less than one-third of upper primary teachers were female teachers. Similar to primary schools, the ratio of female teachers in upper primary schools was much higher in urban areas as compared to that in rural areas. Moreover, predominating and more urbanised districts like Dehradun, Haridwar and Nainital had relatively more female teachers (Table 2.9). This clearly indicates unfair distribution of female teachers among different districts of the state and their strong penchant for urban schools.

Table 2.9

Availability of Female Teachers in Primary and Upper Primary Schools in Uttarakhand

Sl. No.	Districts	Female Teachers in Primary Schools (%)			Female Teachers in Upper Primary Schools (%)		
		Rural	Urban	Total	Rural	Urban	Total
1.	Almora	40.1	74.5	42.5	17.3	55.2	19.8
2.	Bageshwar	37.4	66.0	38.6	13.7	63.6	15.0
3.	Chamoli	52.4	61.9	53.5	11.5	33.1	14.5
4.	Champawat	37.9	52.8	40.1	16.0	40.7	19.2
5.	Dehradun	73.1	89.4	80.0	36.4	78.1	54.3
6.	Garhwal	53.7	61.3	54.3	28.4	55.9	30.9
7.	Haridwar	46.6	75.9	55.7	35.4	73.2	52.6
8.	Nainital	67.9	78.4	70.6	28.9	70.5	38.4
9.	Pithoragarh	54.4	64.6	55.6	19.2	43.4	21.9
10.	Rudraprayag	45.4	51.4	45.6	13.5	23.5	13.8
11.	Tehri Garhwal	47.1	61.7	48.3	21.5	42.2	23.3
12.	Udham Singh Nagar	40.5	64.5	48.7	22.8	51.6	31.6
13.	Uttarkashi	48.4	57.9	49.0	13.7	49.0	15.8
	Uttarakhand	50.92	74.9	55.6	23.2	64.5	31.5

Source: 7th All India School Education Survey (AISES).

Pupil-Teacher Ratio in Schools

Pupil-teacher ratio (PTR) is one of the best educational parameter to measure the quality of education being provided to children. The PTR is used to measure the level of human resources input in terms of number of teachers in relation to the size of pupil population. According to SSA norms, there should be one teacher for every 40 students in primary schools and one teacher for every section in upper primary school. On the basis of the school enrolment and number of teachers, PTR had been computed.

In Uttarakhand state, PTR was 29:1 in primary schools and 19:1 in upper primary schools. Government primary schools have more pupils per teacher as compared to private aided and unaided schools. PTR was 32 in government primary schools as compared to 29 and 22 respectively in private aided and private unaided schools. Overall, pupil-teacher ratio was higher in rural schools (29) as compared to urban areas (27), however this ratio was much higher in government urban primary schools (41 students per teacher) as compared to rural schools (32 students per teacher). But in case of overall upper primary schools, PTR was relatively higher in urban areas (22) as compared to rural upper primary schools (19). Similar to primary schools, private upper primary schools (either aided or unaided) have higher pupil-teacher ratio as compared to government and local bodies schools (Table 2.10).

Table 2.10

Management-wise Pupil-Teacher Ratio in Primary and Upper Primary Schools

Management	*Primary Schools*			*Upper Primary Schools*		
	Rural	*Urban*	*Total*	*Rural*	*Urban*	*Total*
Government	32	41	32	18	23	18
Local body	30	26	28	15	24	18
Private aided	25	32	29	26	24	25
Private unaided	22	22	22	20	21	20
Total	29	27	29	19	22	19

Note: Pupil-teacher ratio has been worked out by including the para teachers.
Source: 7th All India School Education Survey (AISES).

To study the district-wise variation in pupil-teacher ratio (PTR), PTRs are computed for both primary and upper primary schools at district level. Districts Haridwar and Udham Singh Nagar has maximum primary PTR of 43:1, while Pithoragarh district has minimum ratio of 22:1 in primary schools. In case of upper primary schools, pupil-teacher ratio was more than 30 students per teacher in Udham Singh Nagar and Haridwar and it was less than 20 students per teacher in Chamoli, Garhwal, Dehradun, Nainital, Pithoragarh, Rudraprayag, Tehri Garhwal and Uttarkashi districts (Table 2.11). PTR in rural primary schools was relatively higher as compared to that in urban schools in all districts, except Nainital, where PTR in urban primary school was 30 as compared to 27 in rural areas. In case of upper primary school PTR, it was higher in urban areas in most of the districts, except in Almora, Dehradun and Haridwar districts.

Table 2.11

District-wise Pupil-Teacher Ratio in Primary and Upper Primary Schools

Sl.No.	Districts	Primary			Upper Primary		
		Rural	Urban	Total	Rural	Urban	Total
1.	Almora	27	18	26	20	18	20
2.	Bageshwar	28	27	28	21	22	21
3.	Chamoli	24	18	23	16	18	16
4.	Champawat	31	27	31	19	22	20
5.	Dehradun	27	23	25	17	15	16
6.	Garhwal	23	23	23	12	14	12
7.	Haridwar	48	31	43	37	29	33
8.	Nainital	27	30	27	17	22	18
9.	Pithoragarh	22	20	22	18	24	19
10.	Rudraprayag	26	19	25	16	25	16
11.	Tehri Garhwal	27	22	26	17	19	17
12.	Udham Singh Nagar	45	39	43	30	30	30
13.	Uttarkashi	24	19	24	14	15	14
	Uttarakhand	29	27	29	19	22	19

Note: Pupil-teacher ratio has been worked out by including the para teachers.
Source: 7th All India School Education Survey (AISES).

Participation of Children in Schools

An important indicator of educational outcome, the gross enrolment ratio (GER) is the ratio of children enrolled and child population of particular age group. Gross enrolment ratio for primary stage is the ratio of children enrolled at primary stage and child population of age group 6-11 years. In Uttarakhand, GER at primary stage was 104 (combined for boys and girls) in year 2002. The overall GER at primary stage was little bit higher for girls (105) as compared to boys (103), which is also true for rural areas. But in urban areas, GER was 104 for boys as compared to 99 for girl children (Table 2.12). GER more than 100 may be due to children enrolled are of over ages and/or children from other states might have enrolled in Uttarakhand. This may be true as the state is well-known for its good schooling. The state has many good schools, particularly in districts like Dehradun, Nainital and Haridwar.

Table 2.12

Gross Enrolment Ratio in Primary and Upper Primary Schools

Stages	Rural			Urban			Total		
	Boys	Girls	Total	Boys	Girls	Total	Boys	Girls	Total
Primary stage (I-V)	103	107	104	104	99	102	103	105	104
Upper primary stage (VI-VIII)	75	68	72	87	88	88	78	73	76
Combined for primary & upper primary (I-VIII)	92	92	92	97	95	96	93	92	93

Source: 7th All India School Education Survey (AISES).

Figure 2.3

Gross Enrolment Ratio (GER) in Primary and Upper Primary Stages in Districts of Uttarakhand

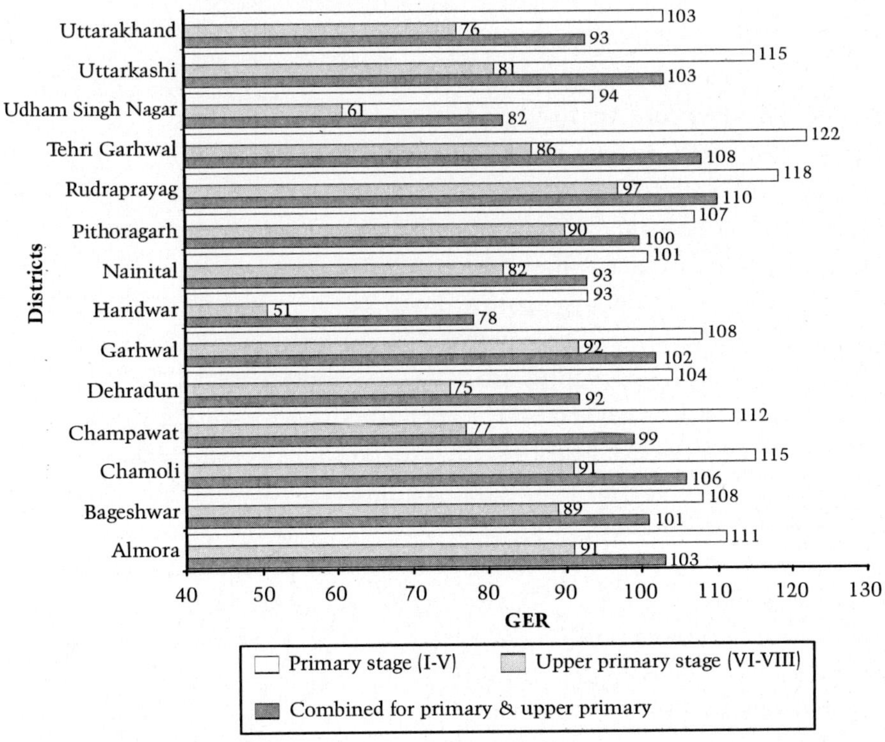

At upper primary stage combined (girls + boys), GER was 76 and it was 78 and 73 for boys and girls respectively. A GER of 76 at upper primary stage indicates that on an average, 24 children per every 100 children of age group 11-14 years are not enrolled at upper primary stage. This indicates that either some children of age group 11-14 years are enrolled in primary classes or they have dropped their studies before reaching the upper primary stage. But a combined enrolment ratio (for primary and upper primary) of 93, still support the hypothesis that some children are not at all attending school or dropped out from school before completing elementary education. Similar to all other indicators, the enrolment of children in primary and upper primary stages is much lower among plain districts as compared to other districts (Figure 2.3). The gross enrolment ratio in upper primary schools was just 51 in Haridwar and 61 in Udham Singh Nagar, which is far behind than the state average of 76 children.

Discussion

The state Uttarakhand is dominantly a rural state and has a historical advantage in literacy in India and in the last many years, considerable actions have been taken to bring education at school level to the rural precincts. Despite all the efforts, the universalisation of elementary education in the state remains a distant dream. Based on above captioned results based on the 7th All India School Education Survey, following observations emerged in regard to elementary education in the state. The analyses show that still 18.6 per cent and 14.0 per cent inhabitations are without primary and upper primary education facilities respectively. The proportion of inhabitations not having educational facilities within inhabitation's peripherals is higher in hilly districts like Champawat, Pithoragarh, Tehri Garhwal, Uttarkashi and Chamoli. More than 80 per cent primary and 70 per cent upper primary schools were purely government schools and less than 1 per cent schools were run by local bodies. Though most of the schools have *pucca* buildings, still about seven to eight per cent of primary and upper primary schools are running in non-*pucca* edifices. Most of the primary schools (72 per cent) have only two teachers, i.e., on an average two teachers are taking care of five classes (1st to 5th stages). More than half primary teachers and one-third upper primary teachers are female teachers. The proportion of female teachers at both primary and upper primary stages was much higher in urban areas as compared to rural areas. The predominating districts like Dehradun, Haridwar and Nainital have relatively more female teachers. This clearly indicates imbalanced distribution of female teachers among different districts of the state and their strong preference for posting in urban areas.

In Uttarakhand, GER at primary stage was 104 (combined for boys and girls) in the year 2002. A GER of more than 100 is an enigma, but this may be due to: a) children for higher ages are enrolled at lower stages, b) children from other districts/states enrolled here, c) some children may be enrolled in more than one school (Rani, 2000). But overall the combined enrolment for primary and upper primary is less than 100 and enrolment at upper primary schools is far less than 100. This reflects a drop-out of children from primary to upper primary, i.e., before completing the eight years of elementary education.

Conclusions

With the help of various government interventions, there has been significant progress in the field of education in Uttarakhand state. A lot of efforts has being going on for educating all children aged 6-14 years, but the dream of achieving 100 per cent elementary education and goals set in SSA, 2001 is still a demanding task. Unless and until all children get access to school, other efforts would not be much effective. Therefore, sincere efforts are needed in the field of accessibility i.e., each habitation should have at least primary and upper primary stage facilities within 1 and 3 km. Government should also make sure that all schools should have their own *pucca* buildings. There is also a need to improve teacher-school ratio and bring down the pupil-teacher ratio, particularly in government schools. The proportion of female teachers needs to be improved, especially at upper primary stage, and they should be uniformly posted in all districts. Now the state government should also resolve to concentrate on putting intensive efforts for addressing the "quality" aspect of education.

References

Census of India (2001). *Total Population of Uttaranchal*. New Delhi: Registrar General and Commissioner of India.

Government of Uttarakhand (2009). *Uttarakhand: At a Glance*. Dehradun: Directorate of Economics and Statistics (downloaded from *http://gov.ua.nic.in/uaglance/)*

Jain, V.K. and S.K. Sharma (2007). "Universilisation of elementary education: Challenges before the country," *University News* 45(11).

MoHRD (2001). "Sarva Shiksha Abhiyan- A programme for UEE", Ministry of Human Resources and Development of Elementary Education and Literacy, New Delhi.

NCERT (2002). *Seventh All India School Education Survey: Guidelines for Survey Offices*. DES&DP. New Delhi.

———. (2007). *Seventh All India School Education Survey: National Reports* (Report I to Report IX), DES&DP, New Delhi.

Rani, Manju (2000). "Determinant of low child education in Uttar Pradesh", MPS *Term Paper* (unpublished). Mumbai: International Institute for Population Sciences.

Sharma, S.K. and V.P. Singh (2007). "Seventh All India School Education Survey- A Statistical Profile on Selected Parameters of School Education", *Journal of Indian Education* 32(4).

Uttarakhand Sabhi Ke Liye Shiksha Parishad (USKLSP) (2007a). Annual Work Plan and Budget, 2007-08. *Uttarakhand State Plan*. Dehradun: State Project Office, Sarva Shikhsa Abhiyaan (downloaded from *www.gov.ua.nic.in/ssaua/)*

———. (2007b). *Educational Statistics Booklet. August*. Dehradun: State Project Office, Sarva Shikhsa Abhiyaan (downloaded from *http://gov.ua.nic.in/ssaua/*).

3 Who Gets Education in Uttarakhand?

Analysis of NFHS-3 Data

Nandita Saikia, Jayanta Kumar Bora and F. Ram

Introduction

Education has been considered as one of the most important determinants of socio-economic status of an individual. Access to education raises the socio-economic status which further can improve the quality of life. There are numerous studies addressing the relationship between education and demographic behaviour; and over the time, it has been proved that education has large and persistent association in two basic components of demography *viz.*, fertility and mortality. It is found that higher socio-economic status (SES) groups exhibited lower rates of all-cause specific mortality than did lower SES groups in the US during 1960s (Kitagawa and Hauser, 1973). In this study, where educational attainment assessed by years of school completed was one of their principal measures of socio-economic status further revealed that improved socio-economic conditions associated with education and income might have a marked effect on the deaths of men 25 to 64 and on deaths of women of all ages 25 and over. Some other study indicates that mortality rates overall and for specific diseases (including heart disease and cancer) are higher in the United States for individuals with lower educational or income status (Steenland *et al.*, 2002). In 1995, low birth weight and infant mortality were more common among children born to less educated mothers. Relationships between maternal education and child health outcomes vary somewhat by racial and ethnic group (Pamuk *et al.*, 1998). Mothers with less than

12 years of education are less likely to have received care in the first trimester of pregnancy than mothers with 16 or more years of education. Also, women with less than a high school diploma are almost 10 times more likely to smoke during pregnancy in United States (Pamuk *et al.*, 1998). In addition, education has been shown to be a powerful and unique predictor of health outcomes—lower levels of education are associated with poor health and higher levels of education are associated with better health. In most countries around the world, whether it is developed or developing, there exists a strong positive relationship between education and health. In most cases, literate women have healthier children, smaller families, and contribute more to family income and community development than do illiterate women. Thus, research provides ample evidence to support the direct relationship between basic education and positive health indicators, lower fertility rates, higher agricultural productivity, higher family income, and other social and economic indicators. In cases where data can be analysed by gender, the education of women is usually a much stronger predictor of positive impact.

The importance of education in India is noteworthy as total fertility rate of India is above replacement level and maternal mortality is still very high. According to NFHS-3, TFR for women with no education is 3.55 whereas same rate for women who have completed 12 or more years of education is only 1.80 which is below replacement level (NFHS-3, 2005-06). Similarly institutional deliveries, particularly in private sector facilities, increase sharply with the mother's education (institutional delivery for women without education and women with education of 12 or more years completed are only 18 and 86 per cent respectively). Thus, education of mothers can play a significant role in order to achieve desired demographic and health goals e.g., reducing TFR and maternal mortality rate. However, accessibility of education is not unbiased with respect to gender in India and this is particularly true in some states like Bihar, UP, Rajasthan and Uttarakhand (Census of India, 2001). Gender disparity in education has been a great concern in Uttarakhand as according to 2001 census, male literacy rate is 83.3 per cent as compared to only 59.6 per cent for females.

Objective of the Study

According to Census of India, the literacy rate of Uttarakhand is higher than the national level literacy. Nevertheless, literacy rate is not evenly distributed among different sections of the society. The Eleventh Five Year Plan for the period 2007-2012 of the state lays strong emphasis on human development, especially through education. In the field of primary education, though access has improved considerably and enrolment is nearly universal, the big challenge is to ensure retention and completion of the upper primary stage, by addressing the problem of dropouts and high rates of wastage due to failure. This paper is trying to examine the existence of gender discrimination in education by different socio-economic subgroups to find out the most vulnerable section of the society for accessing education.

Data and Methodology

Two separate sources of data have been used in order to find out the most vulnerable subgroup of the society with respect to education of Uttarakhand. At first, to find out the rate of literacy by type of residence and sex, principal component analysis (PCA) data from Census 1991 and 2001 have been used.

To obtain the information related to school attendance status of Uttarakhand, National Family and Health Survey 2005-06 has been used. The National Family Health Surveys (NFHS) programme, initiated in the early 1990s, has emerged as a nationally important source of data on population, health and nutrition for India and its states. The 2005-06 National Family Health Survey (NFHS-3), the third in the series of these national surveys, was preceded by NFHS-1 in 1992-93 and NFHS-2 in 1998-99. Like NFHS-1 and NFHS-2, NFHS-3 was designed to provide estimates of important indicators on family welfare, maternal and child health, and nutrition along with information regarding family life education, safe injections, perinatal mortality, adolescent reproductive health, high-risk sexual behaviour, tuberculosis and malaria. NFHS-3 collected information from a nationally representative sample of 109,041 households, 124,385 women aged 15-49, and 74,369 men aged 15-54. The present paper attempts to analyse the school attendance status by different important background characteristics using NFHS-3 household member file for Uttarakhand. The important background characteristics mainly considered here are age, sex, type of residence, standard of living of the household and ethnicity origin of the household head where the member belongs. The standard of living index (SLI) has been considered as a proxy measure of economic condition of the household created on the basis of the type of house, number of rooms, separate room for kitchen, toilet facility, source of drinking water facility, source of lighting, type of fuel used for cooking and other resources and material goods available in the household. The SLI score ranges from 0-14 for low SLI, 15-24 for medium SLI to 25-67 for a high SLI (IIPS and Macro, 2007).

Results and Discussion

There are basically two problems in the educational sector of Uttarakhand. At first, there exists a highly skewed pattern of educational development across the state. While some of the educationally advanced districts like Dehradun and Nainital report literacy rates close to 80 per cent, others like Udham Singh Nagar, Uttarkashi and Haridwar are either closer to the national figure of 65 per cent or below that figure.

Not only are regional inequalities in literacy rates across the state glaring, the fact of gender disparity is a cause of great concern, especially in some of the educationally backward districts of the state like Uttarkashi. Table 3.1 shows that male literacy is always higher than that of female literacy in each district of Uttarakhand. The state-level gender gap in literacy (23.75 units) is higher than that of national level (21.69 units). Some districts *viz.*, Uttarkashi, Chamoli, Rudraprayag, Tehri Garhwal, Pithoragarh seek more attention for improving the female literacy level. However, the gender gap is shrinking fast in the last 10 years as displayed by the relative figure from 1991 and 2001 census.

District-level literacy by type of residence and sex has been shown in Table 3.2. There is no unique pattern in literacy level by type of residence in different districts of Uttarakhand. The gender gap is higher

Table 3.1

Literacy Rate in the Districts of Uttarakhand by Sex from Census 1991 and 2001

	1991				*2001*			
	Female	*Male*	*Diff=M-F*	*Total*	*Female*	*Male*	*Diff=M-F*	*Total*
Uttarkashi	23.57	68.74	45.17	47.23	47.48	84.52	37.04	66.58
Chamoli	40.37	82.01	41.64	61.08	63.00	89.89	26.89	76.23
Rudraprayag	-	-		-	59.98	90.73	30.75	74.23
Tehri Garhwal	26.41	72.10	45.69	48.38	49.76	85.62	35.86	67.04
Dehradun	59.26	77.95	18.69	69.50	71.22	85.87	14.65	78.96
Pauri Garhwal	49.44	82.46	33.02	63.35	68.14	91.47	23.33	77.99
Haridwar	34.93	59.51	24.58	48.35	43.43	61.74	18.31	53.23
Pithoragarh	-	-	-	-	63.14	90.59	27.45	76.85
Champawat	-	-	-	-	67.00	78.00	11.00	73.00
Almora	-	-	-	-	61.43	90.15	28.72	74.53
Bageshwar	-	-	-	-	42.00	58.00	16.00	75.00
Nainital	-	-	-	-	76.00	86.00	10.00	81.00
Udham Singh Nagar	33.30	66.70	33.40	39.30	53.35	75.22	21.87	64.86
Uttarakhand	42.87	75.51	32.64	59.58	60.26	84.01	23.75	72.28
India	32.41	52.63	20.22	52.11	54.16	75.85	21.69	65.38

Table 3.2

District-wise Literacy Rate by Type of Residence and Sex from 2001 Census

District	*Rural*				*Urban*			
	Female	*Male*	*Diff=M-F*	*Total*	*Female*	*Male*	*Diff=M-F*	*Total*
Uttarkashi	34.08	65.92	31.84	52.81	37.39	62.61	25.22	76.25
Chamoli	42.16	57.84	15.68	61.96	37.99	62.01	24.02	77.49
Rudraprayag	43.45	56.55	13.10	61.89	28.39	71.61	43.22	73.61
Tehri Garhwal	38.96	61.04	22.08	53.65	34.44	65.56	31.12	75.97
Dehradun	40.86	59.14	18.28	59.57	43.37	56.63	13.26	76.17
Garhwal	45.67	54.33	8.66	64.59	42.13	57.87	15.74	77.30
Pithoragarh	42.40	57.60	15.20	61.89	42.03	57.97	15.94	79.05
Bageshwar	42.67	57.33	14.66	59.02	42.01	57.99	15.98	74.71
Almora	45.10	54.90	9.80	60.37	41.54	58.46	16.92	82.30
Champawat	38.77	61.23	22.46	56.09	41.55	58.45	16.90	67.93
Nainital	41.29	58.71	17.42	64.31	43.66	56.34	12.68	71.04
Udham Singh Nagar	37.98	62.02	24.04	50.48	40.70	59.30	18.60	59.28
Haridwar	35.67	64.33	28.66	45.58	41.35	58.65	17.30	66.95
Uttarakhand	40.70	59.30	18.60	56.50	41.93	58.07	16.14	70.69

in some districts among the rural residents whereas in some other districts, it is higher among the urban residents. Among the urban residents, females belonging to Rudraprayag and Tehri Garhwal gets least education than their male counterparts. On the other hand, rural females belonging to Uttarkashi, Udham Singh Nagar, Haridwar, Tehri Garhwal and Champawat has lower level of literacy. From Table 3.3, it is clear that the discrimination in school attendance status between male and female is higher in higher education. The percentage gap between male and female in primary education and mid school is 1 and 7 per cent respectively. However, the same rate for high school and above is around 11 per cent. Thus, school attendance status among female decreases as age increases. Looking more crucially at this table, we observe that school attendance status in higher education among urban females is much higher (48.9 per cent for male and 63.2 per cent for female) which is exceptional. Similarly, among all urban residents from primary to high school (for the age group 6-17), school attendance status is almost equal for male and female.

Table 3.3

School Attendance Rate in Uttarakhand by Age, Sex and Type of Residence

Uttarakhand	*Urban*				*Rural*				*Total*			
Age	*M*	*F*	*D=M-F*	*T*	*M*	*F*	*D=M-F*	*T*	*M*	*F*	*D=M-F*	*T*
6-10	91.0	87.4	3.6	89.2	96.1	94.7	1.4	95.4	94.9	92.8	2.1	93.9
11-14	84.8	80.9	3.9	83.1	91.5	83.1	8.4	87.5	89.6	82.6	7.0	86.4
15-17	48.9	63.2	-14.3	56.1	65.9	44.8	21.1	54.9	61.1	49.7	11.4	55.2
6-14	87.9	84.5	3.4	86.3	94	89.3	4.7	91.8	92.4	88.1	4.3	90.4
6-17	78.5	78.8	-0.3	78.6	87.9	78.2	9.7	83.2	85.5	78.4	7.1	82.0

School attendance status by standard of living of the household has been shown in Table 3.4 from which it is clear that as standard of living increases, school attendance status of students also increases. Further, school dropout rate between male and female has been shrinking down with the increase in standard of living. Discrimination is particularly visible in case of higher education. There is a higher percentage of dropouts among the females who belong to household with low standard of living than that of women belonging to household with medium and high SLI. The gender gap in accessing higher education decreases.

Table 3.4

School Attendance Status by Age, Sex and Standard of Living

	Low SLI				*Medium SLI*				*High SLI*			
Age/Sex	*M*	*F*	*D=M-F*	*T*	*M*	*F*	*D=M-F*	*T*	*M*	*F*	*D=M-F*	*T*
6-10	76.9	70.0	6.9	73.7	86.6	76.0	10.6	81.4	88.3	84.1	4.2	86.3
11-14	87.0	83.3	3.7	85.4	95.5	93.7	1.8	94.6	98.2	97.0	1.2	97.7
15-17	84.2	70.0	14.2	77.9	90.4	80.3	10.1	85.6	91.8	87.8	4.0	89.9
6-14	42.9	42.1	0.8	42.5	62.5	39.1	23.4	50.0	67.1	61.3	5.8	64.2
6-17	85.0	77.5	7.5	81.6	93.1	87.5	5.6	90.5	95.1	92.5	2.6	93.9

Table 3.5

School Attendance Status by Age, Sex and Ethnicity of the Household Head

	SC/ST			*OBC*			*General*		
Age/Sex	*Male*	*Female*	*Total*	*Male*	*Female*	*Total*	*Male*	*Female*	*Total*
6-10	84.5	75.7	80.1	77.8	74.8	74.8	89.1	83.1	86.3
11-14	96.0	93.7	95.0	88.9	85.4	87.2	97.0	95.2	96.2
15-17	88.7	81.7	85.2	81.1	73.0	77.0	92.9	86.4	90.0
6-14	54.1	43.2	48.1	47.8	48.0	47.9	68.8	57.5	63.3
6-17	92.7	87.9	90.4	85.4	79.5	82.5	94.7	91.3	93.1

Table 3.5 shows school attendance status by ethnicity of the household. It is clear that school attendance status of students is higher in general category as compared to SC/ST and OBC category. Further, school dropout rate between male and female has been attenuating in SC/ST category as compared to OBC. Discrimination is particularly visible in case of higher education. There is a higher percentage of dropouts among the females who belong to SC/ST category (in the age group 6-14) as compared to general and OBC category.

Conclusion

From this analysis, it is observable that school attendance status at lower primary level, although not hundred per cent, is quite satisfactory for students belonging to different sections of the society. However, as educational level increases, school attendance status by different socio-economic status becomes distinct. Therefore, effort should be taken to reduce dropout rate among mid school and high school level. Further, literacy programme should focus on the illiterate adult especially illiterate women and out-of-school children to reduce gender gap in literacy. The results of our analysis reveal that sex is one of the important factors in determining the school dropouts that has been found higher in socio-economically deprived sections of society comprising mainly the SCs, STs and OBCs.

This study also reveals that male literacy is always higher than that of female literacy in each district of Uttarakhand. Some districts *viz.*, Uttarkashi, Chamoli, Rudraprayag, Tehri Garhwal, Pithoragarh seek more attention for improving the female literacy level. The gender gap is higher in some districts among the rural residents whereas in some other districts it is higher among the urban residents. Among the urban residents, females belonging to Rudraprayag and Tehri Garhwal gets least education than their male counterparts. On the other hand, rural females belonging to Uttarkashi, Udham Singh Nagar, Haridwar and Tehri Garhwal has lower level of literacy.

It is found that in higher education, discrimination in school attendance status between male and female is higher. School attendance status among female decreases as age increases. There is a higher percentage of dropout among the females who belong to household with low standard of living than that of women belonging to household with medium and high standard of living. To gain the various benefits of education on the pace of achieving desired socio-demographic goal, Uttarakhand government should initiate special measures for promoting girl education in the state.

References

Government of India (2002). Census of India, 2001. New Delhi.

Government of Uttar Pradesh and Uttarakhand (2002). Uttar Pradesh and Uttarakhand (Provisional Population 2001). Agra: Sahitya Bhawan Publications.

International Institute for Population Sciences IIPS (2007). *National Family Health Survey, India 2005-2006*. Mumbai: IIPS and ORC Macro.

Kitagawa, E.M. and P.M. Hauser (1973). *Differential Mortality in United States: A Study in Socio-economic Epidemiology*. Cambridge: Harvard University Press.

Pamuk, E., D. Makuc, K. Heck, C. Reuben and K. Lochner (1998). *Socioeconomic Status and Health Chartbook.* Health, Hyattsville, United States: NCHS.

Steenland, K., J. Henley and M. Thun (2002). "All-cause and cause-specific death rates by educational status for 2 million people in two American cancer society cohorts, 1959-1996", *American Journal of Epidemiology* 156:11-21.

4 The Unorganised Sector Workers in Uttarakhand

A Need for Policy Intervention

Bhagwan S. Bisht

Introduction

The unorganised sector workers constitute 92 per cent of the total workforce in the country (NSS 1999-2000) and plays an important role in: (i) providing employment opportunity to a large segment of the working force and contributes to the national product significantly and (ii) the unorganised sector has a crucial role in Indian economy in terms of employment and its contribution to the national domestic product (NDP), savings and capital formation. In this way, the unorganised sector workers contribute nearly 45 per cent of the national income yet do not have any protection from retrenchment or any social security benefits. They work in different employment sectors all the year round with no regular employment and not entitled to have any social security benefits. Almost the same situation is in Uttarakhand.

Objective

The main objective of the study is to present demography, socio-economic status and working condition of the unorganised sector workers in Uttarakhand and also to suggest a work plan for their social security benefits.

Methodology

The findings of this paper are based on the sample study of the unorganised sector workers engaged in tourism activities, brick fields, sand quarries, security services and construction works. This is an empirical study and the information has been collected directly from field sources through interview-schedule and quasi-participant observation method. The total population of unorganised sector workers under study, i.e., 3,75,385 scattered over districts of Uttarakhand constitutes the universe of the present study. Out of the universe, only 8643 workers have been selected through purposive sampling method for study (see Table 4.1).

In this sampling procedure, first of all the area of location of the scheduled employment sectors were identified through pilot survey. At the second step, giving an appropriate representation to all the areas located in hills as well as in plains, the workers engaged in different employments were identified and studied.

Limitation of the Study

The study has been conducted only in those districts/areas where the concentration of workers in the sector under reference is comparatively more.

Findings (Bisht, 2006-07: 1-133)

The information collected directly from field sources exhibit that presently 3,75,385 workers have been engaged with different employment sectors under reference. Out of which only 8,643 workers have been selected for the study. The sector-wise break-up of the workers and the sampled units is presented in Table 4.1.

Out of total 3,75,385 workers, maximum 74.20 per cent are engaged in construction and other works under rural employment schemes, followed by 12.32 per cent workers in brick fields, 6.30 per cent in stone and sand quarries, 5.52 per cent in head load works including coolies and porters and remaining 1.66 per cent workers are engaged in security services. The sample distribution exhibits that out of total 8643 sampled workers, 23.13 per cent are selected from head load works including coolies and porters, 21.05 per cent are from stone/ sand quarries and stone crushers, 21.52 per cent are from construction and other works, 17.36 per cent are from brick fields and the rest 16.94 per cent workers are from security services.

Table 4.1

Sector-wise Break-up of the Workers Engaged in Unorganised Sector and the Sampled Units

Unorganised Sector	*Identified Workers*	*Per cent*	*Sampled Units*	*Per cent*
1 Brick kiln	46,270	12.32	1500	17.36
2. Head load works and coolies/porters	20,795	5.52	1999	23.13
3. Stone/sand quarries/stone crushers	23,622	6.30	1820	21.05
4. Construction and other workers	2,78,472	74.20	1860	21.52
5. Security agencies	6,226	1.66	1464	16.94
Total	3,75,385	100.00	8643	100.00

Sample Profile

The age-wise distribution of the workers in different sectors under reference shown in Table 4.2 exhibits that maximum percentage of the workers i.e., 98.32 per cent engaged in different employment sectors under reference belongs to the age group of 15-60 years of age. Out of this percentage, maximum numbers of the workers are of 21-30 years of age. The data also depict that there are still child-labour workers, which are 0.78 per cent of the total sampled workers engaged with the unorganised sector particularly in sand/stone quarries, brick kiln, head load works and also in construction works respectively. On the contrary, the worker above than 60 years of age are also working with unorganised sectors for eking out their livelihood. Thus, it can be concluded that in spite of the strict Child Labour Act, the child labour practices particularly in unorganised sectors are still being practiced in Uttarakhand. And the family itself is the prime motivator of such practices. On the contrary, the aged workers above 60 years of age are also compelled to work for eking out their livelihoods. There is no provision even for the aged workers.

Table 4.2

Age-wise Distribution of Unorganised Workers in Uttarakhand

Age Group	*Unorganised Workers*					
	Security Services (%)	*Construction Work (%)*	*Porters/ Coolies (%)*	*Quarries/ Stone Crushers (%)*	*Brick Kiln (%)*	*Total (%)*
8-14		01 (0.05)	13 (0.65)	33 (01.81)	20 (1.33)	67 (0.78)
15-20	66 (4.50)	311 (16.72)	309 (15.45)	298 (16.38)	165 (11.00)	1149 (13.30)
21-30	450 (30.74)	596 (32.04)	895 (44.78)	776 (42.64)	450 (30.00)	3167 (36.64)
31-40	443 (30.26)	508 (27.31)	433 (21.67)	440 (24.18)	565 (37.66)	2389 (27.64)
41-50	397 (27.12)	292 (15.70)	252 (12.60)	190 (10.44)	235 (15.68)	1366 (15.80)
51-60	99 (6.76)	132 (7.10)	84 (4.20)	58 (3.18)	54 (3.60)	427 (4.94)
61 & above	09 (0.62)	20 (1.08)	13 (0.65)	25 (1.37)	11 (0.73)	78 (0.90)
Total	1464 (100.00)	1860 (100.00)	1999 (100.00)	1820 (100.00)	1500 (100.00)	8643 (100.00)

The information in Table 4.3 exhibits that both males and females are working in all sectors other than head load works including porters and coolies. But the percentage varies from one employment sector to another. Presently the sampled study proves that only 7.82 per cent female workers against 92.18 per cent male workers are engaged in unorganised sectors under reference. Out of which, maximum percentage of female workers is engaged with construction works, followed respectively by brick kiln and sand/stone quarries.

The information regarding the marital status of the workers shown in Table 4.4 exhibits that the maximum workers, i.e., 78.68 per cent are married, 19.84 per cent are unmarried, 0.83 per cent are widowers, 0.52 per cent are widows, 0.09 per cent are divorced and remaining 0.04 per cent are separated.

Table 4.3

Sex-wise Distribution of Unorganised Workers in Uttarakhand

Sex Group	*Unorganised Workers*					
	Security Services (%)	*Construction Work (%)*	*Porters/ Coolies (%)*	*Quarries/ Stone Crushers (%)*	*Brick Kiln (%)*	*Total (%)*
Male	1457 (99.52)	1507 (81.02)	1999 (100)	1670 (91.76)	1334 (88.93)	7967 (92.18)
Female	07 (0.48)	353 (18.98)	-	150 (8.24)	166 (11.07)	676 (7.82)
Total	1464 (100.00)	1860 (100.00)	1999 (100.00)	1820 (100.00)	1500 (100.00)	8643 (100.00)

Table 4.4

Marital Status of the Unorganised Sector Workers in Uttarakhand

Marital Status	*Unorganised Workers*					
	Security Services (%)	*Construction Work (%)*	*Porters/ Coolies (%)*	*Quarries/ Stone Crushers (%)*	*Brick Kiln (%)*	*Total (%)*
Unmarried	357 (24.39)	373 (20.06)	393 (19.65)	386 (21.20)	206 (13.73)	1715 (19.84)
Married	1105 (75.48)	1395 (75.00)	1585 (79.28)	1425 (78.29)	1290 (86.00)	6800 (78.68)
Divorced	-	02 (0.10)	02 (0.10)	03 (0.17)	-	07 (0.09)
Widows	02 (0.13)	41 (02.20)	-	01 (0.06)	01 (0.07)	45 (0.52)
Widowers	-	45 (02.42)	19 (0.97)	05 (0.28)	03 (0.20)	72 (0.83)
Separated	-	04 (0.22)	-	-	-	04 (0.04)
Total	1464 (100.00)	1860 (100.00)	1999 (100.00)	1820 (100.00)	1500 (100.00)	8643 (100.00)

The nationality and state-wise distribution of workers exhibits that, presently in Uttarakhand, 23.00 per cent Nepali nationals are working with unorganised sectors under reference. The maximum percentage of Nepali workers is engaged in head load works including coolies and porters in tourism sector, followed respectively in stone quarries, construction works and security services. The state-wise distribution of the workers depicts that only 38.92 per cent workers belong to Uttarakhand state while the majority of the workers i.e., 61.08 per cent are from other states of India (Table 4.6). The majority of out-state workers is from UP followed by Bihar, Jharkhand, West Bengal, Rajasthan, Haryana, Himachal Pradesh, Madhya Pradesh, Punjab, Gujarat, Chhattisgarh etc.

Table 4.5

Classification of Workers on the Basis of Nationality and Employment

Nationality	*Employment Sector*					
	Security Services	*Construction Work*	*Coolies & Porters*	*Quarries and Stone Crushers*	*Brick Kiln*	*Total*
Indian	1459 (99.66%)	1567 (84.25%)	629 (31.45%)	1500 (82.42%)	1500 (100%)	6655 (77.0%)
Nepali	05 (0.34%)	293 (15.75%)	1370 (68.54%)	320 (17.58%)	-	1988 (23.0%)
Total	1464 (100%)	1860 (100%)	1999 (100%)	1820 (100%)	1500 (100%)	8643 (100%)

The caste-wise distribution of the workers exhibits that majority of the workers i.e., 54.28 per cent belong to general caste, followed by SCs (21.83 per cent), OBCs (20.41 per cent) and STs (03.48 per cent). This enumeration of data reflects the employment scenario of the different castes in the population and also indicates the increasing trend of unemployment among the general caste population. The educational status of the workers also proves it.

The educational profile of the workers shows that only 37.23 per cent workers engaged with unorganised sector are illiterate, out of which the percentage of the workers belonging to scheduled caste category and OBCs is comparatively more. Among the illiterate workers, maximum percentage engaged with brick kilns, followed by quarries, head load works including coolies and porters and construction works.

Table 4.6

State-wise Distribution of Workers Engaged in Different Employment Sector

State	*Employment Sector*					*Total*
	Security Services	*Construction Work*	*Head Load Workers; Porters/Coolies*	*Quarries/ Stone Crushers*	*Brick Kiln*	
Uttarakhand	1111 (75.89)	1040 (55.91)	464 (23.20)	395 (21.70)	354 (23.60)	3364 (38.92)
Uttar Pradesh	290 (19.81)	276 (14.83)	130 (6.50)	695 (38.19)	1119 (74.60)	2510 (29.00)
Bihar	32 (2.19)	217 (11.67)	16 (0.80)	333 (18.30)	26 (1.73)	624 (7.22)
Chhattisgarh	-	-	-	01 (0.05)	-	01 (0.01)
Rajasthan	-	-	12 (0.60)	01 (0.05)	-	13 (0.15)
Himachal Pradesh	04 (0.29)	-	-	06 (0.32)	-	10 (0.10)
Jharkhand	06 (0.40)	08 (0.43)	04 (0.20)	69 (3.80)	01 (0.07)	88 (1.01)
West Bengal	-	26 (1.40)	02 (0.10)	-	-	28 (0.32)
Nepal	05 (0.34)	293 (15.76)	1370 (68.10)	320 (17.59)	-	1988 (23.00)
Chandigarh	-	-	01 (0.50)	-	-	01 (0.01)
Haryana	12 (0.81)	-	-	-	-	12 (0.13)
Madhya Pradesh	02 (0.13)	-	-	-	-	02 (0.02)
Gujarat	01 (0.07)	-	-	-	-	01 (0.01)
Delhi	01 (0.07)	-	-	-	-	01 (0.01)
Total	1464 (100.00)	1860 (100.00)	1999 (100.00)	1820 (100.00)	1500 (100.00)	8643 (100.00)

Table 4.7

Caste-wise Distribution of Unorganised Sector Workers in Uttarakhand

Caste Category	*Unorganised Workers*					
	Security Services (%)	*Construction Work (%)*	*Porters/ Coolies (%)*	*Quarries/ Stone Crushers (%)*	*Brick Kiln (%)*	*Total (%)*
Scheduled caste	152 (10.39)	415 (22.33)	362 (18.10)	337 (18.51)	621 (41.40)	1887 (21.83)
Scheduled tribe	32 (2.19)	27 (1.45)	86 (04.30)	134 (07.37)	22 (01.47)	301 (03.48)
Other backward classes	126 (8.60)	114 (6.12)	148 (07.41)	591 (32.48)	785 (52.33)	1764 (20.41)
General category	1154 (78.82)	1304 (70.10)	1403 (70.19)	758 (41.64)	72 (04.80)	4691 (54.28)
Total	1464 (100.00)	1860 (100.00)	1999 (100.00)	1820 (100.00)	1500 (100.00)	8643 (100.00)

Table 4.8

Educational Status of Unorganised Sector Workers in Uttarakhand

Educational Status	*Unorganised Workers*					
	Security Services (%)	*Construction Work (%)*	*Porters/ Coolies (%)*	*Quarries/ Stone Crushers (%)*	*Brick Kiln (%)*	*Total (%)*
Illiterate	04 (0.28)	578 (31.07)	810 (40.52)	982 (53.96)	844 (56.27)	3218 (37.23)
Pre-primary	13 (0.88)	263 (14.13)	284 (14.20)	225 (12.37)	165 (11.00)	950 (10.99)
Primary	36 (2.46)	343 (18.44)	336 (16.80)	201 (11.04)	302 (20.13)	1218 (14.09)
Pre-junior high school	57 (3.90)	117 (6.30)	142 (7.10)	99 (5.43)	77 (5.13)	492 (5.69)
Junior high school	429 (29.30)	334 (17.96)	239 (11.96)	159 (8.74)	67 (4.47)	1228 (14.21)
High school	627 (42.82)	115 (6.19)	117 (5.86)	112 (6.16)	39 (2.60)	1010 (11.69)
Intermediate	246 (16.80)	67 (3.60)	54 (2.70)	26 (1.42)	05 (0.33)	398 (4.60)
Graduate	45 (3.08)	37 (1.99)	13 (0.66)	15 (0.82)	01 (0.07)	111 (1.28)
Postgraduate	07 (0.48)	06 (0.32)	04 (0.20)	01 (0.06)	-	18 (0.21)
Others	-	-	-	-	-	-
Total	1464 (100.00)	1860 (100.00)	1999 (100.00)	1820 (100.00)	1500 (100.00)	8643 (100.00)

The occupational profile reveals that the unorganised workers are engaged with different sectors in different capacities, which have been termed as the types/status of workers in the present text. It is observed that the workers are engaged with different employment sectors in the capacity of the wage earners (43.41 per cent), contract labour (22.93 per cent), piece rate labour (20.76 per cent), daily labour (12.72 per cent) and hired labour (0.19 per cent) (see Table 4.9). But the nature of employment show that, the majority of the workers i.e., 58.95 per cent are employed through contractor/sub-contractors, while the rest of the workers are either self-employed (29.50 per cent) or in the capacity of employer (6.91 per cent), and/or employed through group of employment (see Table 4.10). The information thus conclude that the majority of workers get their employment even in unorganised sector only through contractors or the middle men, who have direct or indirect coercion on them and the workers remain under the clutches of the middle men which lead to exploitation of the workers.

Table 4.9

Status/Types of Unorganised Sector Workers in Uttarakhand

Status	*Unorganised Workers*					
	Security Services (%)	*Construction Work (%)*	*Porters/ Coolies (%)*	*Quarries/ Stone Crushers (%)*	*Brick Kiln (%)*	*Total (%)*
Wage earner	-	1572 (84.51)	1894 (94.74)	276 (15.16)	10 (0.67)	3752 (43.41)
Hired labour	-	05 (0.27)	09 (0.45)	02 (0.11)	-	16 (0.19)
Contract labour	1464 (100)	31 (1.67)	05 (0.25)	07 (0.38)	475 (31.67)	1982 (22.93)
Daily labour	-	233 (12.52)	37 (1.86)	798 (43.84)	31 (2.07)	1099 (12.72)
Piece rate labour	-	19 (1.03)	54 (2.70)	737 (40.51)	984 (65.60)	1794 (20.76)
Total	1464 (100.00)	1860 (100.00)	1999 (100.00)	1820 (100.00)	1500 (100.00)	8643 (100.00)

Table 4.10

Nature of Employment of Unorganised Sector Workers in Uttarakhand

Nature of Employment	*Unorganised Workers*					
	Security Services (%)	*Construction Work (%)*	*Porters/ Coolies (%)*	*Quarries/ Stone Crushers (%)*	*Brick Kiln (%)*	*Total (%)*
Self-employment	-	-	1891 (94.60)	659 (36.21)	-	2550 (29.50)
Employer	-	04 (0.21)	87 (4.35)	307 (16.87)	199 (13.27)	597 (6.91)
Employed through group of employment	-	14 (0.75)	01 (0.05)	-	-	15 (0.17)
Employed by individual	-	50 (2.69)	16 (0.80)	59 (3.24)	261 (17.40)	386 (4.47)
Employed through contractor/sub-contractor	1464 (100)	1792 (96.35)	4 (0.20)	795 (43.68)	1040 (69.33)	5095 (58.95)
Total	1464 (100.00)	1860 (100.00)	1999 (100.00)	1820 (100.00)	1500 (100.00)	8643 (100.00)

The wage structure reveals that the majority of the workers (54.59 per cent) are paid Rs.74-100 only per day while there are still 11.06 per cent workers who are paid less than Rs.73.00 only. In all respects, the wages earned by the majority of workers engaged with unorganised sectors under reference is too meagre to satiate their basic needs. However, it can be considered as much as is necessary to keep their body and soul together. So that they can maintain the continuity of the labour force by reproduction process living in the state of pauperism and socio-economic deprivation. The wage structure of the workers is shown in Table 4.11.

The study also concludes that there is no any regular and particular mode of payment to the workers. Some workers are paid only on daily basis (11.69 per cent), some are on weekly basis (15.63 per cent), some are fortnightly (9.30 per cent) and some are on monthly basis (25.95 per cent). There are still some other type of workers who work on piece rate basis (13.84 per cent) and commission basis (0.08 per cent) while 23.51 per cent workers stated that they demand for their wages whenever they need it. But in brief, it can be asserted that the unorganised workers overtly face the problem arising out of the uncertainty of job on the one hand and also of the uncertainty of payment on the other. This state of being creates a new type of psychological insecurity among the workers.

Table 4.11

Rate of Wages of the Workers Engaged in Unorganised Sector in Uttarakhand

Per Day Wage (Rs.)	*Unorganised Workers*					
	Security Services (%)	*Construction Work (%)*	*Porters/ Coolies (%)*	*Quarries/ Stone Crushers (%)*	*Brick Kiln (%)*	*Total (%)*
<51	02 (0.14)		213 (10.66)	69 (3.79)	36 (2.40)	320 (3.70)
51-60	57 (3.89)	16 (0.86)	237 (11.66)	94 (5.16)	154 (10.27)	558 (6.46)
61-72	118 (8.06)	66 (3.55)	162 (8.18)	257 (14.12)	353 (23.53)	956 (11.06)
73	-	464 (24.95)			-	464 (5.37)
74-100	960 (65.58)	1027 (55.22)	720 (36.07)	1185 (65.12)	826 (55.06)	4718 (54.59)
101-150	277 (18.92)	220 (11.83)	169 (8.48)	185 (10.16)	130 (8.67)	981 (11.35)
151-200	42 (2.87)	67 (3.60)	74 (3.75)	28 (1.54)	01 (0.07)	212 (2.45)
201-250	04 (0.27)	-	60 (3.00)	2 (0.11)	-	66 (0.76)
251-300	04 (0.27)	-	163 (8.15)	-	-	167 (1.93)
301-350	-	-	125 (6.25)	-	-	125 (1.45)
351-400	-	-	69 (3.45)	-	-	69 (0.80)
401-450	-	-	02 (0.1)	-	-	02 (0.02)
451-500	-	-	03 (0.15)	-	-	03 (0.03)
501 & above	-	-	02 (0.10)	-	-	02 (0.02)
Total	1464 (100.00)	1860 (100.00)	1999 (100.00)	1820 (100.00)	1500 (100.00)	8643 (100.00)

Table 4.12

Mode of Payment to the Workers Engaged in Unorganised Sector in Uttarakhand

Mode of Payment	*Unorganised Workers*					
	Security Services (%)	*Construction Work (%)*	*Porters/ Coolies (%)*	*Quarries/ Stone Crushers (%)*	*Brick Kiln (%)*	*Total (%)*
Daily basis	-	262 (14.09)	65 (3.25)	683 (37.53)	-	1010 (11.69)
Weekly	-	598 (32.15)	-	676 (37.14)	77 (5.13)	1351 (15.63)
Fortnightly	-	756 (40.65)	-	46 (2.53)	02 (0.13)	804 (9.30)
Monthly	1464 (100.00)	124 (6.67)	-	218 (11.98)	437 (29.14)	2243 (25.95)
Weekly but on Piece rate basis	-	21 (1.13)	-	191 (10.49)	984 (65.6)	1196 (13.84)
Commission based	-	01 (0.05)	-	06 (0.33)	-	07 (0.08)
Others whenever needed	-	98 (5.27)	1934 (96.75)	-	-	2032 (23.51)
Total	1464 (100.00)	1860 (100.00)	1999 (100.00)	1820 (100.00)	1500 (100.00)	8643 (100.00)

Table 4.13

Average Mean of Work-Days in a Week

Day of Week	*Frequency*	*Fx*
1.	14	14
2.	136	272
3.	535	1605
4.	1103	4412
5.	1323	6615
6.	2722	16332
7.	2810	19670
Total	8643	48920

Note: Mean=Σfx/n → Mean = 48920/8643 = 5.66 days.

Average mean of work-days in a week is 5.66 days only.

The study also reveals that the unorganised sector workers do not have any surety of job/work. The enumeration of week, month, season and year-wise availability of work-days depict that an average worker gets only 5 days work in a week, 22 days work in a month, 146 days work in a season of nine months i.e., 270 days and 169 days work in a year. This enumeration of information reflects that the unorganised sector workers in Uttarakhand are leading their life in scarcity of job with meagre wages and also of uncertainty of employment.

Thus, it is evident that an average worker gets only 5 days work in a week.

Table 4.14

Average Mean of Work-Days in a Month

Days (CI)	*f*	*X*	*d*	*fd*	
0-5	11	2.5	-15	-165	
5-10	166	7.5	-10	-1660	-5135
10-15	662	12.5	-5	-3310	
15-20	2163	17.5	0	0	
20-25	2434	22.5	-5	12170	+44240
25-30	3207	27.5	-10	32070	
Total	8643				

Note: Mean = Am+Σfd/n. Σfd = 39105, N = 8643.

Mean = 17.5+39105/8643 = 17.50+4.52=22.2 days.

Average mean of work days in a month is = 22 days only.

Thus, it is evident that an average worker gets only 22 days work in a month.

Table 4.15

Average Mean of Work-Days in a Season of Nine Months (i.e., 270 Days)

C-1	*F*	*X*	*D*	*fd*	
0-30	14	15	-120	-1680	
30-60	162	45	-90	14580	-98070
60-90	849	75	-60	50940	
90-120	1029	105	-30	30870	
120-150	442	135	00	000	
150-180	854	165	30	25620	
180-210	1260	195	60	75600	+155580
210-240	468	225	90	42120	
240-270	102	255	120	12240	

Note: Mean= Am+Σfd/n x (i). Mean=135+57510/5180= 135+11.10= 146.10 days.

Average mean of work-days in a season of nine month (i.e., 270 days) is 146 days only.

Thus, it is evident that an average worker gets only 146 days work in a season.

Table 4.16

Average Mean of Work-Days in a Year

C-1	*F*	*Dx*	*FDx*	
0-60	224	-2	-448	2754
60-120	2306	-1	-2306	
120-180	1674	0	0	
180-240	2372	1	2372	8234
240-300	339	2	678	
300 & above	1728	3	5184	
Total	8643		5480	

Note: Mean= Am+ΣFDx/N.
Mean = 150+(5480/8643)30 = 150+164400/8643= 150+19.02=169.02 days.
Average mean of work-days in a year is = 169 days only.

Thus, it is evident that an average worker gets only 169 days work in a year.

So far as the basic amenities, facilities and working conditions of the unorganised sector workers are concerned, the information depict that the basic amenities like education allowance to the children of the workers, medical allowance/facility, separate hygienic toilets for male and female workers at their work place are almost absent. However, some of the workers informed that drinking water facility remains available at their work place. But there is no other provision for lunch break in general and majority of the workers are not provided any facility like breakfast, lunch and tea with snacks etc.

Even the workers, other than security personnel, are not provided any type of leave, may be that a casual leave, earn leave, medical leave, encashment of leave and maternity leave. However, some of the workers other than security service engaged in quarries/stone crushers and few percentage of construction workers stated that they avail weekly off at their own cost. Some of the workers engaged with stone crushers also stated that they are provided medical leave and also overtime payment for overtime work. But all this depend on the will of the contractor or the owner of the concern.

Table 4.17

Basic Amenities, Facilities and Other Benefits of Unorganised Sector Workers in Uttarakhand

Basic Amenities/ Other Benefits		*Unorganised Workers*					
		Security Services (%)	*Construction Work (%)*	*Head Load Worker (%)*	*Quarries/ Stone Crushers (%)*	*Brick Kiln (%)*	*Grand Total*
Education allowance	Yes	02 (0.13)	-	-	-	-	02 (0.02)
	No	1462 (99.87)	1860 (100.00)	1999 (100.00)	1820 (100.00)	1500 (100.00)	8641 (99.98)
Medical allowance	Yes	12 (0.81)	11 (0.59)	-	-	130 (8.67)	153 (1.77)
	No	1452 (99.19)	1849 (99.41)	1999 (100.00)	1820 (100.00)	1370 (91.33)	8490 (98.23)
Clean drinking water	Yes	1373 (93.78)	1697 (91.23)	1284 (64.23)	589 (32.36)	1500 (100.00)	6443 (74.55)
	No	91 (6.22)	163 (8.77)	715 (35.77)	1231 (67.64)	-	2200 (25.45)
Hygienic toilets	Yes	676 (46.17)	25 (1.34)	33 (1.65)	-	-	734 (8.49)
	No	788 (53.83)	1835 (99.66)	1966 (98.35)	1820 (100.00)	1500 (100.00)	7909 (91.55)
Separate toilets for the female workers	Yes	07 (0.47)	11 (0.59)		-	-	18 (0.21)
	No	1457 (99.53)	1849 (99.41)	1999 (100.00)	1820 (100.00)	1500 (100.00)	8625 (99.79)
Separate toilets for male workers	Yes		11 (0.59)	-	-	-	11 (0.13)
	No	1464 (100)	1849 (99.41)	1999 (100.00)	1820 (100.00)	1500 (100.00)	8632 (99.87)
Lunch break	Yes	02 (0.13)	1429 (76.82)	11 (0.55)	1656 (90.99)	-	3098 (35.84)
	No	1462 (99.87)	431 (23.18)	1988 (99.45)	164 (9.01)	1500 (100.00)	5545 (64.16)

The workers other than security personnel also stated that there is no other provision for economic benefits like bonus, incentive, cash prize, annual increment, house allowance, accommodation allowance, medical facility and conveyance allowance for the workers. But 61.18 per cent workers including 51.04 per cent security personnel, 17.90 per cent construction workers, 3.40 per cent porters and coolies, 29.53 per cent quarries/stone crusher workers and 60.53 per cent brick kiln workers stated that there is a tradition in general that the contractor make available some *kuchcha* accommodation to their workers. But it totally depends on the will of the contractor itself.

Table 4.18

Food-related Facilities to the Workers of Unorganised Sector in Uttarakhand

Food-related Facilities		*Unorganised Workers*					
		Security Services (%)	*Construction Work (%)*	*Porters/ Coolies (%)*	*Quarries/ Stone Crushers (%)*	*Brick Kiln (%)*	*Total (%)*
Breakfast	Yes	19 (1.3)	-	29 (1.45)	31 (1.70)	-	79 (0.91)
	No	1445 (98.7)	1860 (100.00)	1970 (98.55)	1789 (98.3)	1500 (100)	8564 (99.09)
Lunch	Yes	28 (1.91)	-	29 (1.45)	61 (3.40)	-	118 (1.37)
	No	1436 (98.09)	1860 (100.00)	1970 (98.55)	1759 (96.60)	1500 (100)	8525 (98.63)
Tea with snacks	Yes	259 (17.7)	636 (34.19)	29 (1.45)	268 (14.73)	-	1192 (13.79)
	No	1205 (82.3)	1224 (65.81)	1970 (98.55)	1552 (85.27)	1500 (100)	7451 (86.21)
Total		1464 (100.00)	1860 (100.00)	1999 (100.00)	1820 (100.00)	1500 (100.00)	8643 (100.00)

Besides this, there is no other regular provision for pay revision to the workers. But the workers in general stated that the contractor generally increase their wage some times annually, some times bi-annually, some times tri-annually and some times, once in five years with the increase of the dearness in market commodities. This totally depends on the will of the contractors and decided through bargaining between both the parties.

The social security and other benefits related information reveal that some of the security service agencies and stone crusher owners provide social security like PF, EPF, gratuity, ESI and compensation on some particular cases to their workers. While the majority of the workers in general and the workers engaged with construction works, head load works, quarries and brick kiln in particular stated that there is no provision for social security like PF, EPF, ESI etc. Certainly 13.49 per cent workers which include 9.60 per cent security personnel, 12.95 per cent construction workers, 19.50 per cent head load workers, 11.59 per

Table 4.19

Leave Provisions/Leave Facilities to the Workers of Unorganised Sector

Leave Facility	*Unorganised Workers*					
	Security Services (%)	*Construction Work (%)*	*Porters/ Coolies (%)*	*Quarries/ Stone Crushers (%)*	*Brick Kiln (%)*	*Total (%)*
Weekly off	474 (32.38)	17 (0.91)	-	589 (32.36)	-	1080 (12.5)
Casual leave	34 (2.32)	-	-	-	-	34 (0.39)
Earn leave	34 (2.32)	-	-	-	-	34 (0.39)
Medical leave	11 (0.75)	-	-	633 (34.78)	-	644 (7.45)
Encashment of leave	26 (1.78)	-	-	-	-	26 (0.30)
Maternity leave	-	-	-	-	-	-
Overtime payment	94 (6.42)	02 (0.11)	-	258 (14.18)	-	354 (4.10)
Not any	791 (54.03)	1841 (98.98)	1999 (100)	340 (18.68)	1500 (100)	6471 (74.87)
Total	1464 (100.00)	1860 (100.00)	1999 (100.00)	1820 (100.00)	1500 (100.00)	8643 (100.00)

Table 4.20

Wage Revision Pattern for the Workers of Unorganised Sector in Uttarakhand

Wage Revision Pattern	*Unorganised Workers*					
	Security Services (%)	*Construction Work (%)*	*Porters/ Coolies (%)*	*Quarries/ Stone Crushers (%)*	*Brick Kiln (%)*	*Total (%)*
Yes Annual	104 (7.10)	14 (0.76)	111 (5.56)	361 (19.83)	320 (21.33)	910 (10.53)
Bi-annual	10 (0.69)	13 (0.70)	15 (0.75)	-	243 (16.20)	281 (3.25)
Tri-annual	22 (1.50)	-	-	-	07 (0.47)	29 (0.34)
Once in five years	-	-	05 (0.25)	-	-	05 (0.06)
No provision for	1328 (90.71)	1833 (98.54)	1868 (93.44)	1459 (80.17)	930 (62.00)	7418 (85.83)
Total	1464 (100.00)	1860 (100.00)	1999 (100.00)	1820 (100.00)	1500 (100.00)	8643 (100.00)

cent quarry/stone crusher workers and 12.33 per cent brick kiln workers stated that they are covered respectively under individual insurance policy, group insurance policy, Janashree Bima Yojana and also by professional insurance. But the majority of the workers of all employment sectors under reference expressed their ignorance towards any insurance policies. Besides this, there is no any provision for financial support for the workers when they are in need and hardship. Only 4.66 per cent workers including 0.81 per cent security personnel, 1.67 per cent construction works, 0.05 per cent head load workers, 1.49 per cent quarry/stone crusher workers, 22.13 per cent brick kiln workers are of the opinion that the contractor/owners of the respective concerns generally lend individual loans when they are in need. This loan is given totally on personal terms and conditions decided by the money lenders itself. It is observed that only on the basis of this personal loan, the contractors keep the workers under their clutches and make their use as per their choice. This personal loaning system somewhere paves the way for exploitation of the workers.

Thus, it can be concluded that in unorganised sectors under reference there is no any provision for social security to workers. The working conditions are not favourable. The workers work in very harsh and hazardous conditions. No medical facility is available to the workers. No schooling provision is there for the workers' children. No strict and written provision of insurance is there. Even the provision for compensation in any type of accident, has not been existent for the workers. The unorganised workers, who constitute a major part of the existing workforce are deprived of all type of social security and other benefits. Even the basic amenities and the working conditions at their work place are almost unfavourable and totally depend on the will of the contractors and the owners' will.

General Working Condition of the Unorganised Sector Workers

Factories Act, 1948, Section 11 states that there is provision for cleanliness, disposal of waste and effluent and accumulation of dust and fume in any work-room and artificial humidification where needed, suitable lighting—natural or artificial or both, sufficient supply of

Table 4.21

Provisions for Social Security Benefits to the Workers of Unorganised Employment Sector in Uttarakhand

Social Security	*Unorganised Workers*					
	Security Services (%)	*Construction Work (%)*	*Porters/ Coolies (%)*	*Quarries/ Stone Crushers (%)*	*Brick Kiln (%)*	*Total (%)*
PF	361 (24.65)	-	-	27 (1.49)	-	388 (4.49)
EPF	553 (37.78)	-	-	01 (0.05)	-	554 (6.41)
Gratuity	34 (02.33)	-	-	20 (1.10)	-	54 (0.62)
Compensation	07 (00.48)	-	-	-	-	07 (0.08)
ESI	498 (34.02)	-	-	-	-	498 (5.76)
Any other	11 (0.75)	1860 (100.00)	1999 (100.00)	1772 (97.36)	1500 (100.00)	7142 (82.63)
Total	1464 (100.00)	1860 (100.00)	1999 (100.00)	1820 (100.00)	1500 (100.00)	8643 (100.00)

drinking water and also sufficient space for work. But in the present study, it is observed that no other such provision has been made in and around the work place where the unorganised workers have been engaged for earning their livelihood. Virtually, the unorganised sector workers under reference have no favourable and suitable working conditions as desirable according to Factories Act, 1948. The workers generally work in some unhealthy, hazardous and filthy surroundings and live in temporary self-made hutments covered with polythene sheets nearby their work place. Generally, the piece-rate workers like stone/sand quarry workers, brick kiln workers and the workers engaged in road cutting and construction works dwell nearby their work place in such type of temporary hutments, where no basic amenities are available.

Besides this, there are workers who own cheap rented rooms in the nearby localities. Since they cannot afford to spend a high amount for hiring good residential accommodation due to meagre earnings, they are compelled to hire dwelling places in such densely populated and poorly built dirty areas where almost all the basic amenities remain absent.

Such dwelling areas lack sufficient sunlight, fresh air, sanitary services and even fresh drinking water. Such living conditions affect the physical and mental health of the workers and even of their family members and ultimately affect their working capacity. Soon after they come under the grip of some vital diseases like asthma, tuberculosis, diarrhoea, jaundice and many other types of respiratory and gastrointestinal diseases.

The working conditions of the porters and pony-porters, engaged particularly in religious tourism particularly in Yamunotri, Kedarnath, Kailash-Mansarovar route, Tungnath and other areas, where there is no motorable routes available, are inhumane, brutal and animal-like. The litter porters (*dandi-walas*) and basket porters (*kandi-walas*) just carry the pilgrims respectively by litter on their shoulders and baskets on back through the miles-long ups and downs of the hilly tracks full of risk. They do not have any meaning for rest, relaxation, timely meals, sanitation and hygienic conditions. Their only mission is to earn freight by carrying the pilgrims to their destination. Virtually, the porters are used just like a transport animal. Carrying human being by the human being itself reflects the traces of servitude even in the present era of modernisation and advanced technology. Both the parties, the service givers and the service takers, are compelled for this inhumane activity. But the only difference is that the service giver has no any other option of earning one's livelihood and vice-versa, the service taker also has no other safe and comfortable option to reach to one's destination. The former render services to satiate one's hunger of stomach and to save one's family from starvation, while the latter takes the services to make his journey comfortable, subsequently for spiritual bliss and to acquire the peace of mind and soul. In addition, the working condition of pony porters is hellish too. Their working conditions are precarious and full of health hazards. Holding the bushy tail of pony with one hand and the rein of the following pony by the other hand, a porter drive away minimum two and maximum four ponies at a time, and traverse mechanically the ups and downs of the stony, rugged, hilly tracks from morning to night and carry the pilgrims to their destination and thus earn freight to carry on their age-old occupation for living. During this travel, a porter spends the whole day amidst the foul smell coming out of the pony's body and also strong odour of their excreta and urine. The porters seem to have become immunised from the stench arising out of the wastes of the ponies. Hence, on the way to their destination they just take a break for a moment at some halting places, tie the pony with stakes and feed them *gur* and gram while having their breakfast/meal sitting beside the ponies. It seems that the life of a pony porter i.e., mankind is no different from the pony's i.e., the animal. Even at night-time, the porters have to a sleep beside the same place or shade where the ponies are kept. So that they can guard the ponies on one hand and also have some warmth to save themselves from the cold on the other.

Though the local bodies have erected some shades/stables at certain intervals throughout the track for the ponies and the porters, but the maintenance of those shades is worse than any thing and not in a position to serve the purpose. There is a provision for drinking water and of electricity on the way to the place of pilgrimage. But the poor upkeeping system has defeated its meaning. Thus, the pony porters, litter porters and basket porters have sustained their profession any how and serving the pilgrims to help achieve their destination and in turn, earning their living just to keep their body and soul together in wake of scarcity and pauperism.

The brick kiln workers engaged in different brick-fields located in three districts of Uttarakhand namely Udham Singh Nagar, Haridwar and Dehradun are from different states and districts of India. Mostly, the brick kiln workers are working in this sector since their birth. They start their career as brick kiln workers at 5 to 6 years of age while living with their parents working as brick kiln workers. They are basically piece rate contract labourers and work about eight to nine months mostly with effect from the month of October/November every year to mid-June to July next year. During July to September/October, they work as agricultural labourers wherever they get such opportunity, while some of the brick kiln workers migrate to Kashmir in search of job mainly in brick kiln fields. Some of the labourers remain out of job during rainy season. In such cases, the brick kiln workers generally take loan from their owners with this written agreement on stamp papers that they will work for them whenever the work starts in their brick fields. In such cases, the brick kiln owners happily lend money to the workers and negotiate for the cheap rates i.e., Rs. 110-125 for per thousand brick-

pathan. Since the poor and needy workers do not have any option and bargaining capacity hence, they are easily trapped by the owners and remain under their clutches for generations. It is also observed that some of the families are leading covertly the life of a bonded labourer of the brick kiln owners or the contractors who supply labour force to other brick kiln owners. Mr. Nanne, S/o Sri Mouddin (pseudo name) with his wife Mrs. Shahidan and six children ranging from the age one year to 12 years is the best and lively example of this sort. Mr. Nanne's family is working with a brick kiln contractor at Baghora Sitarganj for the last two generations. His father, now passed away, came with his family to work with this brick kiln. He worked throughout his life and transmitted it to his son in legacy. Mr. Nanne is only 30 years of age and has six children, one son and five daughters. In response of a question he stated that more hands generate more earnings, hence he does not have any problem with the large size of family. He is also assured that at least the contractor/brick kiln owner shall provide him shelter at the time of hardship, maybe meagre, however sufficient to keep their body and soul together. This is the notion that has sustained the slavery like conditions among the labourers.

The brick kiln workers just live in very temporary huts made up of the polythene tents beside the brick field or the *kachcha* brick wall covered with grass. An average brick kiln worker performs its work from 8 a.m. to 8 p.m. For this purpose he/she gets up early in the morning by 3.30 to 4.00 a.m. and cooks food for the family, feed the family members and start working with all the family members latest by 8.00 a.m. The worker with his/her partner clear the space for making bricks, dig up the field and collect the soil and pour water on the heap of the soil to get it soaked. Then the wet soil is mixed with the help of spade and also by feet. And when it gets ready, the worker frames it and leaves the *kuchcha* brick to be dried up in the sun.

During the day-long 12 hours of tedious and tiresome work, the workers just have one hour break for having lunch or tea at noon provided they have the means. Being a piece rate labour, the brick kiln owner or the contractor has no other compulsion about their workings. However, they, the owner and contractor, just observe and mind the quality of work done by the piece-rate labourers. In this way, an average brick kiln worker earns Rs. 70 to 80 per day only. The owner just gives an open space to layout the tent or make available the raw material to erect the temporary huts for living, and instal hand pump sets for drinking water. There is no provision of toilets, bathroom and urinal. The workers generally use the adjoining open field for excretion and other toilet purposes. Exceptionally, in some brick fields, the workers themselves have made their temporary toilets by erecting the four walls of *kuchcha* bricks or by wrapping polythene on the upright wooden logs.

The only hand pump set is used for all purposes like drinking water, washing clothings and utensils and taking bath etc. There is no any provision for electricity. Only kerosene oil lamps serve their need for lighting during night time. No medical facility is provided by the contractor and the owners. However, the workers are lent money when they are in need by the contractor/brick field owner and adjust and recover it later on from their wage.

It is observed that the workers from three generation ranging from the age group of 8 to 65 years, work together in brick fields and thus the workers inherited this profession to its posterity in legacy.

The workers engaged in stone/sand quarries and stone crushers are also working in highly hazardous and risky work conditions. The stone crusher workers work in unhealthy environment full of dust and smoke coming out of the crushing machines. The workers have become used to work in such polluted environment. They either do not realise its far-reaching ill and fatal effects on body and mind or if they realise, the economic compulsion forces them to work in such hazardous conditions. In other words, it may be stated that the workers are compelled to work in such unhealthy, polluted, risky and hazardous conditions only for the sake of their livelihood. Besides the working place, the dwelling place of the workers is even more unhealthy and hazardous. The workers engaged in stone/sand quarries and stone crushers, either live in self-made temporary polythene hutments nearby their work place or hire cheap rented rooms in some densely populated dirty localities and live in groups. There are workers who make their temporary hutments nearby their work place and live with their family consisting of wife and children. Such type of workers generally works on piece-rate basis. In such type of piece-rate works, the wife and children of the workers also lend their hands. This system is observed mainly in sand quarries and brick-fields and also in grid-breaking at road side.

Often the workers live a very modest life without any man-made basic amenities and depend by all means on natural resources like fuel wood, drinking water, light, toilets and even for the shelter in order to pass the night. The subjects like education, recreation, modern facilities, hygienic and nutritious food, sanitation, medical facilities and accidental risk-cover are far beyond their access, imagination and priorities. Living at the mercy of nature has become their destiny. They are used to work in inhumane situations at work place as well as their dwellings.

Thus, the poor housekeeping, poor lighting, long working hours, poor work place design, unawareness of possible risks, poor nutrition, inadequate sanitation, ignorance regarding community health and hygiene, poor working conditions altogether reflect the work environment of the unorganised sector workers like brick kiln workers, porters-coolies, workers engaged in quarries, stone crushers and or construction works. There are examples of piece-rate system particularly in brick fields, road construction works mainly in grid-breaking works, which makes working hours irregular and working habits of the workers unsafe.

Suggestions and Recommendations

In view of the crucial role of unorganised sector workers in India's economy, particularly in terms of employment and their contribution to the national domestic product (NDP), savings and also in capital formation on the one hand and the overall problems, the workers generally facing particularly in terms of uncertainty of job, harsh and hazardous working conditions, general socio-economic deprivation, ignorance, lack of technical know-how, etc., on the other hand. In this context, the following suggestions and recommendations can be considered for the identification of the workers and their welfare.

Suggestion and Action Plan

- At the first step, a person willing to work in any scheduled employment under unorganised sector shall have to apply by submitting his/her domicile certificate as verification of national identity, for identity card called 'Unorganised Sector Worker's Identity Card' (USWIC) to the *tehsil* or district level authorised signatory.
- At the second step the authorised signatory, on the basis of the valid domicile certificate of the applicant could issue 'Unorganised sector worker's identity card' to the applicant. The validity of USWIC may be fixed for three to five years duration and may be extended for further three to five years by proper renewal of the USWIC. The scope of the USWIC may be fixed as per norms of the labour ministry of Indian Government.
- At the third step, the worker bearing USWIC would have to get registered with the regional labour and employment department where he/she wishes to work. The registered worker would be issued a registration certificate (RC) on the basis of which he or she will be authorised to work in any scheduled employment in the unorganised sector.
- For the accomplishment of this task, a separate cell/state board within the state can be established with its district/*tehsil* level units/offices. It shall be the duty of the unit/office in-charge to prepare and upkeep a complete unorganised sector worker's profile of the area concerned.
- The contractor or the concern willing to have the services of the unorganised workers should be directed that only those workers bearing the USWIC and registration certificate should be given an opportunity for a job. And the person having no USWIC and RC should be motivated to get USWIC and also to get registered and to have RC first. Such a practice will be helpful to maintain the updated numbers of the workers and also help the department concerned to ensure social security benefits and other welfare measures to the duly valid and registered workers only.

- Only the registered workers having USWIC with RC would be entitled to avail social security benefits and other welfare measures meant for the unorganised sector workers. Such a practice will motivate the workers to get USWIC and also to get registered with the department concerned.
- Both the parties i.e., the contractor or the concern having services of the workers and the workers itself must be liable to abide the provisions related to social security meant for the workers.
- The minimum wage of the workers should be fixed as per price-index and regular revision of wages should be ensured from time to time. This practice will help both the parties in many ways.
- Special care should be taken to safeguard the interests of the workers by providing them social securities of different kinds and other benefits.
- Special awareness programme should be organised periodically for the workers so that they can be made aware of the various provisions, social security benefits, insurance benefits, compensation and welfare measures etc., meant for them.
- Training workshop should be organised for the workers for capacity building, upgrading their skill and awareness level to enable them to find new avenues of employment, and competitive in terms of cost and quality of their product and work.
- Strict provisions related to the working hours, working conditions, insurance, compensation, medical facilities and schooling of the workers' children should be ensured by the department concerned.
- At the same time, the liability of the workers to the work, its quality and also its timely accomplishment should also be fixed.

References

Bisht, B.S. (2007). *Report on Unorganised Sector Workers in Uttarakhand* (Unpublished). Department of Labour and Employment, Govt. of Uttarakhand.

5 Inequalities of Income Opportunity in a Hilly State

A Study of Uttarakhand

Nilabja Ghosh, Sabyasachi Kar
and Suresh Sharma

Introduction

The Indian economy has grown at a fast pace in the recent past and this has resulted in an optimism on most fronts. In such a milieu however, it is extremely important to ensure that all sections of the population share the fruits of this success. The Constitution of India in its Preamble mandated the equality of status and of opportunity to all the citizens and also prohibited any form of discrimination in its Article 15. Yet, inequality in income opportunities has been a steady feature of the Indian economy and society. The persistence of inequalities has always drawn the attention of scholars, activists and policy makers. In the literature, the persistence of underdevelopment in large pockets has been explained by traditional theories such as the 'vicious cycle' (Nurkse, 1953), 'cumulative causation' (Myrdal, 1968) or perhaps by an 'urban bias' in the development process (Lipton, 1977). Although the traditional and modern theories do predict convergence of unequal regions and groups (Lewis, 1954; Kuznets, 1955; Sala-i-Martin, 2002) and spatial diffusion of commercial success (Krugman and Elizondo, 1996), there are numerous empirical examples to the contrary. India's post-reform experience has also failed to indicate spatial convergence in any perceptible degree (Vakulabharanam, 2005; Bhattacharya and Sakthivel, 2003; Kar and Sakthivel, 2003; Marjit and Mitra, 1996). Among the most marginalised sections in India, are people living in geographically fragile areas like the Himalayas, where conventional agricultural and industrial developments face severe constraints. In this paper, we analyse the various types of inequalities in income that characterise these hilly regions even in this era of high growth. It is based on a survey of the Himalayan state of Uttarakhand and examines the factors that lie behind income variation among households in this state. It is obvious that the income earning capability of a household is shaped by its demographic composition. The proportion of the working-aged members in a household would represent its labour power and be an important determinant of the household income. Another factor that could determine the income earning capability of the household is the work experience of the working members symbolising the accumulated learning that creates human capital. However, the advantage of experience has a chance of being nullified under rapid technological change when newer entrants bring more relevant skills making the older experience obsolete. If the market has lesser opportunities for women or if the social norms work against women, the gender composition of the working age members would also matter. Education is another income enhancing factor that is increasingly receiving policy attention in recent times for various reasons. Education is an important door towards higher income opportunity. Besides, it has many other social and inter-generational benefits of immense value. Education is a 'capability' (Sen, 1999 and 2003) that underlies the advocacy of 'investment in man' and has been sometimes considered even more important than physical and tangible capital formation (Myrdal, 1957; 1968). The sources of modern economic growth are sought in the changing quality of labour and capital rather than in the accumulation of conventional units of physical capital and increased application of hours of labour (Kuznets, 1966). A strong empirical regularity is inescapable between the educational attainments of a population and its productivity and performance in the market (Schultz, 1988). Education brings awareness and knowledge of how to make use of available opportunities and resources. It also confers greater bargaining power in the market. In the case of a population engaged in agriculture, empirical investigations have found the returns to schooling of the household heads to be ranging from negative to insignificant positive but when family members' education is also considered, the returns are found significant (Taylor *et al.*, 2000), reflecting the fact that even children's education influences the choice of activities, decisions of resource allocation and the farm incomes. Apart from these intrinsic characteristics of a household, its geographical location also determines its income earning capability. Theories of the urban bias (Lipton, 1977) have shown that urban areas get priority in the development process and this leads to income disparity between rural and urban areas. Thus, households in a rural location will have lower income opportunities compared to urban households. Finally, for a hilly state, household incomes are also determined by altitude. The hilly regions of the state will provide less income earning opportunities than those in the foothills or the plains because the difficulties of communication and the sparsity of population discourage commercial enterprises from building up in the hills.

It is clear from all this that there may be many reasons for inequality of income opportunity to persist in a hilly state. At the same time, there is a conscious public policy motivated to bringing down disparities and promoting balanced development. In this paper, we try to identify which of these are significant for the state of Uttarakhand. Is there a gender bias in income opportunities in this state? How far do educational attainments matter? Does rural residence impact the income possibility of a household and will the spread of educational facilities erase the disparity? Do households in hill areas face similar implications for disparities as households in the plains? These are some of the questions we probe in this paper.

An Overview of Uttarakhand

Uttarakhand is a Himalayan state that has been recently carved out of the state of Uttar Pradesh (UP). More than 90 per cent of the state is in the mountains but a small part lies in the plains. The state is largely rural in character. Due to the harsh topography it is a migration-prone state. The people of Uttarakhand have been described as extremely 'progressive' (Joshi, 1995) as demonstrated by their educational achievements and their liberal revolutionary movements, one of which is symbolised by their achieved emergence as a state separate from Uttar Pradesh. The achievement of a relatively high literacy rate of 72.8 per cent is noteworthy considering that most parts of the state are 'remote' and difficult to access for the welfare directed state machinery. However, significant rural-urban disparity in literacy tarnishes this achievement. For every person not literate in the urban sector, there are on an average 4.9 such persons in the rural region (Census 2001). The corresponding ratio of total populations in the two sectors is less at 2.9. The urban to rural ratio in literacy rate is about 1.2. Tables 5.1 and 5.2 further portrays some of the disparities in basic education with a gender dimension as illuminated by the NFHS data. The rural-urban disparity is most glaring at higher levels of education. A primary data based study also found several social dimensions of inequality in education in the state (Sharma and Ghosh, 2007).

Table 5.1

Basic Educational Attainments and Infrastructure

		Dehradun	*Uttarakhand*	*Uttarkashi*	*Nainital*
Literacy Rate					
Male	Rural	82.74	83.55	87.62	80.42
	Urban	87.21	93.93	87.00	90.37
Female	Rural	55.52	45.10	67.61	61.57
	Urban	74.77	78.48	77.16	79.61
Total	Rural	68.95	64.70	78.02	71.42
	Urban	81.50	87.46	82.40	85.30
Higher Secondary Complete and Above					
Male	Rural	12.10	-	-	-
	Urban	37.40	-	-	-
Female	Rural	4.80	-	-	-
	Urban	32.00	-	-	-
Population Per Total School (Total)					
	Rural	375.02	362.16	371.05	452.27
	Urban	913.40	849.04	973.96	899.23
Population Per Primary School (Total)					
	Rural	506.12	362.16	520.18	632.98
	Urban	1511.31	849.04	1605.87	1521.61
Pupil Per Teacher in Primary School (Total)					
	Rural	28.49	24.78	25.82	25.66
	Urban	26.38	19.03	29.15	22.36

Source: Census 2001, NFHS and NCERT.

The evidence on the gender perception in the state is rather ambiguous. The hill culture has been conventionally credited for superior gender values and this is confirmed by the sex ratio (962 females for 1000 males) which is higher than the all-India figure (933 females for 1000 males) and particularly so in the rural sector (1007). However, this view is far from confirmed when the sex ratio of the 0-6 years age group is considered (908 against 927 in India). Often the gender bias reflects in a society's labour market and its social norms towards women's work participation. Thus in Uttarakhand, male out-migration, rather than gender sensitivity, is a more relevant factor for explaining the overall sex ratio.

Table 5.2

Rural-Urban Disparities in Development from Primary and Secondary Information: Summary Statistics (Urban/Rural)

Development Indicators	*Primary Survey*	*Secondary Source*	*NFHS 1998-99*	*Secondary Data*
Male				
Literate (0)	1.06	1.12	1.04	Census 2001
Primary and above	1.13	-	1.13	
School complete	2.00	-	3.09	
Female				
Literate (0)	1.13	1.29	1.47	Census 2001
Primary and above	1.20	-	1.88	-
School complete	2.00	6.40		
Income (1)	1.77	1.52	-	NSSO 1999-2000

Note: (0) Literate includes only schooled population in primary data.

(1) Rs. per capita per month, primary data are for income (converted) and secondary are consumption expenditure.

Source: Census 2001, NSSO 1999-2000.

Data Sources and Sampling Procedures

Uttarakhand is a newly created state and hence, data paucity is a problem. While secondary data provided by various official sources are utilised for support, this study is mostly based on data collected from a sample survey made over three clusters in three different districts. The clusters chosen purposively for the survey belong to the districts of Dehradun, Nainital and Uttarkashi. The choice of the districts is aimed at covering a broad spectrum of the state. Uttarakhand is roughly triangular in shape and these three districts are located at the three corners. The districts also represent the varied geography present in the state. Uttarkashi is completely hilly, located away from the Indian mainland, relatively more rural and sparsely populated. It is well known for tourism and pilgrimage attractions but is regularly hit by landslides and earthquakes. Nainital is partly hilly and partly plain and is more urbanised and populated. Tourism and forestry are its main sources of income generation. Dehradun, a district in which the state's capital is located, is largely in the plains and is mostly urbanised. It has major industries and reputed institutions in its vicinity. The three districts also present a balanced profile of occupations in agriculture, manufacturing and trade and services as seen from the Census (1991) data.

One urban centre is selected from each district, again keeping a balance in occupation in view. Rishikesh in Dehradun district, Haldwani cum Kathgodam Municipal Board in Nainital district and Uttarkashi M.B. in Uttarkashi district are the urban centres (UC) selected. From a UC, a total of 120 households are chosen by stratified random sampling from among three different urban blocks and with the strata based on the occupational profiles of households. For each UC, six villages are selected at increasing distances from the UC within a radius of about 45 km to demarcate the hinterland. The Village and Town Directory, 1981 (latest) is used to select two villages from each of three 'remoteness' categories, namely least remote—1 to 10 km from the UC; remote—11 to 20 km from the UC; and most remote—31 or more from the UC. In the case of only the large district Uttarkashi, since there are very 'remote' but inhabited villages, the range for the farthest village has crossed the 40 km mark. The selection procedure for the six villages at increasing distance from the urban centre keeps in view different considerations such as the adequacy of the number of households in a village (a minimum of 45 households) and balanced shares of their population engaged in the primary and non-primary sectors. The village population is stratified by farm and occupational classes. A random sample of 40 households is drawn from a village giving a total of 240 households surrounding each UC and 720 households for the rural sector. Along with 360 urban households, a sample of 1080 households is drawn in the two sectors together. The survey was conducted in June-July 2004. The sample households in the rural and urban areas had questionnaires circulated to them soliciting information on various social and economic aspects of their livelihoods.

An Overview of the Three Sample Districts

The population of Uttarakhand is more rural (74.4 per cent) than that in India (72.2 per cent), with a population of 8 million spread over 13 districts. Dehradun crosses the one million mark while Uttarkashi, a spatially large district records a population less than half that of Nainital. The population density of Uttarkashi is only 37 per sq km, that for Nainital is close to the state average of 159, while that of Dehradun is much higher. Going by the Census definition of the rural and urban sectors, Uttarkashi is highly rural with 92 per cent of the population residing in rural areas, while the figure is a much lower 65 per cent for Nainital and 47 per cent for Dehradun. It may be noted that due to population growth, the number of urban centres in this largely rural state has increased over time as the status of villages convert into towns (classification based on Census definition of the two sectors, see Appendix). Also notable in Uttarakhand is the correspondence between geography and urbanisation of a district. More hilly districts remain more rural in population share than those in plains and despite conversions of status, most hilly districts have less than 10 per cent of population in urban areas. The three sample districts confirm this as the most hilly district, Uttarkashi, remains highly rural in contrast to the other two districts (Table 5.3). The advantage of communication in plain areas possibly plays a key role in promoting economic activities that lead to urbanisation and a consequent concentration of population.

Table 5.3

Rural Population: 2001

Districts	*Population*		*Population Density*	*State's Share of Rural Population (%)*		*Share of State Population*
	Total	*Rural*		*Total*	*Rural*	
Uttarkashi	294179	271255	37	3.47	4.30	92.21
Nainital	762912	493126	198	9.00	7.82	64.64
Dehradun	1279083	601965	414	15.08	9.54	47.06
Uttarakhand	8479562	6309317	159	100.0	100.0	74.41

Source: Census of India, 2001.

Data from the State Planning Department, Government of Uttarakhand, reveal a highly concentrated pattern of income as measured by the district domestic products (DDP) in favour of the plain districts. The bar diagram in Figure 3.1 shows that Uttarkashi is at the bottom of the scale, while Dehradun, which is closely followed by Nainital, is at the top. This inequality between the hills and the plains is because Uttarakhand is largely an agriculture-based state but the topography in the hills impose serious impediments to modern agriculture hindering irrigation and mechanisation, and presenting inimical conditions of soil fertility, slope and farm size. The condition is also as hostile for industries. The number of large and medium industries reported (Government of Uttarakhand, 2001) up to March 1998 is 165 generating an employment of 460,000 but of these, 140 units are in Dehradun and Nainital alone. Small industries constituted on the pattern of *khadi* and village industries are more dispersed but the employment of 25000 is not large for the state. Agriculture remains the main livelihood of the people despite the constraints. Horticulture, food processing, pharmaceutical industry, medicinal plants and organic farming are now identified as the strengths of this hilly state. Unemployment is high with unemployed persons in live registers reaching three lakh in 2002-03.

Recent endeavours of the state towards providing greater education to the people with an emphasis on the school level are reflected in the statistics given by the NCERT. The government has been on a drive to provide schools and especially primary schools within close range of the habitations even though the state is known for its scattered population and inaccessibility of many villages. More than 80 per cent of habitations in the state have a primary school within it or in a range of 1 km, there is a school for every 375 population in rural areas compared to 913 in urban areas and the pupils per teacher ratio in primary schools is 28.5 close to 26.4 in urban areas. The enrolment ratio in rural Uttarakhand (105) is higher than at the all-India level (92) and neighbouring Uttar Pradesh (88). Similarly, the pupil-teacher ratio is better than for rural India (44) and rural Uttar Pradesh (61). Uttarkashi now has a better population-to-school ratio in the rural sector (267) compared to Nainital (371) and Dehradun (452). Uttarkashi also has the lowest pupil to teacher ratio among the three districts.

Figure 5.1

Net Domestic Product at Current Prices: 1997-98

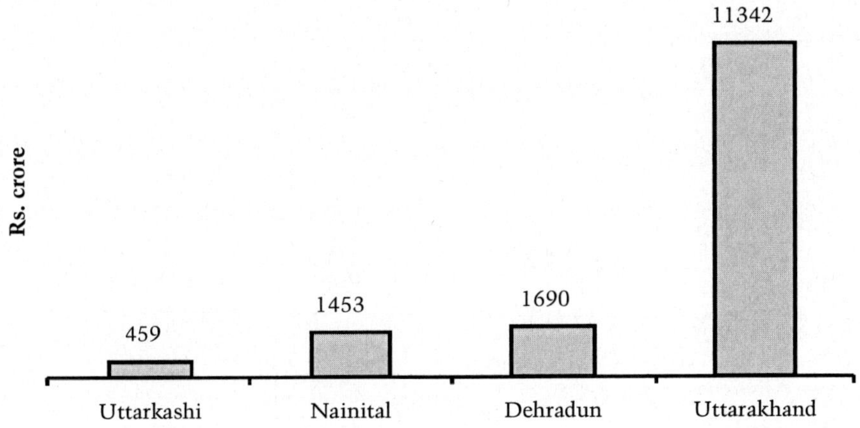

Unequal Income Opportunities

In this section, we use regression analysis to study the different types of income inequalities faced by the people from this state. The endogenous or dependent variable in the regressions is PCIN, the per capita monthly household income. Since we are interested in the income opportunities in the areas where the population resides, we have considered only resident incomes of families, i.e., incomes net of remittances to these families (from outside their places of residence).

We postulate that the exogenous variables that determine the per capita family income include PCW i.e., the labour power of the family (measured as the proportion of family members in the working age group), and AVAGE, which is the work experience of the family (measured by the average age of the working aged members of the family). Apart from these two variables, we include a number of other variables in our regression exercise in order to analyse various types of income inequality in this region.

The regression analysis adopts a multi-step method to investigate the different types of inequalities in income opportunities in these regions. The first step attempts to analyse the gender bias in income opportunities. Accordingly, apart from PCW and AVAGE, equation 1 also includes a variable GENDRATIO, which is equal to the ratio of females to males among the working aged members in a household expressed in percentage. The regression coefficient of this variable clearly captures the income-earning capacity of female-intensive households in this region.

$$PCIN = a_0 + a_1{*}PCW + a_2{*}GENDRATIO + a_3{*}AVAGE \quad ...(1)$$

The second step in the regression exercise attempts to analyse the inequalities in income between skilled and unskilled workers as measured by their education. In order to do this, equation 2 includes three more variables pertaining to the educational attainment of the families. These variables are: (i) school education (PCSC) measured as the percentage of members in the household with education beyond primary stage but only up to school level, (ii) higher education (PCHI) measured as the percentage of members in household with education beyond school level, and (iii) professional education (PCPROF) measured as the percentage of members in household with professional education. Thus, in this study we have considered the education levels of all the household members as a determining force rather than only the education of the household head.

$$PCIN = a_0 + a_1{*}PCW + a_2{*}GENDRATIO + a_3{*}AVAGE + a_4{*}PCSC + a_5{*}PCHI + a_6{*}PCPROF \quad ...(2)$$

Equations 1 and 2 have focused on unequal income opportunities at the household level. We shall next look at sectoral and regional inequalities. The third step is to analyse the urban disparity in income opportunities that go against the rural sector. In order to capture this aspect, equation 3 includes a variable DRURAL, which is a dummy for the rural sector. This variable is used both as a slope dummy to capture the differential returns to education between rural and urban areas and as an intercept dummy to capture other factors that lead to rural-urban disparity in incomes. The rural interaction with professional education is considered irrelevant and omitted due to the unbalanced distribution of education between the sectors and small presence of the category in the rural sector (see Appendix Table A-1).

$$\begin{aligned} PCIN = \; & a_0 + a_1{}^*PCW + a_2{}^*GENDRATIO + a_3{}^*AVAGE + \\ & (a_4{}^*PCSC + a_5{}^*PCHI\,)^*(1+\alpha^*DRURAL) + \\ & a_6{}^*PCPROF + \beta^*DRURAL \qquad \ldots(3) \end{aligned}$$

The fourth step compares the role of the different factors in creating income opportunities between the hills and the plains. Given that the Uttarkashi cluster in our sample is at a high altitude in the mountains while the Dehradun and the Nainital clusters are from the foothills, we have divided the sample into two groups, one consisting of the Uttarkashi cluster representing the hills and the other consisting of the pooled data of the Nainital and Dehradun clusters representing the plains. We have estimated equation 3 separately for these two groups in order to capture the differences between the hills and the plains.

The results of the four regression exercises are presented in Table 5.4. In the first step, equation 1 shows that household income is largely explained by the size of the working age population in the family with a positive and significant effect of experience and a statistically insignificant gender effect. The R^2 values show that at this stage, the fit is poor. In the second step, the inclusion of educational variables improves the fit considerably. Education at any level is found to be income-enhancing and higher education appears to have the strongest influence. The impact of raw labour and experience becomes weaker while the gender effect, which is unfavourable towards female-intensive households, gets stronger although still not statistically significant. The third step captures the rural-urban disparity, and based on the significance levels of the coefficients, both the slope and the intercept effects are retained in the model. Thus, the rural-urban disparity in income opportunities work through two possible channels: first, through the returns to education and second, through other residual sources of income. This disparity brings down the income-earning capacity of all types of education in the rural sector, although the differences are insignificant for school education. In other words, income earned with school education is least affected by rural-urban disparity, but higher education confers much higher earnings to urban individuals compared to their rural counterparts. The equation also shows that labour power is significant even after controlling for all types of educational attainments. This means that even with no education, labour power, measured by the share of working aged members, can enhance household income, but the earning potential increases considerably with higher education of the household members. The coefficient of the gender variable shows that after controlling for other factors, households with a greater share of women in the working age has lower incomes although the coefficient is significant at 10 per cent. This has important implications for a state where the working aged population often tends to be female dominated due to out-migration of males. Finally even after controlling for age, gender and education, the rural household is still likely to earn a significantly lower income than the urban household reflecting a significant dimension of the bias not explained by demography and education. Thus, a household of size 5, with all its members being school educated earns Rs. 2100 more than the one that has no member having more than primary education. Similarly, a household with all its members having higher education is better-off by the substantially greater amount of Rs. 12,650. However the rural household, in the first case is likely to earn Rs. 1814 less and in the second case Rs. 5814 less per month compared to the correspondingly placed households in the urban sector despite comparable educational attainments. Finally for the fourth stage, equation 3 is estimated separately for the hills and the plains.[1] We find that education is a key driver of income in both hills and plains. In the urban sector in both regions, higher education has a bigger impact than

1. An F-test for the two sub-samples is conducted to see that the equations are statistically different though at 10 per cent.

Table 5.4

Sources of Inequality in Income Opportunities: Regression Results

Dependent=PCIN	*Uttarakhand*						*Hills*		*Foothills-Plains*	
Equation No.	1		2		3		3		3	
	Coeff.	*t-value*	*Coeff.*	*t-value*	*Coeff.*	*t-value*	*Coeff.*	*t-value*	*Coeff.*	*t-Value*
CONSTANT	-1797.0	-5.07	-1076.7	-3.86	-746.37	-2.49	-1829.7	-3.19	-172.9	-0.47
PCW	17.34	8.03	6.98	4.55	7.09	4.86	8.35	3.37	5.24	2.82
GENDRATIO	-0.003	-0.009	-0.57	-1.62	-0.46	-1.31	-0.006	-0.009	-0.76	-1.78
AVAGE	58.13	6.51	43.2	5.93	37.5	5.33	56.54	4.38	26.86	3.06
PCSC	—	—	3.44	3.04	4.2	2.1	9.24	2.74	2.92	1.24
PCHI	—	—	23.14	8.21	25.33	5.85	32.32	3.22	23.23	5.61
PCPROF	—	—	25.35	2.56	21.16	2.08	25.26	1.34	21.93	2.13
DUMRUR	—	—	—	—	-222.76	-2.08	49.72	0.25	-285.3	-2.25
Interaction with Rural										
PCSC	—	—	—	—	-1.39	-0.61	-4.43	-1.16	-0.73	-0.26
PCHI	—	—	—	—	-9.37	-1.78	-21.35	-2.14	-5.57	-1.00
R^2 (%)	9.0		27.7		31.0		37.98		27.8	
Durbin-Watson	1.77		1.9		1.98		2.16		1.9	

Source: Based on author's calculation.

other forms of education. There are some differences between the two regions as well. We find that school education has insignificant impact on incomes in the plains while it shows a significant impact in the hills. In contrast, professional education is significant in the plains. Surprisingly, the rural-urban disparity in income from higher education is insignificant in the plains, but the same disparity for higher education is significant in the hills. Another interesting result is that the rural-urban disparity of income from sources other than labour power or education, which is captured by the intercept dummy for the rural sector, is found to be important in the plains but does not emerge in the hills. After controlling for education, raw labour is found to be an important source of income though relatively more powerful in the hills. Further, gender-based disparity is actually not observed in the hills though the sign of the coefficient is negative. It is significant in the plains. This is probably because the agriculture-based and female-dominated economy of the hills makes little distinction between rewarding male and female labour but gender disparity arises in the income-generating sectors in the plains.

Concluding Remarks

This paper examines the inequalities in income opportunities in a hilly region. It is based on the Himalayan state of Uttarakhand, which represents diverse conditions, some of which are advantages while others are constraints. The majority of the districts are in hilly areas and present daunting challenges for both agriculture and industry. The districts of Uttarakhand, the hilly ones in particular, are also highly rural in population share and even the urban areas retain rural characteristics. The lack of opportunities for higher incomes makes these districts migration-prone and the women are usually left behind as workers in the hill economy. Secondary data reveal rural-urban differences in education at various stages and in average income levels. Conversely, there is also evidence of dissemination of education particularly at the school level in favour of rural areas and more important in remote and hilly habitations. This is in line with the nation's endeavours in recent decades to attain universal school education.

The econometric analysis finds that there is significant inequality in income opportunities between skilled and unskilled workers as education is a key driver of income and higher education in particular has a powerful role in increasing income levels. The inequality in income opportunities is also significant between the rural and the urban sectors, with the rural areas facing an adverse bias not only due to the differences in the people's education levels but additionally, because: (i) the returns from various levels of education themselves are relatively lower in the rural sector and (ii) other residual sources not captured by the model work to widen the gap against the rural sector. The results also show that income is somewhat lower in a family that has a higher share of women in the working aged population. Since there is a lot of male migration in Uttarakhand, this gender-based disparity may hurt a number of households in this state. In general, a higher share of dependency expectedly works against the household's welfare and the working aged members both in terms of their share and their length of experience help to make the household better-off. Finally, the results also show that there are differences in the nature of the inequalities between the hilly areas and the plains.

Any policy to promote equality in income opportunity throughout Uttarakhand should be based on an understanding of the nature of the inequalities, which are very different in different parts of the state. Thus, although education has an important income-enhancing power, a rural-urban disparity in returns to higher education is marked in the hills. On the other hand, the same disparity does not characterise the returns to school education in general but in the plains, school education itself has limited benefit. Professional education is relevant only in the plains. Again, rural-urban disparity in income from sources not explained by education, labour, land and gender is apparent only in the plains. Women's share in the workforce brings down household income in the plains but the gender effect is not as apparent in the hills. Raw labour and experience are more important in the hills. Thus, a policy package will have to look for the specific reason for income inequality in a certain area and work out the correct policy relevant for that area.

A policy implication that comes out of the exercise is the well-recognised need for the spread of education in rural and hilly areas. More specifically, our findings emphasise the importance of higher education, in which Uttarakhand is yet to focus attention in the hill areas. Education is particularly important because the present state of agriculture is not found to be income-enhancing in the hills. Another point to note is that there is significant disparity in the returns to education between urban and rural areas. This is a matter of concern as it could only result in more out-migration, discouragement and above all injustice to rural people. This disparity, which is more conspicuous for higher education, could come from the lack of opportunities consistent with the education available in the villages and from the poor quality of education in these areas. The lower returns to higher education can be corrected by redesigning the education system in line with the region's economic prospects and by an integrated approach in planning development. This will also facilitate economic growth. At the regional level, such disparities appear in the hills but the plains demand an emphasis on the spread of education. A focus on both urban and rural development merits attention.

References

Bhattacharya, B.B. and S. Sakthivel (2003). "Regional disparities in growth: A comparison of pre and post-reform period", *Discussion Paper* No. 73/2003. Delhi: Institute of Economic Growth.

Census of India (1981). *Town and Village Directory*, Office of the Registrar General and Census Commissioner, India.

———. (2001a). Uttarakhand *Provisional Population Totals, Series*-6, *Paper-1,* Office of the Registrar General and Census Commissioner, India.

———. (2001b). Uttarakhand *Provisional Population Totals, Series*-6, *Paper-3,* Office of the Registrar General and Census Commissioner, India.

Centre for Monitoring Indian Economy Pvt. Ltd. (2000). *Profiles of Districts*. October.

Dasgupta, Partha (2001). *Human Well-Being and the Natural Environment.* New York: Oxford.

Government of Uttarakhand (2001). *Uttarakhand at a Glance.*

Govinda, R. (2002). *India education report. A Profile of basic education*. Oxford: NIEPA.

International Institute for Population Sciences (IIPS) and Macro International (1998). National Family Health Survey (NFHS-1), 1998-1999: India: Volume I. Mumbai: IIPS.

Joshi, P.C. (1995). *Uttarakhand: Issues and Challenges*. New Delhi: Har-Anand Publications.

Kar, S. and S. Sakthivel (2003). "Regional divergence in India during the era of liberalization: A sectoral decomposition", *Working Paper*. Delhi: Institute of Economic Growth.

Krugman, P. and R. Livas Elizondo (1996). "Trade policy and the third world metropolis", *Journal of Development Economics* 49(1): 137-50.

Kuznets, S. (1955). "Economic growth and income inequality", *The American Economic Review* XLV (1).

———. (1966). *Modern Economic Growth: Rate, Structure and Spread*. New Haven, CT: Yale University Press.

Lewis, W.A. (1954). *Economic Development with Unlimited Supplies of Labour*. Manchester School.

Lipton, M. (1977). Why *Poor People Stay Poor: Urban Bias in World Development*. Cambridge: Harvard University Press.

Marjit, S. and S. Mitra (1996). "Convergence in regional growth rates: Indian research Agenda", *Economic and Political Weekly* 31(33).

Myrdal, Gunnar (1968). *Asian Drama: Inquiry into the Poverty of the Nation*. London: Allen lane, The Penguin Press.

National Sample Survey Organisation (various), *Sarvekshana*.

Nurkste, Ragnar (1953). *Problems of Capital Formation in Under Developed Countries*. Oxford.

Sala-i-Martin, X. (2002). "The world distribution of income: Falling poverty and... convergence, period", *Quarterly Journal of Economics*.

Schultz, T. Paul (1988). "Education investments and returns, in H. Chenery and T.N. Srinivasan (ed.), *Handbook of Development Economics*. Elsevier Science Publishers B.V.

Sen, Amartya (2003). *Human Rights and Asian Values*. New York: Carnegie Council on Ethics and International Affairs.

———. (1999). *Development as Freedom*. New York: Oxford University Press.

Sharma, Suresh and Nilabja Ghosh (2007). "Education for all in rural Himalayas: A study of Uttarakhand", IEG *Working Paper Series* E/284/2007.

Taylor, J. Edward and Antonio Yunez-Naude (2000). "The returns from schooling in a diversified rural economy", *American Journal of Agricultural Economics* pp.287-97.

Vakulabharanam, Vamsi (2005). "Growth and distress in South Indian peasant economy during the era of economic liberalisation", *The Journal of Development Studies* 41(6).

APPENDIX A-5.1

Rural and Urban Sectors: Census Definition

There is no uniform definition of rural and urban areas in the world. The definition used here is as used in Census 2001. The rural-urban demarcations are referred to alternatively as the two sectors. A place is designated as 'urban' if the following criteria are satisfied:

(a) All places with a Municipal Corporation, Municipality, Cantonment Board or Notified Town Area Committee, etc.

(b) All other places satisfying the following criteria:

  (i) A minimum population of 5000,

  (ii) At least 75 per cent of the male working population engaged in non-agricultural pursuits, and

  (iii) A density of population of at least 400 per sq. km.

Primary Data: Household Characters

A-1

Sample Mean Value of Some Household Variables

	Rural	*Urban*
Demography/Employment		
Percentage of working age—male	31.1	33.3
Percentage of working age—female	29.57	29.18
Percentage of members—female	47.75	45.54
Qualifications		
Not educated [0]	51	43
School education[1]	41	40
Higher education—general[2]	8	16
Higher education—professional[3]	0.3	2

Note: [0] Percentage of members not schooled or schooled up to primary.

[1] Percentage of members with only school education.

[2] Percentage of members with higher (beyond school) general education.

[3] Percentage of members with higher (beyond school) professional education. beyond primary stage in household.

B. Fertility and Family Planning

6 Age at Marriage in Uttarakhand

Changing Perspective and Role of Family Systems

Ravi Prakash and
Sulabha Parasuraman

Introduction

Marriage is one of the important social institutions which play an important role in the life of a human being. The study on age at marriage got importance, since long back, due to its strong association and impact on social, economic and demographic situation. Historically, premature and child marriages have been an accepted norm in Indian society. Not only the statistical data but sociological literatures also contain ample evidence to reveal the taboos, social customs and pressures that have perpetuated the custom of early marriage in Indian society. Marriage of females before the attainment of puberty had been a very common feature of the Indian marriage system, even up to the end of the nineteenth century. In fact, it was considered as a matter of pride for parents to have arranged marriage of their daughters before they attain puberty. The basic argument was, since a daughter is a property of another man and his family so it will be safer to marry her as soon as possible i.e., just after the attainment of her puberty. Further, it will be cheaper to get one's daughter married off early in order to escape the iron grip of dowry (Goyal, 1986).

The institution of marriage and family are largely interrelated. While following the custom of early marriage it was said that apart from the socio-economic background of the individual, there is a great role of family from which individual belongs. Most of the studies have agreed that joint family system leads to early marriage of females whereas the nuclear families are associated with late marriage (Timur, 1977; Smith, 1983). Since joint family system was the most common feature of the Indian family system, even in Uttarakhand, it has some say in the existing prevalence of child marriage and in keeping the age at marriage at lower level. But nowadays, the process of educational, industrial and urban development has opened up new opportunities as well as new roles to family members which changes the family mores, values and practices. Now there is nuclearisation of joint families and the family is being transformed from unit of production to unit of consumption.

Although the age pattern of marriage and its determinants have been previously studied by several demographers, but little attention was given to the family context. It is well known that human adaptation involves participation in groups, therefore, it is important to give adequate attention towards the study of group relations which may provide better understanding of the social, cultural, economic and demographic behaviour of people. Unfortunately, so much of demography is focused on the study of individuals that the study of group is comparatively neglected (Yadava, 1997). The present study would like to emphasise on the family aspect and tries to assess its relationship with marriage age. Several authors have argued that the age at marriage is higher for females who belong to nuclear family than those who belong to joint family. But whether this observation is universal irrespective of time and space or it varies according to the different setup, needs reconsideration. This paper is an attempt in this direction which investigates the changing patterns of marriage age in the state of Uttarakhand in past three-four decades, what is the pattern of recent marriages in different family systems (i.e., joint and nuclear) and whether there is any strong influence of family on the age at marriage of individuals or not.

Data and Methods

For the purpose of this study, data from Census (1971-2001) and District Level Reproductive and Child Health Survey (DLHS-RCH)-II (2002-2004) are used. The analysis is divided into two parts. In the first part, age-sex structure data from Census is used to analyse the trends in proportion single and age at marriage by sex and place of residence. The second part of this paper analyses the household level data from RCH-II to investigate the marriage pattern in different family systems of Uttarakhand.

To avoid the lack of uniformity, census data from 1971 onwards have been taken for the analysis. Up to 1951, the census data on marital status was available for 10 years of age interval. In the succeeding censuses, it has been classified in quinquennial age groups. Moreover, there were some changes in the boundaries of the states after Independence. So, in order to maintain the uniformity, it was decided to carry out the analysis for the period 1971-2001 i.e., after the reorganisation of the states. The analysis of census data is made for Uttarakhand as existing today. Uttarakhand is a new state after bi-furcation of Uttar Pradesh into Uttarakhand and Uttar Pradesh against combined Uttar Pradesh till 1991 census. So for analysing the state-level trends and differentials, the age-sex marital status data of Uttar Pradesh is excluded from each census during 1971-1991.

In RCH-II survey, the information is not given that which household is joint and which is nuclear. In order to identify the family by their type, a variable on type of family is constructed using the information on relationship of usual residents with the head of the household in household file. The two indicators, percentage of female and male married below legal age at marriage by type of family and the age at marriage by type of family are used for analyses purpose. The bi-variate analysis is carried out to study the differential in household characteristics of those households where any marriages have been performed since January 1999 by type of family. The chi-square statistic is performed in order to find the association of different household level variable with the legal age at marriage for males as well as females. The zero-order correlation coefficients are used to find out the extent of relationship between age at marriage and household characteristics by family type. Lastly, multiple classification analysis (MCA) is used to estimate the adjusted mean age at marriage for both females and males in the light of available household level predictors.

Variables

The analyses include six independent variables, namely, type of place of residence (urban; rural), religion (Hindu; Muslim; other), caste (SC/ST; OBC; general) and completed years of schooling of household head (no schooling; 1-7 years; 8-10 years; 11 years and more), household standard of living index (low; medium; high), and type of family (nuclear; joint).

Definition of Family

In the present analysis, family type is defined as nuclear and joint family. The nuclear family consists of families where the respondent is living alone, head and spouse who are residing with or without their unmarried children, adult person who are not living with spouse but with the children or head without spouse but with the other relatives who are not married. The other households which do not fall in such categories are considered joint households.

Results

Universality and early marriages are two well-known and important features of Indian marriage system, and persons who remain unmarried after a certain age are socially looked down upon. The tradition of marriage has been visualised as religious and community obligations and not as means to achieve personal happiness. The society, even today, does not approve any one to remain unmarried. Due to these norms, Indian marriages have always shown a high prevalence. Moreover, in most of the cases, these marriages used to take place in early ages of adulthood. Hence, proportion single at certain age (especially at younger ages) may be a good indicator to get more insights about the prevailing marriage custom of any society. The differential in proportion single and mean age at marriage by sex and place of residence is shown in the following subsections.

Proportion Single and Mean Age at Marriage: Trends and Differentials

Differential by Sex

Figures 6.1, 6.2 and 6.3 show proportion of single males and females in five year age groups and singulate mean age at marriage

(SMAM) in Uttarakhand for 1971, 1981, 1991 and 2001. Figure 6.1 reveals that there is an increase in proportion single in all successive censuses, especially at younger age groups 10-14 to 25-29 for both the sexes. In 1971, 93 per cent females were single in the age group 10-14 while in 2001 this percentage reached to the mark of 98 per cent.

Figure 6.1

Proportion of Single Females at Younger Ages, Uttarakhand: 1971-2001

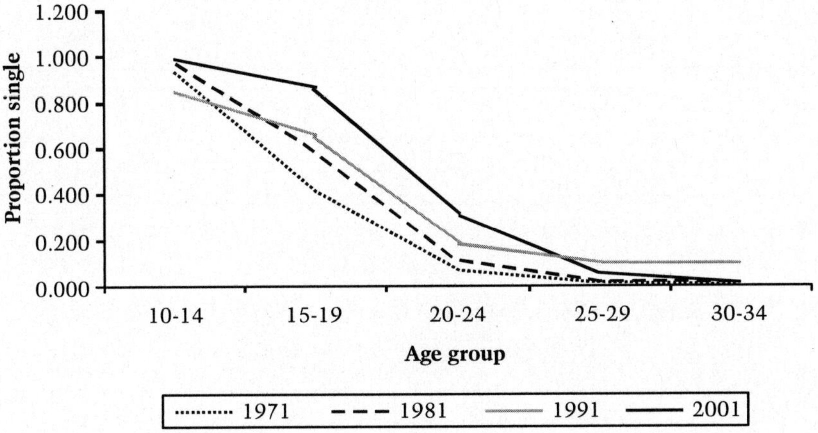

For males, this percentage was around 98 and 99 in 1971 and 2001 respectively. The proportion never married in the age group 15-19 has also been increased from 41 per cent to almost 86 per cent for females and from 87 per cent to 97 per cent for males during the same decades. The increased proportion of never married population in early ages over the period of time indicates the reduction in child marriages and suggests that practically no marriages of girls before age 18 and boys before age 21 in recent decades took place (Figures 6.1 and 6.2).

The singulate mean age at marriage (SMAM) also shows a significant increase in marriage age for both males and females (Figure 6.3). The singulate mean age at marriage shows the average age at which an individual marry hovered around the legal age, for both sexes, since long back. The female age at marriage is estimated as 17.2 years in 1971, 18.4 years in 1981 and has climbed up to 21.0 years in 2001, whereas for

Figure 6.2

Proportion of Single Males at Younger Ages, Uttarakhand: 1971-2001

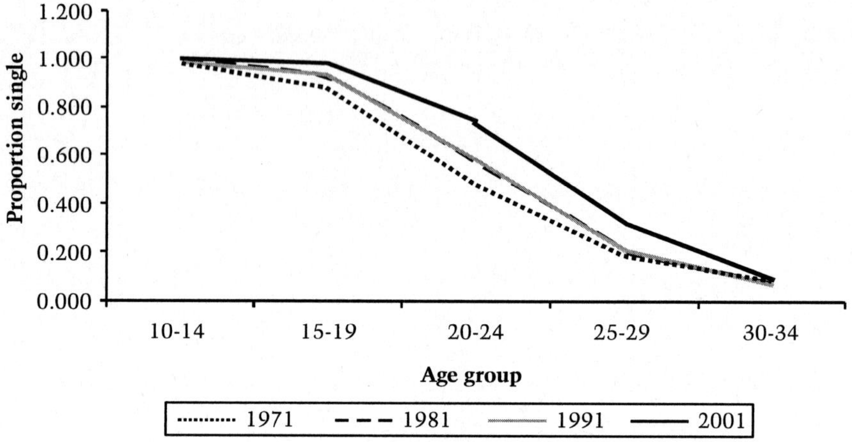

Figure 6.3

Singulate Mean Age at Marriage (SMAM) by Sex, Uttarakhand: 1971-2001

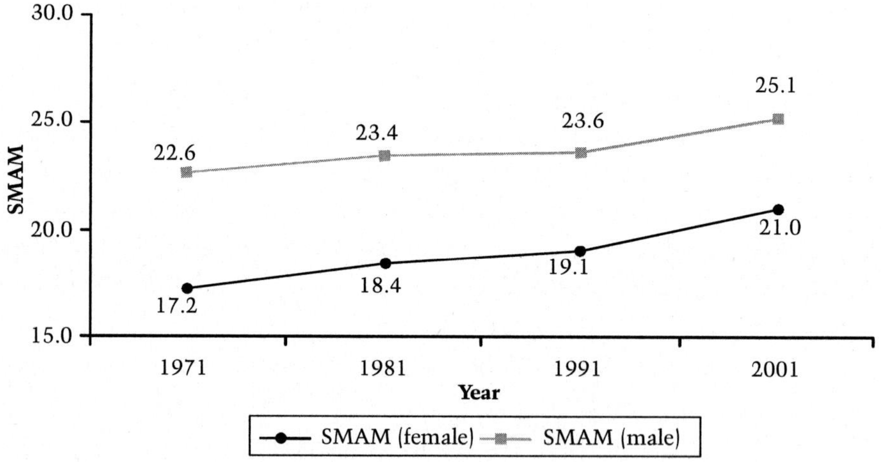

males it reached to approximately 25 years in 2001 as compared to almost 23 years in 1971. The increase in mean age at marriage was not homogeneous during this period and the maximum increase is observed in the decade 1971-1981 for females (about 1.2 years) and during the decade 1991-2001 for males (about 1.5 years). On an average, an increase of 3.8 years for females and 2.5 years for male's age at marriage is observed and the pace of change was almost the same for males and females.

Over the period, there is also reduction in the age gap between the spouse and it is converging in nature. These results indicate that child marriage was not much prevalent in Uttarakhand as compared to Uttar Pradesh where the age at marriage was far behind the legal age in the successive censuses of 1971, 1981 and even 1991 (Prakash and Parasuraman, 2006).

Differential by Place of Residence

The rural-urban differential in nuptiality pattern is clearly visible in India. As discussed above, age at marriage in India and across states is gradually increasing but at the same time, this increase is not equally distributed across the rural and urban parts of the country as well as state.

The result (Table 6.1) shows that proportion single females were substantially higher in urban areas than rural areas. Proportion of single males was also substantially higher in urban areas compared to their rural counterparts. The rural-urban difference in proportion single was higher for females during the decade 1971-1981 than any other decade. Majority of rural females got married by the age 17 years and urban females by 19-20 years in 1971, but in the recent decades these ages have been shifted to 20.6 years and 22.3 years respectively. Almost similar pattern of changes is observed for males too but the level of differences was not so large.

For the state as a whole, the mean age at marriage for females in rural and urban areas is estimated to be around 16.8 years and 19.5 years respectively in 1971, while 20.6 years and 22.3 years respectively in 2001. In case of males, the rural-urban gap is reflected by respective rural and urban estimates of 22.2 and 24 years for 1971 and 24.7 and 26.2 years respectively in 2001. It is also noticed that in the last three decades, the mean ages at which males and females got married in

Uttarakhand varies in the age groups 18-20 and 22-24 for rural females and males respectively, while in the age groups 19-22 and 24-26 for urban one. In rural areas, age gap in mean age at marriage of males and females was of more than five years in 1971 and it reduced to four years in 2001. On the other hand, in urban areas, this gap was slightly lower than the rural areas. The changes in age gap in mean age at marriage followed a consistent pattern and declined consistently over the period of time i.e., during the decades 1971-2001. In other words, it can be said that, in the rural areas there was large age gap in the marriage age because females used to get married at relatively early age while males at somewhat older age, whereas, both females and males of urban areas used to get married at older ages and hence resulted into smaller age gap.

Table 6.1

Proportion Single at Younger Ages, SMAM by Residence, Uttarakhand: 1971-2001

Age Group	*Rural*				*Urban*			
	1971	*1981*	*1991*	*2001*	*1971*	*1981*	*1991*	*2001*
				Female				
10-14	0.9321	0.9676	0.9744	0.9878	0.9712	0.9915	0.9759	0.9858
15-19	0.3750	0.5314	0.7298	0.8518	0.6890	0.8085	0.8736	0.9139
20-24	0.0435	0.0606	0.1217	0.2509	0.2192	0.3093	0.3184	0.4712
25-29	0.0100	0.0093	0.0160	0.0344	0.0464	0.0685	0.0614	0.1083
30-34	0.0044	0.0038	0.0066	0.0096	0.0167	0.0216	0.0238	0.0257
SMAM	16.8	17.8	19.1	20.6	19.5	20.8	20.9	22.3
				Male				
10-14	0.9845	0.9868	0.9864	0.9958	0.9904	0.9940	0.9865	0.9944
15-19	0.8675	0.9122	0.9440	0.9761	0.9267	0.9646	0.9633	0.9818
20-24	0.4211	0.5051	0.5586	0.6952	0.6572	0.7354	0.7566	0.8136
25-29	0.1533	0.1639	0.1887	0.2572	0.2857	0.3148	0.3288	0.4027
30-34	0.0726	0.0567	0.0689	0.0663	0.1221	0.0917	0.0880	0.1094
SMAM	22.2	22.9	23.0	24.7	24.0	24.9	25.0	26.2
Age Gap	5.4	5.0	3.9	4.0	4.6	4.1	4.0	3.9

Family System and Age at Marriage: An Appraisal from Survey Data

It was found in the earlier section that the proportion single at younger ages has increased in the recent past and it adhered somewhat an influence in postponing the singulate mean age at marriage. Now it would be important to see that, other than the changing proportion of single males and females in the recent cohort, what are the possible predictors of changes in age at marriage? Several studies being carried out, for different population subgroups, has shown that the individual level variable like, educational status of individual, their employment status, decision-making status, household level predictors *viz.*, place of residence, religion, caste, the type of family, and the society level factors like dowry demands prevailing at the time of selection of partner and, of course, the horoscope matching determines the marriage age up to a great extent.

Here our interest is at the household level variable rather than the individual level. Although the individual level factors play an important role in determining the marriage age of individual but, there are two prime reasons behind the using of macro level data. First, household or family is one of the most fundamental institutions in Indian society and plays an important role in determining the individuals' behaviour especially the decisions like marriage. Second is the limitation of data. Since the census data only provide age-sex marital status data so it becomes difficult to find out the predictors of marriage age. In such a case, there is no way other than relying on survey data to find out the predictors of age at marriage. The following section deals with different dimensions of age at marriage by taking type of family into account.

Characteristics of Households Where Any Marriage Performed since January 1999

In the RCH-II, 12885 households are interviewed in Uttarakhand. Out of which 53.6 per cent (6902 households) belong to nuclear families while rest of the 46.4 per cent (5983) were joint families. Further, among the nuclear families 11.5 per cent were those where any marriage (either male/female or both) have been performed since January 1999, while among the joint families there were 31.9 per cent such

Table 6.2

Percentage of Households where there was Any Marriage since 1999 of Usual Residents according to Household Characteristics by Type of Family, Uttarakhand: 2002-2004

Household Characteristics	*Type of Family*			
	Nuclear	*No. of HH*	*Joint*	*No. of HH*
Place of Residence				
Rural	12.4	4885	32.1	4459
Urban	9.2	2016	31.2	1524
Religion of HH Head				
Hindu	11.4	5795	31.8	5221
Muslim	11.4	912	32.5	634
Other	15.4	195	30.5	128
Caste of HH Head				
SC/ST	12.2	1320	29.4	914
OBC	9.2	1493	31.1	1304
General	12.1	3845	33.3	3551
Educational Status of HH Head				
Non-literate	18.2	33	38.5	26
1-7 years of schooling	13.2	1246	34.7	1213
8-10 years of schooling	12.4	2012	35.0	1658
11 years and above schooling	9.3	1501	28.7	1178
Household Standard of Living Index				
Low	11.0	2842	27.5	1984
Medium	13.4	1985	32.7	1980
High	10.4	2075	35.4	2019
Total	11.5	6902	31.9	5983

households. For the analysis purpose, those households have been taken into consideration where any marriage has been performed in last three years before the survey.

Table 6.2 shows the percentage of households where any marriage has been performed since January 1999 according to household characteristics by type of family. The table depicts that there are more marriages in joint families than nuclear ones in the recent past. The magnitude of marriage was almost three times higher in the joint families than the nuclear families. On investigating the characteristics of these households, it is evident that proportion of marriage in joint families was almost similar in rural and urban areas, while in nuclear families the proportion of marriages in rural and urban areas varied largely. Similar to the place of residence, in case of religion also, almost same amount of marriage (11.4 per cent) have been performed in Hindu and Muslim headed nuclear families while it differed for the joint families. Further, there are more marriages among the households which belong to general caste and whose head of the household is non-literate. These observations were identical in both types of families. The result also show that in the nuclear families with high standard of living, the extent of marriages in the last three years was lower while in joint families it was a bit higher. Since in joint families new couples do not need independent financial support before their marriage, so the higher percentage of marriages in joint families with high economic status may be attributed to this reason.

Type of Family and Legal Age at Marriage

For analysing the marriage scenario in Uttarakhand, two indicators have been taken into account. These indicators are percentage of marriage below the legal age and mean age at marriage. In order to get more insight about percentage of marriages below the legal age in both type of families, all households are cross-classified by household characteristics, the legal age at marriage and type of family. Table 6.3 shows the per cent distribution of households according to female legal age at marriage and selected household characteristics by type of family. The aggregate level result depicts some reverse results where percentage of female marriages below the legal age is comparatively lower (7.3 per cent) in joint family while higher in nuclear families (10.8 per cent). It contradicts the general finding that the chances of marriage below legal age used to be higher in the joint families. Similarly, by considering all other household characteristics like, place of residence, religion, caste, educational status of household head and household standard of living, it is evident that the magnitude of marriages below the legal age is higher in nuclear families compared to the joint families.

Table 6.3

Percentage of Marriages Performed Below the Legal Age at Marriage by Type of Family according to Sex, Uttarakhand: 2002-2004

Household Characteristics	*Female*		*Male*	
	Nuclear Families	*Joint Families*	*Nuclear Families*	*Joint Families*
Place of Residence				
Rural	12.4	8.3	12.8	11.6
Urban	5.0	4.5	9.3	7.7
χ^2 value:	6.1**	2.7	0.5	3.4***
Religion of HH Head				
Hindu	10.3	6.9	11.5	10.2
Muslim	19.0	12.8	13.0	20.0
Other	0.0	0.0	16.7	0.0
χ^2 value:	4.1	2.9	0.2	10.4*
Caste of HH Head				
SC/ST	19.0	12.3	18.5	22.3
OBC	20.5	10.2	17.9	17.3
General	7.4	5.7	9.1	7.5
χ^2 value:	19.5*	5.7***	3.2	39.2*
Educational Status of HH Head				
Non-literate	0.0	0.0	0.0	0.0
1-7 years	14.8	7.7	18.2	13.8
8-10 years	7.4	7.2	8.3	8.7
11 years and above	0.0	3.0	0.0	3.1
χ^2 value:	18.6*	3.6	9.7**	19.2*
Household Standard of Living Index				
Low	16.8	11.9	15.7	16.4
Medium	7.9	6.1	13.2	9.9
High	2.8	3.6	2.2	6.2
χ^2 value:	22.1*	12.2*	5.5***	22.9*
Total	10.8	7.3	11.8	10.8

Note: Total refers to percentage of marriages in nuclear families and joint families by sex.

* Chi-square test show significant association at 1 per cent level of significance (two-tailed).

** Chi-square test show significant association at 5 per cent level of significance (two-tailed).

*** Chi-square test show significant association at 10 per cent level of significance (two-tailed).

Although there are inconsistencies in result when we compare it between the two types of families, but within the type of family results are consistent. For example, the proportion of marriages below the legal age is higher among the households residing in rural areas, belongs to

Muslim headed households, not fall in general category and also those households in which the standard of living is low. The chi-square test is used to assess the association between household characteristics and the magnitude of marriages below or above the legal age in both types of families. It is found that among the nuclear families, there is a significant association (at 1 per cent significance level) of caste, educational status of household head and SLI with the marriage age while among joint families only caste (at 10 per cent significant level) shows their significant association with the legal age at marriage for females. It concludes that the caste and household standard of living play an important role on age at marriage irrespective of the type of family.

The same table also shows the extent of male marriages below the legal age at marriage in different family systems. The results are found in similar pattern as it was observed for females. The extent of male marriages below the legal age at marriage was higher in the nuclear families (11.8 per cent) than in the joint ones (10.8 per cent). The result shows that the difference in the percentage of households where below legal male marriage has been performed in both type of families, was not much wider (1 per cent) as it was in case of females (3.5 per cent). The result of chi-square test also shows that in the joint families, religion, caste, educational status of household head and SLI have significant association with age at marriage (at 1 per cent level of significance), whereas, in nuclear families only educational status of household head (at 5 per cent significant level) and SLI (at 10 per cent significance level) shows their significant association with the legal age at marriage for males. It concludes that the caste, educational level of household head and household standard of living have more effect on legal age at marriage of males in joint families.

Type of Family and Mean Age at Marriage

The results of the above-mentioned analysis show that the type of family do not possess a significant impact on proportion of marriages below or above the legal age than the other predictors for both the sexes in Uttarakhand. In order to assess the effect of other predictors on age at marriage, we have used a zero-order correlation to quantify the strength of the association between set of independent and dependent variables. In the first step, we did the correlation analysis for both type of families separately and thereafter at aggregate level.

Table 6.4 shows the zero-order correlation coefficients between age at marriage of females and males and selected household characteristics. The result shows a strong significant negative association between female age at marriage and place of residence, caste and household standard of living in both the families. It means the female age at marriage becomes lower in both types of families when we move from urban to rural areas, when we consider those households which fall in socially backward category (SC/ST) and those where the household economic status is lower. On the other hand, religion shows a positive association with female age at marriage at 5 per cent of significance level, but only in joint families. Surprisingly, we did not find any significant association between age at marriage and the educational status of household head for both males and females in both joint and nuclear families. At the aggregate level, when type of family is also included in the model, we observed that it has weak significant (at 5 per cent significance level) negative relationship with female age at marriage. It means that for females, the age at marriage is lower in nuclear families than the joint one.

Table 6.4

Zero-Order Correlation Coefficients between Age at Marriage of Females and Males and Selected Household Characteristics, Uttarakhand: 2002-2004

Variables	*Female*			*Male*		
	Nuclear Family	*Joint Family*	*Combined*	*Nuclear Family*	*Joint Family*	*Combined*
Dependent Variable						
Y: Age at marriage						
Independent Variable						
X_1: Place of residence (1=rural, 0=otherwise)	-0.264*	-0.257*	-0.262*	-0.127	-0.137*	-0.135*
X_2: Religion (1=Hindu, 0=otherwise)	0.023	0.087**	0.057**	0.086	0.084*	0.085*
X_3: Caste (1=SC/ST, 0=otherwise)	-0.190*	-0.152*	-0.176*	-0.141**	-0.144*	-0.144*
X_4: Educational status of HH head (1=Non-literate, 0=otherwise)	-0.038	-0.015	-0.030	0.063	0.021	0.026
X_5: SLI (1=low, 0=otherwise)	-0.292*	-0.244*	-0.271*	-0.182*	-0.223*	-0.217*
X_6: Type of family (1=nuclear, 0=joint)	-	-	-0.059**	-	-	-0.015

Note: * p<0.01, **p<0.05.

In case of males, only caste and SLI has significant negative association with age at marriage in nuclear families, while in joint family except educational status of household head, all other variables are showing their significant association with age at marriage. It is evident from the table that there is not any significant association between age at marriage of male and type of family. That means while taking other variables into consideration, there is not any significant role of type of family in deciding the marriage age of males.

Table 6.5

Adjusted Mean Age at Marriage of Male and Female, Uttarakhand: 2002-2004

Household Characteristics	*Female*	*Male*
Place of Residence		
Rural®	20.6	24.4
Urban	21.2*	24.9**
Religion of HH Head		
Hindu®	20.8	24.6
Muslim	20.3**	23.9**
Other	21.0	25.5
Caste of HH Head		
SC/ST®	20.0	23.5
OBC	20.7	23.1
General	21.0*	25.3*
Educational Status of HH Head		
Non-literate®	20.3	23.8
1-7 years	20.4	24.6*
8-10 years	20.8**	24.5*
11 years and above	21.7*	25.6*
Household Standard of Living Index		
Low®	19.9	23.5
Medium	20.5*	24.5*
High	21.7*	25.4*
Type of Family		
Nuclear®	20.7	24.6
Joint	20.7	24.5
Constant	18.6	21.8
Adjusted R^2	23.2	18.7

Note: ® Reference category. *p<0.01, **p<0.05.

Mean Age at Marriage: Results from Multiple Classification Analysis

In the last section of this paper, the adjusted mean age at marriage is estimated (Table 6.5) using multiple classification analysis (MCA). We could have also computed the simple mean value of age at marriage for both the sexes, but this method is used because it will give the adjusted mean values of age at marriage by taking the effect of other predictors also into account.

The analysis shows that the mean age at marriage for females hovers around the age of 20-21 years while for males this age lies in the range of 23-25 years. The analysis supported our previous finding that the mean age at marriage of males and females is higher in urban areas, households which fall in general category, whose head of the household is educated and households having better standard of living for both the sexes. These results are highly significant (at 1 per cent significance level) for both the sexes. Findings also suggest that Muslims are having lower mean age at marriage of males and females than the Hindus or other religious groups. Surprisingly, we found same mean age at marriage in both type of families for females (20.7 years) and males (24.6 years in nuclear families while 24.5 years in joint families), but these values were not statistically significant. These findings show that the type of family does not have any strong effect on determining the age at marriage of males and females in Uttarakhand. Instead of type of family, the household economic status and caste are more prominent predictors of age at marriage in the state.

Conclusion

In India, very limited statistical information on nuptiality indicators was available prior to first Census, the only source of information being certain references in writing of Hindu mythology (Bhagat, 2002). Since the registration data is also not complete, hence the age-sex marital status data provided by Census and some of the information gathered by different surveys becomes the main source of information for these studies. Previous studies have shown that the age at marriage, particularly of girls, remained quite below the minimum legal age in some parts of Uttar Pradesh, even though the first legislation on age at marriage was already passed in 1929. The findings suggest that the custom of early marriage was not much prevailing in Uttarakhand since 1971 or even before, as it was in Uttar Pradesh (Prakash and Parasuraman, 2006). Over the subsequent decades, there was increase in proportion single at younger ages. The increment in this proportion single at younger ages has led to the increase in marriage age. During these decades, literally no marriages have been performed below the legal age. This was the period when the society had started changing with the modern developments. With the changes in society, there was certain change in the norms and values. Individuals of present generation became more mobile and started to take marriage-related decisions by their own. These changes made individuals free to decide for their own life and have some effect on the age at marriage too.

The findings as to why the amount of marriages below the legal age in nuclear families is high compared to joint families needs some more exploration but up to some extent, it is observed that lower economic circumstances of the joint family results in this way. More clearly, we have observed that among all the households, the economic status of joint families were not better than the nuclear families. It means the postponement of marriage is mainly due to the financial constraints because arrangement of marriage needs adequate financial support. Since economic status of joint families are not good so they require more time for the arrangement of money and this in other way leads to the postponement of marriage age. In the correlation analysis and multivariate analysis too, we observed that the household standard of living have more significant effect on age at marriage of males and females than the other variables like type of family and others. Our findings that the age at marriage is almost same in joint and nuclear families is quite similar to the findings of Unisa *et al.*, 1997 where they conducted a comparative study of two villages in Dehradun and Gorakhpur districts and found that the type of family has nothing to do with age at marriage in the light of other predictors. This means the hypothesis that the age at marriage of males and females seems to be higher in nuclear families do not exist well in all the societies and depends on the time and set-up about which we are talking.

References

Agrawala, S.N. (1962). *Age at Marriage in India.* Allahabad: Kitab Mahal Publication.

Bhagat, R.B. (2002). *Early Marriages in India: A Socio-geographical Study.* New Delhi: Rajat Publication.

Goyal, R.P. (1986). "Age at marriage in India - Emerging trend", *Demography India* 15(2): 239-48.

———. (1988). *Marriage Age in India.* Delhi: B.R. Publishing Corporation.

Kadi, A.S. (1987). "Age at marriage in India", *Asia Pacific Population Journal* 2(1): 41-56.

Hajnal, J. (1953). "Age at marriage and proportion marrying", *Population Studies* 7(2): 111-36.

Malaker, C.R. (1978). "Study of Indian nuptiality", Unpublished Ph.D. Dissertation. Calcutta: Indian Statistical Institute.

Pandey, A. and A. Pandey (1997). "Analyzing female nuptiality pattern at micro level: A case of Madhya Pradesh", *IASSI Quarterly* 16(3 & 4): 212-225.

Prakash, R. and S. Parasuraman (2006). "Age at marriage in Uttar Pradesh: Recent trends and variations", Paper presented in International Conference on *Emerging Issues in Asia Pacific Regions*, organised by International Institute for Population Sciences, Mumbai-88, during 10-13 December.

Smith, P.C. (1983). "The impact of age at marriage and proportions marrying on fertility", in R.A. Bulatao and R.D. Lee (eds.), *Determinants of Fertility in Developing Countries* 2. New York: Academic Press. pp.473-531.

Timur, S. (1977). "Demographic correlates of women's education: Fertility, age at marriage and the family", *International Population Conference* 3:463-495.

Unisa, S., P.C. Saxena and P.K. Bhargava (1997). "Differentials in age at marriage in two selected villages of Eastern and Western Uttar Pradesh", in K. Gupta and A. Pandey (eds.), *Population and Development in Uttar Pradesh*. Delhi: B.R. Publishing Corporation. pp.185-198.

Yadava, R.C. (1997). "Changes in family structure in Uttar Pradesh", in K. Gupta and A. Pandey (eds.), *Population and Development in Uttar Pradesh*. Delhi: B.R. Publishing Corporation. pp.43-50.

7 Economic Differentials of Fertility and Utilisation of Maternal and Child Health Services in Uttarakhand

C.V.S. Prasad and Jalandhar Pradhan

Introduction

The state of Uttarakhand was carved out of Uttar Pradesh on 9th November 2000, by combining 13 districts *viz.*, Almora, Pauri Garhwal, Tehri Garhwal, Bageshwar, Chamoli, Haridwar, Champawat, Nainital, Dehradun, Udham Singh Nagar, Uttarkashi, Pithoragarh and Rudraprayag. These districts are to be grouped into three distinct geographical regions, the high mountain region, the mid-mountain region and the Terai region. Dehradun is the interim-capital city. Uttarakhand has a population of approximately 8.5 million and a total geographical area of 53,483 square kilometres (Census of India, 2001), of which about 60 per cent is under forest cover.

The state of Uttarakhand certainly seems to have a distinct culture, topography, social customs and values, which have contributed to greater performance in socio-demographic parameters than many northern states including Uttar Pradesh. Still fertility in terms of TFR in this state (2.5) is above replacement level and much higher than most of the southern states like Kerala (1.9), Tamil Nadu (1.8) and Andhra Pradesh (1.8) (IIPS, 2007). Further, percentage of women who visited 3 or more times for antenatal care in Uttarakhand (44.9 per cent) is lower than that of national average (52.0 per cent) (NFHS-3, 2005-06). And also percentage of births delivered in a health facility in Uttarakhand (32.6 per cent) is significantly lower than the national average (38.7 per cent). More importantly, the level of fertility remained stagnant over the inter-survey period [NFHS-2 (TFR=2.6) and NFHS-3 (TFR=2.5)]. These slow pace decline in fertility and relatively poor coverage in maternal and child health care services depicts low use of resources, an immediate concern in Uttarakhand.

Studies on fertility levels and their differentials often seek to measure directly the impact of socio-economic factors on fertility. Most of the previous studies gave stress on various dimensions of fertility differentials by age, education, religion, caste etc. However, there are very few studies which addressed the impact of economic status on fertility and utilisation of maternal and child health care services. The major challenge to analyse differentials of fertility and utilisation of maternal and child health care services by economic status, lies in the latter's measurement issues. Though some studies highlight the economic differentials of fertility based on standard of living index (SLI), as a proxy of income measure, which divides the population as low, medium and high standard of living. However, SLI has limited application because of the assumptions and weights given to different components of index, while constructing the index.

In an attempt to provide an alternative measure of economic status, Gwatkin *et al.* (2000) first developed the household asset index as a proxy for wealth/economic status of the sample households at national level based on DHS/NFHS data. On the basis of this index, the entire sample of HHs was divided into five quintiles—the first quintile representing the poorest population and fifth quintile representing the richest category of the population. Using these quintiles, he analysed data to understand the economic differentials of sample HHs and the couples and ever-married women in terms of their fertility, mortality and maternal and child health variables. Since then, use of assets rather than income to capture wealth status has gained ground in the international literature (see, for example, Morris *et al.*, 2000). In order to further validate the use of quintiles as a measure of economic status at HH level, a very significantly close association between HH consumption expenditure pattern and asset-based quintiles was established, and it was argued that asset measurement is a good proxy for income and consumption (Filmer and Pritchett, 1999; Montgomery *et al.*, 2000; Wagstaff, 2005).

In India for the first time, this index was used to study the accessibility and extent of utilisation of RNTCP (Revised National Tuberculosis Control Programme) services by poor people in the states of Kerala, Delhi and Rajasthan (the study was carried out by C.V.S. Prasad and Pramod Padhy). The first author since then along with others attempted to make use of asset quintile to study the economic differentials of various fertility and other aspects. To quote some: Prasad *et al.,* 2006 made an attempt to study the economic differentials of fertility among scheduled caste and scheduled tribe population in India based on asset quintiles. This study found that rich people do exist among SC and ST in significant proportions, though the general caste category followed by OBC account for maximum share of wealth and display significant economic differentials of fertility within SC and ST population groups. In another study using the same economic indicator i.e., asset quintile, the authors addressed the differentials in mother and child health indicators in western states of India using RCH Round-2, Phase-1, 2001-02 district-level household survey (DHS) data. The study concluded that the populations belonging to poorer strata are less benefitted from the government programmes meant for them (Prasad, 2005a). Another study highlighted that, the economic status of the couples/households turned out to be an important and the most dominant determinant of child health indicators followed by mothers' education etc. For instance, the levels of IMR, under five child mortality and other nutritional deficiency indicators were significantly higher among the poorest quintiles compared to that of richest quintile. And also, the accessibility and utilisation of certain child care services were the lowest among the poorer households (Prasad, 2005b). Another study intended to determine the direct and indirect effects of economic and female education variables on fertility variable when other independent variables are kept constant and thereby single out the most important variable. And the finding suggests that economic variable plays a significantly better role in determining the level of fertility in India as compared to that of female literacy (Prasad and Chopra, 2005). The paper also suggested that women should have a minimum education of middle schooling in order to have effect on their fertility.

Further review of the relevant literature indicates that Ahmed (2004), using DHS data of Bangladesh showed that there is differential in contraceptive use, fertility level, unmet need, fertility preference and maternal health care utilisation by socio-economic status. Nguyen and Popkins (2003) using the Vietnam standard of living index based on a survey data, examined inequality effects and trends associated with the economic reform of the Vietnam economy. They found increase in disparity in health outcome variables like stunted children, underweight children, underweight and overweight women and differential in coverage of health insurance among the poorer and rich. Lustig (2000) using the data on study on Mexican health and attitudes towards the recovery process emphasised that inequalities in the utilisation of health services would then be a measurable way of assessing the performance of public policies related to health access. Navaneetham and Dharmalingam (2002) analysing data of NFHS-1 found that women's education and standard of living are most important predicators of receiving antenatal care, TT injection and institutional delivery. Govindasamy (1994) found that the utilisation of health care services is strongly and significantly correlated with women's socio-economic status. He found that standard of living is a significant predicator of the prenatal care, institutional delivery and delivery care. Singh and Singh (2006) using the NFHS-2 data, examined the rich-poor gap in antenatal and delivery care in northeast India. On the basis of household economic well-being index, the result shows that the concentration of women without adequate maternal care is more amongst the poorest economic strata. A study conducted recently among different population groups in the states of Himalayan region shows that the altitude and social hierarchy leads to differentials in fertility and utilisation of maternal and child health care services (Gautam and Kapoor, 2003). The authors explain that the differentials existed because at middle and high altitudes, public health care and other communication facilities are not as easily accessible and available as at low altitudes. Similarly, in the context of social categories, more advanced groups have better access to health and other communication facilities by virtue of the fact that socially higher groups, in general, are more literate and economically better-off. Using different DHS data set, a group of researchers found that inequality in health care utilisation has become an important area of inquiry in economic development given the well-known connection between health, productivity and economic growth (Savedoff and Schultz, 2000; Strauss and Thomas, 1998).

Need for the Study

As mentioned above, NFHS-3 graded the economic status of each of the sample HHs on the basis of asset scores. Using this index, an attempt has been made in this paper to analyse the economic differentials of couples' fertility and use of MCH services in the state of Uttarakhand as such attempt seems to have not been made in this state recently. It is hoped that the findings emerging from the analysis presented in this paper would be useful to the concerned ministry of the state to draw up effective schemes and strategies for increasing the service utilisation among poor people.

Objectives

This paper aims to examine following two objectives:

- To assess the economic differentials of fertility and utilisation of maternal and child health (MCH) services in Uttarakhand.
- To single out the impact of economic variable on fertility keeping other socio-economic covariates constant.

Data and Methodology

National Family Health Survey-3, 2005-06 is being used to examine the above objectives. The focus of the NFHS-3 has been on the utilisation of basic reproductive and child health services such as the coverage of ANC, immunisation coverage, institutional delivery, contraceptive use etc. In addition to the above information, it also provides a wide range of information including household characteristics such as ownership of consumer durables, type of house, source of drinking water, source of lighting, type of fuel for cooking and toilet facility.

The economic index (wealth index) is constructed using household data on assets and amenities. For each household, the asset scores are usually measured as binary variables with value of 1 or 0 according to possession or non-possession of the assets respectively. These scores of all the considered asset variables were normalised and weighted and then pooled for each HH to arrive at the HH asset score. The weight is being obtained by applying principal component analysis on the asset data and as per the value of the pooled score, all the sample households have been arranged in ascending order of magnitude and then divided into quintiles i.e., five groups with equal number of individuals in each. The first quintile represents the poorest and the fifth quintile represents the richest segment of population.

Study/Dependent Variables

Children Ever Born (CEB): Number of children born to the ever-married women aged 15-49 years till date of survey.

ANC Visits: Whether a woman visited a health facility three or more times for receiving antenatal cares during her pregnancy period. Yes=1; No=0.

Tetanus Injection: Whether a woman received at least two TT injections during her last pregnancy period. Yes=1; No=0.

Institutional Delivery: Whether a woman visited any health facility for delivering in case of last live birth. Yes=1; No=0.

Contraceptive Use: Whether a recently married couple is currently using any modern method of contraception. Yes=1; No=0.

Full Immunisation of Children: Whether a child in the age group of 12 to 23 months received one dose each of the BCG and measles vaccines and three doses of the DPT and polio vaccines. Yes=1; No=0.

Independent/Control Variables

A set of independent variables are considered for use in multivariate analysis to see the impact of wealth index on widely used fertility indicator children ever born. These are wealth index, education of mother [middle school and above], caste, residence, working status of the mother, marital duration.

Results

Differentials in Children Ever Born (CEB) by Asset Quintiles

For studying the economic differentials of fertility behaviour of the couples, we considered mean number of children ever born to the ever-married couples till the survey date as a measure of fertility. Analysis of this measure by wealth quintiles is presented in Table 7.1. The table shows that the mean number children ever born (MCEB) vary significantly with the level of wealth quintile in the state of Uttarakhand as well as in the country as a whole. Both in Uttarakhand as well as at national level, the fertility curve showed monotonic decline with increasing economic levels. The mean number of children ever born in the lowest (poorest) quintile is the highest at 2.88 and the lowest in the highest (richest) quintile at 1.65. Such vast difference could be observed at national level as well. The poor-rich ratio [Q1/Q5] shows that the fertility performance of poor people was 1.75 times higher than that of the rich people in Uttarakhand. Such difference perhaps could not be attributed to the differential economic status as difference in the marital duration could partly contribute for the observed differences in the fertility by wealth quintiles. Hence in order to find out the direct contribution, the poor-rich ratio of fertility was worked out in this state after controlling the marital duration. The so computed value was much higher than one (1.2), indicating that economic differentials of fertility do exist in this state.

Table 7.1

Differentials in Fertility Level in Terms of Mean Number of Children Ever Born (MCEB) by Asset Quintiles

Wealth Quintile	*Uttarakhand*	*India*
Q1	2.88	2.97
Q2	2.73	2.64
Q3	2.38	2.28
Q4	2.18	2.00
Q5	1.65	1.60
Total	2.14	2.26
P: R Ratio(Q1/Q5)	1.75	1.86

Differentials in Coverage of TT by Asset Quintiles

Table 7.2 shows that the proportion of pregnant women who received at least two TT injections increased monotonically with the increased economic status. The poor people in this state were more in disadvantageous position with respect to utilisation of this service compared to those at the national level. However, such difference gets reduced with increased economic status and in the higher income bracket, the difference was almost nil. The rich-poor [Q5/Q1] ratio is significantly higher in Uttarakhand (2.5) compared to that of India (1.6).

Table 7.2

Differentials Coverage of Tetanus (Two or More TT) Injections in Uttarakhand and India by Asset Quintiles

Wealth Quintile	*Uttarakhand*	*India*
Q1	37.3	59.7
Q2	42.9	70.2
Q3	64.9	79.3
Q4	70.0	87.2
Q5	92.2	92.9
Total	68.5	76.3
R:P Ratio(Q5/Q1)	2.5	1.6

Differentials in Coverage of Antenatal Care Visits

The proportion of women who visited during their last pregnancy period to any health facility for ANC services (3 or more visits) according to various wealth quintiles is given in Table 7.3. In the state of Uttarakhand, only 12 per cent of women belonging to the poorest wealth quintile have visited three or more times for antenatal care during their pregnancy period, while the corresponding figure was about 78 per cent in the richest quintile. The corresponding figures for India were 27 per cent and 87 per cent respectively. The rich-poor ratio is significantly higher for Uttarakhand (6.5) compared to that of the country as a whole (3.2). In this state the added disadvantage is topography, which affects adversely the accessibility of health facilities for ANC services. The private health facilities were also scanty in the hilly regions of the state.

Table 7.3

Differential in Three or More ANC Visits in Uttarakhand and India by Asset Quintiles

Wealth Quintile	*Uttarakhand*	*India*
Q1	12.1	26.7
Q2	18.6	37.5
Q3	33.2	54.5
Q4	42.5	69.0
Q5	78.4	86.5
Total	44.9	52.0
R:P Ratio(Q5/Q1)	6.5	3.2

Differentials in Institutional Delivery by Asset Quintiles

In this state, the proportion of institutional deliveries (32.6 per cent) was significantly lower than that of India (38.7 per cent). Within this state, significant economic differentials do exist even in this regard too, like at national level. Interestingly the rich-poor ratio, which was (6.2) for Uttarakhand, was slightly lower than that of the nation (6.6). Thus, the analysis shows the dismal picture both at national level and in the state of Uttarakhand in terms of the women from the lower strata of the society not accessing the health facilities for delivery purpose. Compared to the nation, the problem was worse in this state. Perhaps the added disadvantage being its topography.

Table 7.4

Differentials in Institutional Delivery in Uttarakhand and India by Asset Quintiles

Wealth Quintile	*Uttarakhand*	*India*
Q1	11.1	12.7
Q2	8.2	23.5
Q3	15.8	39.2
Q4	30.1	57.9
Q5	69.6	83.7
Total	32.6	38.7
R:P Ratio(Q5/Q1)	6.2	6.6

Differentials in Coverage of Full Immunisation for Children by Asset Quintiles

The vaccination of children against six serious but preventable diseases (tuberculosis, diphtheria, pertussis, poliomyelitis and measles) has been an important intervention in the child survival and motherhood programmes of Government of India. If a child received the required doses of all these vaccines as per the prescribed schedule, he/she was considered as fully immunised. In the NFHS-3, all the children aged 12-23 months were decided as fully immunised either on the basis of the information recorded in the vaccination card if it was shown at the time of survey or by asking relevant questions to their mothers. The proportions of children who received full immunisation were worked out by asset quintiles and the same are presented in Table 7.5. The table shows that although significant economic differentials existed even in this case both in this state and India, as high as about 39 per cent children in Uttarakhand and 24 per cent children in India from the lowest wealth quintile have received all recommended antigens as per the schedule. The rich-poor ratio is 2.1 and 2.9 for Uttarakhand and India respectively. For availing the maternal services such as ANC and delivery services, the woman has to go to health facility, while for immunisation to children or even getting TT injections, the child/woman gets the service being rendered by the service providers almost at their doorstep (*anganwadi* centre or at village central place or at the

Table 7.5

Differentials in Coverage of Full Immunisation in Uttarakhand and India by Asset Quintiles

Wealth Quintile	*Uttarakhand*	*India*
Q1	38.9	24.4
Q2	31.7	33.2
Q3	61.0	46.9
Q4	63.5	55.3
Q5	80.3	71.0
Total	60.0	43.5
R:P Ratio(Q5/Q1)	2.1	2.9

beneficiary residence itself). As per the analysis, presented the former services are far less utilised, while the latter being outreach service, were relatively better utilised. This is an important finding from programme implementation point of view. It appears that looking at the topography, in this state more emphasis is given to outreach services.

Differentials in Contraceptive Use by Asset Quintiles

Contraception is one of the determinants of couples' fertility performance. Hence, this variable was analysed. The level of contraceptive use is better in this state compared to the rest of India, particularly among economically lower strata of the society. However, the rich-poor ratio is significantly high both in Uttarakhand (1.49) and at national level (1.67), indicating presence of economic differentials in this regard as well.

Table 7.6

Differentials in Contraceptive Use in Uttarakhand and India by Asset Quintiles

Wealth Quintile	*Uttarakhand*	*India*
Q1	42.1	34.6
Q2	48.2	43.5
Q3	49.9	49.8
Q4	56.1	55.2
Q5	63.5	58.0
Total	55.4	48.5
R:P Ratio(Q5/Q1)	1.49	1.67

Multivariate Analysis

An attempt has been made to single out the impact of wealth index on the level of fertility controlling-related socio-economic covariates using regression analysis. The dependent variable is children ever born and independent variables are wealth index factor score, education of mother, marital duration, residence, working status of mother, and use of contraception. The results are presented in Table 7.7. The R^2 value shows that the model accounts for 46 per cent variation in the dependent variable and hence, the model is statistically significant. Of all the variables considered in the model, the wealth index stands out as the important determinant with largest beta coefficient, followed by female literacy and other variables. When all other variables are kept constant, a unit change in poverty level of a couple reduces their fertility level by .175 times, while one unit change in the education level (from middle schooling onwards) of the woman would reduce their fertility .079 times. Contraception also turned out as an important determinant.

Table 7.7

Results of Regression Model for Children Ever Born

Covariates	*Standardised Beta Coefficient*	*Sig.*
Wealth index factor score	-0.175	0.000
Education of mother (who completed middle schooling)	-0.079	0.000
Marital duration	0.611	0.000
Residence (Rural=1, Urban=0)	0.006	0.803
Working status (Working=1, Not working=0)	0.020	0.377
Ever used contraception	-0.135	0.000
R^2	0.461	

Conclusions

In this paper, we presented the evidences of economic differentials in maternal and child health indicators in Uttarakhand. On an average, the people in this state are wealthier compared to their counterparts in the rest of the country. Wide economic differentials exist in fertility behaviour of couples and the extent of their utilisation of MCH services both in the state of Uttarakhand and national level. Of the two important determinants of fertility, economic variable emerged as the higher contributing factor than female education. In case of the latter, one should not confine to targeting only wiping out illiteracy but ensure at least providing secondary education for tangible effects on their fertility and FP behaviour and other development. The regression analysis also shows that by and large people after achieving their desired family size, which is generally high, are going for family planning methods. Family welfare programme should target younger couples with lower parity for having better demographic impact. Better child immunisation rates indicate better outreach services. However, like in many states, inaccessibility of health facilities seemed to be the major cause for lower MCH utilisation rates in this state among economically lower strata of the society compared to the richer communities who could afford at least private facilities for availing MCH and FP services. This may indicate that strengthening and extending the outreach services to maternal services would certainly increase the utilisation of these services. This may be achieved by introducing mobile ANC and delivery services. It may be called Mobile Maternal Health Centre (MMHC). This suggestion is made for two reasons: (1) over two-thirds of the Uttarakhand state has a difficult geographic terrain and is characterised by scattered and sparsely populated districts; the efficacy of the traditional 'fixed-location' health care facilities is severely limited by inaccessibility due to adverse topographical conditions. So, the utilisation of maternal and child health care services could be enhanced through community mobile health clinics in the state. (2) the concept of Mobile Health Clinic (MHC) was already initiated in this state to supplement the existing public health facilities. MHC follows a 'fixed day, fixed time and fixed place' approach to provide health care service in remote, hard-to-reach and poorly served hilly areas in the state. Mobile van named "Sehat ki Sawari" was started in 2004 in Chamoli district under the Garhwal division with the help of the Standing Committee on Voluntary Action (SCOVA). The suggested MMHC can be planned on the lines of MHC.

References

Ahmed, S. (2004). "Does family planning program reduce inequality in contraceptive use, fertility and other health care utilization?—Evidence from Bangladesh", Paper presented in Population Association of America (PAA), USA.

Filmer, D. and L. Pritchett (1999). "The effect of household wealth on educational attainment: Evidence from 35 countries", *Population and Development Review* 25(1): 85-120.

———. (2001). "Estimating wealth effects without expenditure data or tears: An application to educational enrollments in states of India", *Demography* 38 (1): 115-132.

Gautam K. and Satwanti Kapoor (2003). "Fertility and mortality differentials among the population groups of the Himalayas", *Bulletin of the World Health Organization* 80 (2).

Govindasamy, P. (1994). "Poverty, women's education and utilization of health services in Egypt", in *Women, Poverty and Demographic Change*. Liege, Belgium: IUSSP.

Gwatkin, D.R. (2003). "Initial country-level information about socio-economic differences in health, nutrition and population", Volumes I and II, *Working Paper* No.99, Washington, DC: The World Bank.

Gwatkin, D.R., S. Rustein, K. Johnson, R. Pande and A. Wagstaff (2000). "Socioeconomic differences in health, nutrition and population", World Bank Health, Nutrition and Population *Discussion Paper*. Washington DC: World Bank.

International Institute for Population Sciences and ORC Macro (2007). National Family Health Survey-3, 2005-06, Mumbai.

Lustig, N. (2000). *Mexico: The Remaking of an Economy*. Washington, DC: Brookings Institution.

Montgomery, M. *et al.* (2000). "Measuring living standards with proxy variables", *Demography* 37(2): 155-174.

Morris, J.N., A.J.M. Donkin and D. Wonderling *et al.* (2000). "A minimum income for healthy living", *Journal of Epidemiology and Community Health* 54: 885-889.

Navaneetham, K. and A. Dharmalingam (2002). "Utilization of maternal health care services in southern India", *Social Science and Medicine* 55:1849-69.

Nguyen, T.M. and B.M. Poplin (2003). "Inequality in health dynamics in Vietnam: Poverty reduction, increased health inequality", *Population-E* 58: 253-64.

Prasad, C.V.S. and P.K. Chopra (2005). "Socio economic determinants of fertility in India", Paper Presented at 27th Annual Conference of IASP Held at PRC Chandigarh, Punjab University, 10-12th February.

Prasad, C.V.S. (2005a). "Certain differentials in mother and child health indicators in western states of India by asset quintiles", Presented at IASP Conference: *Emerging Issues on Population and Health in Western States of India*, held at Goa, 22-23 December.

———. (2005b). "On differentials in the levels of child health care indicators by household asset quintiles", Paper Presented at 27th Annual Conference of IASP held at PRC Chandigarh, Punjab University during 10-12th February.

Prasad, C.V.S., P.K. Chopra and J. Pradhan (2006). "Economic differentials of fertility among scheduled caste and scheduled tribe population in India", Paper Presented at the International Conference on *Emerging Population Issues in the Asia Pacific Region: Challenges for the 21st Century*, hosted by IIPS at Grand Hyatt, Mumbai during December 11–3.

Savedoff, W.D. and T.P. Schultz (eds.) (2000). *Wealth from Health*. Washington, DC: Inter-American Development Bank.

Singh, L.L. and C.H. Singh (2006). "Rich-poor gap in maternal care: A case of northeast India", *Asia Population Studies* (Forthcoming).

Strauss, J. and D. Thomas (1998). "Health, nutrition and economic development", *Journal of Economic Literature* 36(2):766-817.

Wagstaff, A. (2000). "Socioeconomic inequalities in child mortality: Comparisons across nine developing countries", *Bulletin of the World Health Organization* 78 (1): 19-29.

———. (2002). "Poverty and health care inequalities", *Bulletin of the World Health Organization* 80(2).

———. (2005). "The economic consequences of health shocks", *World Bank Policy Research Working Paper* 3644.

8 Unwanted Pregnancy

A Comparative Study of Uttarakhand and Himachal Pradesh

Sujata Ganguly and Sayeed Unisa

Introduction

Women's behaviour during pregnancy, which can affect the health of their infants, may be influenced by their attitude towards the pregnancy (Kost *et al.*, 1998). Mothers with unwanted births have lower quality emotional relationships with their children. In other words, the negative effect of unwanted childbearing is not limited to the child born as a result of unwanted birth. Rather unwanted childbearing leads to a negative family-level effect in terms of mother-child relationship (Barber *et al.*, 1999). Information about women's intention to become pregnant has been used for a variety of purposes from estimating the number of unintended pregnancies to assessing the effects of pregnancy intention on behaviours during pregnancy, birth outcomes, health and development of children born as a result of unintended pregnancies (Joyce *et al.*, 2002).

Joyce *et al.* (2000) concluded from the youth cohort of the National Longitudinal Survey of Labour Market Experiences that the unwanted pregnancy was associated with prenatal and post-partum maternal behaviours, which adversely affect infant and child health, but unwanted pregnancy had little association with birth weight and child cognitive outcomes. Women whose pregnancies were unwanted were more likely to delay prenatal care and to smoke during pregnancy than women whose pregnancies were wanted and were less likely to breastfeed. Although little association between pregnancy intention and measures of child social and cognitive development were found, the effects of other variables such as family income, mother's education and cognitive ability and family structure were significant.

Marston and Cleland (2003) investigated whether children later reported as having been unwanted or mistimed at conception will, when compared with children reported as wanted, show adverse effects when the following criteria are applied: receipt of antenatal care before the sixth month of gestation, supervised delivery, full vaccination of the child and child growth (stunting). The study used data from recent Demographic and Health Survey enquiries in Bolivia, Egypt, Kenya, Peru and the Philippines. In Peru, children unwanted at conception were found to have significantly worse outcomes than other children but in the other countries, a systematic effect was found only for receipt of antenatal care. Weak measurement of the complex concept of wantedness may have contributed to these results. Birth order of the child, with which wantedness was inextricably linked, had more powerful and pervasive effects, with first-born and second-born children being much less likely to show adverse effects.

According to Crissey (2006), prior research has documented a relationship between unintended pregnancy and negative consequences for infants and children. Using the 1988 National Maternal and Infant Health Survey and its 1991 Longitudinal Follow-Up, a composite measure of reported pregnancy intention and birth control use is constructed. This composite measure is compared to more conventional measures through analyses predicting the effects of pregnancy intention on child health, activity and development. Across the different constructions of the pregnancy intention measure, children from unintended pregnancy have poorer outcomes. They are more likely to have less than excellent health, undesirable activity levels and below median scores on a development assessment.

Barber *et al.* (1999) studied the relationships among unwanted childbearing, health and mother-child relationships. It was hypothesised that the unwanted childbearing affects mother-child relationships in part because of the physical and mental health consequences of unwanted childbearing. Impaired mental health hampers women's interaction with their infants and these poor neonatal relationships translate into poor mother-adult child relationships. Using the

Intergenerational Panel Study of Mothers and Children, it was demonstrated that mothers with unwanted births had lower quality relationships with their children from late adolescence (age 18) throughout early adulthood (ages 23 and 31). Furthermore, these lower quality relationships were not limited to the child born as a result of the unwanted pregnancy; all the children in the family suffer. Using the 1987-88 wave of the National Survey of Families and Households, a survey of a national probability sample of US households, it was shown that mothers with unwanted births suffer from higher levels of depression and lower levels of happiness. They spank their young children more and spend less leisure time with them. Hence, it was concluded that experiencing unwanted childbearing reduces the time and attention that mothers give their young children and that these early mother-child interactions set the stage for long-term, lower quality relationships.

Accurate measurement of pregnancy intendedness, including women's attitudes toward pregnancy and motivations to achieve or avoid a pregnancy is important in understanding fertility-related behaviours, estimating unmet need for contraception and building stronger family planning programmes (Speizer *et al.*, 2004). Hence, the broad objective of the paper is to understand the factors underlying unwanted pregnancy and its implications on utilisation of maternal health care in Uttarakhand and Himachal Pradesh.

Data Source

National Family Health Survey-3 (NFHS-3) conducted in the year 2005-06 has been used for the analysis. The NFHS-3 interviewed men of the age group 15-54 and women (never married as well as ever married women) of the age group 15-49. It included questions on several emerging issues such as perinatal mortality, male involvement in maternal health care, adolescent reproductive health, higher risk sexual behaviour, family life education, safe injections and knowledge about tuberculosis. NFHS-3 collected information from a nationally representative sample of 109041 households, 124385 women of the age group 15-49 and 74369 men of the age group 15-54 and covers 99 per cent of India's population living in 29 states (IIPS and MI, 2007a).

Methodology

Unintended pregnancy can have serious health, social and economic consequences. Such pregnancies may be unwanted (a baby is not wanted at any time) or mistimed, yet wanted (a baby is wanted eventually). Hence, in order to determine the pregnancy intention of currently married women, the variable considered is the time when women wanted pregnancy. The specific question asked in NFHS-3 regarding this variable is, "At the time you were pregnant with (NAME), did you want to become pregnant then, did you want to wait until later or did you want no (more) children at all?" (IIPS and MI, 2007b). The entire analysis has been done on the basis of the third part of the question i.e., whether the child was not wanted at all. This question is asked for children born in the last five years preceding the survey. The analysis is restricted to last born surviving children younger than 36 months from singleton births. For the analysis, currently married women have been considered. The unit of analysis are children. For the ease of writing, at places women are referred which implies unwanted children born to women.

The bivariate analysis has been done for studying the percentage distribution of currently married women and percentage of unwanted pregnancy among currently married women by background characteristics in each category. For this purpose, many predictor variables have been used like age, age at first marriage, marital duration, age at first birth, birth order, husband's age, type of place of residence, religion, caste, women's and husband's education, household structure, standard of living, women's working status, exposure to mass media, women's autonomy and contraceptive use.

Further bivariate analyses have been done to study the utilisation of maternal health care services among currently married women by unwanted pregnancy. The variables included are—"How many times did you receive antenatal check-up during this pregnancy?"–This variable has been categorised as none and one or more times; "How many months pregnant were you when you first received an antenatal care for this pregnancy?"–This variable has been re-formed into first, second and third trimester; "At any time before this pregnancy, did you receive any tetanus injections?"; "During this pregnancy, were you given or did you buy any iron folic acid tablets or syrup?"; "During the whole pregnancy, for how many days did you take the tablets or syrup?"; "During this pregnancy, did you take any drug to get rid of worms in your intestines?" (IIPS and MI, 2007b).

Apart from prenatal care, place of delivery which defines natal care has also been taken into account. The specific question asked is "Where did you give birth to (NAME)?". This response has been divided into two categories namely, Home (own or parent's home) and institutional combining public (government/municipal hospital, government dispensary, UHC/UHP/UFWC, CHC/rural hospital/PHC, sub-centre, other public sector health facility) and private (NGO/Trust hospital/clinic, private medical sector/private hospital/clinic/maternity home, other private sector health facility) (IIPS and MI, 2007b).

Selection of the Area

According to NFHS-3 (2005-06), the unwanted pregnancy is 14 per cent in Uttarakhand and around 7 per cent in Himachal Pradesh. This raises a query that both these states are in close proximity with similiar topology, yet these two states vary considerably in the percentage of women reporting unwanted pregnancy. This leads to an emerging research issue to find out the underlying causes for such differentials.

Background Characteristics of Women in Uttarakhand and Himachal Pradesh

In Uttarakhand, majority of women belong to the age group less than 30 years (75 per cent) (Table 8.1). About 55 per cent women have their age at first marriage less than 18 years. Around 28 per cent women have 0-4 years marital duration whereas 40 per cent women have 5-9 years and 32 per cent women have 10 years and above marital duration. Around 53 per cent women have age at first birth below 20 years. Twenty-seven per cent of children are at first birth order. It is 30, 19 and 25 per cent at second, third and fourth birth order respectively.

Table 8.1

Percentage Distribution of Currently Married Women according to Background Characteristics, NFHS-3 (2005-06)

	Uttarakhand		*Himachal Pradesh*	
Background Characteristics	*Per cent*	*Total*	*Per cent*	*Total*
Women's Age (years)				
30 and below	74.55	555	77.06	477
Above 30	25.45	189	22.94	142
Age at First Marriage				
18 and below	55.44	413	32.45	201
Above 18	44.56	332	67.55	418
Marital Duration (years)				
0-4	27.68	206	38.63	239
5-9	39.86	297	43.02	266
10 and above	32.46	242	18.35	113
Age at First Birth (years)				
20 and below	52.66	392	37.77	234
Above 20	47.34	352	62.23	385
Birth Order				
1	26.78	199	31.38	194
2	29.65	221	41.10	254
3	18.86	140	16.51	102
4+	24.71	184	11.01	68
Husband's Age (years)				
35 and below	82.81	605	85.28	526
Above 35	17.19	126	14.72	91
Place of Residence				
Urban	25.08	187	9.43	58
Rural	74.92	558	90.57	560
Religion				
Hindu	84.03	625	96.55	597
Others[1]	15.97	119	3.45	21
Caste				
Scheduled caste	21.85	163	25.94	160
Scheduled tribe	3.31	25	4.67	29
Other backward caste	15.86	118	14.18	88
Others[2]	58.98	439	55.21	341

Contd...

...contd...

	Uttarakhand		*Himachal Pradesh*	
Background Characteristics	*Per cent*	*Total*	*Per cent*	*Total*
Women's Education				
No education	38.33	285	15.21	94
Primary	12.60	94	13.01	80
Secondary	35.54	265	59.93	371
Higher	13.53	101	11.86	73
Husband's Education				
No education	14.41	107	6.45	40
Primary	13.26	98	9.43	58
Secondary	55.66	412	68.93	423
Higher	16.67	123	15.18	93
Household Structure				
Nuclear	38.15	270	28.78	169
Non-nuclear	61.85	437	71.22	418
Standard of Living Index				
Low	17.64	121	8.15	47
Medium	31.60	216	31.25	180
High	50.76	348	60.61	350
Women's Working Status				
Not working	63.47	470	72.93	445
Working	36.53	270	27.07	165
Exposure to Mass Media				
None	22.56	168	10.83	67
Partial	67.27	500	62.55	387
Full	10.16	76	26.61	165
Women's Autonomy				
None	91.35	680	87.24	540
Medium or high	8.65	64	12.76	79
Contraceptive Use				
No	52.23	389	44.69	276
Yes	47.77	356	55.31	342

Note: [1] include Muslim, Christian, Sikh, Buddhist/Neo-Buddhist, Jain, Jews, Zoroastrian/Parsi. Due to very less frequency, all these religious groups have been combined.

[2] include those who do not belong to aforementioned castes.

Around three-fourth of women live in the rural areas. Women in Uttarakhand are mostly Hindus and belong to other caste group. The percentage of women belonging to scheduled tribes is negligible and one-fourth of them belong to scheduled caste. Women mostly have no education or have low level of educational attainment. Husbands mostly have secondary level of educational attainment. Around 62 per cent women live in non-nuclear household. Half of the women belong to high standard of living but majority of them are not engaged in any occupation. Around 67 per cent women have atleast partial exposure to mass media but 91 per cent of women have no autonomy. Around 48 per cent women use contraceptives.

In Himachal Pradesh, the age-wise distribution of women do not show much variation as compared to women in Uttarakhand but the important point to be noted is that majority of women have age at first marriage above 18 years. Around 39 per cent women have 0-4 years marital duration whereas 43 per cent women have 5-9 years and 18 per cent women have 10 years and above marital duration. Around 62 per cent women have age at first birth above 20 years. Thirty-one per cent of children are at first birth order. It is 41, 17 and 11 per cent at second, third and fourth birth order respectively.

Around 91 per cent of women belong to rural areas. Ninety-seven per cent of women are Hindu and 55 per cent of women belong to other caste group. Eighty-five per cent of women and 94 per cent husbands have certain level of educational attainment. Seventy-one per cent women live in non-nuclear household. Around 60 per cent women belong to high standard of living and women belonging to low standard of living are only around 8 per cent. Women mostly are not engaged in any occupation (73 per cent). Women have partial exposure to mass media (63 per cent) but have low autonomy (87 per cent). Around 55 per cent women use contraceptives.

Unwanted Pregnancy

In Uttarakhand, the unwanted pregnancy is high among women who are more than 30 years (31 per cent) whereas 8 per cent women who are less than 30 years of age have reported unwantedness of pregnancy (Table 8.2). However, in Himachal Pradesh, it is 15 and 4 per cent respectively. Uttarakhand shows that unwanted pregnancy is high

Table 8.2

Percentage of Unwanted Pregnancy among Currently Married Women according to Selected Background Characteristics, NFHS-3 (2005-06)

Background Characteristics	*Uttarakhand*	*Himachal Pradesh*
Women's Age (years)		
30 and below	8.11	4.19
Above 30	31.22	15.49
Age at First Marriage		
18 and below	17.68	7.46
Above 18	9.37	6.70
Marital Duration (years)		
0-4	3.88	2.09
5-9	6.73	7.89
10 and above	31.54	14.16
Age at First Birth (years)		
20 and below	17.90	7.26
Above 20	9.63	6.51
Birth Order		
1	1.50	2.58
2	4.07	3.94
3	17.86	11.76
4+	36.61	22.06
Husband's Age (years)		
35 and below	10.08	5.89
Above 35	30.95	13.19
Place of Residence		
Urban	13.90	3.45
Rural	14.16	7.14
Religion		
Hindu	13.28	7.04
Others	17.65	0.00
Caste		
Scheduled caste	19.14	9.38
Scheduled tribe	20.83	13.33
Other backward caste	15.13	3.41
Others	11.39	5.87

Contd...

...*contd*...

Background Characteristics	*Uttarakhand*	*Himachal Pradesh*
Women's Education		
No education	17.83	6.38
Primary	27.66	4.94
Secondary	8.30	7.55
Higher	5.94	5.48
Husband's Education		
No education	22.64	7.50
Primary	20.41	10.34
Secondary	13.11	6.16
Higher	4.88	7.53
Household structure		
Nuclear	18.89	7.10
Non-nuclear	11.44	6.94
Standard of Living Index		
Low	18.33	8.51
Medium	14.81	9.94
High	12.36	5.70
Women's working status		
Not working	12.55	6.07
Working	16.61	7.83
Exposure to Mass Media		
None	17.16	4.41
Partial	14.20	7.51
Full	6.67	6.10
Women's Autonomy		
None	13.82	7.24
Medium or high	15.63	5.06
Contraceptive Use		
No	10.57	3.99
Yes	17.70	9.06
Total	13.98	6.79

among women whose age at first marriage is less than 18 years (18 per cent) and it is 9 per cent among women whose age at first marriage is more than 18 years. Similiar is the pattern for age at first birth. Himachal Pradesh does not show variation according to age at first marriage as well as age at first birth. Unwantedness of pregnancy increases with increase in marital duration in both the states but the magnitude is higher in Uttarakhand compared to Himachal Pradesh. Unwanted pregnancy and birth order shows a direct relation. With increase in birth order, unwanted pregnancy also increases. There is a steep rise at fourth and above birth order.

Unwanted pregnancy is higher in rural areas than urban areas though the difference is nominal. It is 13.9 and 14 per cent in urban and rural areas in Uttarakhand respectively and 3 and 7 per cent in Himachal Pradesh respectively. Scheduled tribe in Uttarakhand reports highest unwanted pregnancy i.e., 21 per cent and it is around 19 per cent among scheduled caste. In Himachal Pradesh, it is around 13 and 9 per cent respectively. Women who have low educational attainment have high unwanted pregnancy. It is 18 and 6 per cent among women who have no education in Uttarakhand and Himachal Pradesh respectively. Twenty-eight and 5 per cent women have unwanted pregnancy with primary education in both the states respectively. Husband's education also shows the similiar pattern. Women in nuclear household have more unwanted pregnancy compared to women in non-nuclear household.

There has been a decline in unwanted pregnancy with rise in the standard of living. It has decreased from 18 per cent to 15 to 12 per cent in Uttarakhand according to low, medium and high standard of living respectively whereas in Himachal Pradesh, it has attained a wedge like pattern. It is 9, 10 and 6 per cent respectively. Women who are working have high unwanted pregnancy. It is 13 per cent among women who are not working and 17 per cent among women who are working in Uttarakhand. In Himachal Pradesh, it is 6 and 8 per cent respectively.

In Uttarakhand, women with no exposure to mass media have high percentage of unwanted pregnancy whereas in Himachal Pradesh the difference is not notable. It is 17, 14 and 7 per cent among women with none, partial and full exposure to mass media in Uttarakhand whereas it is 4,8 and 6 per cent respectively among women in Himachal Pradesh. Women with medium and high autonomy have high percentage (16 per cent) of unwanted pregnancy than women with no autonomy (14 per cent) in Uttarakhand whereas in Himachal Pradesh, the pattern is opposite. It is 5 and 7 per cent respectively. In both the states, it can be seen that women using contraceptives have high percentage of unwanted pregnancy.

Factors Determining Unwanted Pregnancy

The bivariate analysis depicts that unwanted pregnancy is high among certain group of women, for example, older women, those whose age at first marriage is below 18 years, women with higher marital duration, women with children of high birth order, scheduled tribe women, women and their husbands with low level of educational attainment, women in nuclear household, women with low standard of living and those using contraceptives. This is true for both the states. However, in bivariate analysis, the results are unadjusted. There is a possibility that the relation of unwanted pregnancy with other explanatory variables is not independent of influence of one variable over another. Due to this, multivariate binary logistic regression has been applied to get adjusted values. From Table 8.3 it can be seen that, age of women and unwanted pregnancy has direct relation. As age increases, unintended pregnancy also increases. In Uttarakhand, there is 75 per cent and in Himachal Pradesh, there is 3.55 times more probability for women above 30 years age to have unwanted pregnancy. Birth order is another variable that is significant. With increase in birth order, there is drastic increase in unwanted pregnancy in both the states. By controlling other explanatory variables, it can be observed that education is significant to some extent in both the states. In addition to these, exposure to mass media and contraceptive use are significant in Himachal Pradesh. The patterns in multivariate analysis confirm the pattern derived in bivariate analysis.

Utilisation of Maternal Health Care Services

Unwanted pregnancy affects the well-being of women, children and families. In fact, some health experts believe that unwanted pregnancy carried to term are more likely to involve complications. Women with unintended pregnancies may be subject to increased physical abuse by their partners during pregnancy (cited in IGWG and WHO, 2005). The unwanted pregnancy can have its implication on the utilisation of the maternal and child health care services. However, pregnancy intention

Table 8.3

Logit Estimates of the Probability of Unwanted Pregnancy according to Selected Background Characteristics, NFHS-3 (2005-06)

	Uttarakhand		*Himachal Pradesh*	
Background Characteristics	*Exp (β)*	*Sig. level*	*Exp (β)*	*Sig. level*
Women's Age (years)				
30 and below®				
Above 30	1.75	0.12	3.55	0.04
Age at First Marriage				
18 and below®				
Above 18	0.87	0.75	1.65	0.45
Marital Duration (years)				
0-4®				
5-9	0.30	0.06	3.66	0.08
10 and above	0.48	0.30	4.14	0.15
Age at First Birth (years)				
20 and below®				
Above 20	1.15	0.74	1.39	0.62
Birth Order				
1®				
2	3.76	0.09	0.37	0.20
3	25.57	0.00	1.93	0.43
4+	55.83	0.00	6.05	0.07
Husband's Age (years)				
35 and below®				
Above 35	1.84	0.07	0.54	0.27
Place of Residence				
Urban®				
Rural	0.81	0.55	1.88	0.47
Religion				
Hindu®				
Others	0.96	0.92	0.00	1.00
Caste				
Scheduled caste®				
Scheduled tribe	0.82	0.78	1.91	0.48
Other backward caste	0.65	0.32	0.11	0.01
Others	0.69	0.26	0.61	0.29

Contd...

...contd...

Background Characteristics	*Uttarakhand* Exp (β)	*Uttarakhand* Sig. level	*Himachal Pradesh* Exp (β)	*Himachal Pradesh* Sig. level
Women's Education				
No education®				
Primary	3.97	0.00	2.50	0.30
Secondary	1.42	0.43	11.25	0.00
Higher	5.08	0.06	4.03	0.21
Husband's Education				
No education®				
Primary	1.07	0.88	1.10	0.92
Secondary	0.91	0.82	0.55	0.54
Higher	0.21	0.06	2.14	0.51
Household Structure				
Nuclear®				
Non-nuclear	1.44	0.24	1.36	0.52
Standard of Living Index				
Low®				
Medium	0.97	0.95	2.83	0.29
High	1.29	0.61	0.91	0.93
Women's Working Status				
Not working®				
Working	0.85	0.58	0.89	0.80
Exposure to Mass Media				
None®				
Partial	1.13	0.75	5.39	0.04
Full	0.57	0.48	3.79	0.15
Women's Autonomy				
None®				
Medium or high	0.92	0.87	0.31	0.13
Contraceptive Use				
No®				
Yes	1.37	0.26	2.65	0.04

Note: Dependent variable=last born surviving children younger than 36 months from singleton births, and 0=births out of wanted or mistimed pregnancy, 1=Births out of unwanted pregnancy; ®=Reference Category.

has little or no effect on medical supervision at delivery, child vaccination or adequacy of growth, once the impact of socio-economic and demographic characteristics is accounted for; intendedness does appear to independently affect the odds of obtaining adequate prenatal care (Remez, 2003). In the specific behaviours examined, whether pregnancies were wanted exhibits significant net relationships with timing of prenatal care. Women with unwanted pregnancy may initially attempt to deny their pregnancy to themselves and to conceal them from others, either from a desire that the pregnancy "go away" or because of fear of the consequences. Thus, these women may be less likely to obtain prenatal care, especially early in pregnancy (Weller *et al.*, 1987).

Table 8.4 shows that 90 per cent women in Himachal Pradesh with unwanted pregnancy have gone for ANC whereas in Uttarakhand, it is only, 61 per cent. Forty-one, 47 and 12 per cent women in Uttarakhand have gone for first ANC in first, second and third trimester respectively whereas it is 65, 24 and 11 per cent in Himachal Pradesh respectively. Women who have taken tetanus toxoid injections are 71 per cent in

Table 8.4

Percentage Distribution of Selected MHC Services according to Unwanted Pregnancy among Currently Married Women, NFHS-3 (2005-06)

	Uttarakhand			*Himachal Pradesh*		
	Per cent	*Contingency Coefficient*	*Significance Level*	*Per cent*	*Contingency Coefficient*	*Significance Level*
ANC Visit	61.22	0.20	0.00	90.00	0.06	0.36
First ANC visit		0.16	0.01		0.10	0.23
First trimester	40.63			64.86		
Second trimester	46.88			24.32		
Third trimester	12.50			10.81		
Tetanus Toxoid Injections		0.10	0.11		0.19	0.00
None	28.16			2.44		
1	10.68			41.46		
2+	61.17			56.10		
IFA Tablet/Syrup	57.69	0.08	0.09	85.71	0.05	0.44
IFA Tablet/Syrup for more than 90 Days	20.69	0.06	0.44	34.38	0.10	0.11
Place of Delivery		0.13	0.01		0.09	0.08
Home	79.05			53.49		
Institutional	20.95			46.51		

Note: Variable intake of intestinal parasite drug has been dropped because of very less frequency.

Uttarakhand and around 97 per cent in Himachal Pradesh. Similarly, those who have taken IFA tablets or syrup are 58 and 86 per cent respectively in both the states and those who have taken IFA tablets or syrup for more than 90 days are 21 and 34 per cent in Uttarakhand and Himachal Pradesh respectively. 79 per cent of deliveries are home deliveries in the former state whereas it is 53 per cent in latter state.

In Uttarakhand, ANC visit, timing of first visit and place of delivery are significant and have 20, 16 and 13 per cent association with unwanted pregnancy. In Himachal Pradesh, intake of tetanus toxoid injections is significant and has 19 per cent association with unwanted pregnancy.

Summary and Conclusions

Unwanted pregnancy is high in Uttarakhand as compared to Himachal Pradesh. The difference is also quite notable. There are various demographic, social and economic factors that explain this variation. Uttarakhand is a state where three-fourth of the respondents are from the rural areas. Majority of them are Hindu with considerable proportion of them having some level of educational attainment and nearly half of them belonging to high standard of living. However, the autonomy of women is notably low. Moreover, exposure to mass media is quite less.

In Himachal Pradesh, the situation is similar to a certain extent. However, 90 per cent women live in the rural areas. Inspite of such a high percentage of women living in rural areas, most of them have received certain level of education. Furthermore, about more than half of them have age at first birth more than 20 years. As compared to women in Uttarakhand, women belonging to high standard of living are high. In terms of exposure to mass media and autonomy, Himachal Pradesh shows better existing situation. In short, it can be concluded that women are in a better position in Himachal Pradesh than the women in Uttarakhand.

Unwanted pregnancy is higher in Uttarakhand (14 per cent) as compared to Himachal Pradesh (7 per cent). The analysis further points out that age of women and unwanted pregnancy has direct relation. As age increases, unintended pregnancy also increases. Birth order is another variable that is significant. With increase in birth order, there is drastic increase in unwanted pregnancy in both the states. By controlling other explanatory variables, it can be observed that education is significant to some extent in both the states. In addition to these, exposure to mass media and contraceptive use are significant in Himachal Pradesh.

The utilisation of maternal and child health care services is quite low in Uttarakhand. In every aspect like, ANC care, timing of first ANC, intake of tetanus toxoid injections, intake of IFA tablets or syrups or intake of IFA tablets or syrups for more than 90 days and place of delivery, Himachal Pradesh shows better performance. From this, it may be concluded that unwanted pregnancy is higher in Uttarakhand than Himachal Pradesh and the utilisation of maternal and child health care services is yet to be improved.

Throughout, there are certain situations where exact explanation for the queries cannot be given. There may be certain reasons behind it e.g., the question on pregnancy intention can suffer from number of limitations like if son is born after four daughters then that son is not considered unwanted. On the contrary, the daughters may be considered unwanted. Hence, preferences for a particular sex composition can create bias. Another important factor is that of replacement as well as insurance effect i.e., to have more children for compensating child loss. The unwantedness of the child can become wanted after its birth e.g., 4 in 10 married women who said that they wanted no more children and subsequently had a birth reported that birth as wanted and said their reaction to it had been positive. Only seven per cent of those who said they wanted more children reported a subsequent birth as unwanted (Westoff, 1980). Moreover, the respondent may respond so as to present a favourable image to the interviewer. Hence, such situation can create response bias. Besides, there are cases where there are non-numeric responses when question on ideal number of children is asked. The influence of the family members can also be important in determining the pregnancy intention.

References

Barber, J.S., W.G. Axinn and A. Thornton (1999). "Unwanted childbearing, health, and mother-child relationships", *Journal of Health and Social Behavior* 40(3): *231-257*.

Crissey, S.R. (2006). "Effect of pregnancy intention on child well-being and development: Combining retrospective reports of attitude and contraceptive use", *Population Research and Policy Review* 24(6): 593-615.

IGWG and WHO (2005). *A Summary of the 'So What?' Report*. Department of Women and Health Family and Community Health, WHO, Geneva, Switzerland.

International Institute for Population Sciences (IIPS) and Macro International (2007a). National Family Health Survey, 2005-2006: India, IIPS, Mumbai. Volume I.

———. (2007b). National Family Health Survey, 2005-2006: India, IIPS, Mumbai. Volume II.

Joyce, T.J., R. Kaestner and S. Korenman (2000). "The effect of pregnancy intention on child development", *Demography* 37(1): 83-94.

———. (2002). "On the validity of retrospective assessments of pregnancy intention", *Demography* 39(1): 199-213.

Kost, K., D.J. Landry and J.E. Darroch (1998). "The effects of pregnancy planning status on birth outcomes and infant care", *Family Planning Perspectives* 30(5): 223-230.

Marston, C. and J. Cleland (2003). "Do unintended pregnancies carried to term lead to adverse outcomes for mother and child? An assessment in five developing countries", *Population Studies* 57(1): 77-93.

Remez, L. (2003). "Unintended pregnancy is linked to inadequate prenatal care, but not to unattended delivery or child health", *International Family Planning Perspectives* 29(3): 146-147.

Speizer, I.S., J.S. Santelli, A. Afable-Munsuz and C. Kendall (2004). "Measuring factors underlying intendedness of women's first and later pregnancies", *Perspectives on Sexual and Reproductive Health* 36(5): 198-205.

Weller, R.H., I.W. Eberstein and M. Bailey (1987). "Pregnancy wantedness and maternal behaviour during pregnancy", *Demography* 24(3): 407-412.

Westoff, C.F. (1980). "Women's reactions to pregnancy", *Family Planning Perspectives* 12(3): 135-139.

9 Communication, Accessibility and Condom Use

Insights from Uttar Pradesh and Uttarakhand, NFHS-3, 2005-06

Manoj Kumar Raut, Daliya Sebastian and Satyaban Sahu

Introduction

> *One in three of all deaths related to pregnancy and childbirth could be avoided if women who wanted effective contraception had access to it*
>
> *(Source:* "Contraceptives Save Lives", July 11, 2008, World Population Day, UNFPA*).*

Population stabilisation is an issue concerning most of the countries in the developing world. It is more so in India and similarly, in one of its state, the largest of all, in Uttar Pradesh (UP). One of the gravest problem, that many countries in the early stages of demographic transition are facing is the burgeoning population problem. To address this issue, national family planning programmes, which began in the mid-20th century have evolved rapidly to meet the information and service needs of target groups.

India is the second most populous country in the world with a population of 1028.7 million, projected to become the most populous country in the world by 2028 (UN projections). It is a land of multiplicities and diversities. It is characterised by regional imbalances like a large north-south divide in health and development. In India, the high levels of fertility and mortality is contributed mostly by a group of states now termed as Empowered Action Group (EAG) states, formerly referred to as BIMARU states. These eight states are Bihar, Jharkhand, Uttar Pradesh, Uttarakhand, Madhya Pradesh, Chhattisgarh, Orissa and

Rajasthan. These eight states constitute 45 per cent of the total population of India and account for 59 per cent of the total poor in India. These states alone contribute to more than half (55 per cent) of the estimated live births, infant deaths (54 per cent) and maternal deaths (58 per cent) in India (estimates based on SRS data).

Family Planning in India

India is the one of the first countries in the world to adopt a family planning programme way back in 1951. But it has yet to achieve net replacement levels of fertility in all states. Family planning in India has also undergone several transformations. In the 1980s, though, the efforts to encourage the use of reversible methods were initiated, the trend and pace of spacing methods over terminal methods has been quite gradual. The use of any family planning method in India has risen from 40.7 per cent during NFHS-1 to 48.2 in NFHS-2 to 56.3 per cent in the recently concluded NFHS-3. The method-mix has shown a gradual shift in favour of spacing methods over terminal methods. As a spacing method, condom use in India has risen from 2.4 per cent during NFHS-1 to 3.1 in NFHS-2 to 5.2 per cent in the recently concluded NFHS-3.

So, this paper tries to understand the factors enabling higher condom use in Uttarakhand in comparison to Uttar Pradesh. This may offer some insights to the programme planners and implementers to achieve improvement in condom use considering the striking difference in the level of TFR in both these states. Both Uttar Pradesh and Uttarakhand are EAG states. According to Census 2001, UP, with a population of 166 million, 70 districts and 107,452 villages is considered to be a mini-India. Uttarakhand has been recently carved out of UP, the most populous state in India. After being recently carved out of this state, it was subsequently rechristened as Uttarakhand. Though Uttarakhand has been carved out of UP, there is a lot of variation between both the states. The TFR of UP is still at 3.8 children per woman compared to 2.6 per woman for Uttarakhand (NFHS-3, 2005-06). It is really a matter of utmost concern in UP with a population double the size of Uttarakhand, which has a population of 84.8 million with 13 districts and 16,826 villages. The crude birth rate of UP is 29.1 compared to 20.1 for Uttarakhand per 1,000 mid-year population (SRS, 2008) (See Table 9.1). Uttar Pradesh is

Table 9.1

Key Demographic Indicators

Sl. No.	*Indicators*	*Uttar Pradesh*	*Uttarakhand*	*India*
1.	Population (in number)	166,197,921	8,489,349	1,028,610,328
2.	Percentage of scheduled castes	21.1	17.9	16.2
3.	Percentage of scheduled tribes	0.1	3.0	8.2
4.	Overall sex ratio (females/1000 males)	898	962	933
5.	Sex ratio (0-6 years) (females/1000 males)	916	908	927
6.	Crude birth rate (CBR)*	29.1	20.1	22.8
7.	Crude death rate (CDR)**	8.6	6.7	7.5
8.	Natural growth rate (in %)	21.4	14.2	16.0
9.	Total fertility rate (TFR) (children per woman)	3.8	2.6	2.7
10.	Infant mortality rate (IMR)***	67	44	53
11.	Literacy rate (in %)	56.3	71.6	64.8
12.	Contraceptive prevalence (any method) (in %)	43.6	59.3	56.3
13.	Administrative divisions (no. of districts)	70	13	593

Note: * Number of live births per 1,000 mid-year population.

** Number of deaths per 1,000 mid-year population.

*** Number of infant deaths per 1,000 live births.

Source: *Sample Registration System, 2008; Census 2001; NFHS-3, 2005-06.*

Figure 9.1

Total Fertility Rate (TFR) of India and States Expressed in Children Per Woman, NFHS-3, 2005-06

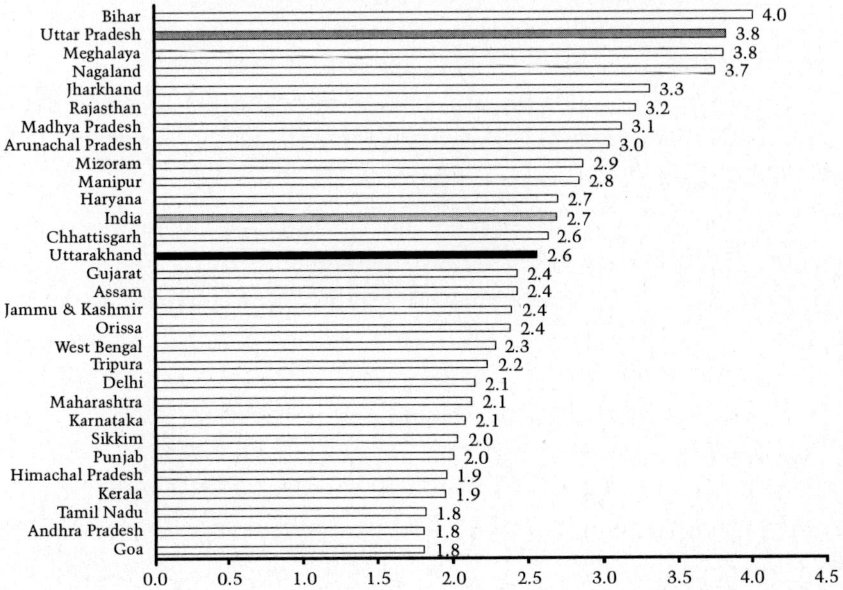

Figure 9.2

Infant Mortality Rate of India and States Expressed in Number of Infant Deaths Per 1,000 Live Births, Sample Registration System: 2008

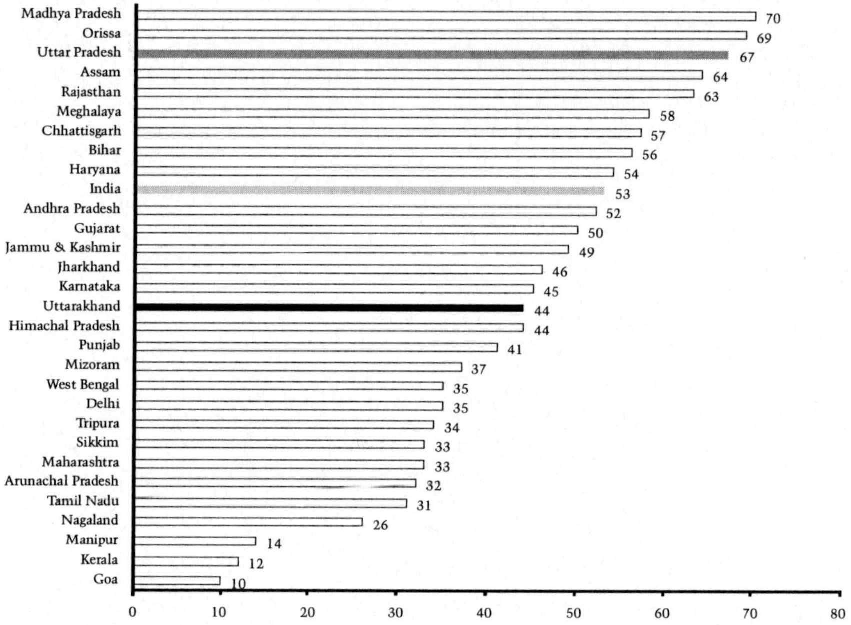

characterised by high levels of both fertility as well as mortality, with a TFR of 3.8 (NFHS-3, 2005-06) and IMR of 67 infant deaths per 1,000 live births (SRS, 2008) and MMR of 440 maternal deaths per 100,000 live births (SRS, 2004-2006).

Contraceptive prevalence in both the states: There is a lot of variation with regards to the contraceptive use in both the states. The use of any method in UP is below half at 43.6 per cent compared to 59.3 per cent in case of Uttarakhand, which is above the national average (56.3). With regards to the method mix, the variation is overwhelming. The use of any modern method in Uttarakhand is 55.5 per cent compared to just 29.3 per cent in case of UP. Among the modern methods, the percentage of female sterilisation is about double in case of Uttarakhand (32.1) compared to UP (17.3). Male sterilisation is about nine times in case of Uttarakhand (1.8) compared to UP (0.2). Similarly, current condom use is about double at 15.7 for Uttarakhand compared to UP (8.6). So, this study tries to find out the factors responsible for the higher condom use as a means of contraception in Uttarakhand, which can be a precedent for Uttar Pradesh to increase the use of condom as a means of birth spacing.

Table 9.2

Contraceptive Use in Uttar Pradesh, Uttarakhand and India in 2005-06: (NFHS-3)

Sl. No.	*Current Use of Contraception by Type of Methods*	*Uttar Pradesh*	*Uttarakhand*	*India*
1.	**I. Any Method**	43.6	59.3	56.3
2.	*Type of Methods*			
3.	*Any Modern Method*	29.3	55.5	48.5
4.	Female sterilisation	17.3	32.1	37.3
5.	Male sterilisation	0.2	1.8	1.0
6.	Pill	1.7	4.2	3.1
7.	IUD	1.4	1.5	1.7
8.	Injectables	0.1	0.1	0.1
9.	Condom/*nirodh*	8.6	15.7	5.2
10.	Other modern method	0.1	0.1	0.0
11.	*Any Traditional Method*	14.3	3.8	7.8
12.	Rhythm	11.3	2.1	4.9
13.	Withdrawal	2.5	1.7	2.5
14.	Folk method	0.5	0.0	0.3
15.	**II. Not Currently Using**	56.4	40.7	43.7
	Total (I+II)	100.0	100.0	100.0

Note: IUD : Intra-Uterine Device.

Source: *NFHS-3, 2005-06.*

Mass Media and Interpersonal Channels of Communication

Mass media channels include radio, films/movies, television, newspapers and magazines. Interpersonal channels include counselling; outreach activities; advocacy; and information provided by health professionals and social services workers, religious and community leaders, traditional health practitioners, women's and youth organisations, community councils and organisations, school programmes and groups, trade union and labour group leaders, government services, non-governmental and voluntary organisations, and business leaders. Small media channels include posters, cassettes, leaflets, brochures, slide sets, videos, flip charts, flash cards, t-shirts, badges, etc. Traditional media consist of traditional folk arts, story tellers, puppet shows, plays, theatre, role plays, music, dance performances, comedy, magic, festivals, etc. New communication technologies include computer networks, global telephone systems, new multimedia technologies, etc. Interpersonal communication is especially effective when supported by appropriate small media such as leaflets, posters, flip charts, video, role play, songs and drama. Family planning programmes around the world employ different types of communication media after segmenting the population, based on their specific and peculiar needs and choices (Piotrow *et al.*, 1997).

Literature Review

A lot of studies have been carried out on the possible determinants of family planning and contraceptive use. Saksena and Rastogi (1988) investigated the reach of 12 different media of communication through which people are exposed to family planning. This included interpersonal, print and audio-visual media namely home visits, group meetings, entertainment/cultural programmes (puppet shows, religious songs/recitals, folk drama etc.), radio, films, family planning posters, television, wall-paintings/hoardings, pamphlets/leaflets, exhibitions, newspapers and magazines. The results show that radio played an important role in disseminating family planning information in the survey areas. They also showed that media exposure seemed to help reduce misconceptions, fears and apprehensions regarding birth control methods.

Murphy and Boggess (1998) have studied the extent to what young men's attitudes explain increase in condom use over time. Between 1988 and 1995, young men's attitudes toward partner appreciation of condom use, condom-use embarrassment and pleasure reduction from condom use, all changed in a direction suggestive of more consistent condom use. However, attitudes related to pregnancy prevention and AIDS avoidance changed in a direction suggestive of less-consistent condom use. Changes over time in the strength of the relationship between three attitude measures (masculinity, pleasure reduction and partner appreciation) and condom use also were predictive of lower levels of condom-use consistency.

Bankole *et al.* (1999) have also investigated the determinants of trends in condom use by using data from the 1988 and 1995 National Surveys of Family Growth to evaluate trends in condom use—either use alone or use with another highly effective method (dual method use). Logistic and multinomial regression analyses were carried out to analyse the influence of women's characteristics on condom use. Current condom use rose significantly between 1988 and 1995, from 13 per cent to 19 per cent of all women who had had sex in the past three months. Multivariate analyses showed that women in the early stage of a relationship (six months or less in duration) were much more likely than those in a long-standing relationship (five years or more in length) to use the condom (odds ratio, 1.5). In both 1988 and 1995, younger women and better educated women were more likely to be currently using the condom than were older or less-educated women. For example, in 1995, women younger than 18 were 1.8 times as likely as 40-44-year olds to be using condoms, and college graduates were 1.5 times as likely as high school graduates to do so. Further, women who were not in a union and either had never been married or were formerly married were more likely to be current condom users in 1995 than were married women (odds ratios, 1.5-1.9). Poor women were less likely than higher income women to be condom users in 1995 (odds ratios, 0.7-0.8), but poverty had made little difference in 1988.

Multivariate findings on differential use by country suggest that choice of contraceptive method was related to health care policy, service provision, and differences in provider preferences. Contraceptive decisions were primarily based on reproductive status, country, educational level and religious beliefs rather than on the characteristics of the method (Oddens and Lehert, 1997).

Caron *et al.* (1993) used logistic regression analysis to find out the relationship between condom-related behaviours and attitudes toward condoms, sexuality and the double standard among a self-selected group of 330 first-year college students. The majority (86.4 per cent) of respondents had engaged in sexual intercourse, and 34.2 per cent of those subjects reported two or more new sexual partners since arriving at college. Although 80.3 per cent of those who had engaged in sexual intercourse since arriving at college reported using a condom, only 20.7 per cent of students who had ever engaged in sexual intercourse reported using a condom every time.

Bhat (1996) also has shown that mass media exposure plays an important role in shaping the regional variation in fertility in India.

One such paper has discussed the impact of mass media exposure and how it leads to an increase in use of contraceptives (Retherford and Mishra, 1997). According to them, in the absence of statistical controls, exposure to family planning messages increase intended future use of contraception by 12 per cent and when, residence, education and number of living children are statistically controlled, this increase reduces to 7 per cent. Srivastava (1988) in a study among two ethnic Muslim groups of *momin* and *kokni* has reiterated the role of mass communication in explaining inter-spousal communication.

Westoff and Bankole (1999) in a study of mass media and reproductive behaviour in Pakistan, India and Bangladesh have shown that in Pakistan, 34 of the 59 multivariate results in both surveys demonstrate significant media effects. In India, 26 of 32 tests show significant effects and in Bangladesh, 39 out of 64 show significant results for the two surveys (1992-93 and 1996-97).

Sohail and Rossem (2002) have also shown that mass media exposure significantly increased the likelihood of that a man or a woman would discuss use of the female condom in the future in Tanzania. It has also been demonstrated by them that though peer educators and providers had a limited coverage, they had a stronger impact than mass media on individual's intention to use a female condom. The contacts with peer educators and providers can be considered as similar to interpersonal communicators, who can perform both the knowledge and persuasion function of development communication.

Dwivedi and Ram (2006) have analysed data from Indian National Family Health Survey-1 (INFHS-1) and INFHS-2 of Uttar Pradesh and have also found that women who are exposed to mass media were more likely to use more contraception compared to those who were not exposed.

Objectives

- To study the relationship between different socio-demographic characteristics and condom-use behaviour amongst users of condom and non-users of any contraceptive method.
- To explore the factors enabling condom use in the states of Uttarakhand and Uttar Pradesh.

Materials and Methods

Materials: Data

The data used in this paper is from the third India National Family Health Survey (INFHS, 2005-06). The 2005-06 National Family Health Survey (NFHS-3) is the third in the NFHS series of surveys. The first NFHS was conducted in 1992-93, and the second (NFHS-2) was conducted in 1998-99. All three NFHS surveys were conducted under the stewardship of the Ministry of Health and Family Welfare (MoHFW), Government of India. The MoHFW designated the International Institute for Population Sciences (IIPS), Mumbai, as the nodal agency for the surveys. Funding for NFHS-3 was provided by the United States Agency for International Development (USAID), the United Kingdom Department for International Development (DFID), the Bill and Melinda Gates Foundation, UNICEF, UNFPA and the Government of India. Technical assistance for NFHS-3 was provided by Macro International, Maryland, USA. Assistance for the HIV component of the survey was provided by the National AIDS Control Organisation (NACO) and the National AIDS Research Institute, Pune (NARI). NFHS-3 interviewed 124,385 women aged 15-49 and 74,369 men aged 15-54 to obtain information on population, health and nutrition in India and each of its 29 states. The survey is based on a sample of households that is representative at the national and state levels. The survey provides trend data on key indicators and includes information on several new topics, such as HIV/AIDS-related behaviour, attitudes toward family life, education for girls and boys, use of Integrated Child

Development Scheme (ICDS) services, men's involvement in maternal care and health insurance. For the first time, NFHS-3 provides information on men and unmarried women. In addition, HIV prevalence is measured at the national level and for selected states. The NFHS-3 fieldwork was conducted in two phases by 18 research organisations between November 2005 and August 2006 (IIPS and MI, 2007).

Methods

The paper tries to understand the factors enabling condom use in the states of Uttar Pradesh, the largest state in India and the state carved out of it, Uttarakhand among currently married women in the age group of 15-49 years. In addition to bivariate analysis, multivariate analysis was performed to control for the effects of other correlated factors, as results from bivariate analyses could be thoroughly misleading, for example, contraceptive use could be higher in urban areas not because the type of place of residence has something to do with contraceptive use, but because urbanites are more educated and have a higher standard of living. So, in order to arrive at the true significance of each factor independently keeping all other at their mean values, it is necessary to control or nullify the effects of other factors. In this way, multivariate analyses helps to separate out the independent effect of a factor from the effects of other correlated factors or covariates. For analysis purpose, a sample of respondents was selected from the two states of those who are either currently using condom or those who are not using any contraceptive method amongst currently married women. So, as the dependent variable is categorical and dichotomous in nature with two categories, non-use of any contraceptive method=0 and current use of condom=1. Binomial or binary logistic regressions were carried out to explore factors influencing or enabling condom use. Logistic regression can be used to predict a dependent variable on the basis of independents and to determine the per cent of variance in the dependent variable explained by the independents; to rank the relative importance of independents; to assess interaction effects; and to understand the impact of covariates. Logistic regression applies maximum likelihood estimation after transforming the dependent into a logit variable (the natural log of the odds of the dependent occurring or not). In this way, logistic regression estimates the probability of a certain event occurring. Note that logistic regression calculates changes in the log odds of the dependent, not changes in the dependent itself as OLS regression does. The multiple logit model can be expressed as:

$$\ln\left(\frac{P}{1-P}\right) = \alpha + \beta_1 x_1 + \beta_2 x_2 + \ldots \beta_i x_i + e$$

- P is the probability that the event Y occurs, P(Y=1);
- P/(1-P) is the "odds ratio";
- In[P/(1-P)] is the log odds ratio, or "logit";
- β_1, β_2, β_i here refers to beta coefficients;
- x_1, x_2, x_i here refers to the independent variables;
- *e* is the error term;
- Interpretation of βi
  - o Increase in log-odds for a one unit increase in x_i with all the other X_is constant.
  - o Measures association between X_i and log-odds adjusted for all other X_i.

The model goodness-of-fit was assessed by the difference of the log likelihood values, which is similar to the chi-square difference and it follows a chi-square distribution with degrees of freedom (*df*) equal to the difference of the *df* between the fitted model and null model. The formula is as given below:

$$G = \chi^2 = -2LL_{null} - (-2LL_k)$$

where,
G stands for deviance statistic,
χ^2 stands for model chi-square,
$-2LL_{null}$ stands for null model with just the constant,
$-2LL_k$ stands for the k model containing all the predictors.

In addition to the difference in deviance, the proportion of unaccounted for variance that is reduced by adding variables to the model is the same as the proportion of variance accounted for, or R^2 has also been displayed in the tables 9.6 and 9.7. In Statistical Package for

Social Scientists (SPSS), there are two modified versions of this basic idea, one developed by Cox and Snell and the other developed by Nagelkerke. Because this R-squared (R^2) value cannot reach 1.0, Nagelkerke modified it. The correction increases the Cox and Snell version to make 1.0 a possible value for R-squared. This is computed as follows:

Nagelkerke Pseudo R^2

$$R^2 = \frac{1-\left[\frac{-2LL_{null}}{-2LL_k}\right]^{2/n}}{1-(-2LL_{null})^{2/n}}$$

This version of the Pseudo R^2 has been considered here, which measures the strength of association, where the null model is the logistic model with just the constant and the *k* model contains all the predictors in the model.

Predictors Used in the Model

In all, five models have been analysed here. In Model 1, only the composite mass media variable consisting of exposure to radio, TV and newspaper is entered and it is used as an independent variable. In Model 2, all the mass media variables are entered, all independently as well as the composite mass media variable consisting of exposure to radio, TV and newspaper. Model 3 enters the variables related to accessibility to condom and Model 4 enters the composite mass media variable and the socio-demographic variables. In Model 5, all the above including the socio-demographic variables are entered (See Table 9.3). The mass media variables used as predictors are reading newspaper, listening to radio, watching TV and specifically reading news regarding family planning in the newspaper, listening to news about family planning on radio and watching similar things on TV. The accessibility predictors include the source of condoms; either from government/municipal hospitals, private hospitals or clinics or doctors or from pharmacy or drug stores. The other socio-demographic predictors include current place of residence, previous place of residence, age of the respondent (currently married woman in the age bracket of 15-49 years of age), her education, her husband's education, number of sons and daughters dead, standard of living index, woman's current work status and the mass media and accessibility covariates (See Table 9.4).

Table 9.3

Model Design

Models	*Model 1*	*Model 2*	*Model 3*	*Model 4*	*Model 5*
Variables	Mass media as a composite variable including exposure to TV, radio and newspaper (MMV)	Only mass media variables independently as well as a composite variable including exposure to TV, radio and newspaper (MMVI+MMV)	Only variables related to accessibility to condom (ACV)	MMV+ACV+ Socio-demographic variables (SDV)	MMVI+MMV + ACV + socio-demographic variables (SDV)

Table 9.4

Predictors Used in the Model

Predictors Used in the Model	*Definition*	*Uttar Pradesh* *N*	*Uttar Pradesh* *%*	*Uttarakhand* *N*	*Uttarakhand* *%*
N		2270	100.0	1701	100.0
Background - Community Level					
Current residence	0 for rural	1227	54.0	1317	77.4
	1 for urban	1044	46.0	384	22.6
Previous residence	0 for countryside	1770	78.0	1443	84.8
	1 for city/town	500	22.0	259	15.2
Background - Individual Level					
Education of the woman	0 for non-literate	485	21.4	1166	68.5
	1 literate	1785	78.6	536	31.5
Education of the husband	0 for non-literate	379	16.7	567	33.4
	1 literate	1892	83.3	1134	66.6
Religion	0 for Hindu	2006	88.3	1427	83.9
	1 for Muslim	126	5.6	247	14.5
	2 for other religions	138	6.1	27	1.6

Contd...

...contd...

Predictors Used in the Model	*Definition*	*Uttar Pradesh* N	*Uttar Pradesh* %	*Uttarakhand* N	*Uttarakhand* %
Demographic					
Current age of the woman	0 for 15-24 years	745	32.8	696	40.9
	1 for 25-34 years	759	33.4	572	33.6
	2 for 35-49 years	767	33.8	434	25.5
Number of sons dead	0 for sons surviving	2119	93.3	1472	86.5
	1 for sons dead	151	6.7	230	13.5
Number of daughters dead	0 for daughters surviving	2124	93.5	1471	86.5
	1 for daughters dead	147	6.5	230	13.5
Socio-economic					
Standard of living index	0 for low	597	26.3	707	41.6
	1 for medium	759	33.4	447	26.3
	2 for high	914	40.3	547	32.2
Woman's current work status	0 for not working currently	1427	62.9	1031	60.6
	1 for working currently	843	37.1	670	39.4
Communication Covariates					
Mass media exposure	0 for no exposure	135	5.9	905	53.2
	1 for partial exposure	1271	56.0	650	38.2
	2 for complete exposure	864	38.1	146	8.6
Newspaper	0 for does not read	1093	48.1	1362	80.0
	1 for reads	1177	51.9	340	20.0
Radio	0 for does not listen	805	35.5	1328	78.1
	1 for listens	1465	64.5	373	21.9
TV	0 for does not watch	255	11.3	1045	61.4
	1 for watches	2015	88.7	656	38.6
Read about FP in newspaper	0 for has not read	1538	67.7	1439	84.6
	1 for read	733	32.3	262	15.4
Heard about FP on radio	0 for has not heard	1070	47.1	1463	86.0
	1 for has heard	1201	52.9	239	14.0
Seen about FP on TV	0 for has not seen	554	24.4	1183	69.6
	1 for has seen	1716	75.6	518	30.4
Accessibility					
Condoms from government/ municipal hospital	0 for no	1786	78.7	1218	71.6
	1 for yes	484	21.3	484	28.4
Condoms from private hospital/clinic	0 for no	2080	91.6	1589	93.4
	1 for yes	190	8.4	112	6.6
Condoms from pharmacy	0 for no	1715	75.5	1183	69.5
	1 for yes	556	24.5	519	30.5
Dependent Variable used in the Model					
Current use of condom	0 for non-users	2117	93.3	1534	90.2
	1 for users	153	6.7	167	9.8

Note: The columns N refer to absolute number.

Findings

In Table 9.5, the results of bivariate analysis have been presented. The significance levels of the association has been tested with chi-square tests. Chi-squares tests have only been run for 2x2 contingency tables of cross tabulation. Tables 9.6 and 9.7 present the results of the logistic regression analyses carried out taking five models into consideration. The findings of the logistic regression analyses shows that there is a lot of variation between the two states with regards to the factors influencing current use of condom. When only the mass media variables are entered in the model, in case of Uttarakhand, it accounts for 28 per cent of the variance explained which is quite low at 8 per cent in case of Uttar Pradesh. The findings show that mass media is an important factor influencing condom use in Uttarakhand unlike Uttar Pradesh. In case of Uttarakhand, those who have complete exposure to

Table 9.5

Current Use of Condom by Socio-Demographic Variables among Currently Married Women in the Reproductive Age of 15-49 Years, Uttar Pradesh & Uttarakhand (NFHS-3, 2005-06)

Background Covariates	*Definition*	*Uttar Pradesh*			*Uttarakhand*		
		Non-Users (%)	*Users (%)*	*N*	*Non-Users (%)*	*Users (%)*	*N*
N		2117	153	2270	1534	167	1701
Background-Community Level							
Current residence							
	0 for rural	94.9	5.1	1227	95.6	4.4	1318
	1 for urban	91.3	8.7**	1043	71.6	28.4**	384
Previous residence	0 for countryside	94.4	5.6	1770	93.1	6.9	1443
	1 for city/town	89.4	10.6**	501	73.7	26.3**	259
Background-Individual Level							
Education of the woman	0 for non-literate	98.4	1.6	485	96.7	3.3	1166
	1 literate	91.9	8.1**	1785	75.9	24.1**	536
Education of the husband	0 for non-literate	97.4	2.6	379	96.5	3.5	567
	1 literate	92.4	7.6**	1892	87.0	13.0**	1134
Religion	0 for Hindu	93.5	6.5	2005	91.1	8.9	1427
	1 for Muslim	89.0	11.0	127	88.7	11.3	247
	2 for other religions	93.5	6.5.	138	59.3	40.7	27

Contd...

...contd...

Background Covariates	*Definition*	*Uttar Pradesh*			*Uttarakhand*		
		Non-Users (%)	*Users (%)*	*N*	*Non-Users (%)*	*Users (%)*	*N*
Demographic							
Current age of the woman	0 for 15-24 years	95.0	5.0	744	93.7	6.3	695
	1 for 25-34 years	90.4	9.6	759	85.5	14.5	572
	2 for 35-49 years	94.4	5.6	767	90.8	9.2	434
Number of sons dead	0 for sons surviving	93.3	6.7	2119	88.9	11.1	1472
	1 for sons dead	92.1	7.9 n.s.	151	98.7	1.3**	229
Number of daughters dead	0 for daughters surviving	93.0	7.0	2124	89.6	10.4	1472
	1 for daughters dead	96.6	6.7	146	93.9	6.1*	230
Socio-economic							
Standard of living index	0 for low	97.8	2.2	597	97.3	2.7	708
	1 for medium	96.4	3.6	758	94.2	5.8	447
	2 for high	87.7	12.3	915	90.1	9.9	548
Woman's current work status	0 for not working currently	93.6	6.4	1427	88.5	11.5	1031
	1 for working currently	92.8	7.2 n.s.	843	92.8	7.2**	670
Communication Covariates							
Mass media exposure	0 for no exposure	99.3	0.7	134	98.0	2.0	905
	1 for partial exposure	94.1	5.9	1271	85.4	14.6	650
	2 for complete exposure	91.1	8.9	865	63.3	63.7	147
Newspaper	0 for does not read	96.2	3.8	1093	95.2	4.8	1362
	1 for reads	90.5	9.5**	1177	70.0	30.0**	340
Radio	0 for does not listen	93.0	7.0	805	92.8	7.2	1328
	1 for listens	93.4	6.6 n.s.	1465	81.0	19.0**	373
TV	0 for does not watch	97.7	2.3	256	97.4	2.6	1045
	1 for watches	92.7	7.3**	2015	78.7	21.3**	656
Read about FP in newspaper	0 for has not read	96.2	3.8	1537	94.9	5.1	1439
	1 for read	87.2	12.8**	733	64.5	35.5**	252
Heard about FP on radio	0 for has not heard	94.9	5.1	1069	97.2	2.8	1183
	1 for has heard	91.8	8.2**	1201	74.1	25.9**	518
Seen about FP on TV	0 for has not seen	96.8	3.2	554	91.8	8.2	1462
	1 for has seen	92.1	7.9**	1716	80.3	19.7**	239
Accessibility							
Condoms from government/ municipal hospital	0 for no	94.8	5.2	1786	93.0	7.0	1217
	1 for yes	87.6	12.4**	484	83.2	16.8**	483
Condoms from private hospital/clinic	0 for no	93.7	6.3	2080	90.8	9.2	1590
	1 for yes	2117	153**	190	81.3	18.8**	112
Condoms from pharmacy	0 for no	96.4	3.6	1715	95.9	4.1	1183
	1 for yes	83.6	16.4**	555	77.3	22.7	519

Note: Chi-square value *: significant at 5 per cent level; **: significant at 1 per cent level; n.s.: not significant.

The columns N refer to absolute number.

Table 9.6

Odds Ratios from Multivariate Logistic Regression Analysis of the Likelihood of Condom Use among Currently Married Women in the Reproductive Age of 15-49 Years, Uttar Pradesh & Uttarakhand (NFHS-3, 2005-06)

Covariates		*Uttar Pradesh (N=2805)*			*Uttarakhand (N=1135)*		
		Model 1	*Model 2*	*Model 3*	*Model 1*	*Model 2*	*Model 3*
Background - Community Level							
Current residence							
	0 for rural®						
	1 for urban						
Previous residence	0 for countryside®						
	1 for city/town						
Background - Individual Level							
Education of the woman	0 for non-literate®						
	1 literate						
Education of the husband	0 for non-literate®						
	1 literate						
Religion	0 for Hindu®						
	1 for Muslim						
	2 for other religions						
Demographic							
Current age of the woman	0 for 15-24 years®						
	1 for 25-34 years						
	2 for 35-49 years						
Number of sons dead	0 for sons surviving®						
	1 for sons dead						
Number of daughters dead	0 for daughters surviving ®						
	1 for daughters dead						
Socio-economic							
Standard of living index	0 for low®						
	1 for medium						
	2 for high®						
Woman's current work status	0 for not working currently ®						
	1 for working currently						
Communication Covariates							
Mass media exposure	0 for no exposure®						
	1 for partial exposure	5.585*	2.511		8.408**	3.840*	
	2 for complete exposure	8.702**	2.349		28.528**	8.517*	
Newspaper	0 for does not read®						
	1 for reads		1.517			1.094	

Contd...

...contd...

Covariates		*Uttar Pradesh (N=2805)*			*Uttarakhand (N=1135)*		
		Model 1	*Model 2*	*Model 3*	*Model 1*	*Model 2*	*Model 3*
Radio	0 for does not listen ®						
	1 for listens		0.621			0.755	
TV	0 for does not watch ®						
	1 for watches		1.699			0.724	
Read about FP in Newspaper	0 for has not read®						
	1 for read		2.688**			2.494**	
Heard about FP on Radio	0 for has heard ®						
	1 for not heard		1.326			0.661	
Seen about FP on TV	0 for has seen®						
	1 for has not seen		1.071			3.616**	
Accessibility							
Condoms from government/ municipal hospital	0 for no®						
	1 for yes			1.812**			1.130
Condoms from private hospital/clinic	0 for no®						
	1 for yes			0.965			1.261
Condoms from pharmacy	0 for no®						
	1 for yes			4.639**			6.271**
Pseudo R^2 x 100		2.0	8.0	11.3	21.3	28.4	15.4

Note: Dependent variable: Current use of condom.

*: significant at 5 per cent level; **: significant at 1 per cent level. ®-refers to Reference Category.

mass media like newspaper, radio and TV are 8.5 times more likely to be currently using condom than those who have not been exposed to any kind of mass media. If seen separately for different types of mass media, those who have read about family planning in newspaper (OR: 2.494, CI: 1.374-4.527) are 2.5 times more likely to use condom compared to those who have not read about family planning in the newspaper and or having watched it on TV (OR: 3.616, CI: 1.707-7.659) are 3.6 times more likely to use condom. Both are significant at 1 per cent level. Though these separately are insignificant, when all the variables are entered, partial (OR: 3.491) and complete exposure (OR: 7.378) to mass media are found to be still significant at five per cent level. In addition to this, urban area as a place of residence, literacy of the woman, religion and standard of living index were found to be significant predictors of current use of condom. In case of UP, reading newspaper (OR: 2.688) is only a significant predictor among the mass media factors. Other than this,

Table 9.7

Odds Ratios from Multivariate Logistic Regression Analysis of the Likelihood of Condom Use among Currently Married Women in the Reproductive Age of 15-49 Years, Uttar Pradesh & Uttarakhand (NFHS-3, 2005-06)

Covariates		*Uttar Pradesh (N=2805)*		*Uttarakhand (N=1135)*	
		Model 4	*Model 5*	*Model 4*	*Model 5*
Background - Community Level					
Current residence					
	0 for rural®				
	1 for urban	0.976	0.933	2.673**	2.317**
Previous residence	0 for countryside®				
	1 for city/town	0.983	0.986	1.298	1.316
Background - Individual Level					
Education of the woman	0 for non-literate®				
	1 literate	2.443*	2.086*	4.169**	3.347**
Education of the husband	0 for non-literate®				
	1 literate	1.064	1.037	0.750	0.755
Religion	0 for Hindu®				
	1 for Muslim	1.632	1.724*	3.247**	3.254**
	2 for other religions	0.696	0.678	1.878	1.937
Demographic					
Current age of the woman	0 for 15-24 years®				
	1 for 25-34 years	1.434	1.403	2.278**	2.171**
	2 for 35-49 years	0.917	0.889	2.190*	2.058*
Number of sons dead	0 for sons surviving®				
	1 for sons dead	2.411**	2.401*	0.164**	0.177**
Number of daughters dead	0 for daughters surviving ®				
	1 for daughters dead	0.618	0.645	1.676	1.537
Socio-economic					
Standard of living index	0 for low®				
	1 for medium	1.492	1.468	1.971*	2.378*
	2 for high®	3.634**	3.366**	2.592**	2.331*
Woman's current work status	0 for not working currently ®				
	1 for working currently	1.716**	1.723*	1.377	1.350
Communication Covariates					
Mass media exposure	0 for no exposure®				
	1 for partial exposure	2.135	2.370	2.801**	3.491*
	2 for complete exposure	1.870	2.527	4.618**	7.378*

Contd...

...contd...

Covariates		*Uttar Pradesh (N=2805)*		*Uttarakhand (N=1135)*	
		Model 4	*Model 5*	*Model 4*	*Model 5*
Newspaper	0 for does not read®				
	1 for reads		0.911		0.768
Radio	0 for does not listen ®				
	1 for listens		0.590		0.781
TV	0 for does not watch ®				
	1 for watches		1.241		0.525
Read about FP in Newspaper	0 for has not read®				
	1 for read				1.781
Heard about FP on Radio	0 for has heard ®				
	1 for not heard		1.722*		0.735
Seen about FP on TV	0 for has seen®				
	1 for has not seen		0.704		2.486
Accessibility					
Condoms from Government/ municipal hospital	0 for no®				
	1 for yes	1.584*	1.485	0.606**	0.570
Condoms from private hospital/clinic	0 for no®				
	1 for yes	0.942	0.865	0.561*	0.545
Condoms from pharmacy	0 for no®				
	1 for yes	3.411**	3.150**	1.492*	1.348
Pseudo R^2 x 100		18.1	19.3	37.9	39.1

Note: Dependent variable: Current use of condom.

*: significant at 5 per cent level; **: significant at 1 per cent level. ®-refers to Reference Category.

among the accessibility factors, those sourcing condoms from government hospitals and buying it from pharmacies or drug stores are found to be more likely users of condom. In addition to this, the literacy of the woman, religion and mothers whose sons are dead, standard of living index are significant predictors of current condom use. It is revealing that in both the states, Muslims are observed to more likely use condom than Hindus, more so in case of Uttarakhand (OR: 3.254) and UP (OR: 1.724), which are both significant at one per cent level (See Table 9.7). In the models 1, 2 and 4, mass media as a composite variable has been taken as well as it has been taken as separate component variables of exposure to radio, TV and newspaper. So, to test whether multi-collinearity may have impacted on the findings, another model was tested by only taking the composite variable of mass media only. The results were found to be similar (See Table 9.7). Mass media emerged as the most significant factor after controlling for the socio-demographic and accessibility variables in case of Uttarakhand unlike UP.

Conclusions

Communication and accessibility are two important aspects which link the age-old chain of demand and supply. This study tries to establish the factors enabling condom use in Uttarakhand and to find out whether these factors can be responsible to enhance condom use in UP, which is the mother state. Condom as a means of contraception as well as a preventive against the deadly HIV virus is quite effective. Gradually, in addition to male condoms, female condoms have also been invented and are in use recently, though they are at an initial stage. The female condom has been placed and positioned as preventive, female controlled method, which has proven to be a preventive against common STIs and HIV. It also establishes the autonomy of women. But the initial problems with insertion and the cost factor are limiting its use to a substantial extent. Male condoms have been in use for a long time for the effective triad of benefits of contraception, HIV and STI prevention. In this analysis, mass media emerges as the most significant factor in influencing condom use in Uttarakhand, which can really be a learning experience for UP to carry out mass media campaigns in newspaper, radio and TV on family planning, which can be linked as a hook for interpersonal communicators at village level like the grassroot health outreach workers like ANM, male health worker, health guides, AWWs and ASHAs, who in turn can drive home the message of using contraceptive methods. Access to contraception and use is quite vital to improve the high fertility and mortality situation in the most populous state of India, Uttar Pradesh.

References

Bankole, A., J.E. Darroch and S. Singh (1999). "Determinants of trends in condom use in the United States, 1988-1995", *Family Planning Perspectives* 31(6): 264-271.

Bhat, Mari P.N. (1996). "Contours of fertility decline in India: A district level study based on the 1991 census", in K. Srinivasan (ed.) *Population Policy and Reproductive Health.* New Delhi: Hindustan Publishing Corporation.

Caron, S.L., C.M. Davis, W.A. Halteman and M. Stickle (1993). "Predictors of condom-related behaviors among first-year college students", *The Journal of Sex Research* 30(3): 252-259.

Department of Health & Family Welfare (2002). "Workshop proceedings on reproductive & child health and population policy issues in Uttaranchal", Govt. of Uttaranchal and Policy Project, The Futures Group International, New Delhi. May 2-3, Dehradun.

Dwivedi, L.K. and F. Ram (2006). "Change and determinants of contraceptive use in Uttar Pradesh", in Arvind Pandey (ed.), *Biostatistical Aspects of Health and Population, India*. Hindustan Publishing Corporation.

International Institute for Population Sciences (IIPS) and Macro International (2007). National Family Health Survey (NFHS-3), 2005–06: India: Volume I. Mumbai: IIPS.

Murphy, J.J. and S. Boggess (1998). "Increased condom use among teenage males, 1988-1995: The role of attitudes", *Family Planning Perspectives* 30(6): 276-280.

Oddens, B.J. and P. Lehert (1997). "Determinants of contraceptive use among women of reproductive age in Great Britain and Germany", *Journal of Biosocial Sciences* 29: 415-435.

Piotrow, P.T., D.L. Kincaid, J.G. Rimon II, and W. Rinehart (1997). *Health Communication: Lessons from Family Planning and Reproductive Health*. Centre of Communication Programs, Johns Hopkins School of Public Health, USA: Praeger Publishers.

Population Reference Bureau (2005). *World Population Datasheet.*

Powers, D.A. and X. Yu (2000). *Statistical Methods for Categorical Data Analysis*. CA: Academic Press.

Registrar General of India (2001). "Maternal mortality in India: 1997-2003 - Trends, causes and risk factors", Registrar General of India, New Delhi, in collaboration with Centre for Global Health Research University of Toronto, Canada.

————. (2009a). *Special Bulletin on Maternal Mortality in India, Sample Registration System: 2004-2006*.

————. (2009b). *SRS Bulletin* 44(1), October.

Retherford, R.D. and V. Mishra (1997). "Media exposure increases contraceptive use," *NFHS Bulletin* 7: 1-4.

Rogers, E.M. (1973). *Communication Strategies for Family Planning.* New York: Free Press.

Rogers, E.M. and F.F. Shoemaker (1971). *Communication of Innovations: A Cross-cultural Approach.* New York: Free Press.

Saksena, D.N. and S.R. Rastogi (1988). "The reach and effectiveness of media for popularizing the family planning programme", *Journal of Family Welfare* 35: 26-38.

Singhal, A. and E.M. Rogers (1989). *India's Information Revolution*. Sage Publications.

Sohail, A. and R.V. Rossem (2002). "Impact of mass media campaigns on intentions to use the female condom in tanzania", *International Family Planning Perspectives* 28(3): 151-158.

Srivastava, H.C. (1988). "The role of mass media in interspouse communication among urban momin and kokni muslims", *Journal of Family Welfare* 35: 50-60.

Westoff, C.F. and A. Bankole (1999). "Mass media and reproductive behaviour in Pakistan, India and Bangladesh", *DHS Analytical Reports*. USA: Macro International Inc.

Zavier, Francis. A.J., P.N. Mari Bhat and S.C. Gulati (2005). *Levels and Determinants of Contraceptive Use*. Delhi: Population Research Centre, Institute of Economic Growth.

C. Utilisation of Health Services

10 Interactions with Health Workers and Reproductive Behaviour

Evidence from Uttarakhand

Puspita Datta and
Chayan Roy Choudhury

Introduction

In many developing countries, including India, attempts to stabilise the population are seriously trapped by the problem related to contraceptive acceptance and thereby, fail to bring changes in the preferences for smaller family. Unless and until people started accepting the contraception and realise the benefits of small family, it is not possible to achieve the targeted population stabilisation. In India, almost all women have some knowledge about contraception, but still the proportion of them using any effective method is less. Contraceptive acceptance is limited by a number of barriers, including fears and misunderstandings about contraceptives and their side effects. In many areas, the difficulty of obtaining regular supplies of contraceptives is a major factor. This problem is particularly prominent in rural areas, where majority of India's populations are residing. When government think about the options for reducing fertility in traditional societies, deliberations often focus on the means for making the practice of modern contraception as convenient as possible, although operational strategies differ from setting to setting. A common element, shared among many programmes, is the deployment of village workers to canvass households and promote contraceptive use. Originally viewed as a means of providing information about family planning, household services have also become an important way to disseminate contraceptive supplies (Phillips *et al.*, 1996).

Social interaction may be one mechanism for the exchange of contraceptive information. Studies in Kenya and elsewhere have demonstrated that women frequently talk to one another about fertility and contraceptive use during the course of their daily routinc (Rutenberg and Watkins, 1997). Through these informal discussions, women may learn about others' experiences with particular contraceptives, they may evaluate the appropriateness of different methods for their own situation and they may assess whether social norms favour the use of family planning. By promoting informal discussions about family planning within a group with a diverse membership, social clubs play a mediating role in the diffusion of new information and innovative behaviours (Boulay and Valente, 1999). From the results of a study in Iran, it seems probable that the health workers did not substantially alter attitudes toward contraceptive use in the villages. Rather, the increase in contraceptive use occurred among those persons who already approved contraception, mainly among women in the middle childbearing years (25-40). The auxiliary health worker provides a viable means for dcveloping countries to upgrade the health and living conditions of rural populations. Health workers also provide knowledge of better health care and reproductive care and discussed about family planning which is one of the major influencing factors behind lowering fertility rates. The results of this study indicate that such health workers do have the potential to raise the level of contraceptive use among rural women and thus to lower fertility (Zeighami *et al.,* 1977).

The diffusion of ideas and practices has played an important role in fostering the transition to lower fertility in Europe and, more recently, in developing countries (Bongaarts and Watkins, 1996). As information about contraceptive methods becomes more widespread, couples begin to understand that they can control their fertility and make conscious choices about the size of their families. Accordingly, the desire for children may change as exposure to new ideas alters individuals' aspirations for themselves and their families. In a social system characterised by strict patriarchal controls and extensive female seclusion in Bangladesh, the presence of a female family planning worker acts as a link to modern ideas about reproductive choice in which the role of women shifts from passive toward more active modes of decision-making. By mobilising demand for family limitation, mediating familial and religious conflicts with regard to contraception, alleviating fears of an alien technology and delivery system, and facilitating access to family planning methods, the worker's presence contributes to contraceptive use (Simmons *et al.*, 1988).

Bairagi (2001) argues that over the years, the gap between actual fertility rates and desired fertility rates (around two sons and a daughter) may have been narrowed to a point where a decline in TFR will only come from further structural changes. If this explanation holds, and if diffusion of knowledge about family planning can be sustained by peers and family members (Simmons, 1996), the need for family planning health workers may indeed be unnecessary. But the per cent of new people attaining reproductive age and the per cent of non-users, combined, are still quite significant, at least for the foreseeable future, and because studies have shown notable increases in discontinuation in contraception rates when field worker contact is relaxed, the health workers role should continue to be important (Andaleeb, 2004). Outreach effects arise from crystallising existing demand for contraception rather than from fostering changes in the demand for children. Outreach helps women implement their preferences, but plays a relatively minor role in shaping those preferences (Phillips *et al.*, 1996).

On the assumption that their interactions not only increases the awareness and accessibility, it also improves the preference level of people and as a consequence of this improved knowledge level, people's reproductive choice and performance can change. It will be worth observing the impact of interactions with health workers on contraceptive behaviour as well as fertility behaviour. Uttarakhand has 16,414 villages with about 75 per cent population living in the rural areas. Given the poor paying capacity and scattered location of settlements in hilly districts (93 per cent hilly area), the population is almost entirely dependent on the public health delivery system. In rural areas, health workers play a major role in delivery of health services, specially to motivate and make people aware about family planning and various aspects of maternal and child health care, because they can directly interact with the people. Against this backdrop, this paper tries to observe, how far interactions and discussions with health workers about various matters motivate people to use contraceptives, to choose type of contraceptives, future intention to use contraceptive methods among those who do not use any method and future intention to have child, preferred waiting time for next birth, etc., for the state of Uttarakhand, using National Family and Health Survey-3 (2005-06) dataset.

Considering the nature of work they do, ANM (auxiliary nurse and midwives), LHV (lady health visitors), AWW (Anganwadi workers), MPW (multipurpose workers), ASHA (accredited social health activist); all are regarded as health workers. In the NFHS-3 (2005-06), all women were asked about their interactions with health workers and about different methods of contraception during last three months before the survey. The question on health worker visit in NFHS–3 was restricted to last three months prior to the survey. This constraint of less time span reduced the sample size to 553. This limitation of the data restricts us to the experiences of the women for a small time span which may not be sufficient enough to draw any robust conclusion. The proportion of women in different background characteristics and types of different services received during interactions with the health workers in Uttarakhand provides the platform for our current discussion. In the focal part of the study, it explains whether interactions with health workers make any difference in the contraceptive behaviour of the women in Uttarakhand and after that whether the interactions bring changes in the desire for more children and preferred future birth and waiting time for next birth. On the above basis, a current situational analysis of manpower in Uttarakhand and evidences and experiences of other countries are provided to strengthen the concluding facts.

Results and Discussions

The visit by the health worker varied with the socio-economic and demographic status of the women concerned. In the present study, only 19 per cent of the total women in Uttarakhand had interaction with health workers in the past three months before the survey and more than half of these women belonged to the age group 20-29 (Table 10.1). Most of these women resided in the rural areas, thus confirming with

Table 10.1

Proportion of Women Interacting with Any Health Worker in Past Three Months by Selected Background Characteristics, Uttarakhand, NFHS-3

Characteristics of Women	*Frequency*	*Percentage of Women Visited by HW*
Age of the Women		
15-19	71	12.9
20-24	132	23.9
25-29	152	27.4
30-34	80	14.4
35-39	61	11.0
40-44	33	5.9
45-49	25	4.5
Place of Residence		
Urban	91	16.4
Rural	462	83.6
Educational Attainment		
No education	178	32.1
Incomplete primary	19	3.4
Complete primary	62	11.1
Incomplete secondary	180	32.5
Complete secondary	53	9.6
Higher	62	11.2
Working Status		
Not working	314	56.8
Working	238	43.0
Number of CEB		
0	103	18.6
1	81	14.6
2	139	25.1
3	93	16.7
4+	139	25.0

the rural priority of the health workers responsibilities. With the rural nature of the women in consideration, it is expected to have more women with no or very little education. As the home visit by the health workers are more prevalent, the non-working women staying at home are more probable to have interaction with the health workers. Most of these women have two or more children. More than half of the surveyed women belonged to the higher SLI group, the effect of which was reflected accordingly on the proportion of women having interaction with the health workers (Table 10.2).

Table 10.2

Proportion of Women Interacting with Any Health Worker in Past Three Months by Economic Status, Uttarakhand, NFHS-3

Economic Status of Women	*Frequency*	*Percentage of Women Visited by HW*
Standard of Living Index		
Low	61	11.3
Medium	160	29.8
High	304	56.5
Not *de jure* resident	13	2.5
Household has BPL Card		
No	404	73.2
Yes	133	24.1
Not *de jure* resident	13	2.4
Wealth Index		
Poorest	22	3.9
Poorer	72	13.0
Middle	130	23.6
Richer	178	32.2
Richest	151	27.3

A variety of issues were discussed by the health worker while providing service. The issues that were discussed can be broadly categorised into family planning services, maternal and child health care, hygiene and nutritional aspects, etc. Among these issues, it is observed that immunisation is the most important (50.7 per cent) that has been discussed with the health workers, followed by family planning as the next most important issue (Table 10.3). The prevalence of the women with two or more children may have influenced this outcome and resulted in a dubious negligence of the family planning issue by the health workers.

Table 10.3

Proportion of Women who Received Various Services from Health Workers in Past Three Months, Uttarakhand, NFHS-3

Services Discussed by Health Workers in Past Three Months	*Frequency*	*Percentage*
Family planning	81	14.8
Immunisation	279	50.7
Antenatal care	28	5.0
Delivery care	14	2.6
Delivery preparedness	1	0.2
Postnatal care	10	1.8
Disease prevention	6	1.1
Medical treatment for self	42	7.6
Treatment for sick child	17	3.1
Treatment for other persons	4	0.8
Malaria control	NA	NA
Supplementary food	29	5.2
Growth monitoring of child	10	1.9
Early childhood care	10	1.8
Pre-school education	42	7.6
Nutrition/health education	32	5.8
Family life education	43	7.8
Menstrual hygiene	18	3.2
Other	67	12.2

The personal communication with the health workers brings in the change in contraceptive behaviour and beliefs. It is observed from Table 10.4 that those who were visited by any health worker, there is almost an 11 percentage point difference between the women who ever used any contraceptive and the women who never used, with ever user on the higher side of the scale. The difference for the women who were not visited is very less and the percentage is higher for the women who never used. The intention to use by the women those who never used any contraceptive method is seen to be higher for those who had any interaction with health workers. The women those who are exposed to the interaction are more tilted towards using modern methods. There is no difference in the percentages of the women who are not visited and visited and are using traditional method. Non-users intending to use contraceptive method increases with the interaction with the health workers, *vis-à-vis* the does not intend to use decreases with the same. The growing intention to use after the interactions are converted in demand for the contraceptives along which the unmet need for contraceptive increases which is clearly observed from the results of Table 10.4. It is noteworthy that there is a higher unmet need and current use of limiting method compared to spacing methods, after the interaction with health workers. A study by Zavier and others (2004) also showed that preference for permanent as well as temporary methods would rise if the users had an opportunity to interact with health workers about various methods. This result from Uttarakhand indicates that the existence of personal interaction with the health workers affects method selection.

Table 10.4

Contraceptive Behaviour of Women in Uttarakhand according to the Interaction/Non-Interaction with Health Workers (HW)

Contraceptive Bahaviour	*No Interaction by HW*	*Interaction by HW*
Ever Use of any Contraceptive		
Never	51.6	44.5
Yes, used	48.4	55.5
Intention to Use Contraceptives among Never Users		
In next 12 months	9.2	23.3
Use later	18.3	31.8
Unsure about use	3.6	7.2
Does not intend	17.5	12.8
Current Contraceptive Use and Future Intentions		
Using modern method	39.8	41.8
Using traditional method	2.7	2.7
Non-user intends to use	15.7	30.4
Does not intend to use	12.5	11.4
Unmet Need for Contraception		
Unmet need to space	2.7	4.9
Unmet need to limit	3.9	7.4
Type of Contraceptive Currently Using		
Using to space	3.5	5.8
Using to limit	38.9	38.7

The most important aim of contraceptive promotion through the health workers is that the direct and personal interactions about contraception ultimately make women more knowledgeable and at the same time it brings changes in the fertility behaviour, such as spacing between births, desire for more children. In this connection, Arends-Kuenning and others (1996) concluded that, "Outreach does not have a significant effect on persuading women to have fewer children, but it plays a very important role in helping them to meet their reproductive goals". As women who are exposed to the health worker interaction are more likely to use contraception both for spacing and limiting, more than 41 per cent of them wants no children in future compared to those women who are not having any interactions with health workers (Table 10.5). The proportion of women who want to have another child is more, though less than the proportion who do not want any more children, is higher among the women who interact with health workers. Among those women who wants more children in future, a higher

Table 10.5

Fertility Preference, Desire for Children and Preferred Waiting Time for Next Birth in Future in Uttarakhand according to the Interaction/Non-Interaction with Health Workers (HW)

	No Interaction by HW	*Interaction by HW*
Fertility Preference		
Have another	13.5	21.2
Wants no more	27.5	41.4
Desire for More Children in Future		
Wants within 2 years	7.6	8.3
Wants after 2+ years	5.6	12.0
Preferred Waiting Time (grouped)		
<12 months	34.9	20.5
1 year	21.6	18.8
2 years	18.8	19.7
3 years	13.6	24.8
4 years	5.2	6.0
5 years	3.4	6.0
6+ years	0.3	0.0

proportion preferred waiting time for the next birth after 2 years and more if the women was visited by any health worker. For better understanding the fact that whether health worker interaction affect the desire for children and preferred waiting time for the next birth, the analysis was carried out according to the number of children ever born (CEB). It is seen from Table 10.6 that after two children, women do not want any more children is higher for those who interact with health workers compared to the women with no such interaction. The proportion of women going for sterilisation is higher after two children among those who never interact with health workers and it is smaller among those who have interactions. The differences can be visible for the women who have two children or more because, it is found from the NFHS-3 that most of the women's ideal number of children is two. It also implies that women are trying to achieve ideal family size or the gap between ideal family size and actual family size is reducing as their

Table 10.6

Desire for Children and Preferred Waiting Time for Next Birth in Future by CEB of Women in Uttarakhand according to the Interaction/Non-Interaction with Health Workers (HW)

HW Interaction/CEB	*0*	*1*	*2*	*3*	*4+*	*Total*
			Fertility Preference			
No Interaction by HW						
Have another	15.8	62.2	8.5	3.7	3.5	13.6
No more	1.3	30.1	56.6	38.1	39.1	27.5
Sterilised	0.2	2.0	28.6	55.2	52.0	26.0
Interaction by HW						
Have another	21.4	67.5	17.0	10.1	5.1	21.2
No more	3.9	23.8	66.7	44.9	52.2	41.3
Sterilised	0.0	1.3	14.8	41.6	39.7	20.6
			Preferred Waiting Time			
No Interaction by HW						
Wants within 2 years	9.7	29.1	5.8	1.3	2.3	7.6
Wants after 2+ years	5.4	32.1	2.5	1.9	1.2	5.6
Interaction by HW						
Wants within 2 years	8.7	23.5	8.1	5.6	1.5	8.5
Wants after 2+ years	12.6	42.0	8.1	3.4	3.7	12.1

preference for no more children after two children is increasing and this is influenced by the health worker interaction factor. Low level of sterilisation may happen due to the fact that the women who interact with health workers have better knowledge about the spacing methods of contraception. Due to the same reason, preferred waiting time for next births among the women who want to have more children in future is higher for those who have any interactions with health workers compared to those women who do not interact.

So far the paper discussed about the health workers' interactions and impact of their interactions on the women in Uttarakhand. It is clear that the health workers are an important means of health service delivery and to implement the family planning programmes effectively at the grassroot level. Table 10.7 shows the current situation of health manpower in the state of Uttarakhand. It can be observed clearly from the statistics that there is a shortfall of health workers of various levels, even in many cases the number of positions sanctioned by the state government is less than the required number.

Table 10.7

Health Manpower Statistics in Uttarakhand: 2007

Health Professionals	*Required [R]*	*Sanctioned [S]*	*In Position [P]*	*Vacant [S-P]*	*Shortfall [R-P]*
Health worker (female)/ANM at sub-centre	1765	1765	1604	161	161
Health worker (female)/ANM at SCs & PHCs	1997	1950	1785	165	212
Health worker (male) at sub-centres	1765	855	656	199	1109
Health assistants (female)/LHV at PHCs	232	160	159	1	73
Health assistants (female)/LHV at PHCs	232	160	159	1	73
Health assistant (male) at PHCs	232	552	417	135	*
Nurse midwife/staff nurse at PHCs & CHCs	575	145	129	16	446
Total specialists (surgeons, OB&GY, physicians & paediatricians)	196	163	79	84	117

Source: *Bulletin of Rural Health Statistics*, Ministry of Health and Family Welfare (As on March 2007).

Conclusion

The study has been carried out mainly to understand the role of health workers in promoting contraceptive behaviour and thereby bring changes in the fertility preferences among the married women of Uttarakhand. On a similar course of thought as was discussed in the previous studies done on different countries with different social set-ups, the present study emphasises on the findings that the role of the health workers, those who are directly interacting with the clients, facilitate the contraceptive belief and behaviour.

The poor road connectivity, difficult hilly terrain, small scattered settlements, lack of infrastructure and manpower contributes to problems of access to health service delivery. It is found that Uttarakhand has shortfall of health manpower, especially health workers of different level. This paper shows apart from indicating a problem of health service delivery, how shortfall of health workers can be a problem for bringing changes in reproductive behaviour in favour of smaller family and thereby this paper strengthens the need for adequate health manpower resources. The recent situation of Uttarakhand from the NFHS-3 dataset reveals that only around 19 per cent women had interacted with health workers during last three months, indicating the neglect of field work on the part of these workers. So the issue is not only lack of health workers in promoting contraceptive methods and reproductive health care awareness, but also in home visits. Therefore, it is highly essential to reexamine and redefine the roles and responsibilities of existing health workers and family welfare staff in particular, in order to utilise this human resource in a more efficient manner.

References

Andaleeb, Syed Saad (2004). "Family planning field workers in Bangladesh as influence agents: Some policy implications", *Journal of Health & Population in Developing Countries* (URL: *http://www.jhpdc.unc.edu/* date published 4 May 2004).

Arends-Kuenning, Mary, Mian Bazle Hossain and Barkat-e-Khuda (1996). "The effects of family planning programs on fertility preferences: Evidence from Bangladesh", Paper presented at the Population Association of America Annual Meeting, New Orleans, 9-11 May.

Bairagi, R. (2001). "Demographic transition in Bangladesh: What happened here in the 20th century and what is next?", Paper presented at the *International Union for the Scientific Study of Population*, 24th General Conference, Salvador, Brazil, 18-24 August.

Bongaarts, J. and S.C. Watkins (1996). "Social interactions and contemporary fertility transitions", *Population and Development Review* 22(4): 639-682.

Boulay, Marc and Thomas W. Valente (1999). "The relationship of social affiliation and interpersonal discussion to family planning knowledge, attitudes and practice", *International Family Planning Perspectives* 25(3): 112-118.

Freedman, Ronald (1997). "Do family planning programs affect fertility preferences? A literature review", *Studies in Family Planning* 28(1): 1-13.

Phillips, James F., Mian Bazle Hossain and Mary Arends-Kuenning (1996). "The long-term demographic role of community-based family planning in rural Bangladesh", *Studies in Family Planning* 27(4): 204-219.

Rutenberg, N. and S.C. Watkins (1997). "The buzz outside the clinics conversations and contraception in Nyanza Province, Kenya", *Studies in Family Planning* 28(4): 290-307.

Simmons, Ruth (1996). "Women's lives in transition: A qualitative analysis of the fertility decline in Bangladesh", *Studies in Family Planning* 27(5): 251-268.

Simmons, Ruth, Laila Baqee, Michael A. Koenig and James F. Phillips (1988). "Beyond supply: The importance of female family planning workers in rural Bangladesh", *Studies in Family Planning* 19(1): 29-38.

Zavier, A.J. Francis, T.R. Dilip and V. Prakash Narayanan (2004). "Interactions with family planning workers and dynamics of method selection in rural India," Paper submitted for the XXVIth annual conference of Indian Association for the Study of Population, would be held at Annamalai University, during 9th-11th February.

Zeighami, Elaine, Bahram Zeighami, Iraj Javidian and Susan Zimmer (1977). "The rural health worker as a family planning provider: A village trial in Iran", *Studies in Family Planning* 8(7): 184-187.

11

Inhibiting Factors in the Utilisation of Public Health Care Services by the Rural People in Uttarakhand

Evidence from National Family Health Survey-3

Anita Bhargava and Satyaban Sahu

Introduction

India, a signatory to the Alma Ata Declaration, had committed itself to achieve Health for All by 2000 AD. In India, HFA (Health for All) included a package of health services to all segments of the population giving priority to the underprivileged and vulnerable sections of the society (Uma, 2004).

Primary health care is essential health care, which is based on practical, scientifically sound and socially accepted methods. It should be universally accessible to every individual and the family in the community and the cost of the health care should be affordable (Prakasam, 1995). Primary health care can be defined as "essential health care and universally accessible to all citizens and at a cost that the community and country can afford" (WHO, 1978). The delivery of primary health care is the foundation of rural health care system and forms an integral part of national health system. Though 70 per cent of the rural population is aware of the existence of PHCs and SCs, only a third of them utilise the same and are dissatisfied with the quality of inputs and services (Srinivasan, 2002).

Primary health care is delivered to the rural population through primary health care centre by bringing health care as close as possible to where the people live and work. In India, a large proportion of population lives in rural areas and hence, the health care system has been extended to rural masses through PHCs, sub-centres (SC) and health guides, *dai*/TBA (traditional birth attendant) (Prakasam, 1995).

The Government of India has launched a National Rural Health Mission (NRHM) in the year 2005; with its objectives to provide integrated comprehensive and effective primary health care to the unprivileged and vulnerable sections of the society, especially women and children by improving access, availability and quality of public health services. The key strategy of the mission include: ensure intra and intersectoral convergence, strengthening public health infrastructure, increasing community participation, creating village level cadre of health workers, fostering public-private partnerships, emphasising quality services and enhanced programme management inputs (Ojha, 2006). The same NRHM was launched in the states with the main focus to strengthen primary health care through grassroot level public health interventions based on community ownership.

Many health problems were included in the Tenth Five Year Plan among which few major problems were persistent gaps in manpower and infrastructure in government sector especially at the primary health care level, in remote rural, tribal and urban slum areas where health care needs are greatest, massive inter-state/inter-district/urban-rural differences in performances as assessed by health and demographic indices; availability and utilisation of services are poorest in the most needy remote rural areas in states/districts, increasing dual diseases burden of communication and non-communicable diseases because of ongoing demographic, lifestyle and environmental transitions and escalating costs of health care, ever widening gaps between what is possible and what the individual or the country can afford etc.

This five year plan has tried to enhance the quality of services and strengthen linkages between secondary care institutions. Efforts such as horizontal integration of all aspects of the current vertical programmes including supplies, monitoring, information, education, communication and motivation (IECM), training administrative arrangements and implementation so that they are integral components of health care; there will be progressive convergence of funding, implementation and family welfare programmes under a field of administration beginning at and below district level, improving the efficiency of the existing health care system in the government, private and voluntary sectors and building up appropriate linkages between them and building up an effective system of disease surveillance and response at the district, state and national level as a part of existing health services etc. Also, a major thrust will be given to mainstream ISM&H system and utilise ISM&H practitioners by ensuring that ISM&H clinics are located in the primary, secondary and tertiary care institutions providing complimentary system of care these institutions and ISM&H care is funded as a part and parcel of funds provided for these institutions etc.

Background of the Study

Uttarakhand was earlier known as Uttaranchal which came into existence on 9th November 2000 as the 27th state of the Republic of India. The state comprises 13 districts of the erstwhile Uttar Pradesh, namely Almora, Bageshwar, Chamoli, Champawat, Dehradun, Haridwar, Nainital, Pauri Garhwal, Pithoragarh, Rudraprayag, Tehri Garhwal, Udham Singh Nagar and Uttarkashi. The state of Uttarakhand is spread over an area of 55,845 km and the population is 84,79,562 (Bhatt, 2003). The state is the 11th most sparsely populated state and being a hilly one, the population density of the state is 159 per sq. kms. The poor road connectivity, difficult hilly terrain, small-scattered settlements, lack of infrastructure and human power contributes to the problems of access to health service delivery.[1]

The state is broadly divided into two geographic regions—Kumaon and Garhwal. According to NFHS-2 survey, 78 per cent of the population of Uttarakhand lives in rural area.[2] About 88 per cent of its area is hilly or mountainous terrain; the remaining area lies in the plain. Seventy per cent of the population lives below the poverty line compared to the national average of 26 per cent.[3] In context of quality of health care,

1. Soft copy of the article downloaded from the site: *http://www.whoindia.org/EIP/HSR/Report/Uttaranchal/UttaranchalBw.pdf*
2. *http://medind.nic.in/haa/t04/i1/haat04ip127.pdf.*
3. Soft copy of the article downloaded from the site: *http://www.south.du.ac.in/fms/idpad/case studies/IDPAD%20case%203%20UMHRC%%20clinic. 2\%20% uttaranchal*

three-quarters of households in Uttarakhand use private doctors private hospitals/clinics for treatment and only 23 per cent normally use the public medical sector. Even among households with a low standard of living, only 22 per cent normally use the public medical sector.

When regression was run using the standard of living and type of residence as independent variable and type of health care services used by the people of the state, the highly significant (type of place of residence significant at .001 level and standard of living at .000 level) results showed that there is an overt impact of both the conditions in the state. On contrary, noticeably, the section of the population with high level of standard of living utilises the government and municipal hospitals (54 per cent) and other health services provided by the government. But at the same time, this section also takes advantages of private health clinics of almost about 51 per cent.

Uttarakhand has a network of government health institutions.

Table 11.1

Health Infrastructure of Uttarakhand

Particulars	*Required*	*In Position*	*Shortfall*
Sub-centre	1294	1631	-
Primary health centre	214	222	-
Community health centre	53	49	4
Multipurpose worker (female)/ ANM at sub-centres and PHCs	1853	1636	217
Health worker (male) MPW (M) at sub-centres	1631	616	1015
Health assistant (female)/LHV at PHCs	222	181	41
Health assistant (male) at PHCs	222	417	-
Doctors at PHCs	222	182	40
Obstetricians and gynaecologists at CHCs	49	34	15
Physicians at CHCs	49	4	45
Pediatricians at CHCs	49	18	31
Total specialists at CHCs	196	71	125
Radiographers	49	30	19
Pharmacists	271	287	-
Laboratory technicians	271	32	239
Nurse/midwife	565	129	436

Source: RHS Bulletin, March 2006, Ministry of Health and Family Welfare, Government of India.

It is noticeable that most of the government health facilities are located in urban areas and the plains and people in hilly areas have to travel at least 20-25 kms to reach a health service.[4] With a collaboration of Government of Uttarakhand, the Technology Information, Forecasting and Assessment Council (TIFAC) and Birla Institute of Scientific Research (BISR), there had been an initiation of Uttarakhand Mobile Hospital and Research Centre (UMHRC) for a period from 2002-2007. It provides health services in the hilly regions of the state under a three-way public partnership. The motive behind UMHRC was to provide health care and diagnostic facilities to poor and rural people at their door step.[5]

People report that women in hilly areas are very vulnerable. Most are poor and cannot afford private medical services when they are available but most areas have no facilities at all. No medicines available, doctors not available at the health centres, doctors refuse to work in interior villages due to problems in hilly areas, government hospital has no emergency services, most of the areas have no medical facilities and medicines are ineffective are the cited reasons by the people of the state which makes the government health facilities underutilised.[6]

A study done in Andhra Pradesh by Prakasam (1995) reveals that those women who are not attending the PHC expressed that they do not have faith or got bad treatment. Nearly 18 per cent of the proportion of his sample size revealed that they prefer to go to private doctor for treatment. Also, it was found that the people perceived that the doctor at PHC is careless and demands money. Also, the people have negative attitude towards PHC and those who are having positive attitude towards PHC, they are dissatisfied with the services. Furthermore in conclusion of his paper, he has stated that nearly 77 per cent of the rural masses are not utilising the family planning services through PHC but they prefer to have such services from private nursing homes.

---

4. Soft copy of the article downloaded from the site: *http://www.south.du.ac.in/fms/idpad/case studies/IDPAD%20case%203%20UMHRC%%20clinic. 2\%20% uttaranchal*

5. Ibid.

6. Ibid.

A similar study done in the same state by Vijaykumar and Chakrapani (1995) also has the similar findings regarding the utilisation of the public health services by the rural people. Majority of respondents considered physical accessibility of the PHC as a primary reason of not availing the health services to a large extent. Also they counted poor transport facilities, poor and low economic status of the rural people, poor qualities of drugs, lack of required medicines and treatment, and shortage of doctors in PHCs as other determining factors in not using the public health services. Apart from these cited reasons, the study had also observed that illiteracy and lack of health consciousness had resulted in most of the people not being aware of the illness at a stage when prevention is possible. The PHC could not sustain for a longer period of time due to the non-availability of the doctors to run the PHC.

The utilisation of government health services is far below the desired level—only 37 per cent people utilise government health facility whenever they need. It means that the government services have not yet come to the expectation of people. The low contacts by the female health workers have also reflected in low utilisation of MCH services, which were female-oriented. Almost three-fourth of the users of health and family welfare services had reported one or the other problems with the use of the programme services. The main problems were poor health services, ineffective medicines and money which were being charged by the staff for the services (Agarwal, 1990).

A study done by Sharma and Hardeep (2003) slowed that the patients would prefer to avail health services from private doctors but because of financial constraints, they have to depend upon government doctors only. A number of patients remarked that most of the times, doctors were not present in the unit and if present, their rude behaviour, indifferent attitude towards patient's feelings and sentiments further aggravated patients' problems. Such factors shape the perception of the people towards the service quality, which ultimately influence their level of satisfaction towards the government health services.

A similar study carried out by Duggal (1994) in Jalgaon district of Maharashtra also cites the reasons that why the people do not use public health services. They said that the inconvenient or far away location (45 per cent); lack of personal attention (23 per cent); long waiting period or loss of wage due to long waiting (17 per cent) and poor quality treatment or inadequate facilities make public health care under-utilised.

The district-level household survey (2002) in the districts of Uttarakhand suggests that the condition of the public health services is poor and lacks in basic needs of the patients. For example in Dehradun, nearly 10.8 per cent women who needed to visit health facility had visited private health facility. The percentage of women visiting private health facility is higher—12.9 per cent in urban areas as compared to 9.6 per cent in rural areas. The per cent of women who needed to visit health facility and visited government health facility are more in urban areas as compared to rural areas (Dehradun, district-level household survey, 2002). In Uttarkashi, nearly 7.1 per cent women who needed to visit health facility had visited private health facility. The percentage of women visiting private health facility is higher (26.3 per cent) in urban areas as compared to 6.2 per cent in rural areas (Uttarkashi, district-level household survey, 2002). In Nainital, percentage of women visiting private health facility is higher (8.4 per cent) in urban areas as compared to 5.5 per cent in rural areas (Nainital, district-level household survey, 2002). Similar kind of preference to private health care facility is found in other districts of the state. Generally, the women reported that they face the problem of long waiting time for getting services of the government health facility, inconvenient location of the centre, prolonged waiting at the centre, personal manners, technical skills of the physicians and other staff is not satisfactory. In addition, high charges of services, medicines being not given or of bad quality are also alleged by the women who desired to seek the government health care facilities.

Rationale of the Study

Though it is also observed that the functioning of the public health service outlets in some states like the four southern states—Kerala, Andhra Pradesh, Tamil Nadu and Karnataka—is relatively better, because some quantum of drugs is distributed through the primary health system network, and the patients have a stake in approaching the public health facilities (NHP, 2002), but on the basis of the background of the study it can be concluded that more or less the utilisation of public health care services in the country is not up to the satisfactory level.

Objectives

1. Comparison between rural and urban population for the utilisation of public health care services of the state.
2. Determinants/controlling factors/hindering factors in providing the public health care services to the poor people of the rural areas.

Data Source and Methodology

National Family Health Survey-3 (NFHS-3) published in 2005-06 and IIPS was the nodal agency in conducting the survey, which was used to evident and support the objectives of the paper.

To make the data useful, SPSS was used to show the data analysis. The Uttarakhand state file was extracted from the data and bivariate analysis, correlations and regression analysis were used to make the data compatible with the study.

Findings and Discussions

Background Characteristics of the State

Table 11.2 describes the background characteristics of the state. As stated in the beginning, 78 per cent of the population in the state resides in rural areas. The type of residence directly influences the utilisation of health care facilities.

There are many causal factors in the state, which directly or indirectly affect the health of the population. From the data, it is evident that there is a clear variation in the utilisation of health care services by the rural and urban population. Only 47 per cent of the urban and 43 per cent of the rural population avail government health care services whereas the population prefers to seek treatment from private sector as 51 per cent of urban and 55 per cent of the rural population prefer to go to private health care facilities. The practice of traditional treatment has very insignificant position in utilisation of health care services.

Table 11.2

Background Characteristics

	Category of Health Facilities Available				
	Government Facility	*Private Facility*	*Traditional Treatment*	*Other Facility*	*N*
Type of Place of Residence					
Urban	47.1%	51.4%	0.4%	1.1%	749
Rural	43.4%	54.8%	0.4%	1.5%	1,910
Total	44.4%	53.8%	0.4%	1.4%	2,659
Sex of Household Member					
Male	43.9%	54.4%	0.4%	1.3%	2,240
Female	47.0%	50.8%	0.5%	1.7%	419
Total	44.4%	53.8%	0.4%	1.4%	2,659
Age of Head of HH					
15 to 59 years of age	45.6%	52.6%	0.5%	1.3%	1,977
Above 60 years	40.8%	57.4%	0.3%	1.5%	681
Total	44.4%	53.8%	0.4%	1.4%	2,658
Marital Status of HH					
Never married	**50.0%**	48.6%	0.0%	1.4%	70
Ever married	44.3%	53.9%	0.4%	1.4%	2,588
Total	44.4%	53.8%	0.4%	1.4%	2,658

It is also noticeable that men are more likely to avail private health services, that is 54 per cent in comparison to 51 per cent females.

Socio-Economic Characteristics

Table 11.3 highlights the socio-economic characteristics of the state. Among cultural factors, religion plays an important role in availing the health care services in the state. As a whole, only 44 per cent of the population is utilising government health care services and others seek the treatment from private sector. Among Hindus, 52 per cent population avail the private facility and only 46 per cent population avail the government health care facilities. Similar is the case with other religions category where 80 per cent of them are utilising private health care facilities.

Table 11.3

Socio-Economic Characteristics

	Category of Health Facilities Available				
	Government Facility	*Private Facility*	*Traditional Treatment*	*Other Facility*	*N*
Religion of the Head of the HH					
Hindu	46.2%	51.9%	0.5%	1.5%	2,324
Muslim	40.2%	58.7%	0.0%	1.1%	189
Christian	**50.0%**	50.0%	0.0%	0.0%	6
Other religions	19.9%	79.4%	0.0%	0.7%	141
Total	44.4%	53.8%	0.4%	1.4%	2,660
Type of Caste or Tribe of the Household Head					
Scheduled caste	44.6%	53.4%	0.6%	1.5%	545
Scheduled tribe	33.3%	64.0%	1.3%	1.3%	75
Other backward class	44.9%	54.1%	0.5%	0.5%	401
None of above	44.8%	53.4%	0.3%	1.5%	1,633
Total	44.4%	53.8%	0.4%	1.4%	2,654
Household Structure					
Nuclear	46.0%	51.9%	0.5%	1.6%	1,591
Non-nuclear	42.0%	56.7%	0.3%	1.0%	1,067
Total	44.4%	53.8%	0.4%	1.4%	2,658

The standard of living index also plays an important role in determining the utilisation of health care services. Those having high level of index, around 57 per cent of them seek health services from private sector and 53 per cent of the population of low standard of living is using government health care services in comparison to private sector. The wealth index also figures out the same scenario. The people having poorest wealth index are availing more government health care services, that is 55 per cent and it has kept on declining as the wealth index increases from poorest to richest. The wealth index of richest utilises only 43 per cent of the government health care services.

Exposure to Mass Media

Table 11.4 gives a description on exposure to mass media which is one of the most important factors which control the utilisation of health care services in the state. When people have no exposure then they are using 19 per cent of the health care services and inclined towards traditional treatment. But if they are exposed to mass media, then there is a significant change in the treatment-seeking perception. Sixty-seven per cent of the population who are partially exposed to mass media are using government health care services.

Table 11.4

*Exposure to Mass Media**

	Category of Health Facilities Used				
	Government Facilities	*Private Facility*	*Traditional Treatment*	*Other Facilities*	*Total*
No exposure	18.6	18.7	25.0	16.7	18.6
Partial exposure	66.8	66.6	50.0	66.7	66.6
Total exposure	14.7	14.8	25.0	16.7	14.8
Total	100	100	100	100	100

Note: * Exposure to mass media includes here watching TV, listening to radio and reading newspaper; N=859.

Table 11.5 unveils the major reasons regarding why the population does not avail government health care services. Mostly the population had reported that the government health care services suffer with poor facilities for example basic medical equipments, beds and necessary treatment facilities etc., followed by long waiting period to get the appropriate treatment.

Table 11.5

Reasons for Household Member for Not Using Government Facility

	Type of Place of Residence		
Reasons	*Urban*	*Rural*	*Total*
No nearby facility	19.1%	30.7%	27.4%
Facility timing not convenient	8.6%	8.0%	8.2%
Health personnel often absent	5.2%	9.2%	8.1%
Waiting time too long	27.4%	18.3%	20.9%
Poor quality of care	30.7%	37.8%	35.8%
Payment required	.0%	0.7%	0.5%
Medicine not provided	.0%	0.1%	0.1%
Others	1.9%	1.3%	1.4%

In rural area though the government health care services such as PHCs and CHCs are not located nearby, 31 per cent of them are availing them because they are not in a position to avail the private health care facilities due to their poor economic conditions.

As mentioned above, in the beginning the state is a physically challenged state which is prone to natural disasters such as landslides, earthquakes and floods etc. These physical factors also control the utilisation of health care services among the population.

Also, these calamities are very frequent especially in the rainy season and hence, inhibit the utilisation of the health care services in the state. The transport and communication infrastructure is still not developed fully which also plays important role in the accessibility of the services. The remote place of the state are yet not connected with the major road lines as well as *pucca* road and therefore, it declines the utilisation of the services.

Conclusion

From the data, it is evident that the state of health in the state is challenged by physical, socio-economic and cultural factors. The situation is worse in the districts like Chamoli, Pithoragarh, Tehri Garhwal etc. But the health care services' conditions are found in a better condition in Dehradun because it is very much developed and better connected to transport and communication facilities. Also, the government health care facilities are more accessible by the population. As mentioned in the article by Roy (1985), the WHO has identified a number of supportive activities essential for successful implementation of primary health care which are enumerated below:

1. Community involvement and participation.
2. Intra- and inter-sectoral coordination.
3. Development and mobilisation of resources.
4. Involvement of managerial processes.
5. Health manpower development.
6. Medical and health services research including innovative approaches.
7. Development and application of appropriate technology.

Recommendations

As recommendations are concerned, it can be said that the Panchayati Raj system should be emphasised in rural areas to make the government health care services extensively and efficiently utilised by the rural people. Mobile health care services should be enhanced in the rural areas which are located at remote areas. Also, the rural population should be encouraged to avail the government health care services. It should be made free or of less cost. Emphasis should also be made to the maternal and child health care since they are at a high risk of getting diseases because of the poor conditions associated with their style of living.

In this way surely in future, health for all can be achieved by the state.

References

Agarwal, A.K. (1990). "Quality in health services", *Health and Population-Perspectives and Issues* 13(1&2): 31-35.

Bhatt, S.C. (2003). *The District Gazetteer of Uttaranchal.*

Duggal, Ravi (1994). "Health care utilization in India", *Health for the Millions* 2(1): 10-12.

International Institute for Population Sciences (2003-04). Reproductive and Child Health; District level Household Survey- Nainital. Mumbai: IIPS.

National Health Policy (NHP) (2002). Soft copy downloaded from the site: *http://mohfw.noc.in/np2002.htm*

Ojha, Rabindra Nath (2006). "National rural health mission", *Kurukshetra* 54(8): 29-31.

Prakasam, C.P. (1995). "Utilization of primary health care services in a rural set up", *Health and Population-Perspectives and issues* 18(1&2): 70-80.

Ramachandran, Prema (1994). "Health care during the Tenth plan", *Yojana* 47(1): 60-69.

Roy, Somnath (1985). "Public health Services in India", *Health and Population Perspectives and issues* 8(3): 135-157.

Sharma, R.D. and Chahal Hardeep (2003). "Rural health care and patient satisfaction", *Journal of Rural development* 22(3): 363-379.

Srinivasan, S. (2002). "Primary health care services in rural India", *Kurukshetra* 50(12): 22-27.

Uma, H.R. (2004). "Financing of health services in India under five year plans", *Kurukshetra* 52(3): 19-21.

Upreti, B.C. (2004). *Uttaranchal (Issues and Challenges of Development and Change).* Kalinga Publications.

Vijaykumar, S. and C. Chakrapani (1995). "Availability, accessibility and utilization of rural health services", *Journal of Family Welfare* 41(3): 52-60.

WHO (1998). *Health Promotion Glossary.* Geneva: World Health Organization.

12 Home to Institutional Deliveries

A Long Perspective in Uttarakhand

Sanjay Rode

Introduction

All the pregnant women require advance medical care and skilled birth attendants. This is mainly because every year, more than 136000 women unnecessarily suffer from ill-health and die during the pregnancy and childbirth in India (WHO, 2006). The safe motherhood programme provides the antenatal and postnatal care and promotes institutional deliveries. The major aim of this programme is to reduce the infant, maternal mortality and morbidity. Every woman has the right to acquire information on contraceptives, newborn care and the maternity related medicines. The women are expected to register in a health facility, when the pregnancy gets confirmed. They must visit to the health facility at least three times during pregnancy and get the required medicines and knowledge of childcare. During the prenatal visits, the women are made aware of institutional deliveries and they are expected to deliver the baby in the health facility. An emergency case can be managed during the institutional delivery. The births attended by the unskilled health persons increases the probability of both maternal and infant mortality and morbidity.

In Uttarakhand, infrastructure facilities such as roads, irrigation, electricity and communication are less developed in hilly districts. Because of low industrialisation and services sector development in hilly districts, most of the households are involved in the primary sector. The women are doing variety of labour-intensive activities other than household chores. Every day, women have to perform different activities such as carry water, firewood, fodder for the animals, childcare, cooking etc. Other than the regular activities, women are also involved in all sort of agricultural tasks. Household food security is depending on the cultivable land, number of domestic animals and source of fodder. Because of steep slope of the hills and lack of transport facilities, women are carrying the maximum load on their back. They spend maximum physical energy to perform different manual tasks. The pregnancy and illness severely affects women's health in Uttarakhand. They have less time to take rest or transfer the daily chores on the other members. Also, the health care services are located far away from the villages.

Across the villages, roads are not properly maintained and built. The heavy rainfall and low density of population are the main reasons of poor road network. In order to visit the nearest health care facility, women have to walk certain distance to reach the main road. Then they have to wait for the transport buses or jeeps, which are not frequently available. The cost of travelling, user charges, outside food, waiting time etc., are higher for the poor households. The quality of care, opening hours, availability of health persons is also important. Therefore, most of the poor pregnant women prefer delivering at home. The skilled health persons such as doctors, trained *dais*, nurses are not available across the villages. Birth attended by the unskilled or untrained *dai* cannot provide the proper hygiene and expected medical care during delivery. It affects the morbidity and mortality of mothers and children in the state. The educated women are more careful about their health care needs. They use the nearest health care facilities very efficiently and effectively. Thus, women those who have received antenatal care during their pregnancy are more likely to deliver the baby in the health care facility.

The Government of Uttarakhand has planned to provide adequate health care facilities to all women and children and it is promoting the institutional deliveries. The programme of maternal and child health is very comprehensive but the involvement of households and women is very low. The government must promote the women's education; self-help employment and women's autonomy. Similarly, the investment in the irrigation, road development and health care facilities will improve the health of women and children in the state. Such steps will help to reduce the maternal and infant mortality and morbidity in the state.

Data and Methodology

Data for this study is obtained from International Institute for Population Sciences (IIPS). Government of India launched the reproductive child health (RCH) programme in 1996-97. The main focus behind the programme is to generate district level data on utilisation of the services provided by government health facilities. Therefore, it was decided to undertake District Level Household Survey (DLHS) under the RCH programme in the country. The fieldwork of round one of RCH was conducted during the year 1998-99 into two phases. The data of round one is not available for analysis. The fieldwork of round two was completed during 2002-2004. During phase one, half of the districts household data was collected in the state. The remaining half of the districts household data was collected in the second phase. In the round two, total of 9641 currently married women (age 15-44 years) were interviewed. This survey has comprehensively collected the information on the women's age, education, contraceptive knowledge of different methods, current use of any contraceptive method, availability of contraceptive methods, problem related to current method, antenatal care and place of delivery. The postnatal complications and treatment taken from the different sources is also taken into consideration. The lower and upper bound maternal deaths are measured for every 100,000 live births.

The DLHS-RCH II data is processed in the Stata 8 version. The multinomial logit regression model is used to understand the socio-economic reasons behind the place of delivery of women in the state.

Safe Motherhood Programme

Safe motherhood programme aims to prevent pregnancy-related deaths and disabilities. The safe motherhood programme needs care, understanding—by the family, community, health care facilities and government. They need to ensure that all pregnant women get essential care like adequate nutrition, regular check-ups, immunisation and supplementary iron. The period of pregnancy extend from the time of conception to 42 days after delivery. The total period of the pregnancy is divided into three periods: the antenatal, natal and the postnatal check-ups. The antenatal period is the period from conception to the onset of labour. In order to provide the adequate care during this period, it is necessary to first recognise the signs of pregnancy. All the pregnant women should be registered with the auxiliary nurse and midwife (ANM) in the sub-centre as soon as she becomes pregnant. It is essential to provide routine care and timely screening to identify risk factors like anaemia, pelvic disproportion and blood pressure, and take remedial action. The pregnant women must visit to the sub-centre or any other health centre at least three times during this period. During these visits, women should undergo routine medical check-ups like measurement of height, weight, blood pressure and anaemia, and that there is no other health problem. The measurement of foetal height, heart sound and growth is necessary. But according to the survey in Uttarakhand, 34.5 per cent women have not visited to any health care facility during their pregnancy. Only 49.6 per cent women had three antenatal visits.

Place of Deliveries

It is safest to have delivery in an institution with appropriate medical facility. Delivery in a hospital also ensures newborn care. It can reduce the incidence of infant mortality substantially. In such an institution, emergency conditions like bleeding, obstructed labour requiring operation can be promptly attended. Such events may not be predicted in advance and also cannot be handled at home. Usually, the household and pregnant women together decide the place of delivery. The numbers of socio-economic, demographic, cultural, infrastructure factors are responsible for the place of delivery of women. The poor households are trying to maximise their economic gain out of the risk involved in delivery of the mother. The risk behaviour is also depending on the number of factors such as distance of public and private health facility, quality of care, availability of doctors/nurse, waiting time etc. It is difficult to examine because they are different for different households and women.

Table 12.1

Place and Type of Deliveries

(Per cent)

Place of Delivery	*Rural*	*Urban*	*Total*
Government/municipal hospital	7.0	22.1	10.6
Government dispensary	0.8	0.7	0.8
UHC/UHP/UFWC	0.1	0.0	0.1
CHC/rural hospital	0.3	0.1	0.2
Primary health centre	0.6	0.9	0.6
Sub-centre	0.0	0.0	0.0
NGO/trust hospital	0.1	0.7	0.2
Government ISM hospital/clinics	0.1	0.2	0.1
Private ISM hospital/clinics	1.2	1.7	1.3
Private hospital/clinics	6.2	22.1	10.0
Home	83.6	51.4	76.0

Source: Computed from DLHS-RCH II, (2006).

The above table shows that, 76 per cent of births have taken place in the home. In the private hospital/clinics, only 10 per cent of the births took place. In the government/municipal hospital, 10.6 per cent births have taken place in the state. As far as urban area is concerned then there is no difference in the (22.1 per cent) births which took place in the government/municipal hospitals and private hospital/clinics.

In the urban area, around half of the births took place at home. In the rural area, 83.6 per cent births took place at home. In the government/municipal hospital (7 per cent) and private hospital/clinics (6.2 per cent) the reported births are lower. If we combine all the births, which took place in the public health facility in the state, then it is only 12.6 per cent. In the private health facility, total 11.3 per cent births took place. Such lower deliveries in the public and private health care facilities are the major concern in the state.

Geographical Distribution of Place of Deliveries

It is important to examine the geographical distribution of the place of deliveries. The health care facilities are poorly developed across the border districts. The households have to visit the district and city hospitals in order to get the reliable, affordable, efficient health care facilities.

Table 12.2

Place of Deliveries in Different Districts

(Per cent)

Districts	*Rural*			*Urban*			*Total*		
	Public	*Private*	*Home*	*Public*	*Private*	*Home*	*Public*	*Private*	*Home*
Almora	0.6	0.4	7.2	3.0	1.7	3.4	0.7	1.2	6.3
Bageshwar	0.5	0.3	5.8	2.1	1.7	4.1	0.6	0.9	5.4
Chamoli	0.6	0.3	5.2	0.8	1.1	4.5	0.5	0.6	5.0
Champawat	0.6	0.1	7.1	0.5	1.9	4.8	0.5	0.6	6.5
Dehradun	0.8	0.8	4.1	4.2	3.5	6.5	1.4	1.6	4.6
Garhwal	0.8	0.6	4.5	2.6	2.6	2.2	1.1	1.2	4.0
Haridwar	1.0	1.7	8.0	2.6	3.1	2.7	2.0	1.4	6.7
Nainital	0.6	0.7	6.2	2.5	1.7	8.9	1.0	1.1	6.9
Pithoragarh	1.0	0.2	5.6	3.9	0.9	4.2	0.4	1.7	5.3
Rudraprayag	0.9	0.6	8.1	0.6	0.3	1.6	0.5	0.8	6.6
Tehri Garhwal	0.6	0.6	5.6	1.4	2.5	2.1	1.0	0.8	4.8
Udham Singh Nagar	0.2	1.0	6.4	0.2	2.5	6.1	1.3	0.2	6.4
Uttarkashi	0.6	0.2	9.7	0.5	0.1	0.3	0.2	0.6	7.5
Total	9.0	7.4	83.6	24.8	23.9	51.4	11.3	12.7	76.0

Source: Computed from DLHS-RCH II, (2006).

Above table shows, that the Uttrakashi district has the highest number of deliveries which are taking place at home (7.5 per cent). The births reported at home in the rural area (9.7 per cent) of Uttarkashi are higher. It is followed by the Nainital (6.9 per cent) district. In Nainital, the births reported at home in urban area (8.9 per cent) are higher. The lowest home deliveries are reported in Deharadun (4.6 per cent) and Garhwal (4 per cent) district. In Dehradun district, the births reported at home in rural area (4.1 per cent) are lower as compare to other districts in the state. In the same district, the births reported in urban public (4.2 per cent) and private (3.5 per cent) health care facilities are higher. The lowest deliveries in public health facilities are reported in Uttarkashi (0.2 per cent) and Pithoragarh (0.4 per cent) district. The districts such as Uttarkashi, Chamoli and Champawat have reported the lower deliveries in the public and private health care facilities. These districts are the border districts of the Uttarakhand state. The health care facilities are located far away from the villages. The lower transport facilities and higher transport cost, waiting time are the causes of lower use of public and private health care facilities. The regular visits of women are not possible because of the above reasons.

Socio-Economic Characteristics and Type of Deliveries

It is important to understand the socio-economic characteristics of women, who had a delivery at home, public and private health care facility. Such socio-economic factors are important in order to decide the place of delivery of any woman. Table 12.3 shows few characteristics.

In the rural area, 63.8 per cent deliveries are taking place at home. In the public health facility, 6.8 per cent and in the private health facility 5.6 per cent deliveries are taking place. In the urban area, only 12.2 per cent deliveries are taking place at home. There is no much difference in deliveries, which are taking place in the public and private health facilities. According to religion, the Hindu women (67.5 per cent) have more deliveries at home. Among the Muslim women, 8.1 per cent deliveries took place at home. The Sikh women had more (0.3 per cent) deliveries in the private health care facility. According to caste, 13.9 per cent scheduled caste women delivered at home. Among the other backward caste, 12.9 per cent women had delivery at home. Among the other caste, 45.7 per cent of women had delivery at home. Among the other caste women, few deliveries have taken place in the public (8.7 per cent) and private (7.7 per cent) health care facility. The standard of living index is sole determinant of the place of delivery of women. It is used as a proxy of household income. The women from the higher standard of living index are expected to deliver a baby in the public or private health care facility. The table shows that the women of lower standard of living index have (39.9 per cent) more home deliveries. The deliveries in the public health care facilities (2.6 per cent) are higher than the private (1.6 per cent) health care facilities among the women of lower standard of living index.

Table 12.3

Socio-Economic Characteristics of Women Who had Delivery

Socio-Economic Variables	*Public (Per cent)*	*Private (Per cent)*	*House (Per cent)*	*Total Women (Number)*
Rural	6.8	5.6	63.8	2824
Urban	5.9	5.6	12.2	876
Religion				
Hindu	11.6	9.6	67.5	3281
Muslim	0.9	1.3	8.1	381
Christian	0.2	0.1	0.1	13
Sikh	0.1	0.3	0.2	23
Caste				
Scheduled caste	1.6	0.9	13.9	610
Scheduled tribe	0.3	0.2	1.5	72
Other backward caste	1.8	2.3	12.9	631
Other caste	8.7	7.7	45.7	2297
Do not know	0.3	0.1	2.0	
Standard of Index				
Low standard of living index	2.6	1.6	39.9	1631
Medium standard of living index	4.5	2.1	24.8	1166
High standard of living index	5.6	7.6	11.2	903
Age of Women				
15-19	0.3	0.1	1.9	86
20-34	11.6	10.6	67.3	3309
35-44	0.9	0.6	6.8	305
Mother's Education				
Secondary school	5.3	3.2	32.1	1503
Graduate	3.9	4.1	7.2	563
Postgraduate	1.2	2.2	0.8	155
Husband's Education				
Secondary school	5.2	3.8	44.1	1965
Graduate	5.0	4.5	16.0	343
Postgraduate	1.5	2.4	2.8	249
Antenatal check-up	10.6	9.8	37.2	2130

Source: Computed from DLHS-RCH II, (2006).

In the higher standard of living index, nearly 11.2 per cent deliveries took place at home. In the private health care facilities, more (7.6 per cent) deliveries took place as compared to the public health facilities (5.6 per cent). In the age group of 20-34, more deliveries took place at home (67.3 per cent). There is no much difference in terms of deliveries, which are taking place in the public (11.6 per cent) and private health care facilities (10.6 per cent) in the same age group. In the 35-44 age group, very few deliveries are reported (6.8 per cent) at home. Mother's education play an important role as far as the place of delivery is concerned. The educated women are always delivering the baby in the public or private health care facility. The educated women are more conscious about their own and child health. They take all the precautions and necessary measures against any problem. The table shows that, 32.1 per cent secondary school studied women had delivery at home. Such women prefer more (5.3 per cent) deliveries in the public health care facilities than the private (3.2 per cent) health care facilities. In the postgraduate category, the women preferred deliveries in the private health care facilities (2.2 per cent) than the public health care facilities (1.2 per cent). The home deliveries among the postgraduate women are low at 0.8 per cent. It means that higher education among women steadily reduces the home deliveries. It also reduces the deliveries at the public health facilities. Private health care facilities are providing quality health care facilities at higher prices. During the delivery of the woman, the role of husband is very important. His education is considered important because of his control of monetary resources and the decision about the place of delivery. If the husband is more educated then the woman may get better health care during the delivery. Table 12.3 shows that home deliveries are more where husbands have secondary school of education (44.1 per cent). If the husbands are postgraduate then the home deliveries (2.8 per cent) are very low. The antenatal care is most important for the women during the pregnancy. Very few women had received the antenatal care in the state. There is no difference among the women who had delivery at public (10.6 per cent) and private (9.8 per cent) health care facility.

It is important to understand the deliveries of women, which are taking place in the urban and rural area according to standard of living index. The pregnant women in the rural area have less access to health care facilities and skilled health persons. The health care facilities provided by the private health care sector are expensive and they are beyond the control of poor households. The poor women of rural area have no choice but to deliver the baby at home.

Figure 12.1

Place of Deliveries according to Standard of Living Index in Rural Area

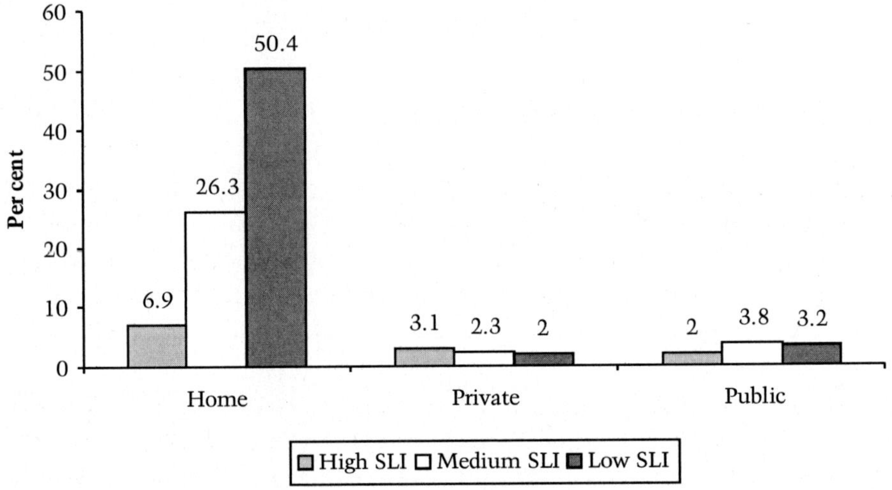

Figure 12.1 shows that, half of the deliveries of rural women in the lower standard of living index are taking place at home. In the high standard of living index only 6.9 per cent deliveries are taking place at home. The richer households have more access to jeep, car and other necessary transport facilities during the delivery. They can easily reach the public or private health facility within a short period of time or bring the private health person at home. But it is not possible for the poor households to provide for the emergency care.

In the rural area, only 2 per cent women of lower standard of living index had delivery in the private health care facility. Such deliveries are increasing according to increase in the standard of living index. In the higher standard of living index, 3.1 per cent deliveries are taking place in private health care facility. The women of higher standard of living index in the rural area are (2 per cent) less likely to deliver the baby in the public health care facility. The deliveries of rural women of medium standard of living index are (3.8 per cent) more in the public health care facilities.

In the urban area, the women have more access to the health care facilities. The distance, opening hours, availability of the health care persons is higher as compared to the rural health facilities. Therefore, urban women are more likely to deliver the baby in the public or private health facilities.

Figure 12.2

Place of Deliveries according to Standard of Living Index in Urban Area

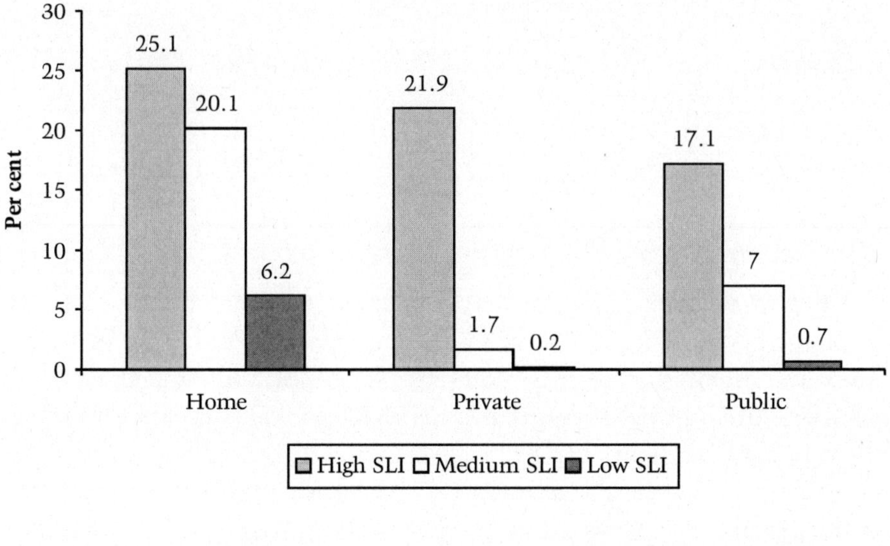

In the urban area, home deliveries in the lower standard of index are (6.2 per cent) low. But home deliveries in the higher standard of living index (25.1 per cent) are more. It would be because of three reasons. Firstly, health care facilities are located near to households. Therefore, the household can reach health facility during an emergency. Secondly, the sample may consist of newly urban residence of women. Thirdly, the sample size may be low and does not represent ideal picture of home deliveries in urban area. Around 21.9 per cent women of high standard of living index had delivery in private health facility. In the lower standard of living index, it is only 0.2 per cent. In the public health facility, the women of higher standard of living index (17.1 per cent) have more births. The women of lower standard of index in urban area (0.7 per cent) are less likely to deliver the babies in the public health facilities.

Table 12.4

Deliveries Conducted at Home

(Per cent)

Deliveries Conducted	*Rural*	*Urban*	*Total*
Doctor	1.7	2	1.7
ANM/nurse	8.2	23.8	10.7
Trained *dai*	8.3	17.3	9.7
Untrained *dai*	64.4	50.7	62.2
Relatives	16.3	5.8	14.6
None	1.1	0.4	1.1

Source: Computed from DLHS-RCH II, (2006).

It is now clear that, the maximum deliveries are taking place at home in the rural area. The women from the lower standard of living index are delivering the baby at home. It means that higher number births are attended by the untrained *dai* (62.2 per cent) in the state. The relatives (14.6 per cent) are also attending the deliveries of women. The births attended by the trained *dais* (9.7 per cent), ANM/nurses (10.7 per cent) and doctors (1.7 per cent) are lower in the state. In the rural area, the untrained *dais* attain 64.4 per cent deliveries. In the urban area, half of the deliveries are attained by the untrained *dai*. The births attended by the ANM/nurse in urban area (23.8 per cent) are quite higher than the rural (8.2 per cent) area.

Maternal Deaths in Uttarakhand

The most commonly used measure of maternal mortality is the number of maternal deaths during a given time period per 100000 live births. This is a measure of the risk of deaths once the women have become pregnant. The main causes of maternal deaths are hemorrhage, anaemia, sepsis, and complications from abortions, obstructed birth and toxemia. It is calculated as follows,

$$E\ (MD_t) = Y_{it}{}^{*}CMMR/1000000$$

Where,

- MD_t= Expected death of women, who suffered from different pregnancy-related complications in particular year.
- Y_{it}= Population of women in the ith age group in period t.
- CMMR= Current maternal mortality ratio.

We have estimated the age-wise maternal death in the state for the current year. For lower bound, maternal mortality ratio (MMR) is taken as 343 whereas for upper bound MMR, it is 695 per 100000 women (Ranjan, 2004). Table 12.5 shows the maternal death in current year.

Table 12.5

Estimated Maternal Deaths in the State

Age Group	*Maternal Deaths in the State (Number)*	
	Lower Bound	*Upper Bound*
20-24	1110	2062
25-29	996	1851
30-34	837	1556
35-39	774	1439
40-44	622	1456
45 +	524	924
Total	4863	8988

Source: Ranjan (2005).

The estimated maternal deaths due to various complications are higher in the state. Every year, minimum 4863 maternal deaths would be taking place in the state. There is large variation in maternal deaths in the rural and urban area. The deaths in the border districts would be higher than the plain surface region/districts. The MMR for the state is under-represented because the inhabited villages in the state are comparatively higher. Secondly, because of physical topography and climatic conditions, it is difficult for the households to reach up to health facility at the right time. The households are scattered across the wide area and transportation facilities are not available near to the village or household. These characteristics add to the total maternal deaths in the state.

Multinomial Logit Regression Results

It is important to understand the socio-economic factors and their correlation as far as choices of the deliveries are concerned. Health care facilities may provide the maximum facilities such as patient-friendly relations and lower user charges fees etc. But the household socio-economic factors are also important. The household must demand the institutional care and deliveries. The internal choice factors of households are important and it must get the match with the facilities provided by health care facilities. The multinomial logit model allows us to differentiate between women's choices based on public, private health care facility or home delivery.

The model is defined as follows.

$$\Pr(y_i = j) = \frac{\text{Exp}(X_i B_j)}{1 + \sum_j^J \exp(X_i B_j)}$$

and

$$\Pr(y_i = 0) = \frac{1}{1 + \sum_j^J \exp(X_i B_j)'}$$

Where for the ith women, y_i is the observed outcome and X_j is a vector of explanatory variable. The parameters B_j are estimated by maximum likelihood. The results of the model are explained in the following table.

Table 12.6

Multinomial Logit Regression Results

Variables	*Public vs. Private*		*Public vs. Home Delivery*	
	Co-efficient (Standard Error)	*T value*	*Co-efficient (Standard Error)*	*T value*
Rural	0.48*(0.17)	2.85	0.80*(0.13)	5.92
Religion				
Hindu	20.43*(0.71)	28.42	1.50(1.90)	0.79
Muslim	21.20*(0.76)	27.80	1.89(1.91)	0.99
Christian	19.71*(0.67)	23.12	-0.67(2.04)	-0.33
Sikh	22.47*(1.05)	21.23	1.46(2.06)	0.71
Caste				
Scheduled caste	0.72(0.62)	1.16	0.09(0.41)	0.23
Scheduled tribe	0.72(0.76)	0.94	-0.37(0.52)	-0.71
Other backward caste	1.23**(0.60)	2.04	0.09(0.40)	0.24
Other caste	0.85(0.58)	1.45	0.22(0.39)	0.58
Standard of Index				
Low standard of living index	0.33(0.22)	1.44	0.48**(0.15)	3.26
High standard of living index	1.06*(0.19)	5.61	-0.18(0.14)	-1.23
Age of Women				
20-34	0.44(0.57)	0.78	0.24(0.36)	0.65
35-44	0.13(0.63)	0.21	0.01(0.42)	0.03
Mother's Education				
Secondary school	-0.38(0.24)	-1.63	-0.63*(0.16)	-3.64
Graduate	-0.01(0.28)	-0.04	-1.29*(0.21)	-6.07
Postgraduate	0.39(0.34)	1.14	-1.97*(0.32)	-6.18
Husband's Education				
Secondary school	0.52(0.33)	1.58	0.19(0.22)	0.89
Graduate	0.49(0.37)	1.33	-0.01(0.25)	-0.02
Postgraduate	0.84**(0.40)	2.08	0.03(0.31)	0.10
Antenatal check-up	0.02(0.21)	0.11	-0.94*(0.14)	-6.66
Constant	-23.30(1.13)	1.13	0.35(1.97)	0.18
LR $chi^2(40)$ = 1080.01	Prob > chi^2 = 0.00			
Log likelihood = -2112.98	Pseudo R^2 = 0.20			

Note: * Significant at 1 per cent; ** significant at 5 per cent; *** significant at 10 per cent.

Public health facilities are providing the reliable, consistent, affordable, patient-friendly services in the rural and urban area. The follow-up visits are also possible with lower economic burden on households. The government has made adequate measures to provide the universal health care to all women and children. The private health care facilities are providing efficient and better health care facilities but they are profit-maximising services. The poor people have always the first preference to use the public health facilities. Therefore, we have compared the deliveries of public health facilities with deliveries in the private health care facilities. The deliveries in the public health care facilities are also compared with the home deliveries. Table 12.6 shows that, the private health care facilities are positively related to the rural area, Hindu, Muslim, Christian and Sikh religion, other backward caste, and higher standard of living index in comparison to the public health care facilities. The home deliveries are positive in the rural area, lower standard of living index. The home deliveries are negatively related to women's education and antenatal check-up in reference to deliveries in public health facility.

Private health care facilities are positively related to the rural women. The rural women those who are from higher income group like to have delivery in the private health facility. They can access the quick, efficient and affordable care from private health care facility. The Hindu, Muslim, Christian and Sikh religion is positively related to private health facility. There is no religious difference as compared to deliveries in the private health care facility. The women from any religion have the right to access and use the private health care facilities. As far as caste of the women is concerned, other backward caste women are delivering more in the private health care facility as compared to the public health care facility in the state. The women in the higher standard of living index are more likely to deliver baby in the private health care facility. The women of higher standard of living index have more economic resources to pay for the hospital fees, medicinal charges and transport etc.

The home deliveries are more prevalent in the rural area. In rural area, health facilities are located far away from the house. The distance from the main road, waiting time for vehicle, monetary cost of travelling and the non-performing of any economic activities are quite higher for the poor women in the rural area. The pregnant women cannot walk for longer distance during complication. Therefore, emergency transportation facilities are required at shorter distances. In the Uttarakhand state, the rural households are scattered across the hills and villages. Because of physical structure and hills the roads are not adequately developed. Therefore, most of the pregnant women are forced to give births at home. The women of the lower standard of living index cannot afford the delivery in the private health facility. Delivery at home with unskilled *dai* or relative does not have very high economic cost or burden. The women have to perform different activities at home such as carry drinking water, firewood, fodder, cooking etc. The pregnant women cannot spend enough time in the public or private health care facilities for delivery. The secondary, graduate and postgraduate studied women are less likely to deliver the baby at home. The educated women clearly understand the risk involved to her and baby in the home delivery. They choose the public or private health facility in advance and it depends on their economic resources and nearest available health care facility. They have more knowledge of the location, quality of care and the cost of the delivery. Those women who have not visited for antenatal care are more likely to deliver the baby at home. The prenatal visits are important because it provides maternal medicines and educate women about care of newborn and child health. In order to improve the access of the institutional deliveries, the policies of improving standard of living index, mother's education, and antenatal care is important.

Policy Implications

The safe motherhood programme is providing the antenatal care to pregnant women, promoting institutional care and postnatal care. All the pregnant women are expected to register in the health facility and get the maternal medicines, knowledge about diet, newborn care and the measure the movement of fetus. The emergency care can be managed during the institutional delivery. Such efforts by the health facilities are important in order to reduce the maternal, infant morbidity and mortality. The low birth weight of babies, anaemia, diarrhoea, proper breastfeeding can be managed through effective health interventions. In Uttarakhand, more than one-third of pregnant women have not been visiting to any kind of health care facility. Only half of the women surveyed, had completed the least three antenatal visits. In the state, three-fourth of the deliveries took place at home. In the rural area, every fourth out of fifth delivery is taking place at home. The birth reported in the government/municipal hospital and private health facilities are low and they are almost same. The border districts such as Uttrakashi, Chamoli and Champawat have higher home deliveries and lower deliveries in the public and private health care facilities. The women of lower standard of living index have more deliveries at home. The less educated husbands do not allow their wives to deliver a baby in the public or private health care facility. The women of lower standard of living are more likely to use the public health care facilities than the private health care facilities and *vis-á-vis* in the higher standard of living index women.

The government needs to provide more technical and higher education to the girls. The promotion of self-help employment opportunities will help the households to maximise their income. There is need of massive awareness through radio and television about the maternal and child health. Government must train at least one untrained *dai* from each village. Medical kit for delivery of women should be given to trained *dais*. Such trained *dai* of each village can provide the regular information on number of pregnant women and their antenatal check-up, institutional deliveries and postnatal complications. It will be indirect link between primary health centre and the pregnant women in the villages. The ANM/nurse can work along with trained *dais* and get the necessary information, maternal medicines of pregnant women in each village. Emergency care during complicated pregnancy should be provided through the mobile vans. Government must fulfill all vacant seats in all public health care facilities. Immediate appointment of lady health officers will curb the home deliveries in the state. Health staff must be given more incentive and encouragement to work in the rural and hilly districts. There is need of multiple measures to reduce the home deliveries in the state. The traditional agriculture and cropping pattern needs crop diversification. Farmers must be given training of cultivating cash crops. For that more investment in canal irrigation facilities is required. Farmers need to provide the ready-made market of their agricultural products. The investment in the rural roads is urgent and important. Government must take urgent steps because three-fourth of deliveries are taking place at home. Any delay in the effort will lead to many unaccountable women and infant deaths in the state. Improvement of maternal and child health through various alternatives policies is important in the state.

References

Greene, William H. (2003). *Econometric Analysis*. Delhi: Pearson Education Private, Ltd.

Pandey, Sanjay, Ravi Shankar, CMS Rawat and V.M. Gupta (2007). "Socio-economic Factors and Delivery Practices in an Urban Slum of District Nainital, Uttranchal", *Indian Journal of Community Medicine* 32(3): 210-211.

Ranjan, A. (2005). "Obstetric Risk in Central India", in Alok Ranjan *et al.* (eds.), *Obstetric Risk in Central India*. University of Southhampton, Southampton, UK.

International Institute for Population Sciences (2006). *District Level Household Survey (DLHS-2)*. Mumbai: IIPS.

WHO (2002). "Reducing Risks, Promoting Healthy Life", *World Health Report-2002*. Geneva: World Health Organization.

———. (2006). *Annual Report-2006: Department of Making Pregnancy Safer*, Family and Community Health. Geneva: World Health Organization.

Appendix A-12.1

The standard of living index is calculated by adding the following scores

Source of drinking water: 3 for tap (own), 2 for tap (shared), 1 for hand pump and well and 0 for other.

Type of house: 4 for *pucca*, 2 for semi-*pucca*, and 0 for *kuchcha*.

Source of lightening: 2 for electricity, 1 for kerosene and 0 for other.

Fuel for cooking: 2 for LPG gas/electricity, 1 for kerosene and 0 for other.

Toilet facility: 4 for own flush toilet, 2 for own pit toilet, 1 for shared toilet and 0 for no toilet.

Ownership of items: 4 each for car and tractor, 3 each for television, telephone and motorcycle/scooter and 2 each for fan, radio/transistor, sewing machine and bicycle.

The total of the score vary from the lowest of a 0 to maximum of 40. On the basis of total score, households are divided into three categories as:

1. Low – if total score is less than or equal to 9.
2. Medium – if total score is greater than 9 but less than or equal to 19 and
3. High – if total score is greater than 19.

13 Understanding the Determinants of Breastfeeding Practices and its Discontinuation in Uttarakhand

Archana Kujur and Sulabha Parasuraman

Introduction

Breastfeeding is a major determinant of infant health and survival, birth spacing and prevention of childhood infections. It is critical for nourishing the health and development of newborns and infants. Several empirical studies have concluded that breastfeeding reduces morbidity and mortality of infants and children, and promotes maternal health, both in developing and developed nations (Koosha *et al.*, 2008; Li *et al.*, 2005; Nicoll and Williams, 2002; Lawrence, 2002; Chhabra *et al.*, 1998; Yngve and Sjöström, 2001). Studies have highlighted the benefits of breastfeeding, especially exclusive breastfeeding, particularly in poor environment where early introduction of milk is critical due to the risks associated with pathogen's contamination and over-dilution of milk leading to risk of morbidity and undernutrition (Huttly *et al.*, 1997; Cunningham *et al.*, 1991). There is no artificial feeding formula capable of qualitatively replacing breast milk, its important nutrient and disease-resisting constituents (WHO, 2001).

In case of India, in spite of the almost universal practice of breastfeeding, the performance is far from satisfactory owing to low rates of early initiation, exclusive breastfeeding and the timing of complementary feeding practices (Patel *et al.,* 2008). Studies have noted that an inappropriate breastfeeding practice significantly elevates the risk for all cause mortality. One of the goals set by India's Population Policy, 2000 is the reduction of infant mortality rate to 30 by the year 2010. On the other hand, the fourth Millennium Development Goal (MDG) focus on the reduction of child mortality, and the target for this goal is to reduce the mortality rate of children under five by two-thirds, between 1990-2015. This is also reflected in the Tenth Five Year Plan (2002-2007), which states that infant mortality rate to be reduced to 45 per thousand live births by 2007 and 28 per thousand live births by 2012. Recent evidence suggests that the infant mortality rate in India has been declining. The National Family Health Survey (NFHS) surveys have shown declining trends in the infant mortality from 79 per thousand live births (NFHS-1, 1992-93) to 68 per thousand live births (NFHS-2, 1998-99), which further reduced to 57 per thousand live births (NFHS-3, 2005-06).

Infant mortality is a sensitive indicator of human development. High mortality and morbidity among infants and children below 5 years occurs on account of inadequate care, asphyxia during birth, premature birth, low birth weight, acute respiratory infections, diarrhoea, vaccine preventable diseases, malnutrition and deficiencies of nutrients, including Vitamin A. Diarrhoea is one of the leading causes of mortality and morbidity among infants. NFHS-2 (1998-99) shows that 19.2 per cent children suffered from diarrhoea during the two weeks preceding their survey. About 7 per cent of total deaths among infants in India are due to diarrhoea (*Family Welfare Yearbook*, 1998). Keeping the goals and policies related to infant and child mortality in mind, Department of Family Welfare initiated several policies and programmes. Among them, one is the "Implementation of exclusive breastfeeding up to the age of 6 months and appropriate practices related to complimentary feeding", which is the single most cost-effective intervention of reducing infant mortality. In addition, it is also the ideal method of infant feeding and helps in delayed return to fertility in the mother and acts as natural contraceptive.

Malnutrition has also been responsible, directly or indirectly, for 60 per cent of the 10.9 million deaths annually among children under five years in the world, of which 2.42 million deaths occur alone in India. Over two-thirds of these deaths, which are often associated with inappropriate feeding practices, occur during the first year of life. Not more than 35 per cent of infants worldwide are exclusively breastfed during the first four months of life; complementary feeding frequently begins too early or too late, and foods are often nutritionally inadequate and unsafe (WHO, 2003).

On investigating the causes behind child mortality, diarrhoea was the leading one and accounted for 4.6 million deaths across the world annually. Efforts to control diarrhoea over the past decades have been based on multiple, potentially powerful interventions implemented more or less simultaneously. One of the important interventions likely to have had an impact on mortality caused by diarrhoea includes the promotion of breastfeeding (WHO, 2000). Infants who initiated breastfeeding within the first 3 days of life had 26 per cent lower rate of diarrhoea during the first 6 months of life compared with infants who initiated after 3 days. Timing of initiation of breastfeeding and diet were independently predictive of the rate of diarrhoea. Further, early initiation was associated with a longer duration of exclusive breastfeeding (Clemens *et al.*, 1999).

Breastfeeding is an unequalled way of providing ideal food for the healthy growth and development of infants; it is also an integral part of the reproductive process with important implications for the health of mothers. As a global public health recommendation, infants should be exclusively breastfed for the first six months of life to achieve optimal growth, development and health. Thereafter, to meet their evolving nutritional requirements, infants should receive nutritionally adequate and safe complementary foods while breastfeeding continues for up to two years of age or beyond. Exclusive breastfeeding from birth is possible except for a few medical conditions, and unrestricted exclusive breastfeeding results in ample milk production. Breast milk is the natural first food for babies, it provides all the energy and nutrients that the infant needs for the first months of life, and it continues to provide up to half or more of a child's nutritional needs during the second half of the first year, and up to one-third during the second year of life. Breast milk promotes sensory and cognitive development, and protects the infant against infectious and chronic diseases. Exclusive breastfeeding reduces infant mortality due to common childhood illnesses such as diarrhoea or pneumonia, and helps for a quicker recovery during illness (WHO, 2003).

Study carried out by Popkin *et al.* in 1990 among the low income countries, found that the breastfeeding duration is normal in Asian countries, but there is neglect on the other aspects of infant feeding. Khan (1990) has argued that in India, although breastfeeding is still almost universal, particularly in rural areas, there are indications that in certain segments of the population, such as the educated and urban elite, the duration of breastfeeding is declining. Unfortunately, this trend is also slowly trickling down to some disadvantaged urban segments of the population such as slum dwellers. However, it has also been observed that in India, particularly in rural areas, women continue to breastfeed their children exclusively for up to 8 months and in some cases even 12 months. Khan has also argued that the normal practice is to delay the initiation of breastfeeding considerably, at least in some parts in India, so that the colostrum will not be fed to the child. There also appears to be a relatively long delay, often exceeding six months post-partum, in the introduction of food supplementation. Studies in India have also shown that the newborn are breastfed for the first time only 48 to 72 hours after their birth. In a small proportion of cases, initiation of breastfeeding is reported after 24 hours or between 13 and 24 hours. However, in some of the tribal areas, breastfeeding is initiated within 6-12 hours. Initiation of early breast-feeding has also been reported from other states (Belavady and Gopalan, 1959; Mudgal *et al.*, 1979; Khan and Basu, 1987).

Need for the Study

One of the strategies of the government to reduce infant mortality is the promotion of exclusive breastfeeding which is the single most cost-effective intervention for reducing infant mortality, especially in the case of poor and the underserved. Uttarakhand is a newly formed state where the infant mortality rate is 67 per thousand birth according to Census 2001, which needs immediate attention. The mean breastfeeding duration is 25 months and the mean duration of exclusive breastfeeding is only 7 months according to NFHS-3 report (IIPS & Macro International, 2007) which is a cause of concern. From the above literatures, we have already gathered the idea that breastfeeding is a very important component of reducing infant mortality and improving child survival. Therefore, this study aims to systematically examine the socio-economic and demographic factors which determine ever breastfeeding and also understand relevant factors which determine the hazard of discontinuation of breastfeeding.

Data

The present study used data from the third round of National Family and Health Survey (NFHS-3) conducted in the year 2005-06. The NFHS is a national representative survey, conducted on the similar lines of Demographic and Health Survey (DHS) in several developing countries, primarily to provide important indicators of population and health, i.e., fertility, mortality, family planning, maternal and child health indicators, etc., both at the national and state level. For the present study, kids file has been used to compute various estimates of breastfeeding practices which includes, breastfeeding status, initiation of breastfeeding and prelacteal feeding. For bivariate analysis of initiation of breastfeeding and prelacteal feeding, last-born child of a women during five years preceding the survey have been included. For the binary logistic regression and Cox proportional hazards model, and for computation of ever breastfeeding in bivariate table, children born in the five years preceding the survey were included.

Methods

Bivariate tables have been generated for the state, across different background characteristics. Binary logistic regression is carried out to determine the various factors influencing ever breastfed status. Cox proportional hazards analysis has been used to see the net contribution of different background factors on stopping of breastfeeding, which combines the features of life table and regression (Cox, 1972). Application of the Cox hazards model was proposed as appropriate for analysis of the duration of breastfeeding (Huffman, 1987; MacDonald, 1981). The benefit of using such a multivariate life-table model is that censoring of nursing by either the survey or the deaths of children are taken care of. The technique of the proportional hazards model is similar to regression analysis but also useful to analyse the process of survival, in which termination may occur at any time (in that case, stopping of breastfeeding or termination of breastfeeding). It also models the influence of a set of variables on the hazard of termination. This method is useful to assess the net effect of an explanatory factor on the hazard of termination (stopping of breastfeeding) of a process controlled for the effects of other factors. In the following analysis, the primary aim is to estimate the net effect of different background factors on stopping of breastfeeding. The theoretically pertinent predictor variables used are: education of the mother, standard of living index, religion of household head, caste of household head, age of the mother, sex of the child and place of residence.

Results

Bivariate Analysis

The bivariate analysis has been carried out to understand the unadjusted distribution of ever breastfeeding initiation, initiation of breastfeeding and prelacteal feeding according to selected demographic and socio-economic characteristics as reported in Table 13.1. We have categorised the initiation of breastfeeding in three following types: i) immediately: breast feeding from immediately to half an hour of birth, ii) Within an hour: from half an hour to one hour and iii) Within a day: includes breastfeeding initiation from more than one hour to one day. The level of ever breastfeeding in Uttarakhand is considerably lower that many states of India, which is not very positive indicator for the state, but interestingly we find that the state shows very little difference in ever breastfeeding, initiation of breastfeeding and prelacteal feeding among children of different sex. If we look at the ever breastfeeding among the women of different age groups, we find that it is higher for the women in age group 35 and above (95 per cent), as compared to women in the age group 15-24 (89 per cent). This may indicate gradual increase in the breastfeeding among women with increment in age. Immediate initiation of breastfeeding is again highest for the women in the age group 35 and above (36 per cent), followed closely by women in the age group 15-24 (33 per cent) and lowest (28 per cent) for 25-34 age group women. We also find that prelacteal feeding is also higher for the women of the age group 35 and above (48 per cent).

Table 13.1

Percentage Distribution of Ever Breastfed, Initiation of Breastfeeding and Prelacteal Feeding across Different Background Characteristics, Uttarakhand: 2005-06

Background Characteristics	*Ever Breastfed*	*Initiation of Breastfeeding* *Immediately*	*Within an Hour*	*Within a Day*	*Prelacteal Feeding*
Child Characteristics					
Sex					
Male	89.6	31.2	16.7	31.8	45.9
Female	90.7	28.7	21.0	31.7	44.0
Family Characteristics					
Mother's Age (years)					
15-24	89.0	32.9	15.0	30.2	46.6
25-34	90.1	27.7	20.8	32.8	43.8
35+	94.8	36.4	15.4	30.2	47.8
Education					
No education	90.3	31.2	16.0	32.8	45.2
Primary	91.9	26.6	20.2	33.7	45.2
Secondary	89.3	30.4	20.8	28.7	43.5
Higher	90.1	29.0	19.4	34.6	48.2
Religion					
Hindu	90.6	32.3	19.5	31.2	40.7
Others	87.5	17.2	13.4	35.0	69.7
Caste					
SC/ST	88.9	26.4	18.3	36.3	45.4
OBC	87.5	28.7	15.4	26.9	57.2
Others	91.4	31.9	19.6	31.1	41.8
Standard of Living Index					
Low	93.7	35.7	20.0	25.2	36.5
Medium	89.8	33.8	13.9	35.6	40.4
High	88.6	27.3	19.2	32.3	51.4

If we look into the ever breastfed status by the education of the women, we do not find very wide variation. Nearly 90 per cent women with no education and similar per cent of women with higher secondary education have ever breastfed their children. Similarly, we do not find much conspicuous differences in the initiation of breastfeeding and prelacteal feeding according to the education of the women. Religion also does not show significant difference, but the percentage of ever breastfeeding (91 per cent) and immediate initiation of breastfeeding (32 per cent) is higher for the Hindu women, whereas prelacteal feeding is (41 per cent) 30 per cent less among Hindu women as compared to women belonging to other religion (other religions include Muslims, Christians and Jains). Caste groups show consistent variation in prelacteal feeding; almost 60 per cent women belonging to other backward class (OBC) carry out prelacteal feeding as compared to 46 per cent among scheduled caste or scheduled tribe (SC/ST) categories women, and 42 per cent by other caste groups. Higher percentage of women belonging to low SLI (94 per cent) had ever breastfed their children, initiate immediate breastfeeding (36 per cent) and lower percentage of women with low SLI (37 per cent) gave prelacteal feeding, as compared to women belonging to other SLI groups.

Multivariate Analyses

Binary Logistic Regression Analysis

Binary logistic analysis has been carried out to find the determinants of ever breastfeeding after adjusting for the confounding variables in Table 13.2. The result from the logistic regression analysis suggests that all the variables in the model were significantly associated with the odds for ever breastfeeding. Through the analysis, we find that the women who were educated up to primary level were less likely (24 per cent) to ever breastfeed their children as compared to women who have not received any education. If the sex of the child was female, then women were less likely (17 per cent) to be breastfed as compared to the male child. Women's age seems to be significant predictor of ever breast-feeding. Contrary to the percentage distribution result of bivariate analysis where higher percentage of women in low SLI ever breastfed their children, we find that women belonging to medium SLI (62 per cent) and high SLI (75 per cent) were more likely to ever breastfeed their children, as compared to women belonging to low SLI. Similar result is also found in case of religion and caste, where women belonging to religion other than Hindu were more likely to breastfeed, women belonging to SC/ST (49 per cent) and women belonging to OBC caste (43 per cent) were more likely to beastfeed their children. Women residing in urban areas were also more likely (64 per cent) to breastfeed their children than their counterparts.

Table 13.2

Odds Ratio Showing the Likelihood for Affecting Ever Breastfeeding according to Selected Demographic and Socio-Economic Covariates, Uttarakhand: 2005-06

Explanatory Variables	*Exp(B)*
Mother's Education	
Illiterate ®	1.00
Primary educated	0.763***
Secondary educated	0.995
Higher secondary educated	0.836
Mother's Age R^2	1.00***
Standard of Living Index	
Low ®	1.00
Medium	1.620***
High	1.753***
Religion	
Hindu®	1.00
Others	1.09***
Caste	
General®	1.00
SC/ST	1.493***
OBC	1.435***
Place of Residence	
Rural®	1.00
Urban	1.649***
Sex of the Child	
Male®	1.00
Female	0.836***

Note: P Values: *** $p < 0.01$; ** $p < 0.05$; * $p < 0.10$. ®-Reference category.

Cox Proportional Hazards Analysis

The Cox proportional hazards analysis shows the relative risk for discontinuation of breastfeeding (relative to the risk for the reference category) for children after adjusting for demographic and socio-economic covariates in Table 13.3. Most of the covariates show significant effect on the hazard of discontinuation of breastfeeding. It is observed from Table 13.3, that the hazard of discontinuation of breastfeeding was positively associated with women education as women with higher level of education were significantly more likely than less

Table 13.3

Cox Proportional Hazards Regression Model to Determine the Risk Factors for Discontinuation of Breastfeeding, Uttarakhand:2005-06

Explanatory Variables	*Exp(Beta)*
Education of the Mother	
Illiterate ®	1.00
Primary educated	0.853***
Secondary educated	1.036***
Higher secondary educated	0.987***
Age of the Mother (in completed years)	1.003***
Standard of Living Index	
Low ®	1.00
Medium	1.501***
High	1.584***
Religion	
Hindu ®	1.00
Others	1.218***
Caste	
General ®	1.00
SC/ST	1.376***
OBC	1.227***
Place of Residence	
Rural ®	1.00
Urban	1.58***
Sex of the Child	
Male ®	1.00
Female	0.912***

Note: P Values: *** $p < 0.01$; ** $p < 0.05$; * $p < 0.10$. ®-Reference category.

educated women to discontinue breastfeeding her child. For example, primary educated women were 15 per cent less likely to discontinue breastfeeding than only 2 per cent higher secondary educated women. Interestingly, contrary to general notion, we found that the hazard for discontinuation of breastfeeding was lower (9 per cent) for female children than her male counterparts.

The hazard of discontinuation of breastfeeding among children increases with the increase in the standard of living for both medium (50 per cent) and high standard (58 per cent) of living as compared to children belonging to low SLI. The hazard of discontinuation of breastfeeding is higher if the woman's education is up to secondary level. Children who belong to religion other than Hindu have higher (21 per cent) hazard of discontinuation of breastfeeding. The hazard for discontinuation of breastfeeding is also higher for children belonging to SC/ST (37 per cent) and OBC (22 per cent) caste groups. The hazard for discontinuation of breastfeeding for children residing in urban area is higher (58 per cent) than for children residing in rural area.

Summary and Conclusion

Breastfeeding is an important component for the betterment of the health of the child, improve the immunity and protect it from frequent occurrences of ailments such as diarrhoea, which in the long run may cause poor health condition and poor nutritional level, therefore breastfeeding is an important and cost-effective way of bringing in an improvement in the morbidity and mortality conditions of the children. In the state of Uttarakhand, 90 per cent children are ever breastfed but this percentage is low as compared to other states and also lower than the national average (94 per cent), therefore there is need to increase the lever of ever breastfeeding percentage. The percentage of immediate initiation of breastfeeding is around 30 per cent which needs to be considerably increased.

We find variation in ever breastfeeding, initiation of breastfeeding and prelacteal feeding across the selected demographic and socio-economic characteristics. Increase in the educational level does not show increase in the percentage of ever breastfeeding which may be a cause of concern and raise concerns over the effect of education on the maternal behaviour. It may also be attributed to improper or incomplete knowledge about breastfeeding. Binary logistic regression shows education of the women and sex of the children to be significant determinants of ever breastfeeding. However, SLI, caste groups, place of residence and religion also play an important role in determining ever breastfeeding.

Cox regression shows that the improvement in education and SLI increases the hazard of discontinuation of breastfeeding which may be because of the lack of proper understanding of the importance of breastfeeding. Therefore, it is important for the government to take proper measures to disseminate information regarding the importance of breastfeeding through mass media and public awareness. Although the analysis does not show consistent result which may not lead to a solid policy recommendations, it does give us further scope to do in-depth research to understand the associated cultural factors affecting the breastfeeding practices in the state of Uttarakhand.

References

Akin J., R. Bilsborrow, D. Guilkey, B. Popkin, D. Benoit, P. Cantrelle, M. Garenne and P. Levi (1981). "The determinants of breast-feeding in Sri Lanka", *Demography* 18(3):287-307.

Belavady, B. and C. Gopalan (1959). "Studies of lactation and dietary habit of Nilgiri Hill tribes", *Indian Journal of Medical Research* 47: 221.

Breastfeeding Promotion Network of India (BPNI), Maternity Benefit Act 1961. Accessed online at *http://www.bpni.org/maternity_protection_law.html*

Chhabra P., V.L. Grover, O.P. Aggarwal and K.K. Dubey (1998). "Breastfeeding patterns in an urban resettlement colony of Delhi", *Indian Journal of Pediatrics* 65:867-72.

Clemens J., R.A. Elyazeed, M. Rao, S. Savarino, B.Z. Morsy and Y. Kim (1999). "Early initiation of breastfeeding and risk of infant diarrhea in rural Egypt", *Pediatrics* 104: e3.

Cox, D.R. (1972). "Regression models and life-tables", *Journal of the Royal Statistical Society* 34(2): 187-220.

Cunningham A.S., D.B. Jelliffe and E.F. Jelliffe (1991). "Breast-feeding and health in the 1980s: A global epidemiologic review", *Journal of Pediatrics* 118(5):659-666.

Currò, V., R. Lanni, F. Scipione, V. Grimaldi and P. Mastroiacovo (1997). "Randomized controlled trial assessing the effectiveness of a booklet on the duration of breastfeeding", *Arch Dis Child* 76:500-3.

Department of Women and Child Development (2001). *National Policy for the Empowerment of Women*. India.

———. (2004). *National Guidelines on Infant and Young Child Feeding.* India.

Huffman, S.L. (1987). "Nutrition and fertility in Bangladesh: Breastfeeding and post partum amenorrhoea", *Population Studies* 41(3): 447-462.

Huttly, S.R., S.S. Morris, V. Pisani (1997). "Prevention of Diarrhoea in Young Children in Developing Countries", *Bulletin World Health Organization* 75(2):163-174.

IIPS and Macro International (2007). *National Family Health Survey (NFHS-3), India.* Mumbai: International Institute for Population Sciences.

International Institute for Population Sciences (IIPS) (1998-99). *National Family and Health Survey. India (NFHS-2).* Mumbai.

———. (2004). *Reproductive and Child Health District-Level Household Survey-2004.* Mumbai.

Khan, M.E. and J.K. Basu (1987). *Breastfeeding among working women in organized and unorganized sector*, Report submitted to ICMR, New Delhi. Baroda: ORG.

Khan, M.E. and S. Rao (1989). "Accessibility and utilization of family welfare services by couples below poverty line", Report submitted by ORG, Baroda to the Ministry of Health and Family Welfare, Government of India.

Khan, M.E. (1990). "Breastfeeding and weaning practices in India", *Asia-Pacific Population Journal* 5(1).

Kishor, S. and K. Gupta (2004). "Women's empowerment in India and its states evidence from the NFHS", *Economic and political weekly 694-712.*

Koosha, A., R. Hashemi Fesharaki and N. Mousavinasab (2008). "Breast-feeding patterns and factors determining exclusive breastfeeding", *Singapore Medical Journal* 49(12): 1002-1006.

Lawrence, R.A. (2002). "Peer support: Making a difference in breastfeeding duration", *Canadian Medical Association Journal* 166: 42-43.

Li, R., N. Darling, E. Maurice, L. Barker, L.M. Grummer-Strawn (2005). "Breastfeeding rates in the United States by characteristics of the child, mother, or family: The 2002 National Immunization Survey", *Pediatrics* 115: e31-7.

MacDonald, J. (1981). "A new methodological approach for the analysis of WFS current status breastfeeding data", *World Fertility Survey Technical Bulletin* 1732. Voorburg, Netherlands: International Statistical Institute.

Mudgal, S., V.J. Rajput, M. Chansoria and K.K. Kaul (1979). "Tribals of Madhya Pradesh-A 'knowledge, attitudes and practice' survey of infant feeding practices", *Indian Pediatrics* 16(7): 617-622, July.

Nicoll, A. and A. Williams (2002). "Breastfeeding", Arch Dis Child 87: 91-2.

Patel, A., N. Badhoniya and M. Dibley (2008). "Breastfeeding and infant feeding practices in India-A review of demographic and health surveys and national family health survey", *Solution Exchange for MCH Community Newsletter*, Breastfeeding Month Special.

Popkin, B.M., L. Adair, J.S. Akin, R. Black, J. Briscoe and W. Flieger (1990). "Breastfeeding and diorrheal morbidity", *Pediatrics* 86: 874-882.

Population Commission (2000). *National Population Policy 2000,* India. New Delhi. Accessed online at *http://populationcommission.nic.in/npp.htm*

Registrar General of India (2006). *Sample Registration System Bulletin 2006*. New Delhi.

Sivakami, M. (2003). "The impact of maternal work participation on duration of breastfeeding among poor women in South India", *Asia-Pacific Population Journal* 18(3).

World Health Organization (2000). *Bulletin of the world Health Organization*. Special Theme: Child mortality, 78(10).

———. (2003). *Global Strategy for Infant and Young Child Feeding*. Geneva: WHO.

———. (2001). *Global Strategy on Infant and Young Child Feeding*. Geneva: WHO.

Yngve A. and M. Sjöström (2001). "Breastfeeding in countries of the European Union and EFTA: Current and proposed recommendations, rationale, prevalence, duration and trends", *Public Health Nutrition* 4:631-45.

14 Social Health Insurance and Social Security in Uttarakhand

Avishek Hazra and Subrata Lahiri

Introduction

A question that remains of paramount importance in a majority of the world's countries is how their health financing systems can provide sufficient financial risk protection to all of the population against the costs of health care. A crucial concept in health financing policy towards universal coverage is that of society risk pooling whereby all individuals and households share the financing of total health care costs. The larger the degree of risk pooling in a health financing system, the less people will have to bear the financial consequences of their own health risks, and the more they are likely to have access to the care they need.

While nations declare similar admirable goals to provide their citizens with equal access to a reasonable quality of health care and to prevent health-caused impoverishment, the reality is starkly different. This is clear from the fact that over 80 per cent of the total health financing is private financing, much of which is out-of-pocket payments (i.e., user charges) and not any prepayment schemes. Public spending in health care is very low at 17 per cent and our national health policy NHP (2002) has recognised this.

Carrin and James (2004) in their paper noted that for achieving universal coverage, there are essentially two main options. One is a health financing system whereby general tax revenue is the main source of financing health services. These health services are usually provided by a network of public and contracted private providers, often referred to as a national health service. Secondly, there is social health insurance (SHI). Workers, self-employed, enterprises and government pay contributions into a social health insurance fund. The base for workers' and enterprises' contributions is usually the worker's salary. SHI either owns its own provider networks, works with accredited public and private health care providers, or uses a combination of both.

Financing through health insurance is realised in India in most of the health and population policies developed in the recent past. On health insurance, the policy directions provided by NHP 1983 stated—"Besides mobilizing the community resources, through its active participation in the implementation and management of national health-related programmes, it would be necessary to devise well-considered health insurance schemes for health promotion and also ensuring that the community shares the cost of the services, in keeping with its paying capacity". In this context, NHP 1983's reliance was not on private health insurance with its public health goals; rather, its emphasis was openly on community mobilisation, sharing and participation (for cost sharing), according to ability to pay (Sharma, 2002).

Understanding social gradients responsible for poor health as well as improved health is very important. Researchers opine that wealth alone does not determine the health of a nation's population. Some low-income countries, Costa Rica, China, Sri Lanka, Cuba and the state of Kerala in India have achieved good and equitable health in spite of relatively low levels of national wealth (Marmot, 2008). While talking on strategic thinking to improve public health and life chances, Prof. Sir Michael Marmot (Chair of the World Health Organisation's Commission on Social Determinants of Health) exemplifies the Indian government for providing work guarantees as a way to lift people above the national poverty line, since poverty and hunger are closely linked. He also recommends setting up robust social protection systems in all poor countries so that people in low-wage settings are able to afford and access health care.

Uttarakhand: Geography and Demography

The state of Uttarakhand was created by combining the hilly districts of Uttar Pradesh on 09.11.2000. These districts are Uttarkashi,

Chamoli, Rudraprayag, Pauri, Tehri, Dehradun, Pithoragarh, Champawat, Nainital, Almora, Bageshwar, Haridwar and Udham Singh Nagar. The districts have been grouped into two distinct divisions—Garhwal division and the Kumaon division on the basis of homogeneity, contiguity and socio-cultural affinity. The state is surrounded by Himachal Pradesh in the west, Uttar Pradesh in the south, Nepal in the east and China in the north. It has a population of 8.5 million, 20th rank in terms of population size. About 78 per cent of the population of the state lives in rural areas. Total area 53,483 sq.km, 18th in terms of area. The population density per km is 159 which is less than 1/4th of population density of Uttar Pradesh (689). The state is 11th most sparsely populated state in the country. About 36 per cent of the state's population is younger than 15 years and only 5 per cent is aged 65 or above. The literacy rate—age 7 and above is 84 per cent for males, 60 per cent for females and 72 per cent for the total population. The poor road connectivity, difficult hilly terrain (93 per cent of area in hills), small scattered settlements, lack of infrastructure and human power contribute to problems of access to health service delivery. Given the poor paying capacity and scattered location of settlements in hilly districts, the population is almost entirely dependent on the public health delivery system while the presence of the private sector tends to be concentrated in the plains.

Objectives and Data

The present paper focuses on the risk-pooling mechanisms and particularly the social health insurance in India in general and Uttarakhand in particular. Supporting by existing literature, in its first part the paper emphasises about the importance of social health insurance as a healthy option for health care financing and in the second part, it talks about a particular social health insurance scheme—Employees State Insurance Scheme (ESIS). Along with various reports and documents, NFHS-3 data (2005-06) has been used to substantiate the paper. For the first time in NFHS-3, information on health care prepayments or health insurance of household members have been collected from the head of the household and is given in the household data file. And that provides a chance to have an idea about the state-wise health insurance coverage.

Social Health Insurance: Concept and Importance

Mossialos and Thomson (2002) define social health insurance (SHI) in the following way: "SHI contributions are not related to risk, are levied on earned income and collected by a body at arm's length from government-otherwise it amounts to an earmarked payroll tax. Contributions are usually compulsory and shared between the employee and employer". Gupta and Trivedi (2004) in their article mentioned that literature of SHI have admitted that social health insurance has no uniformly valid definition, but two characteristics are crucial (Normand and Busse, 2002). Firstly, insured people pay a regular, usually wage-based contribution and secondly, independent quasi-public bodies act as the major managing bodies of the system and as payers for health care.

A mainstay of SHI is the separation of financing of care from provision and the creation of an independent body responsible for the management of the fund (Mossialos and Thomson, 2002). An anticipated benefit is the "independence of the insurer from the government and the increased responsiveness to the patient or consumer" (Mossialos and Thomson, 2002). In the recent years, the interest in implementing SHI—especially in developing countries—has helped crystallise some of the conceptual problems as well (Gupta and Trivedi, 2004). SHI in comparison with private insurance tends to create a much larger risk pool and contributions are not risk-related. Under SHI, membership is also compulsory, which reduces the likelihood of adverse selection, whereby insurance is favoured and bought by those anticipating needing health care (e.g., elderly, chronically ill).

Social health insurance meant for social security is one of the principal methods of health financing. Twenty-seven countries have established the principle of universal coverage via this method. Several low and middle-income countries are currently interested in extending their existing health insurance for specific groups to eventually cover their entire populations. For those countries interested in such an extension, it is important to understand what characterises a well performing SHI scheme and how long the transition from incomplete to universal coverage could be expected to take. In India, the current methods of financing the health care, the underfunded government health services and the fee for private health services, are clearly unsatisfactory.

With regard to SHI, a number of conditions need to be satisfied and key questions need to be answered before a country can embark on its extension or establishment. These questions relate firstly, to the labour market. If the self-employed and informal sector workers dominate the labour market, how feasible is it to register and collect contributions from them? Furthermore, if payroll contributions are scheduled to occupy a major share of total SHI contributions, will they increase labour costs to such an extent that they will have a negative impact on employment? Secondly, is sufficiently skilled administrative staff present so as to build up and run the SHI institutions? Thirdly, will there be a legal framework that determines, among others, the objectives of the country's SHI scheme, the rights and duties of insured members, the roles and functions of the organisation(s) that are operating SHI? Fourthly, is a health care infrastructure in place that will be able to provide the health services that are part of the SHI benefit package?

Gupta and Trivedi (2004) rightly mentioned that in India, the concept of SHI is still imperfectly understood, and often all the existing health schemes are discussed in the context of SHI (WHO, 2003a; b). There have been very few attempts within the country to have policy discussions around the overall health insurance scenario, and where and how different types of insurance fit in the overall scheme of things. Most of the discussions have merely been descriptive in nature, and have not gone beyond the rhetoric that greater health insurance is needed.

It has been mentioned earlier that social health insurance is meant for social security of the population. Now what is social security and why do we need it? Social security protects not just the subscriber but also his/her entire family by giving benefit packages in financial security and health care. Social security schemes are designed to guarantee at least long-term sustenance to families when the earning member retires, dies or suffers a disability. Thus, the main strength of the social security system is that it acts as a facilitator—it helps people to plan their own future through insurance and assistance.

In the Indian context, social security is a comprehensive approach designed to prevent deprivation, assure the individual of a basic minimum income for himself and his dependents and to protect the individual from any uncertainties. The state bears the primary responsibility for developing appropriate system for providing protection and assistance to its workforce. Social security is increasingly viewed as an integral part of the development process. It helps to create a more positive attitude to the challenge of globalisation and the consequent structural and technological changes.

In the post-Independence period, provision of social security to the working population has been one of the thrust areas of government. Prior to Independence, there was only one enactment in the area of social security namely the Workmen's Compensation Act, 1923. After Independence, several schemes for the benefits of working population have been launchcd. Employees State Insurance Act, 1948 is one important among the many.

Employees State Insurance Scheme (ESIS) and Central Government Health Scheme (CGHS) are the social health insurance schemes functioning in India. ESIS is one of the major flagships of the health insurance scheme directly run by the government. ESIS of India is an integrated social security scheme aimed to provide social protection to workers and their dependents only in the organised sector. The scheme was introduced right after Independence. Employees covered under the scheme are entitled to medical facilities in sickness, maternity and death or disablement due to an employment injury or occupational hazard. The scheme is mainly financed by contributions raised from employees covered under the scheme and their employers, as a fixed percentage of wages. Those who earn not more than Rs. 7500 per month would come under the purview of ESI scheme. The employees earning not more than Rs. 40 a day as wages are exempted from payment of their part of contribution. The state government bears certain percentage of expenditure on medical benefit per annum within per capita ceiling and other additional expenditure beyond the ceiling. Though the ESI Act was in action since 1948, in recent years we observe some changes. Such alterations are made mainly to suit the newly emerging needs for employees, not only in organised sector but the scheme is now targeted to cover employees in unorganised sectors as well.

Social Health Insurance in Uttarakhand

In this section, we talk about a particular social health insurance scheme, *viz.*, Employees State Insurance Scheme (ESIS). Having stated that ESIS aims to provide social protection to workers and their dependents only in the organised sector, it is worth mentioning that the workforce participation rate in Uttarakhand is 36.93, slightly lower than that of national level value of 39.26 and the organised sector employees hold a share of 3.2 per cent of the total population in this state. The per cent share of organised sector employees to the total workers in the state is 8.7 per cent. As per the available estimate, in the year 2005, there were 749012 employments in 328595 enterprises existing in the state of Uttarakhand.

A brief statistics about the ESIS is given in Table 14.1. ESIS were functioning in 22 states in the year 1999 and in the year 2005, the scheme was running in 25 states. As per the latest available estimate, the total number of ESI beneficiaries in the year 2005 was 32973200. With the help of 6960 insurance medical officers (IMOs) and 2135 insurance medical practitioners (IMPs), medical services are provided to the beneficiaries through 144 ESI service hospitals and 1427 ESI service dispensaries. Among a total of 8400526 ESIS employees in India, 27089 are in Uttarakhand (Table 14.2). 29044 insured persons (IPs) and 36126 families are provided medical services in ESI hospitals and dispensaries in Uttarakhand (Table 14.3).

The growth rate of enterprises (excluding crop production and plantation) is 6.21 (4.8 at the national level). It has been found that per cent share of capital expenditure towards social security and welfare to total expenditure has decreased, and the revenue expenditure has increased over time.

Quite interestingly, findings in the NFHS-3 data reveal that the percentage of household having at least a member covered by any health

Table 14.1

Employees State Insurance Scheme (ESIS) at a Glance in India

	1999	*2005*
States/UTs covered	22	25
No. of centres	642	718
No. of employees	8085200	7570200
No. of insured persons/family units	8819050	8498250
Total beneficiaries	34217900	32973200
ESI hospitals	130	144
ESI dispensaries	1452	1427
Insurance medical officers	6234	6960
Insurance medical practitioners	2722	2135

Source: Rajya Sabha Unstarred Question No.836 dated 29.11.2006 (obtained from *www.indiastat.com*)

Table 14.2

Number of ESIS Employees in EAG States in India

State	*2002*	*2006*
Bihar	29850	36714
Chhattisgarh	29250	38575
Jharkhand	56500	92492
Madhya Pradesh	237100	190985
Orissa	114300	120333
Rajasthan	248850	319677
Uttarakhand	17900	27089
Uttar Pradesh	429650	516685
India	7159350	8400526

Source: Rajya Sabha Unstarred Question No.836 dated 29.11.2006 (obtained from *www.indiastat.com*)

insurance or health scheme in the state of Uttarakhand is higher (6.8 per cent) compared to the national level (4.9 per cent). Although there is not much difference in the state level and national level values in the percentage of households with at least a member having ESIS, in Uttarakhand, a higher percentage of households (2.5 per cent) is informed to have at least a member having Central Government Health Scheme (CGHS) compared to the national level (1.0 per cent). Another remarkable finding that may be highlighted is that among the EAG

Table 14.3

State-wise Number of Workers and Families Provided Medical Services in ESI Hospitals and Dispensaries in India: 2004-05

States	*2004-05*	
	IPs	*Families*
Bihar	48584	42332
Madhya Pradesh	710759	921615
Orissa	427744	516872
Rajasthan	993120	1311232
Uttar Pradesh	597136	739245
Chhattisgarh	119126	144576
Jharkhand	92533	96558
Uttarakhand	29044	36126

Source: Lok Sabha Starred Question No.131, dated 27.02.2006 (obtained from *www.indiastat.com*)

states, Uttarakhand ranks first in terms of health insurance coverage as a whole and also in terms of coverage of social health insurance.

Conclusion

The health insurance coverage in general and social health insurance in particular in Uttarakhand is better than other states and also than the national level figures. In the 11th five year plan (2007-2012), the objective of Directorate of Medical Health & Family Welfare of Uttarakhand is "Health for All". This cannot be achieved unless and until the poorer strata of the population get equal access to utilise health care facilities as the wealthier section receive. The inequity in terms of health care utilisation can be narrowed through bringing the poor under some shade of financial protection, i.e., through some risk-pooling mechanism like health insurance and more particularly social health insurance.

In the recent times, the Government of India has expanded the social security for the workers in the unorganised sector, who constitute 93 per cent of our workforce. In Uttarakhand also, the per cent share of unorganised sector workers is quite high (91 per cent). In the wake of wide ranging social inequalities, regional disparities, unemployment and poverty, nations throughout the world presently are striving to rebuild

Figure 14.1

Per cent of Capital Expenditure Towards Social Security and Welfare to Total Expenditure in Uttarakhand: 2001-2007

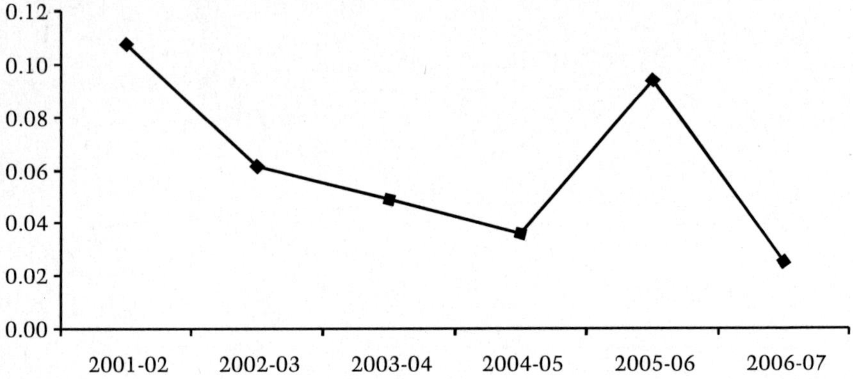

Figure 14.2

Health Insurance Coverage in Uttarakhand and India: 2005-06

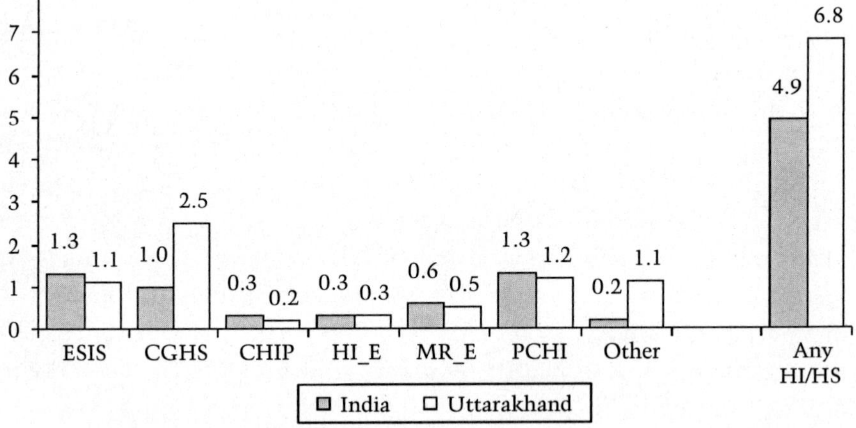

Note: ESIS: Employees State Insurance Scheme; CGHS: Central Government Health Scheme; CHIP: Commercial Health Insurance Programme; HI_E: Health insurance provided by employer; MR_E: Medical reimbursement through employer; PCHI: Privately purchased commercial health insurance.

Figure 14.3

Social Health Insurance Coverage in EAG States: 2005-06

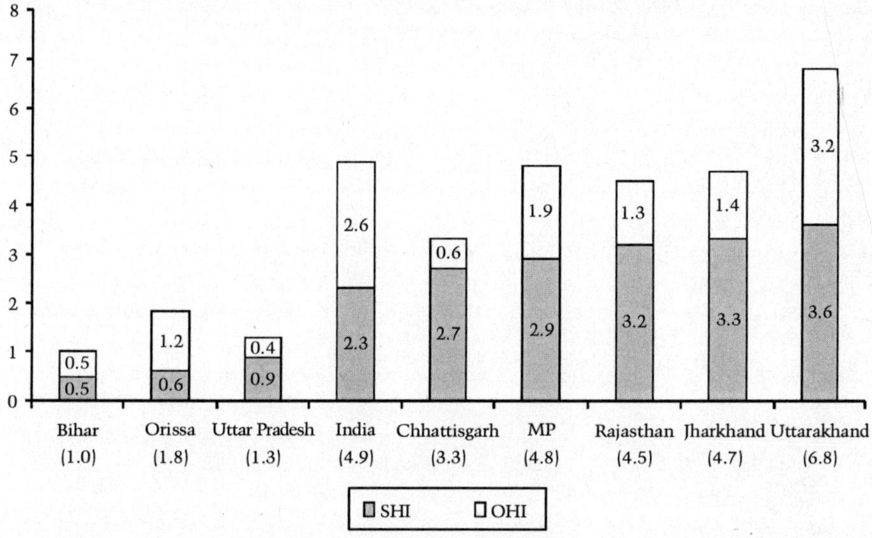

Note: SHI: Social Health Insurance; OHI: Other Health Insurance.

their socio-economic order from below. If the aspirations of the people are to be fulfilled, the vision must evolve from the grassroots level. Bhatt (2002) in an article stated that the need of the hour in the state is to ensure actual sharing of power with the people, seeking their fullest participation and fulfilling their hopes and felt needs. However, it should be categorically mentioned that introducing or implementing social health insurance may not serve the purpose it is meant for. Responsiveness of the system and people's awareness towards benefits of health insurance is equally important for better functioning of such schemes.

References

Bhatt, K.N. (2002). "Decentralized development in Uttarakhand", *PUCL Bulletin.*

Carrin, Guy and Chris James (2004). "Reaching universal coverage via social health insurance: Key design features in the transition period", *Health Financing Policy Issue Paper.* Geneva: World Health Organization.

Deshpande, N. (2004). "Out of pocket expenditure for availing primary health care in Uttaranchal", Unpublished paper.

Government of Uttarakhand (2005). "Uttarakhand Health and Population Policy 2005", Department of Medical Health and Family Welfare, Government of Uttarakhand.

Gupta, I. and M. Trivedi (2004). "Social health insurance redefined: Health for all through coverage for all", *IEG Working Paper.* New Delhi: Institute for Economic Growth.

Marmot, M. (2008). "Reduce social inequity to avoid ill health", An interaction with Sir Michael Marmot on strategic thinking to improve public health and life chances, New Delhi: Public Health Foundation of India (PHFI).

Mossialos, E. and S. Thomson (2002). "Voluntary health insurance in the European Union: A critical assessment", *International journal of health service* 32(1): 19-88.

Normand, Charles and Reinhard Busse (2002). "Social health insurance financing", in E. Mossialos, A. Dixon, J. Figueras and J. Kutzin (eds.), *Funding Health Care: Options for Europe*. Buckingham, PA: Open University Press. pp.59-79.

Sharma, B.B.L. (2002). "Health financing in India: Some issues", Workshop Proceedings on *Health Policy Issues and Health Programmes in Uttaranchal* held at Mussoorie during 9-10 May.

WHO (2003a). *Social Health Insurance*. Report of a regional expert group meeting held during 13-15 March at New Delhi, WHO Regional Office for South East Asia.

———. (2003b). *Social Health Insurance*. Report of a regional consultation held during 7-9 July 2003 at Bangkok, Thailand, WHO Regional Office for South East Asia.

D. Gender Issues

15

Indicators of Women's Empowerment and their Determinants among Currently Married Women of Uttarakhand

An Analysis of NFHS-3 Data

N. Audinarayana

Introduction

The role of the status of women or women's autonomy in the process of social and economic change has assumed importance at the international level after the first major United Nations Conference on Women held in 1975. Demographers are now specifically interested in the study of the status of women, because it is one of the most important factors in the process of demographic transition. Several empirical studies confirmed that improvement in various dimensions of the status of women reduces fertility, maternal mortality, infant and child mortality, and promotes rapid implementation of family planning programmes (for a critical review one can see Dyson and Moore, 1983; Mason, 1985; Mahadevan *et al.*, 1989; Basu, 1992). In patriarchal societies like India, the status and empowerment of women within the society in general and within their households in particular plays an important role in promoting change in reproductive attitudes and behaviour. In view of this, enhancement of women's status has emerged as an important policy objective in the development plans of many less developed countries and proposed/taken solid efforts to improve the women's position at society level through various factors that are closely associated with it.

Measuring women's empowerment at household/family level is not an easy task because of its multi-dimensionality and complex nature. The concept itself has changed over a period of time such as the 'status of women', 'women's position', 'women's autonomy', 'women's empowerment', 'gender stratification', 'gender systems', 'gender equity', etc. Even today we are not fully aware of many of the dimensions of the concept of women's empowerment, the order of importance of such dimensions and their influence on major demographic processes. Further, the factors that affect women's empowerment also vary widely and may differ across different settings as well as over time (Mason, 1995; Jejeebhoy, 2000; Agarwala and Lynch, 2006; Barrett, 2007). In view of the importance given to women's empowerment, in Indian context, attempts have been made to collect first-hand information from women through the National Family Health Surveys (1998-99 and 2005-06) so as to measure certain indicators of women's empowerment. Making use of such data for Uttarakhand during the NFHS, 2005-06, in this paper, an attempt is made to understand the degree of women's empowerment focusing on three dimensions *viz.*, women's decision-making power at household level, access to financial resources and freedom of movement. Attempt is also being made to examine the principal determinants of these three indicators of women with the help of a multivariate technique.

Theoretical Propositions and Past Research

Researchers in the past widely used women's educational level and their participation in income generating activities as the best proxies for measuring the status of women at macro level; however, in the recent past these have been widely recognised as the best characteristics that would enhance the women's autonomy in decision-making at the family level, access to economic resources and freedom of movement. This is because educated women may be exposed to more egalitarian views on gender and her education may lead family members to have a greater respect for her opinions, which in turn enhance their empowerment at family/society level. In addition to these, it is likely that marital households with moderate and higher wealth status may provide an opportunity to women to inculcate more modern ideas about gender equality and thereby, empowered better than those women belonging to households of 'poorest' wealth index. Of course, to a certain extent this may depend upon the setting where they live. Women residing in urban areas have favourable attitudes towards gender equality, in addition to having comparatively higher education and more participation in income generating activities. These in turn are likely to enhance their chances to participate in decision-making at household level, have access to monetary resources and freedom of movement from their households to community and society at large.

Women's empowerment to a certain extent varies according to the religious values to which they adhere. In general, in India, it is widely argued that Muslim women suffer with lower status, whereas Christian women enjoy slightly better status than Hindu women. This may be mainly because of the fact that Christians are better educated and modernised in their attitudes and way of living than the Hindus, followed by the Muslims. Likewise, among Hindus, women from scheduled castes/tribes are likely to experience lower empowerment than those from other backward castes and others (upper castes). This is mainly because of the reason that every caste has been ascribed a status according to the social status of the occupation of its members (including women). In general, higher caste people will have more education and higher occupational/economic status and thereby, higher status of women too, as compared to lower castes, especially the scheduled castes/tribes. Exposure to mass media also enhances women's empowerment since such an exposure largely disseminates less traditional views of women's role in the household, encouraging greater women's decision-making power and freedom of movement outside home. Women's age and duration of marital life too tend to boost up their status at household level because of their increasing role in marital household and control over spouse and other family members. Likewise, producing more number of children also would promote their autonomy at family level. Earlier research carried out in India as well as in selected less developed countries supported these propositions mostly in the expected direction (Jejeebhoy, 1991; 2000; Basu, 1992; Thenmozhi, 1992; Mason, 1995; Jejeebhoy and Sathar, 2001; Rahman and Rao, 2004; Agarwala and Lynch, 2006; Audinarayana and Thenmozhi, 2006; Barrett, 2007).

Data and Methods

Data for the present paper was drawn from the National Family Health Survey–3, 2005-06 (NFHS-3) conducted during April-June 2006 in Uttarakhand state. In all, 2953 ever married women (15-49 years) were interviewed for the survey purpose from 2659 households and the response rate was 91.2 per cent (for more details see IIPS and Macro International, 2007). However, study of this type (on women's empowerment) would be appropriate for those of currently married women and moreover, the relevant data would also be mostly available for such women only. In addition to this, data for some background characteristics of women was either 'missing', 'do not know' or 'not reported'. In view of these problems, comparable data for women only was included in the logistic regression analyses (see Table 15.3), whereas in the case of women's empowerment indicators all women for whom such data is available was made use of (see Table 15.2).

Dependent Variables: For the purpose of analysis, from the data available for the various items, three following indicators of women's empowerment have been calculated and considered here as dependent variables.

Women's decision-making power: This variable is computed based on the data of women's participation in decision-making of four household tasks (see Table 15.2). If women participating in decision-making exclusively by 'themselves' or 'jointly with their husband' in all the four household tasks are categorised into one group and scored as '1' and if not assigned a score of '0'.

Women's access to resources: This variable is computed based on the information whether women have a bank or savings account or not, and whether they have money for their own use or not. From this information, all those women who have either a bank or savings account, or has money for own use have been grouped into one category and assigned a score of '1' and if not given a score of '0'.

Women's freedom of movement: This variable is computed based on the information whether women are allowed to go to three specified places on their own or not. From this information, all those women who are allowed to go to all the three places under consideration are grouped into one category and assigned a score of '1' and if not a score of '0'.

Explanatory Variables: All those background variables of women which are likely to affect (based on the theoretical background and past research) one or the other indicators of women's empowerment and data available for the same in the NFHS-3 have been considered for this study. For an overall understanding of these variables, the frequencies have been computed and presented in Table 15.1. Most of these variables are self-explanatory, except two—women's exposure to mass media (index) and household wealth index of the households.

Women's exposure to mass media (Index): This variable is computed based on the information available for three mass media channels—frequency of reading newspaper or magazines, frequency of listening to radio and frequency of watching television. The scores assigned to the responses for each of the mass media channels are as follows: not at all – 0, less than once a week – 1, at least once a week – 2 and almost every day – 3. Pooling these scores for each woman, the total number of women have been categorised into four groups *viz.*, not exposed to any of the three mass media channels (score 0), exposed to mass media channel at a 'lower' extent (scores 1-3), 'moderate' extent (scores 4-5) and 'higher' extent (scores 6-9).

Household wealth index: In NFHS-3, wealth index of household has been computed based on 33 household assets and housing characteristics. For this purpose, each household asset is assigned a weight (factor score) generated through principal component analysis, and the resulting asset scores are standardised in relation to a normal distribution with a mean of zero and standard deviation of one. Each household is then assigned a score for each asset, and the scores were summed for each household; individuals are ranked according to the score of the household in which they reside. The sample is then divided into quintiles i.e., five groups with an equal number of individuals (20 per cent) in each at national level. However, at state level the quintiles may not be equal in size (for more details see IIPS and Macro International, 2007).

Table 15.1

Characteristics that Affect Indicators of Women's Empowerment in Uttarakhand

Characteristics	*Percentage*	*Frequency*
Place of Residence		
Rural	72.3	2135
Urban	27.7	818
Women's Present Age (in years)		
15–24	38.6	1141
25–34	31.0	916
35–49	30.3	896
Religion		
Hindus	85.8	2534
Muslims	8.0	236
Christians	6.2	183
Caste Background		
Scheduled castes/tribes	24.8	731
Other backward castes	16.2	477
Others	59.0	1744
Women's Educational Status		
Illiterate	32.6	962
Primary school (1-4 classes)	32.2	952
Middle school + (5+classes)	35.2	1039
Women's Work Status		
Not working	55.3	1633
Working, but not paid	27.2	818
Working for cash/kind	17.0	502
Women's Exposure to Mass Media (Index)		
No exposure at all (score 0)	19.1	558
Lower (scores 1–3)	36.0	1058
Moderate (scores 4–5)	24.4	717
Higher (scores 6–9)	20.6	608
Duration of Marriage (in years)		
0–9	35.7	1052
10–19	34.6	1021
20 +	29.8	880
No. of Living Children		
0–1	33.2	981
2–3	29.9	884
4 +	36.8	1058
Household Structure		
Non-nuclear	48.9	1397
Nuclear	51.5	1460
Household Wealth Index		
Poorest	4.9	164
Poorer	14.5	428
Middle	20.3	598
Richer	23.8	712
Richest	36.6	1081
Total	100.0	2953

Note: Frequency for certain characteristics would not add up to 2953, because of missing data for some respondents.

Logistic Regression Analysis

In order to find out the principal determinants of the three indicators of women's empowerment, logistic regression analysis is carried out here since all the three dependent variables are dichotomous as discussed earlier. All the background variables of women are used as explanatory variables and are categorised in nature. In this analysis, the net effects of each of the categories of the independent variables on the dependent variables are computed based on odds ratios and corresponding p-values in comparison with a reference category (of the independent variable), controlling for all other independent variables used in the model (Kendall, 1975).

Results and Discussion

Indicators of Women's Empowerment in Uttarakhand

Data provided in panel 1 of Table 15.2 show that about 56-60 per cent of the currently married women have participated in making decisions either by themselves or by jointly with their husband about their own health care, household purchases for daily needs and visiting to family or relatives, whereas just about 50 per cent of them are able to participate in making decisions in the case of large household purchases. The overall decision-making power of the women (making decisions in all the four issues under consideration) works out as 36 per cent only. When women were enquired about their access to resources (panel 2), about 36 per cent reported that they have money for own use, whereas just about one-fifth have a bank or savings account. The per cent of women who have access to either of these resources comes to about 43 per cent. In the case of women's freedom of movement (panel 3), as high as 60 per cent of women reported that they are usually allowed to go alone to market followed by allowed to go alone to health facility, whereas about 45 per cent of women said that they are mostly allowed to go on their own to places outside the village/community where they normally reside. The per cent of women who are allowed to go to all these three specified places with full freedom comes to about 43 per cent. All these figures, by and large, show that a reasonably moderate proportion of women are empowered in terms of decision-making power, level of access to economic resources and freedom of movement to selected places in the society.

Table 15.2

Indicators of Women's Empowerment in Uttarakhand

Indicators of Women's Empowerment	*Percentage*	*Frequency*
Women's Participation in Decision-Making		N = 2076
Own health care	60.6	1258
Making large household purchases	49.5	1027
Making household purchases for daily needs	56.5	1173
Visit to family or relatives	56.1	1165
Decision-making in all four issues	36.0	747
Women's Access to Resources		N = 2935
Have bank or savings account	20.2	593
Has money for own use	36.1	1059
Access to either of the resources	43.2	1268
Women's Freedom of Movement		N = 2949
Allowed to go to market	60.0	1770
Allowed to go to health facility	56.4	1663
Allowed to go to places outside the village/community	44.7	1318
Freedom of movement to all three specified places	42.8	1262

Determinants of Women's Decision-Making Power in Household Matters

Results provided in column 2 of Table 15.3 show that controlling for other variables under consideration, women residing in urban areas, belonging to Christianity, completed middle school education and above, and from nuclear households have greater likelihood of decision-making power at household level ($p<0.001$ or $p<0.01$ in all cases) compared to their counterparts. Likewise, the odds of household decision-making power are 1.69 and 1.40 times higher for women little older in age (35-49 and 25-34 years, respectively; $p<0.05$ and $p<0.10$, respectively), 1.56 times higher for those exposed to mass media channels at a higher level ($p<0.05$) and 1.55 times higher for those in whose case duration of marriage is 20 years or longer ($p<0.05$) as against their counterparts from younger age group, not exposed to any mass media or exposed to a lesser extent and who have completed lesser marital durations. It is

Table 15.3

Results of Logistic Regression Analyses on Indicators of Women's Empowerment in Uttarakhand

Explanatory Variables	*Decision-Making Odds Ratio & Level of Sig.*	*Access to Resources Odds Ratio & Level of Sig.*	*Freedom of Movement Odds Ratio & Level of Sig.*
Col. 1	Col. 2	Col. 3	Col. 4
Place of Residence (Ref: Rural)	1.000	1.000	1.000
Urban	1.754***	1.277+	1.158
Women's Age (Ref: 15-24)	1.000	1.000	1.000
25–34	1.402+	1.190	1.559**
35–49	1.689*	1.745*	2.088***
Religion (Ref: Hindus)	1.000	1.000	1.000
Muslims	0.841	0.680+	0.759
Christians	1.689**	1.335	1.651**
Caste Background (Ref: SC/STs)	1.000	1.000	1.000
OBCs	1.036	0.722*	0.925
Others	1.097	1.329*	1.047
Women's Education (Ref: Illiterates)	1.000	1.000	1.000
Primary school	1.046	1.203	1.421**
Middle school +	1.469**	1.594***	1.542***
Women's Work Status (Ref: NW)	1.000	1.000	1.000
Working, but not paid	1.631***	1.567***	1.860***
Working for cash/kind	1.196	2.912***	2.050***
Women's Exp. to MM (Ref: No)	1.000	1.000	1.000
Low	1.030	1.553+	0.899
Fair	0.941	2.352***	1.359
Good	1.563*	1.267	1.598**
Duration of Marriage (Ref: 0-9 years)	1.000	1.000	1.000
10–19 years	1.277	1.177	1.191
20 + years	1.555*	0.847	1.469+
No. of Living Children (Ref: 0-1)	1.000	1.000	1.000
2–3	1.659*	0.962	0.619*
4 +	1.517+	1.242	0.623*
Household Structure (Ref: Non-Nuclear)	1.000	1.000	1.000
Nuclear	1.951***	1.113	1.174
Household Wealth Index (Ref: Poorest)	1.000	1.000	1.000
Poorer	0.646+	1.151	1.550*
Middle	0.792	1.372*	1.666***
Richer	0.796	2.055***	2.370***
Richest	0.876	2.871***	2.622***
-2 Log likelihood	2388.713	2445.979	2545.745
Chi-square	219.168	399.320	344.867
(d.f.) Level of sig.	(23) 0.000	(23) 0.000	(23) 0.000
Number of cases	1991	2076	2086

Note: + = $p<0.10$, * = $p<0.05$, ** = $p<0.01$, and *** = $p<0.001$.

striking to note that the likelihood of women's power in making household decisions is conspicuously higher among those who are working, but not paid as against to those who are not working in the past 12 months preceding the survey ($p<0.001$), whereas such positive net effect is also noticed in the case of women working for cash/kind, but statistically insignificant. Another interesting point noted here is that the odds of women's decision-making power are observed as significantly higher (1.66 and 1.52 times; $p<0.05$ and $p<0.10$, respectively) among those who have 2-3 children and 4 or more children than those who do not have a child or have only one child. Surprisingly, women's household wealth index, on the whole, exhibited net negative effect on women's decision-making power and even turned out as significant to a lesser extent ($p<0.10$) in the case of those belonging to households classified as 'poorer' as against to those who belonging to the households' wealth index is the 'poorest'. Women from OBCs and other caste groups, by and large, have exhibited better decision-making power as against to those from SC/ST communities, but statistically the magnitude of effects turned out as insignificant.

Determinants of Women's Access to Resources

From Table 15.3 (column 3), it is noted that, controlling for other variables under consideration, women who have education up to middle school level and above, working for cash/kind as well as working, but not paid, exposed to mass media at a fair extent and belonging to households that are categorised as 'middle', 'richer' and 'richest' in terms of wealth index have shown higher odds of access to economic resources ($p<0.001$ in all cases except 'middle' wealth index for which $p<0.05$ level) than their counterparts. Women from older age group (35-49 years), and from communities other than SC/STs have exhibited better access to financial resources than those from younger age group (15-24 years) and SC/ST communities ($p<0.05$ in both the cases). It is obvious to note that women living in urban areas have shown fair access to monetary resources than their rural counterparts, but statistically to a lesser significant level ($p<0.10$). Another conspicuous point noted here is that the odds of women's access to resources is comparatively much lower among the Muslims ($p<0.10$) as against the Hindus. Other variables included in the model *viz.*, marital duration, number of living children and household structure did not exhibit neither consistent nor significant net effects on women's access to financial resources.

Determinants of Women's Freedom of Movement

Data given in column 4 of Table 15.3 show that, controlling for other variables under consideration, women from higher reproductive age groups (25-34 and 35-49 years), belonging to Christianity, completed primary as well as middle school education and above, working for the last 12 months (both for cash/kind and not paid), whose level of exposure to mass media is higher and belonging to households that are better in terms of wealth index reported to have greater likelihood of freedom of movement ($p<0.001$ or $p<0.01$ in all cases except in the case of households of 'poorer' wealth index in which case the $p<0.05$ level is at moderate) compared to their counterparts. On the other hand, it is striking to note that women who have 2-3 and 4 or more children have exhibited lesser chances of freedom of movement ($p<0.05$ in both the cases) than those who do not have a single child or have only one child. Women who spent longer marital duration (20 years or more) have shown comparatively higher likelihood of freedom of movement than those who have spent fewer years of marital life. Urban residence, caste background other than OBCs and SC/ST and nuclear household structure though exerted positive net effects on women's freedom of movement, statistically they did not turn out as significant.

Conclusions and Implications

On the whole, in Uttarakhand state, women seem to be empowered much below average level in terms of three indicators *viz.*, participation in decision-making at household level, access to financial resources and freedom of movement from home to community/society. With a few exceptions, women who are better educated, working (paid in cash/kind and not paid), and older in age have shown higher decision-making power, access to resources and freedom of movement. Women belonging to the households that are said to be 'middle', 'rich' and 'richest' in wealth index have exhibited greater access to financial resources and freedom of movement, but appear to be less at decision-making power at household level (though results did not turn out significant). On the other hand, women living in nuclear family set-up and urban areas have shown greater propensity in making decisions at household level. Women's exposure to mass media to a fair and good extent turned up as a significant predictor in the case of one or the other indicators of women in positive direction. Higher number of living children, on the one side, seems to enhance women's decision-making power; on the other side, it curtails their freedom of movement to a moderate extent. As expected, compared to Hindu women, Christian women have exhibited higher empowerment (significant with decision-making power and freedom of movement), whereas Muslim women have exhibited lower empowerment (mild significant only with access to resources). However, caste *per se* did not show consistent net effect on the three indicators of women's empowerment.

Based on these findings, the following policy implications are suggested.

1. Schemes related to girls' education should be implemented throughout the country without loss of time. Topics related to involving the females in decision-making, freedom of movement and various aspects gender equality and related issues have to be incorporated into their curriculum, which will enable them to understand the importance of women's empowerment at household and society level.
2. Women in general and unmarried girls in particular may be encouraged to participate in income generating activities both within and outside their home. For this purpose, vocational training programmes and reservation for females in employment may be provided and implemented effectively. Further, part-time employment outside the home also gives them a better access to financial resources and motivate them to plan and utilise such resources, in addition to have greater freedom of movement and chances of participating in decision-making at household level.
3. Strategies have to be evolved to impart the importance of women's empowerment and its role not only in demographic sphere but also in the household, community, society and nation at large to

all people. For this purpose, various mass media channels as well as other formal and informal channels have to be effectively made use of.

References

Audinarayana, N. and N. Thenmozhi (2006). "Gender discrimination at the family level and its determinants in an urban setting", in Packiam, L. (ed.), *Gender Discrimination in Indian Society*. New Delhi: Allied Publishers Private Limited. pp. 75-83.

Agarwala, Rina and Scott M. Lynch (2006). "Re-fining the measurement of women's autonomy: An international application of a multi-dimensional construct", *Social Forces* 84(4): 2077-2098.

Barrett, Kenley (2007). "The determinants of female decision-making power and its demographic implications: An analysis of northern and southern India", *Demography India* 36(1): 1-20.

Basu, Alaka, M. (1992). *Culture, the Status of Women, and Demographic Behaviour.* New York: Oxford University Press.

Dyson, Tim and Mick Moore (1983). "On kinship structure, female autonomy, and demographic behaviour in India", *Population and Development Review* 9(1): 35-60.

International Institute for Population Sciences (IIPS) and Macro International (2007). *National Family Health Survey (NFHS-3), 2005-06: India: Volume I.* Mumbai: IIPS.

Jejeebhoy, Shireen J. (1991). "Women's status and fertility: Successive cross-sectional evidence from Tamil Nadu, India, 1970-80", *Studies in Family Planning* 22(4): 217-23.

———. (2000). "Women's autonomy in rural India: Its dimensions, determinants, and the influence of context", in Harriet B. Presser and Gita Sen (ed.), *Women's Empowerment and Demographic Processes.* New York: Oxford University Press. pp. 204-238.

Jejeebhoy, Shireen J. and Zeba A. Sathar (2001). "Women's autonomy in India and Pakistan: The influence of religion and region", *Population and Development Review* 27(4): 687-712.

Kendall, M. (1975). *Multivariate Analysis.* London: Charles Griffin & Company.

Mahadevan, K., Akbar Aghajanian, R. Jayasree, and G.S. Moni (1989). "Status of women and population dynamics: A conceptual model", in K. Mahadevan (ed.), *Women and Population Dynamics: Perspectives from Asian Countries*. New Delhi: Sage Publications. pp. 321-345.

Mason, Karen O. (1985). *The Status of Women: A Review of its Relationships to Fertility and Mortality.* New York: The Rockefeller Foundation.

———. (1995). *Gender and Demographic Change: What do we Know?* Leige, Belgium: International Union for the Scientific Study of Population.

Rahman, Lupin and Vijayendra Rao (2004). "The determinants of gender equity in India: Examining Dyson and Moore's thesis with new data", *Population and Development Review* 30(2): 239-268.

Thenmozhi, N. (1992). "Status of women and fertility in an urban setting", Unpublished Ph.D. thesis. Coimbatore: Bharathiar University.

16 Gender-based Violence and Consequences on Sexual Reproductive Health of Women in Uttarakhand

C.P. Prakasam

Introduction

There has been a growing recognition globally about the implication of violence against women and its influence on health and well-being of women. In the developing countries where marriage is universal, more so in India, violence by husband against their wives, commonly called domestic or spousal violence, is one of the most common forms of gender-based violence. Research revealed that gender-based violence affects a range of health outcomes, both for women who experiences it and for their children (Garcia-Moreno *et al.*, 2006; Hindin *et al.*, 2008; Kishor and Johnson, 2006). The health consequences of violence against women include non-fatal outcomes such as injury, unwanted pregnancy, alcohol/drug abuse, HIV/AIDS etc., and long-term outcomes include organ damages, chronic disabilities, mental disorders, depression and adverse pregnancy outcomes. Abused women are less likely to seek prenatal care and more likely to give birth to low weight babies. Research studies conducted in India (Jejeebhoy and Cook, 1997; Jejeebhoy, 1998; Ramasubban and Singh, 1998) showed association between domestic violence and reproductive health problems. Further Rob Stephenson and others (2006), in their study showed positive relation between severity of domestic violence and risk of gynaecological morbidity. Apart from that, sexual violence may cause vaginal, anal or urethral trauma, leading to an elevated risk of infection (Campbell, 2002).

Research studies also revealed that socio-economic variables (background variables) influences reproductive and sexual health due to violence. It has been observed that high-level domestic violence has been reported in both rural and urban areas *viz.*, place of living (Rao, 1997; Jejeebhoy, 1998; Jeyaseelan *et al.*, 2007). A multi-level analysis carried out by Koenig *et al.* (2006) revealed that a community environment of violent crime was associated with elevated risks of both physical and sexual violence, further higher socio-economic status was found to be protective against physical but not sexual violence. A community-based study in rural Gujarat (Visaria, 1999) revealed that two-thirds of the surveyed women reported some form of psychological, physical or sexual abuse. It is noted that each form of abuse cuts across all age, caste and education lines. Despite the observed marital abuse among young brides, the relationship of age and duration of marriage with violence was weak and the factors underlying of abuse include the failure to perform duties and responsibilities, economic stress, inadequate dowry, alcohol use, and hierarchical gender relations. With this backdrop, understanding the magnitude of domestic violence (physical, emotional and sexual) and its principal determinants on reproductive and sexual health variables have become an important research component.

Objectives

In this paper an attempt is made to analyse gender-based violence (physical, emotional and sexual violence) against currently married women, particularly attitude of women towards it and prevalence of domestic violence in Uttarakhand. Also, it examines the inter-relationship between gender-based violence and reproductive and sexual health problems.

Data and Methodology

To achieve the objectives, data were collected from NHFS-3 for the state Uttarakhand (IIPS and Macro International, 2007). By using conflict tactics scales (CTS), NFHS-3 collected data on domestic violence. Spousal physical and sexual violence is measured by set of questions listed in Appendix A-1. For the present study, information on

1547 currently married women has been analysed. List of variables considered for analysis is given in Table 16.1.

The analysis was carried out in three stages. Initially, currently married women ever experienced and experienced in past 12 months, physical, emotional and sexual violence by selected socio-economic variables (background variables) have been analysed to understand the prevalence of gender-based violence in Uttarakhand. In the second stage, the reasons for justifying husband beating with the background variable have been analysed to know the attitude of currently married women in Uttarakhand towards violence. Finally, major predictors (determinants) of currently married women experiencing physical and sexual violence in Uttarakhand have been analysed by applying logit regression analysis and risk-ratio of sexual health problems due to physical and sexual violence has been calculated.

Table 16.1

List of Variables by Category Considered for Analysis

Category of Variables	*Variables*
Background variables	Age
	Marital duration
	Type of place of residence
	Religion
	Wealth index
	Work status
	husband living with the respondent
	Partner's education
	Partner's occupation
Sexual reproductive health	Reason for not having sex: husband has STD
	Reason for not having sex: husband has affairs
	Had STD in last 12 months
	Had genital-sore ulcer in last 12 months
	Had genital discharge in last 12 months
Gender-based violence	Have ever experienced physical violence since age 15
	Have experienced physical violence in past 12 months
	Have ever experienced emotional violence since age 15
	Have experienced emotional violence in past 12 months
	Have ever experienced sexual violence since age 15
	Have experienced sexual violence in past 12 months

Figure 16.1

Prevalence of Violence by Age of Currently Married Women in Uttarakhand

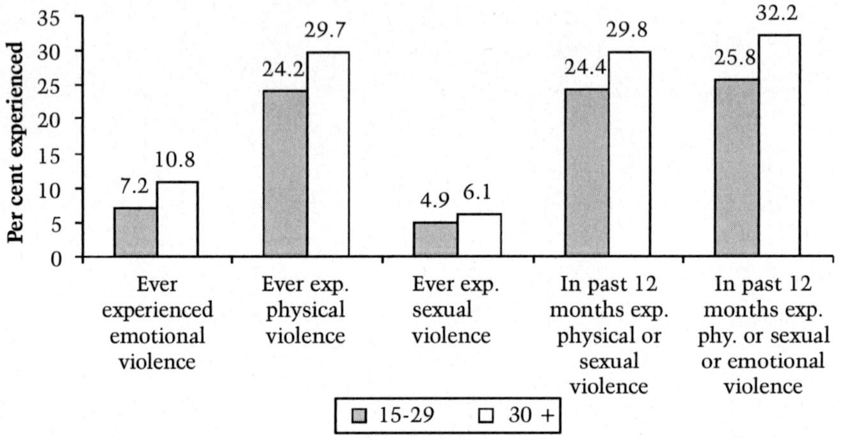

Results

Prevalence of Gender-based Violence by Background Variables

Percentage of currently married women who have experienced violence ever and in the past 12 month's period according to physical, emotional and sexual violence by age group shows that highest percentage of women experiences physical violence (Figure 16.1) followed by emotional and sexual violence. Nearly 30 per cent women above 30 years of age experienced physical violence and 24.2 per cent in the age group of 15-29 years. Women experiencing any type of violence in past 12 months is found to be high for 30 years and above age group (32.2 per cent) than the younger age group. It has been observed that more than 74 per cent women with 10 years and more marital duration (Table 16.2) were found to experienc gender-based violence. Significant association (chi-square test) between marital duration and gender-based violence with ever and past 12 months except 'ever experienced sexual violence'. Further, more than 80 per cent of currently married women in Uttarakhand (Table 16.2) living in rural areas and belonging to Hindu religion experienced violence.

Table 16.2

Percentage of Currently Married Women who have Experienced Violence Ever and in the Past 12 Months Period according to Type of Violence by Background Characteristics in Uttarakhand, NFHS-3 Data

Background Characteristics	*Gender-based Violence*				
	Ever Experienced Emotional Violence	*Ever Experienced Physical Violence*	*Ever Experienced Sexual Violence*	*In Past 12 Months Experienced Physical or Sexual Violence*	*In Past 12 Months Experienced Physical or Sexual or Emotional Violence*
Marital Duration					
0-4 years	6.5	9.2	14.0	9.4	8.8
5-9 years	16.9	16.7	9.7	16.9	17.2
10+	76.6	74.1	76.3	73.7	74.0
χ^2	**	**	NS	**	**
Type of Place of Residence					
Urban	26.6	22.7	19.4	22.0	22.6
Rural	73.4	77.3	80.6	78.0	77.4
χ^2	NS	**	*	**	**
Religion					
Hindu	87.7	84.4	80.6	84.7	84.9
Non-Hindu	12.3	15.6	19.4	15.3	15.1
χ^2	NS	*	*	**	**
Wealth Index					
Poor	34.4	30.9	33.3	31.2	30.6
Middle	18.8	23.9	21.5	24.0	23.3
Rich	46.8	45.3	45.2	44.7	46.1
χ^2	**	**	*	**	**

Note: χ^2 calculated between who have experienced violence "yes" or "no"; **p<.001, *p<.01, N.S=Not Significant.

Attitude towards Gender-based Violence

To study the attitude of gender-based violence (physical, emotional and sexual violence) against currently married women in Uttarakhand, information regarding acceptance of husband beating for particular reason has been derived from NFHS-3 and listed in Table 16.3. Husband beating is justified by currently married women for the reasons 'if wife goes without telling husband', 'neglects house or children', 'argues with husband', 'refuse to have sex with husband', and 'does not cook food properly'. Table 16.3 shows reasons for justifying husband beating by currently married women in Uttarakhand by socio-economic and reproductive health variables. Results show that percentage of women who agrees at least one reason found to be significantly high among non-Hindu (religion), rural areas (place of residence), having wealth index as "poor", and with illiterate partner.

Table 16.3

Reason for Justifying Husband Beating by Currently Married Women in Uttarakhand, NFHS-3 Data

	Percentage who Agree with Specific Reasons						
Variables	*Percentage Who Agree with at Least One Reason*	*Wife Goes Without Telling Husband*	*Wife Neglects House or Children*	*Wife Argues with Husband*	*Refuse to Have Sex with Husband*	*Wife Does Not Cook Food Properly*	*Number of Currently Married Women*
1. *Age*							
15-19	44.8	34.3	40.3	37.3	16.4	34.3	67
20 29	40.6	28.5	34.8	31.5	13.5	23.8	785
30-39	39.8	29.3	34.2	28.4	14.3	21.9	761
40-49	40.8	27.5	30.8	29.5	14.8	23.4	461
ψ^2=	NS	NS	NS	NS	NS	NS	
2. *Marital Duration*							
<5 years	35.7	25.3	31.1	28.1	13.1	21.8	367
5-10 years	44.7	29.6	36.4	31.7	11.6	24.1	398
>10 years	41.5	29.5	33.8	30.2	15.3	23.6	1309
ψ^2=							
3. *Religion*							
Hindu	38.7	26.9	32.2	28.1	13.3	21.6	1801
Non-Hindu	52.6	40.9	44.5	43.3	19.7	35.0	274
ψ^2=	**	**	**	**	NS	**	
4. *Place of Residence*							
Urban	29.2	18.7	24.3	22.4	8.9	14.5	593
Rural	45.0	32.8	37.7	33.2	16.3	26.9	1481
ψ^2=	**	**	**	NS	NS	**	
5. *Husband Living*							
With	41.2	29.2	34.4	31.0	14.3	23.9	1825
Stays outside	35.5	25.4	29.4	23.4	12.9	19.4	248
ψ^2=	NS	NS	NS	NS	NS	NS	

Contd...

...contd...

Variables	*Percentage who Agree with Specific Reasons*						
	Percentage Who Agree with at Least One Reason	*Wife Goes Without Telling Husband*	*Wife Neglects House or Children*	*Wife Argues with Husband*	*Refuse to Have Sex with Husband*	*Wife Does Not Cook Food Properly*	*Number of Currently Married Women*
6. *Wealth Index*							
Poor	52.2	39.9	45.6	40.2	21.9	34.5	406
Middle	48.0	36.7	40.7	36.2	18.1	27.8	425
Rich	34.1	22.4	27.7	24.7	10.3	18.3	1243
Ψ^2=	**	**	**	NS	**	**	
7. *Work Status*							
Not working	38.5	26.0	30.4	29.1	13.1	20.5	1144
Working	42.9	32.3	38.1	31.3	15.5	27.0	930
Ψ^2=	NS	NS	NS	NS	NS	NS	
8. *Partner's Education*							
No. educated	55.4	39.0	48.3	46.0	23.8	39.0	323
Educated	37.6	26.8	31.1	27.1	12.4	20.4	1743
Ψ^2=	**	**	**	**	NS	**	

Note: **P<.001 *P<.01. Ψ^2: Chi square test for association.

In rural areas, majority of women live in poor socio-economic condition where, husband beating wife is a common affair in many families. Women in rural areas may not consider it as a serious matter as they are accustomed to it.

Act of Gender-based Violence

It has been observed under physical violence that most of currently married women experienced "slap" from their spouse since 15 years of age (ever slapped). More than 70 per cent of women ever experienced severe physical violence such as "strangle or burn" or "threatened or attacked with knife/gun or other weapon" (Table 16.4). Under the category of sexual violence, around 92 women expressed that spouse physically forced sex when not wanted, during their lifetime. The "forced sex act" by husband may lead to unwanted pregnancy, repeated abortions and other gynaecological problems. This would lead to physical and mental disturbances which affect the health of women and their children.

Table 16.4

Percentage Currently Married Women who Experienced Physical and Sexual Violence by Act of Violence in Uttarakhand, NFHS-3

Act of Gender-based Violence	*Per cent of Currently Married Women who Experienced (Yes)*
Physical Violence	
1. Spouse ever pushed, shook or threw something	74.6
2. Spouse ever slapped	94.8
3. Spouse ever punched with fist or something harmful	81.9
4. Spouse ever kicked or dragged	70.0
5. Spouse ever tried to strangle or burn	74.6
6. Spouse ever threatened or attacked with knife/gun or other weapon	73.3
Sexual Violence	
1. Spouse ever forced other sexual acts when not wanted	4.8
2. Spouse ever physically forced sex when not wanted	92.0

Inter-Relationships

To understand the factors influencing gender-based violence by sexual reproductive health variables and socio-economic variables, logit regression analysis was carried out. From Tables 16.2 and 16.3, it was evident that prevalence of gender-based violence and attitude towards physical, emotional and sexual violence are different across background variables with limited exceptions. Hence, logit regression analysis has been carried out by considering socio-economic variables and sexual reproductive health variables. The results are listed in Table 16.5.

Physical Violence

Logit regression analysis shows that marital duration, partner's education and partner occupation significantly influences currently married women for the exposure of physical violence (Table 16.5). The probability of currently married women experiencing physical violence with marital duration of 5 to 10 years and more are found to be less than women with less years of married life. Women with educated partner and husband staying outside experiences high risk of physical violence than women with illiterate and partner staying with her, controlling for other variables (Table 16.5).

Sexual Violence

Sexual violence which has been measured by self-reported physical force to have unwanted sex and to perform any sexual act was influenced by socio-economic variables and sexual health variables. The logit regression analysis shows that (Table 16.5) among the socio-economic variables, partner's education alone is found to have been contributory factor for sexual violence. When sexual health variables are considered, partner's education, genital discharge and partner drinks alcohol are the factors which determine sexual violence (Table 16.5).

Risk Ratio due to Violence

Logit regression analysis explained the influence of socio-economic variables determining physical and sexual health problems. To understand the risk of getting sexual health problems due to physical and sexual violence, relative risk (risk ratio) has been calculated. Relative risk is the ratio of sexual health problems among the currently married women who were exposed to violence to that of not exposed. The calculated relative risk of sexual health problems with physical and sexual violence is given in Table 16.6. Due to physical violence, currently married women were at risk of getting genital discharge 1.87 times more than women without violence. Further, getting genital sore/ulcer was found to be twice at risk than women without physical violence and it was 1.09 times with any STD in the last 12 months (Table 16.6).

Risk of experiencing genital discharge due to sexual violence was found to be 2.74 times more among currently married women than who are not exposed to sexual violence (Table 16.6). Similarly, the risk ratio for genital sore/ulcer and any STD in last 12 months was 2.19 and 1.04. From the risk ratio, it has been observed that currently married women who were exposed to violence are likely to face genital problems and STD than other women who were not exposed to spousal violence.

Table 16.5

Logit Regression Analysis Results of Physical and Sexual Violence with Background Variables among Currently Married Women in Uttarakhand, NFHS-3 Data

Background Variables	*Physical Violence*			*Sexual Violence*		
	Exp(B)	*95.0% C.I. for EXP(B)*		*Exp(B)*	*95.0% C.I. for EXP(B)*	
		Lower	*Upper*		*Lower*	*Upper*
Age Group						
15-19	1.000			1.000		
20-29	.847	.308	2.328	1.385	.287	6.680
30-39	1.289	.844	1.968	1.218	.563	2.634
40-49	1.200	.866	1.661	1.068	.585	1.951
Marital Duration						
<5 years	1.000			1.000		
5-10 years	.509*	.310	.837	.771	.322	1.846
>10 years	.656	.441	.974	.400	.171	.937
Type of Place of Residence						
Urban	1.000			1.000		
Rural	.770	.567	1.045	.628	.342	1.155
Religion						
Hindu	1.000			1.000		
Non-Hindu	.659	.455	.955	.456	.245	.849
Working						
Not working	1.000			1.000		
Working	.961	.745	1.240	.856	.530	1.382
Partner's Education						
No education	1.000			1.000		
Educated	2.291**	1.657	3.168	1.386*	.772	2.488
Partner's Occupation						
Unemployed						
White collar job	1.367	.682	2.741	1.472	.431	5.020
Blue collar job	.579**	.426	.786	1.096	.625	1.922
Wealth Index						
Poor	1.000			1.000		
Middle	1.346	.957	1.892	1.622	.868	3.028
Rich	1.230	.892	1.696	1.209	.651	2.244
Husband Lives in House						
Living with her	1.000			1.000		
Staying elsewhere	1.535	1.011	2.330	1.238	.550	2.788
Genital Discharge						
Yes *(ref)*						
No				.292**	.171	.497
Partner Drinks Alcohol						
Yes						
No				.452*	.282	.722
Constant	.358**			.096		
-2 Log Likelihood	1673.84			638.0		
100 x R-	1			74		
Square	11.7			4.5		

Table 16.6

Risk Ratio of Sexual Health Problems due to Gender-based Violence among Currently Married Women in Uttarakhand, NFHS-3 Data

Type of Gender Violence	*Relative Risk of Sexual Health Problem*		
	Had Genital Discharge in Last 12 Months	*Had Genital Sore/Ulcer in Last 12 Months*	*Had any STD in Last 12 Months*
Physical violence	1.87	2.00	1.09
Sexual violence	2.74	2.19	1.04

Note:

$$\text{Relative Risk} = \frac{\text{Incidence of sexual health problems among currently married women exposed to violence}}{\text{Incidence of sexual health problems among currently married women who are not exposed to violence}}$$

Conclusion

This paper examines the physical and sexual violence against currently married women in Uttarakhand by analysing NFHS-3 data. It has been observed that one-fourth of women expressed that they have (ever) experienced physical violence and around five per cent with sexual violence.

- Age-wise, it has been observed that more number of women belonging to 30 years and above face physical and sexual violence than younger age group (15-29 years). Nearly two thirds of currently married women with marital duration more than 10 years, living in rural area, belonging to Hindu religion expressed that they had ever experienced violence.
- To understand the attitude towards violence, the results revealed that percentage of women who justifies husband beating with at least one reason was found to be significantly high among non-Hindu (religion), rural areas (place of residence), having wealth index as "poor", with illiterate partner. In rural areas, majority of women living in poor socio-economic condition are likely to accept wife beating as a social and family norm.
- More than 70 per cent of currently married women expressed that "spouse ever slapped" as the important reason followed by punched with fist or some harmful instrument. Highest

percentage of women expressed that they had "forced sex when not wanted".

- The probability of currently married women experiencing physical violence with marital duration 10 years and more were found to be higher than other age group.
- Partner education, genital discharge and partner drinks alcohol are the factors which determine sexual violence.
- Currently married women who experienced physical or sexual violence are at risk of getting genital disorders and this risk ratio ranges from 1.04 to 2.74.
- Women who experienced sexual violence were 2.74 times at risk of genital discharge in last 12 months than women who are not exposed to sexual violence.

From the above large survey data analysis, it was evident that most of the women are experiencing physical violence. Currently married women living in rural areas should be educated about gender issues and gender rights. Intervention programmes should be imparted to women along with their husbands (men) focusing on violence and consequences on sexual and reproductive health.

References

Campbell, J.C. (2002). "Health consequences of intimate partner violence", *Lancet* 359 (9314):1331-1336.

Garica-Moreno, C., H.A. Jansen, M. Ellsberg, L. Heise and C.H. Watts (2006). "Prevalence of intimate partner violence: Findings from the WHO multi-country study on women's health and domestic violence", *Lancet* 368(9543):1260-9.

Hindin, M.J., S. Kishor and D.L. Ansara (2008). "Intimate partner violence among couples in 10 DHS countries: Predictors and health outcomes", *DHS Analytical Studies No.18*. Calverton, Maryland, USA: Macro International Inc.

International Institute for Population Sciences (IIPS) & Macro International (2007). *National Family Health Survey (NFHS-3), 2005-06, India:* Volume I. Mumbai: IIPS.

Jejeebhoy, S. and R.J. Cook (1997). "State accountability for wife-beating: The Indian challenge", *Lancet* 349 (suppl.1): 10-12.

Jejeebhoy, S. (1998). "Associations between wife-beating and foetal and infant death: Impressions from a survey in rural India", *Studies in Family Planning* 29(3): 300-308.

Jeyaseelan, Lakshman, Shuba Kumar, Nithya Neelakantan, Abraham Peedicayil, Rajamohanam Pillai and Nata Duvvury (2007). "Physical spousal violence against women in India: Some risk factors", *Journal of Biosocial Science* 39(5): 657-670.

Kishor, S. and K. Johnson (2006). "Reproductive health and domestic violence: Are the poorest women uniquely disadvantaged?", *Demography* 43(2): 293-397.

Koenig, M.A., R. Stephenson, S. Ahmed, S.J. Jejeebhoy, J. Campbell (2006). "Individual and contextual determinants of domestic violence in north India", *American Journal of Public Health* 96(1): 132-138.

Ramasubban, R. and Bhanwar Singh (1998). "Ashaktapana (weakness) and reproductive health in a slum population in Mumbai, India", in Obermeyer Carla M. (ed.), *Cultural Perspectives in Reproductive Health.* Oxford University Press.

Rao, Vijayendra (1997). "Wife-beating in rural south India: A qualitative and econometric analysis", *Social Sciences & Medicine* 44(8): 1169-1180.

Stephenson, Rob, Michael A. Koenig and Saifuddin Ahmed (2006). "Domestic violence and symptoms of gynaecological morbidity among women in north India", *Family Planning Perspectives* 32(4): 201-208.

Visaria, Leela (1999). "Violence against women in India: Evidences from rural Gujarat", summary report in: *Domestic Violence in India: A Summary Report of Three Studies*, by Barbara Buton, Nata Duvvury, Anuradha Rajan, and Nisha Varia. Washington DC.: International Centre for Research on Women. *http://www.cedpa.org*

APPENDIX A-16.1

In NFHS-3, spousal physical, sexual and emotional violence is measured using the following set of questions:

Evidences of Physical Violence:

(Does/did) your (last) husband ever does any of the following things to you:

- Slap you?
- Twist your arm or pull your hair?
- Push you, shake you or throw something at you?
- Punch you with his fist or with something that could hurt you?
- Kick you, drag you or beat you up?
- Try to choke you or burn you on purpose?
- Threaten or attack you with a knife, gun, or any other weapon?

Evidences of Sexual Violence:

- Physically force you to have sexual intercourse with him even when you did not want to?
- Force you to perform any sexual acts you did not want to?

Evidences of Emotional Violence:

- Say or do something to humiliate you in front of others?
- Threaten to hurt or harm you or someone close to you?
- Insult you or make you feel bad about yourself?

17 Inequalities in Maternal and Child Health Care in Selected States of India

Whether Social Structure or Economic Differentiation Matters?

Sandhya Rani Mahapatro

Introduction

Health is considered as a major component of human development. As stated by Dreze and Sen (1995), health and education can promote the freedom and ability of individuals to make use of available opportunities. In order to ensure 'Health for All', equal access to health care has been considered as one of the prime concern in areas of health research. Earlier, millions of maternal and child death in India occured due to inadequate health care facilities. Accordingly, a large number of primary health care centres (PHC) have been set up as a part of government's 'Health for All' programme so that it is easily accessible without any constraint. Though, maternal and child health care in India is an important component of public health system (Bose and Tyagi, 1983; Ghosh, 1989), still there exist huge inequalities in health and nutritional status in the society, particularly among the poor sections of the population. Maternal and child health care services are more likely to sharpen inequality in utilisation. The dimensions of inequality prevailing in India are varied. The inequality that exists among regions, class, caste and gender hinders the overall development of society. It is feared that such inequality might intensify in the liberalisation era. However, several programmes in India are trying to narrow down various dimensions of inequality.

India is a signatory to UN's "Health for All" and it is committed to address the wide disparities in various dimensions of health such as incidence of diseases, disability, death, care-seeking behaviour, diagnosis and treatment. An individual's age, economic status, ethnicity, caste, gender etc., could lead to such inequality in health. Among all these domains, caste and economic status of the individual plays a significant role. However, it is not clear if the inequalities are based on caste or financial status. Hence, in this study an attempt is made to understand whether the inequality in maternal and child health care is due to social structure or due to economic differentiation in the three states of India that is Uttarakhand, Jharkhand and Chhattisgarh by taking these objectives into account: firstly, to examine the extent of differential in maternal and child health and nutritional indicators by social groups and secondly, to examine the extent of economic differentiation in such health and nutritional indicators.

With this background, the paper is organised in the following manner: the second section gives a background profile of the three states by their socio-economic characteristics. The next section gives a brief review of relevant literature relating to socio-economic differentiation and its impact on maternal and child health. Section 4 describes the data and methodology used for the study. In section 5, the empirical findings of the study have been given. Finally the study ends by summarising the results followed by possible policy implication.

Profile of the Study Population

Uttarakhand, Jharkhand and Chhattisgarh have distinct geographical and topographical characteristics. Chhattisgarh and Jharkhand are on a plateau, while Uttarakhand is on the lap of the middle and lower Himalayas. All three are land-locked states. For administrative purposes, Jharkhand is divided into four divisions and 22 districts, Uttarakhand and Chhattisgarh into 13 and 16 districts respectively.

Uttarakhand is a state with 8.49 million people, accounting for one per cent of total population of the country. The state being a hilly one, is the most sparsely populated state in the country. Seventy-two per cent of total population of state is literate which is higher than the national average. Chhattisgarh is a state which fulfils the long-cherished demand for the tribal people. It is a state of 21 million people which accounts for 2.5 per cent of total population of the country. The decadal growth rate is lower than the national average. The state of Jharkhand with a population of 27 million population accounts for three per cent of total population of the country. Jharkhand is one of the mineral-rich regions in the country.

Table 17.1

Socio-Economic and Demographic Characteristics of the Three States

Variables	*Year & Source*	*Uttarakhand*	*Jharkhand*	*Chhattisgarh*
Total Population (million)	Census 2001	8.49	26.94	20.83
CBR	SRS (2006)	20.5	26.2	27.4
CDR	SRS (2006)	7.2	8	7.7
TFR	SRS (2004)	3.6	3.5	3.4
IMR	SRS (2006)	42	49	60
Sex ratio	Census 2001	962	941	989
Decadal growth rate	Census 2001	20.4	23.4	18.3
MMR	SRS (2001-2003)	517	371	379
Social Variable				
Literacy	Census 2001			
Male		83.3	67.3	77.4
Female		59.6	38.9	51.9
Total		71.6	53.6	64.7
Life expectancy	SRS (2004)			
Male		—	61.8	57.5
Female		—	69.9	57.2
Economic Variables				
GSDP (in crore)	(2004-05)	11057	26788	—

To understand the socio-economic inequality, the distribution of women by caste and wealth index is shown in Table 17.2. For the purpose of study, OBC and others are combined into one category considered as general. Caste-wise distribution of women in all the three states shows that in Uttarakhand, less than five per cent women belong to ST category whereas two-fifth of population belongs to SC category and more than 70 per cent women are general. Compared to

Uttarakhand, in Chhattisgarh and Jharkhand more than 50 per cent of population belong to general category, 30 per cent of women belong to ST category and it is less than 20 per cent for SC.

Table 17.2

Distribution of Women by Caste and Wealth Index in the Three States

Variables	*Uttarakhand*	*Jharkhand*	*Chhattisgarh*
Caste			
SC	23.4	12.0	15.4
ST	4.2	30.3	30.5
General	72.4	57.7	54.1
Wealth Index			
Poorest	8.0	57.2	44.2
Poorer	16.8	16.2	26.9
Middle	23.1	10.8	14.6
Richer	24.2	9.5	7.3
Richest	27.9	6.3	7
Total	100.00	100.00	100.00

To know the economic inequality in these three states, the wealth index is used as appropriate measure. The distribution of women by wealth index shows that proportion of women in Uttarakhand falling in poorest quintile is 8 per cent whereas it is 28 per cent in richest quintile. As compared to Uttarakhand, in Chhattisgarh 44 per cent people fall under poorest quintile and 57 per cent in Jharkhand whereas it is about 7 per cent for the richest quintile. This shows that economic inequality is higher in Jharkhand, followed by Chhattisgarh and though inequality exists but it is low in Uttarakhand.

Review of Literature

It is widely recognised that the determinants of health are social and economic rather than purely medical. Of various dimensions of inequality, caste and economic status become the major predictors of maternal and child health. Hence, this section gives a snapshot of relevant literature on such dimensions.

Caste is a major indicator of health outcomes and mandates the need for interventions that change social structures. The Indian society is stratified in such a way that there are glaring inequalities among different social groups. Caste occupies a prime role especially in Indian society as it, by and large, governs the status of the household. Social stratification system determines the living condition, privileges, obligations and other cultural practices surrounding the life of a person which in turn affects their perception regarding health, knowledge of health care and accessibility of health care practices. Caste is also likely to influence the health behaviour of individuals. Caste differences may lead to disparities in accessibility, utilisation and quality of health care services. In a health care research study, caste system has been identified to be an indicator of health. The studies show a caste-based inequality in health.

Caste is an important factor in the social system, particularly in rural communities that exerts and influences the utilisation of maternal and child health services. It is one of the important dimensions of social backwardness. Women belonging to oppressed sections of the society are generally prohibited from various health care facilities and hence, the maternal and child care received by them are poor as compared to other social groups. Among the social groups, those belonging to scheduled caste and scheduled tribe (SC/ST), live in relative isolation and are often restricted easy access to common facilities in spite of legal provisions prohibiting such discrimination. Moreover, a health worker may also be reluctant to visit localities or hamlets of SCs/STs (Sivakami and Kulkarni, 2003). Various studies show that there exist a strong association between caste and utilisation of maternal care services (Govindasamy and Ramesh, 1997; Shariff, 1999). There exists differentials in health care indicators between SC, ST, OBC and women in other category even after controlling for socio-economic factors in some states of India (Roy *et al.*, 2004).

Evidence from various studies suggests that not only caste results in poorer health status and negative health outcomes but economic status of the household also greatly influences the utilisation of health care services. Based on the Demographic Health Survey (DHS) data for more than 50 countries, it was found that the poorest quintiles are far worse than better-off groups on a range of health outcomes, including childhood mortality and nutritional status (Carr, 2004). On an average, a child from the poorest health quintile is twice as likely as a child in richest quintile to die before age 5. Similarly, the study showed that the people in the poorest quintile are less likely than those in better-off quintile to use basic health services such as immunisation, maternity care and family planning. In Indian context, the disparities in health outcome and health care utilisation is even larger among the rich and poor. The estimated under five mortality of poorest quintile is 141 per 1000 live births, as compared to 46 per 1000 live birth for the richest. Ahmed (2004) using DHS data of Bangladesh showed that there is differential in contraceptive use, fertility level, unmet need, fertility preference and maternal health care utilisation by socio-economic status. Many studies show that women from low income class or low standard of living are at a disadvantage in utilising maternal health care (Kanitkar and Sinha, 1989; Bhatia and Cleland, 1995; Obermeyer and Potter, 1991; Obermeyer, 1993; Majumdar *et al.*, 1994). In almost all the studies, economic ability has been identified as one of the most significant barriers of access to utilisation of health care. Wagstaff (2002) while doing cross-national comparison on health inequalities found that poor children in poor countries are less likely to get immunised in spite of increased incidence of diarrhoea among the poor quintiles. Income of the household exerts considerable influence in child survival, particularly in the early years of life and the likelihood of a child getting immunised increases with the economic status of the household (Gage *et al.*, 1997). Use of maternal care services is positively related and probability of child health was found to be inversely related with household wealth status (Rustein and Johnson, 2004).

From the review of the above literature, the major issue which comes in to focus is that the poorer and the socially weaker sections of the society are at a disadvantageous condition in utilisation of health care services and nutritional status. Although a large number of primary health centres and sub-centres has been created in order to reach out to the marginalised group, bridge the gap between the social groups and as a part of government's "Health for All" programme, most of the states in India still are far away from this goal. Hence, in this paper an attempt is made to examine the extent of inequalities in maternal and child health and nutrition in the newly formed states of Uttarakhand, Jharkhand and Chhattisgarh with a special focus on social and economic groups. Further, it also assesses the net effect of these groups on health and nutrition after controlling for other socio-economic and other demographic characteristics of the individual.

Data Source

This study uses the data from National Family Health Survey-3, a large scale sample survey that was carried out by International Institute for Population Sciences (IIPS) under the aegis of the Government of India. The NFHS-3 covered a sample of over 109,041 sample households, 124,385 women aged 15-49. It provides estimates for the country as a whole and all the 29 states. The survey was conducted with the primary objective of providing reliable and comparable estimates of various demographic features like fertility, infant mortality, child health, family planning, reproductive health, women's empowerment, HIV related information etc., for different states of India.

Apart from this, it also gives data on basic socio-economic characteristics of household and women like their educational attainment, their economic status etc. The survey also provides information on social groups namely, scheduled castes (SC), scheduled tribes (ST), other backward classes (OBC) and others.

Methodology

The following indicators of the health and nutrition are examined in the present paper.

- *Full immunisation:* Children who received one dose each of the BCG and measles Vaccines and three doses each of the DPT and polio vaccines are considered as fully immunised.
- *Underweight:* Children whose weight-for-age is below minus two SD from the median reference of population.
- *Anaemia:* Children whose haemoglobin level is less than 11.0g/dl.

- *Full ANC:* Full ANC is that the minimum of three antenatal visits, two or more TT Injection received and receipt of more than hundred IFA tablets/syrup.
- *Safe delivery:* Safe delivery is considered as the institutional delivery performed in health institutions.
- *Anaemia level:* Women whose haemoglobin level is less than 11.0g/dl.

Bivariate analysis is used to carry out the extent of differential in health and nutritional indicators among the individuals belonging to different caste and income groups.

Besides, logistic regression analysis is used to assess the influence of certain variables on the probability of occurrence of an event. Three sets of separate logistic regression have been carried out for each of the health and nutritional indicator for women and child. The response variable for maternal health care includes full ANC, safe delivery and anaemia level of women. Likewise for children, the dependent variables consist of child immunisation, body mass index and anaemia level in children. The explanatory variables for the study mainly consist of caste and wealth index which is used as the proxy for economic status of the household. Besides, other variables like education, religion, age of women, birth order and place of residence is taken here. Here the study tries to see, after controlling for other variables, to what extent caste and economic differentials influence the maternal and child health care indicators.

Empirical Findings

Distribution of Women in Different Social Groups by Background Characteristics in Uttarakhand, Jharkhand and Chhattisgarh

The social inequality by caste in all the three states by background characteristics of women are shown in the Table 17.3. The background characteristics include age of women, education of women, wealth index, religion and place of residence. It may be seen that 78.4 per cent SC women in Uttarakhand live in rural area whereas it is more than 80

Table 17.3

Distribution of Women in Different Social Groups by Background Characteristics

	Uttarakhand				*Chhattisgarh*				*Jharkhand*			
Background Variables	*SC*	*ST*	*General*	*Total*	*SC*	*ST*	*General*	*Total*	*SC*	*ST*	*General*	*Total*
Residence				1234								
Urban	21.63	10.81	24.79	290	19.61	4.88	25.76	325	16.88	4.19	23.39	273
Rural	78.37	89.19	75.21	944	80.39	95.12	74.24	1413	83.12	95.81	76.61	1380
Wealth Index				1234				1738				1654
Poorest	11.33	6.08	7.08	99	68.51	75.53	45.2	994	45.69	68.52	30.17	732
Poorer	25.21	42.57	12.56	207	14.49	11.57	19	282	29.59	18.64	30.92	446
Middle	28.67	16.22	21.68	285	6.32	5.91	14.25	187	15.63	9.24	17.14	240
Richer	16.22	27.48	26.6	299	7.55	5.43	12.1	166	6.95	2.79	9.88	120
Richest	18.57	7.66	32.08	344	3.13	1.57	9.45	109	2.14	0.81	11.89	116
Religion				1234				1732				1653
Hindu	95.31	82.88	80.3	1035	95.68	48.6	69.52	1149	98.47	99.05	94.3	1594
Muslim	3.3	13.06	13.14	134	2.04	0.91	29.7	305	0	0	5.25	46
others	1.39	4.05	6.56	65	2.28	50.49	0.78	278	1.53	0.95	0.46	13
Education of Women												
No education	55.31	72.97	35.29	513	74.64	74.07	61.48	1162	55.49	69.29	44.62	890
Primary	13.2	15.31	12.45	157	12.35	8.23	11.94	189	20.11	12.79	22.24	315
Secondary	28.15	9.91	37.18	419	11.68	16.12	23.37	343	22.34	17.05	26.92	384
Higher	3.34	1.8	15.08	145	1.33	1.59	3.21	43	2.06	0.87	6.22	65
Age of Women								1737				1653
15-24	31.65	53.83	28.3	372	51.59	40.93	49.24	817	42.32	40.31	45.23	716
25-34	59.52	44.37	63.74	765	37.39	48.61	43.54	770	45.11	50.62	49.97	817
35-49	8.83	1.8	7.96	97	11.02	10.45	7.23	150	12.57	9.06	4.8	120

per cent for Chhattisgarh and Jharkhand. Similarly, about 90 per cent ST women in Uttarakhand live in rural area and it is 95 per cent for Jharkhand and Chhattisgarh. The economic differential among the caste groups is remarkable in these three states. In case of Uttarakhand, 11 per cent of SC are classified in the poorest quintile as compared to 7 per cent among ST and 8 per cent among general. In case of Jharkhand and Chhattisgarh, the proportion of poor is relatively higher for ST and SC compared to others. In Chhattisgarh, 75 per cent of ST fall under poorest quintile, for SC it is 69 per cent, followed by general which is 45 per cent. This pattern is similar for Jharkhand. The religion differential among the caste group is sharp which shows that proportion of Hindu is higher for all the caste as compared to Muslims and others. This is true for all the states. The educational differential by caste shows that the proportion of women who are illiterate is higher among SCs followed by STs and general. In Uttarakhand, it is 73 per cent for ST, 55 per cent for SC and 35 per cent for others.

Differential in Maternal and Child Health Status by Social Groups in the Three States

Table 17.4 presents the extent of inequality in all the seven MCH indicators between the caste groups. From the table, it is found that SC and ST have poorly performed in all the health and nutritional indicators as a whole in comparison to general.

Table 17.4

Health and Nutrition Status by Castes/Tribes

	Uttarakhand				*Jharkhand*				*Chhattisgarh*			
Health & Nutrition Indicators	*SC*	*ST*	*Non-SC/ST*	*N*	*SC*	*ST*	*Non-SC/ST*	*N*	*SC*	*ST*	*Non-SC/ST*	*N*
Child Indicator												
Full immunisation	54.1	41.9	63.0	219	25.07	31.5	39.1	303	47.8	42.2	52.9	284
Received BCG	78.3	71.0	85.9		63.85	75.2	73.5		79.5	81.2	87.9	
Received DPT	57.8	71.0	70.1		32.65	39.3	44.1		62.1	62.3	63.8	
Received polio	72.7	71.0	83.4		63.85	80.5	81.5		82.6	82.5	87.3	
Received measles	65.1	56.5	74.5		44.61	42.5	52.6		62.1	55.6	66.4	
Nutritional Status				1030				1387				1442
Stunting	54.9	47.9	41.4		53.48	55.2	46.5		57.7	52.6	53.3	
Wasting	21.3	21.4	18.0		29.59	40.2	29.3		14.8	27.1	17.7	
Underweight	44.9	50.3	35.3		56.79	65.5	53.0		46.4	53.3	44.8	
Anaemia level	73.5	72.3	57.5		76.44	80.5	64.6	1300	69.0	78.1	69.4	1295
Women Indicator												
Safe delivery	24.4	7.9	36.9	1227	15.24	7.9	24.7	1726	11.3	3.9	21.1	1653
Full ANC	19.3	9.2	30.1	869	13.51	12.2	26.4	1196	20.3	15.1	27.5	1197
3 & more visits	38.8	22.9	50.7	833	27.79	25.9	43.0	1193	48.0	48.1	59.6	1195
TT injection	63.2	65.1	71.0	867	63.88	54.2	75.7	1193	76.3	68.2	78.4	1192
IFA tablets	36.2	24.3	46.6	527	21.49	29.5	31.0	579	21.9	24.7	32.2	876
Anaemia level	60.0	71.4	53.1	2839	72.58	85.0	62.4	2779	51.9	74.0	50.3	3776
Undernutrition	37.9	48.9	26.6	2735	39.30	47.01	42.01	2624	38.4	50.4	40.9	3582

Looking into the full immunisation coverage, say for Uttarakhand it is 42 per cent among ST, followed by SC that is 54 per cent and by general that is 63 per cent. This pattern is same for Chhattisgarh. Whereas in Jharkhand it is found that full immunisation coverage is lowest among SCs that is 25 per cent, 31 per cent for STs and 39 per cent for general. If we compare full immunisation coverage between the three states, it is found that the coverage is lower in Jharkhand as compared to Uttarakhand and Chhattisgarh. Out of various components of immunisation, it is found that the coverage of measles is lower as compared to other vaccination in all the three states.

Coming to nutritional status, it is found that proportion of underweight children is higher among STs followed by SCs and general. In Jharkhand, it is 66 per cent for ST, 57 per cent for SC followed by general. This pattern is same for other two states. Looking into the nutritional status of women, it is higher for ST that is 48 per cent, 37 per cent for SC and 26 per cent for general in Uttarakhand. But in Jharkhand, it is higher for ST that is 47 per cent followed by others, that is 42 per cent and SCs. This pattern is same for Chhattisgarh.

Similar is the case with anaemia level both for children and women. It is observed from the table that anaemia level is higher in all the three states among all the groups particularly among STs. In Jharkhand more than 80 per cent children and women among STs become anaemic. In Uttarakhand only, proportion of anaemic children is higher among SCs followed by ST and general.

Looking into other programme-related indicators, the situation is the same and is much sharper. If we observe the safe delivery case in Uttarakhand, it is 8 per cent STs followed by SCs that is 24.4 per cent and general that is 37 per cent. This pattern is same for the other two states. In Chhattisgarh, the differential is much higher. Only 4 per cent of STs go to health institutions.

If we look into the results it is found that in all states, the proportion of women going to health institutions for delivery is lower among all the groups. And it is much lower for Chhattisgarh compared to the other two states. In Uttarakhand even though economic inequality is low among the caste groups, still there exists social inequality in utilisation of these services.

In case of antenatal care, it is observed that the coverage of complete ANC is lowest for STs followed by SCs and general. In Uttarakhand, the coverage of full ANC is 9 per cent for ST, 19 per cent for SC and 30 per cent for general. Like safe delivery, full ANC coverage is lower in all the three states. The possible reasons for not utilising these services are lack of awareness among women, lack of accessibility of these services, both physical and economical.

Economic Differential in Maternal and Child Health Status in the Three States

Table 17.5 presents economic inequalities in these three states with respect to all seven indicators selected for the analysis. Wealth index is used to examine the extent of inequality prevailing in different income groups with respect to such indicators. The differential in full immunisation coverage varies directly with wealth quintile in Chhattisgarh. In Jharkhand, it is lowest for poorest followed by middle, poorer and so on. Whereas in Uttarakhand, it is lowest for poorer followed by poorest, middle, richer and richest.

Looking into the safe delivery case in Uttarakhand, it is 8 per cent for poorer followed by poorest that is 12 per cent, 16 per cent for middle, 30 per cent for richer and 70 per cent for richest. Similarly, in Chhattisgarh it is 4 per cent for poorest, 5 per cent for poorer, 17 per cent for middle, 37 per cent for richer and 88 per cent for richest. This shows that not only inequality exists among the income groups but also the extent of inequality is sharp. This situation is same with coverage of FANC.

Looking into the table, it is found that, though inequality exists among the income groups with respect to such indicators, the extent of inequality is higher in safe delivery and coverage of FANC in all the states.

There are certain other correlates of health and nutrition indicators except caste/tribe or income. If higher percentages of SC/ST or low income group people do not go for FANC or if they are anaemic, that may not be due to their caste *per se* or due to their low income. It can be due to certain other factors. Thus, besides caste and wealth index, a

Table 17.5

Health and Nutrition Status by Wealth Index

Health & Nutrtion Indicators	*Uttarakhand*						*Jharkhand*						*Chhattisgarh*					
	Q1	*Q2*	*Q3*	*Q4*	*Q5*	*N*	*Q1*	*Q2*	*Q3*	*Q4*	*Q5*	*N*	*Q1*	*Q2*	*Q3*	*Q4*	*Q5*	*N*
Child Indicator																		
Full immunisation	39.1	32.4	60.4	63.3	80	219	24.5	41.5	28	62	76.3	304	37.0	48	53	68	94.4	285
Receive BCG	55.9	73.0	82.9	86.6	95.7		63.5	82.6	77	90	100		76.8	89.1	84.2	100	100	
Receive DPT	39.1	45.1	70.5	69.2	84.5		29.7	50.2	40	67	79.2		52.2	65.4	60.6	86	100.0	
Receive polio	61.5	57.5	80.6	88.4	92.9		73.7	91.3	80	87	88.1		78.6	87.7	90.6	83	100.0	
Receive Measles	55.9	40.0	73.0	80.9	87.1		39	60.6	36	70	85.2		49.3	67.3	63.5	90	94.4	
Nutritional Status						1030						1390						1445
Stunting	62.5	63.6	53.1	46.4	22		55	53	43	47	13.5		58.1	59.1	49.9	50	20.4	
Wasting	25.9	25.4	23.5	16.4	11.9		36	32.4	32	24	17.3		24.6	15.9	20.6	11	15.8	
Underweight	57.4	54.1	44.2	39.8	18.2		63.5	61.2	49	49	17.1		55.6	51.2	40.3	31	17.8	
Anaemia level	77.7	69.4	67.3	58	51.6	887	76.9	68.7	59	64	47.3	1303	76.1	74.9	67.8	66	52.7	1297
Women Indicator																		
Safe delivery	11.6	8.1	16	30.2	69.8	1227	5.39	15	28.6	42.3	91.9	1729	3.7	4.91	17.1	37	88.0	1665
Full ANC	9.3	7.3	15.5	24.5	52.9	870	9.7	19.8	33.1	36.9	65.3	1200	14.2	19.6	23.6	44	58.2	1198
3 & more visits	13.1	20	34.7	45.1	80.5	833	18.8	40.2	58.3	62.9	89.2	1196	41.8	50.5	63.3	84	92.2	1196
TT injection	37.0	43	64.8	71.6	92.5	868	56.1	79.1	81.3	82.9	95.3	1196	65.6	75.1	85.4	91	90.5	1193
IFA tablets	33.6	25	25.1	39.2	60.3	527	19.2	27.3	37.9	34.3	62.2	579	22.7	22.4	26.1	40	63.6	876
Anaemia level	61.6	56	60	59.2	48.2	2842	76.6	71.4	64	60	55	2786	65.4	56.5	55.3	48	43.9	3768
Undernutrition	39.9	43	37	31	18.3	2738	50	47.8	47.7	35.1	17.5	2630	52.7	46.9	41.1	32	16.4	3585

Note: Q1 = Poorest; Q2 = Poorer; Q3 = Middle; Q4 = Richer; Q5 = Richest.

set of independent variables are taken for examining the differentials in health and nutritional status between the individuals belonging to different socio-economic groups. These are type of residence, women's education, religion of the women, age of the mother, sex of the child, birth order, work status of women, exposure to mass media etc. For this, logistic regression is carried out to capture the significance of other variables.

Results of Logistic Regression

Maternal Indicators

FANC: Differential between SC women and general regarding full ANC disappear in all the three states, whereas in Jharkhand and Chhattisgarh 'ST' women are less likely to get FANC. The programmes should focus specifically on the STs. Except caste, in Jharkhand it is found that women belong to richest quintile are more likely to FANC. Thus, in Jharkhand it is income which matters in utilisation of ANC.

Safe Delivery: Differential between SC/ST women and women in general category disappear in all the three states. Thus, here caste does not play any role. Economic factor plays an important role here. In Uttarakhand, women belonging to richer quintile are three times more likely to go to health institutions, in Jharkhand it is two times and in Chhattisgarh four times.

Anaemia: It is found that ST women are two times more likely to get anaemic in all the three states. SC women in Uttarakhand and Chhattisgarh are more than one time likely to be anaemic than general.

Undernutrition: Differential between SC/ST and general persist regarding BMI in Uttarakhand. The odds of having low BMI is 2.07 for ST and 1.47 for SC in Uttarakhand, whereas in Jharkhand and Chhattisgarh, SC women are less likely to be underweight compared to general. In Chhattisgarh, it found that women belonging to richest quintile have low BMI. This is the case with Jharkhand also.

Table 17.6

Results of Logistic Regression for Women

	Uttarakhand				*Jharkhand*				*Chhattisgarh*			
	Full ANC	*Safe Delivery*	*Anaemia*	*Under-nutrition*	*Full ANC*	*Safe Delivery*	*Anaemia*	*Under-nutrition*	*Full ANC*	*Safe Delivery*	*Anaemia*	*Under-nutrition*
Caste												
General [R]												
SC	1.01	1.12	1.29*	1.47*	0.72	0.72	1.36**	0.8*	0.82	1.04	1.01	0.74***
ST	0.44	0.38	2.01*	2.07*	0.38*	0.88	2.62***	0.92	0.66*	0.61	2.48***	1.03
Wealth Index												
Q1[R]												
Q2	0.87	1.63	0.78	0.78	1.61*	1.73*	0.89	0.91	1.17	0.92	0.85*	0.80***
Q3	1.2	1.92	0.98	0.98	3.09***	2.14**	0.69**	0.95	1.42	2.49**	0.85	0.70***
Q4	1.69	3.53**	0.96	0.96	3.48***	2.61***	0.62***	0.56***	2.45**	4.96***	0.65***	0.49***
Q5	2.42	7.85***	0.71	0.71	4.52***	16.07***	0.55***	0.25***	1.72	22.59***	0.55***	0.23***
Place of Residence												
Urban[R]												
Rural	0.61**	0.59**	1.18	1.45***	1.05	0.44**	1.01	0.94	0.61**	0.25***	0.81**	1.13
Religion												
Hindu[R]												
Muslim	1.62	0.77	1.74***	1.31	1.07	0.83	0.89	1.13	0.7	3.02**	0.96	0.95
Others	1.21	4.86***	1.12	1.08	1.49	0.35**	1.1	0.98	0.98	0.73	0.73	1.52*

Contd...

...contd...

	Uttarakhand				*Jharkhand*				*Chhattisgarh*			
	Full ANC	*Safe Delivery*	*Anaemia*	*Under-nutrition*	*Full ANC*	*Safe Delivery*	*Anaemia*	*Under-nutrition*	*Full ANC*	*Safe Delivery*	*Anaemia*	*Under-nutrition*
Education												
No[R]												
Primary	1.84*	1.17	0.96	0.95	1.53	0.8	1.01	0.74**	1.13	0.98	0.87	0.96
Secondary	3.10***	1.93***	0.95	0.97	1.38	2.90***	0.92	0.73***	1.33	1.7	0.80**	0.9
Higher	7.83***	10.54***	0.74**	0.67**	3.47***	15.63***	0.81	0.87	3.07**	4.42***	0.76	0.76
Age of Women												
15-24[R]												
25-34			1	0.57***			1.04	0.69***			0.85*	0.74***
35+			0.77***	0.51***			1.17	0.53***			0.91	0.45***
Birth Order												
1[R]												
2	0.69*	0.52***			0.79	0.51***			0.81	0.44***		
3	0.47**	0.41***			0.69	0.32***			0.69	0.23***		
4+	0.61	0.41***			0.69	0.30***			0.61**	0.20***		
Full ANC												
No[R]												
Yes		2.23***				2.13***				1.36		

Note: *<=0.10 **<=0.05 ***<=0.01; R= Reference Category.

Table 17.7

Results of Logistic Regression for Children

	Uttarakhand			*Jharkhand*			*Chhattisgarh*		
	Full Immunisation	*Malnutrition*	*Anaemia*	*Full Immunisation*	*Malnutrition*	*Anaemia*	*Full Immunisation*	*Malnutrition*	*Anaemia*
Caste									
General[R]									
SC	0.97	1.18	1.79***	1.00	0.96	1.59**	0.44	0.89	0.97
ST	1.18	1.11	1.78	1.01	1.14	1.56**	0.71	1.09	1.29
Wealth Index									
Q1[R]									
Q2	0.63	0.91	0.63	1.12	1.03	0.76	2.44**	0.93	0.99
Q3	1.27	0.69	0.61	0.88	0.74	0.59**	0.69	0.67**	0.75
Q4	1.45	0.64	0.43**	1.29	0.75	0.68	4.23***	0.56**	0.71
Q5	2.47	0.33***	0.38***	6.68*	0.22***	0.40***	2.12	0.43**	0.31***
Place of Residence									
Urban[R]									
Rural	0.71	1.67**	1.09	0.68	1.09	1.08	1.44	1.10	0.58***
Religion									
Hindu[R]									
Muslim	0.53	1.78**	1.84**	1.24	0.86	1.19	0.61	0.77	1.73
Others	4.72	0.99	1.07	0.49	1.38	1.25	0.90	0.64	0.20**

Contd...

...contd...

	Uttarakhand			*Jharkhand*			*Chhattisgarh*		
	Full Immunisation	*Malnutrition*	*Anaemia*	*Full Immunisation*	*Malnutrition*	*Anaemia*	*Full Immunisation*	*Malnutrition*	*Anaemia*
Education									
No[R]									
Primary	0.63	0.76	0.75	1.42	0.79	0.62**	0.45*	1.04	0.85
Secondary	2.24*	0.62***	0.86	2.55**	0.66**	0.80	2.35***	0.61***	0.72*
Higher	0.86	0.39*	0.69	1.24	0.30**	0.71	3.81	0.29***	0.56
Age of Child									
< 1 year[R]									
<25 months		1.43	1.75**		2.42***	0.92		1.31	0.81
25+		2.23***	0.59**		2.31***	0.34***		1.30*	0.25***
Birth Order									
1[R]									
2	0.82			0.83			0.87		
3	0.83			1.37			0.58		
4+	0.37*			0.82			0.52***		
Anemia of Women									
No[R]									
Yes			2.08***			2.49***			1.58***

Note: *<=0.10 **<=0.05 ***<=0.01; R= Reference Category.

Child Health Indicators

Full Immunisation: Differential between SC/ST and general disappear regarding immunisation. This also happens in different income groups.

Malnutrition: Differential between SC/ST and general disappear regarding malnutrition. This states that caste does not have any effect on malnutrition. In Chhattisgarh, it is income which plays a significant role for this. This is the case with Uttarakhand and Jharkhand.

Anaemia: Differential between SC and general persist in Uttarakhand and Jharkhand regarding anaemia. The odds of having anaemia for SC is 1.8 in Uttarakhand, 1.6 in Jharkhand but in Chhattisgarh, caste does not have any effect on anaemia.

Conclusion

The broad idea of the present paper is to understand the inequalities in maternal and child health and nutritional indicators. Caste and wealth quintiles are used as the basis of analysis to capture the inequalities. The study focuses on three states which are the newly formed states of India and lagging behind in various socio-economic and demographic indicators. It is found that there is greater inequality in these health and nutritional indicators by distribution of wealth and by different social groups. Instead of caste and wealth, certain other factors are also contributing to this such as educational level of women, age of women, religion, birth order etc. In all the indicators STs are lagging behind, followed by SCs and general. The level of immunisation, ANC and safe deliveries, the three main components of RCH services and also other nutritional indicators varies directly with the wealth index in both the states of Jharkhand and Chhattisgarh whereas in Uttarakhand, it is the poorer quintile who are lagging behind in all three RCH indicators. The result of logistic regression shows that caste is not a significant predictor except for anaemia of women; whereas, wealth index has a significant predictor in many indicators. This implies economically weaker sections do receive less care than other sections. In other words, economic factors play a significant role in access to and utilisation of maternal and child health care rather than caste. Though inequality persists in all indicators both by caste and distribution of wealth, the extent of inequality is relatively higher for ANC and safe delivery as compared to other indicators for all the three states. Hence, there is a need not only to find out the reasons for inequality in such indicators but also more programmatic stress should be given to improve ANC and safe delivery for poorer section of the society. As the deprivation in MCH indicators are mainly attributable to low income rather than low social status, there is a greater need to focus on the weaker and disadvantaged section of the society in the health care matter. There is a need to address the difficulties faced by the poor in obtaining various health care facilities.

References

Ahmed, S. (2004). "Does family planning program reduce inequality in contraceptive use, fertility and other health care utilization? Evidence from Bangladesh", paper presented in Population Association of America (PAA), USA.

Bhatia, J.C and J. Clealand (1995). "Determinants of maternal care in a region of South India", *Health Transition Review* 5: 127-142.

Bishoyi, D. (2005). "Economic inequality in utilization of reproductive and child health services: A comparative study of Orissa and Bihar", Seminar paper presented in IIPS.

Bose, A. and R.P. Tyagi (1983). "Rural health services: present status", in Bose, A. and P.B. Desai (eds.), *Studies in Social Dynamics of Primary Health Care*. Delhi, India: Hindustan Publishing Corporation. pp. 104-122.

Carr, D. (2004). "Improving the health of the world's poorest people", *Health Bulletin* 1: 1-34.

Dreze, J. and A. Sen (1995). *India Economic Development and Social Opportunity*. Delhi: Oxford University Press.

Gage, A.J., A.E. Sommerfelt and A.L. Piani (1997). "Household structure and childhood immunization in Niger and Nigeria", *Demography* 34: 295-309.

Ghosh, S. (1989). "Child health and survival- Its relationship with maternal health", in Singh, S.N., M.K. Premi, P.S. Bhatia and Ashish Bose (eds.), *Population Transition in India* I. Delhi, India: B.R. Publishing Corporation. pp. 267-280.

Govindasamy, P. and B.M. Ramesh (1997). "Maternal education and the utilization of maternal and child health services in India", *National Family Health Survey Subject Reports*, Number 5. Mumbai, India: International Institute for Population Science and Calverton, USA: Macro International Inc.

International Institute for Population Sciences and ORC Macro (2007). *National Family Health Survey-2005-06*. Mumbai, India.

Kanitkar, T. and R.K. Sinha (1989). "Antenatal care services in five states of India", in Singh, S.N., M.K. Premi, P.S. Bhatia and Ashish Bose (eds.), *Population Transition in India* II. Delhi, India: C.R. Publishing Corporation. pp.201-212.

Majumdar, P.K., R. Tiwari, B. Ram and B.N. Bhattacharya (1994). "Study on utilization of maternity and child health services in rural Jammu, India", *Health and Population Perspectives and Issues* 17: 4-34.

Negi, N.S. (2007). "Utilization of maternal and child health services among tribals in Chhattisgarh", M. Phil Dissertation presented in IIPS.

Obermeyer, C.M. (1993). "Culture, maternal health care and women's status: A comparison of Morocco and Tunisia", *Studies in Family Planning* 24: 354-365.

Obermeyer, C.M. and J.E. Potter (1991). "Maternal health care utilization in Jordan: A study of patterns and determinants", *Studies in Family Planning* 22: 177-187.

Pandey, A., Nandini Roy, D. Sahu and Rajib Acharya (2004). "Maternal health care services: Observation from Chhattisgarh, Jharkhand and Uttaranchal", *Economic and Political Weekly* 39(7): 713-720.

Roy, T.K., Sumati Kulkarni and Y. Vaidehi (2004). "Social Inequalities in health and nutrition in selected states", *Economic and Political Weekly* 39(7): 677-683.

Rustein, Shea O., and K. Johnson (2004). "The DHS wealth index", *DHS Comparative Reports* 6. Maryland, USA: ORC Macro.

Shariff, A. (1999). *India Human Development Report: A Profile of Indian States in the 1990s.* New Delhi, India: Oxford University Press.

Sivakami, M. and P.M. Kulkarni (2003). "Are Socially and economically weaker sections deprived of maternal health care in Tamilnadu in India", *Journal of Health and Population In Developing Countries*, 7 August, pp. 1-15.

Wagstaff, A. (2002). "Poverty, and Health care inequalities", *Bulletin of the World Health Organization* 80(2): 97-105.

E. HIV/AIDS

18 Perceived Risk and Vulnerability to HIV of Youth in Uttarakhand

Dhananjay W. Bansod
and Benoy Peter

Introduction

HIV transmission among general population often occurs through their sexual partners, who also have an infected sexual partner/s among the high risk groups. Among the general population, women, youth and adolescents are the most vulnerable. Physiologically, young people are more vulnerable to STIs than adults; girls more than boys. Gender imbalances, societal norms and economic dependence contribute to this risk. Lack of access to correct information (almost 73 per cent of young people have misconceptions about modes of HIV transmission), tendency to experiment and an environment which makes discussing issues around sexuality taboo adds to their vulnerability. In India, people in the age group of 15-29 years comprise nearly a quarter of the country's population; however, they account for 31 per cent of AIDS burden (NACO, 2007). This clearly indicates that young people are at a high risk of contracting HIV infection.

Young women are biologically more vulnerable to HIV infection than young men—a situation aggravated by their lack of access to information on HIV and even lesser power to exercise control over their sexual lives. Early marriage also poses special risks to young people, particularly women. This is especially relevant for India, where almost every second girl is married off by the time they are 18 years of age. In India, women account for around one million out of 2.5 million estimated number of people living with HIV/AIDS. Their heightened vulnerability has both biological and socio-economic reasons. Early marriage, violence and sexual abuse against women are the major socio-economic reasons of their vulnerability to HIV infection. Their biological construct makes them more susceptible to HIV infection in any given heterosexual encounter.

AIDS is a development and gender issue (Seidel, 1993). Social inequality between men's and women's roles and positions is cited as being most responsible for the spread of HIV/AIDS in India. Because of their subordinate role, middle and lower class and especially village women, are more sexually vulnerable. They tend to have limited knowledge of the problems and the risks associated with the HIV virus. Women have less knowledge of how to avoid HIV 'and also less social power to oppose risk conditions'. "Lack of social and physical access to health services for women further increases their vulnerability to the HIV virus" (Pachauri, 1994).

A joint report on the AIDS pandemic by UNAIDS and the WHO stated that AIDS is affecting women and girls in increasing numbers such that globally, almost 50 per cent of all people living with HIV are female and 76 per cent of young people (aged 15–24 years) living with HIV in Sub-Saharan Africa are female. The report also pointed to steep increases in HIV infections in East Asia, Eastern Europe and Central Asia between 2002–2004 (UNAIDS/WHO, 2004). In India, women account for 21.3 per cent of all AIDS cases (Sharma *et al.*, 2001).

The nation is clearly divided into low risk states in the north, and high risk states in the south (NACO, 2004). High risk states are those states where the sero-prevalence rate is above 1 per cent. Low risk states are states in which the sero-prevalence rate is below 1 per cent. The National AIDS Control Organisation (NACO) recognises that the southern states of India are considered to be at highest risk and areas of lowest risk are states in the northern half of the country.

Globally, it is known that there is a lack of HIV knowledge among youth between the ages of 15-24. The World Health Organization (WHO) states that youths are at the epicentre of preventing the progression of the HIV/AIDS pandemic. The WHO estimates that youths aged 15 to 24 comprise 50 per cent of all new HIV infections and consequently must be targeted for education in decreasing transmission and reducing the stigmatisation of an HIV diagnosis (WHO, 2004).

Globally available evidence suggests that age at puberty is falling (Winter, 1992) while age at marriage is rising. The amount of time young people experience between puberty and first marriage has increased. This means that the first sexual experience and childbearing may take place for many in a different personal and social context. There are some other factors too, which may encourage premarital sexuality; such as the changing mores, massive urbanisation influence of modern mass media and information technology, migration of younger people to towns and cities in search of jobs and better lifestyle, erosion of traditional customs and social norms which had been main discouraging barriers for premarital sex in the past (Tiwari and Kumar, 2002).

The study conducted by Tiwari and Kumar (2002) in Delhi and Lucknow among youths aged 15-24, found that about one-quarter to one-third youths indulged in premarital sex and hardly one-fifth of always use a condom. Around one-tenth of the females always used condom. Quite a high percentage of respondents replied female sex workers (FSWs) or friends/relatives as sex partners. This implies that there is a multiple partner relationship and has serious implications as infections from FSWs may be transmitted to friends and relatives. It has been also found that one-third to half of the respondents do not have knowledge on various aspects of sex and to manage problems arising out of premarital sex. Khasakhala and Mturi (2008) conducted a survey among unmarried and unemployed out-of-school youth to study risky sexual behaviour. It was found that for these youth, contextual and probably social factors appear to be the main determinants of risky sexual behaviour for both males and females.

In the light of literature and availability of data, the study is an attempt to understand and compare the socio-cultural determinants of vulnerability among young men and women in Uttarakhand, India.

Objectives of the Study

The study is an attempt to understand the factors influencing the knowledge and behaviour of youth in Uttarakhand that would decide their vulnerability to HIV/AIDS. The specific objectives are:

- To assess the factors influencing youths' vulnerability to HIV.
- To understand the sexual behaviour and their determinants among youth in Uttarakhand.
- To examine the gender differentials in the sexual behaviour of the youth.

Methodology

Data will be used from National Family Health Survey (NFHS-3), which was conducted during 2005-06. For the first time, NFHS-3 provides information on men and unmarried women. The survey is based on a sample of households, which is representative at the national and state levels. NFHS-3 conducted interviews with almost 199,000 women aged 15-49 and men aged 15-54 throughout India. NFHS-3 tested more than 100,000 women and men for HIV infection and also collected information on HIV/AIDS-related attitudes and behaviour. Multivariate statistical analyses were carried out exploring the NFHS-3 data for Uttarakhand, keeping in view the above objectives of the study.

Profile of Youth

Among men, 60 per cent of them were from the late adolescent age and the rest were from the early adulthood stage. Two-thirds of them were from rural areas whereas the other one-third were from urban Uttarakhand. Near about 90 per cent of the women had secondary education or above educational qualification. But five per cent of the men had no formal schooling. Except for 11.6 per cent, all young men were from the never married category. Hindus constituted more than four-fifths of them. Muslims constituted the second highest proportion of religious groups with slightly more than 10 per cent among the total. Two-thirds of the youth were either from the richer or richest layers of wealth. The poorest constituted five per cent of youth and poorer category constituted near about 15 per cent of the young population surveyed (Table 18.1).

Table 18.1

Frequency Distribution of Young Men in Uttarakhand by Selected Background Characteristics

Background Characteristics	*Frequency*	*Percentage*
Age		
15-19	193	60.2
20-24	128	39.8
Place of Residence		
Urban	111	34.5
Rural	210	65.5
Education		
No education	15	4.7
Primary	24	7.5
Secondary & higher	282	87.9
Marital Status		
Never married	284	88.4
Married	37	11.6
Religion		
Hindu	271	84.5
Muslim	34	10.5
Others	16	5.0
Wealth Index		
Poorest	17	5.3
Poorer	43	13.4
Middle	63	19.7
Richer	75	23.4
Richest	123	38.2
Recent Sexual Activity		
Never had intercourse	256	80.0
Active in last four weeks	30	9.4
Not active in last four weeks	35	10.6
Heard of STI		
No	21	6.5
Yes	300	93.5
Ever Heard of AIDS		
No	21	6.5
Yes	300	93.5
Total	321	100.0

Among the young women, more than half of them are from the late adolescent group and the rest from early adulthood (Table 18.2). Three quarters of them are from rural area and two-thirds were unmarried.

Table 18.2

Frequency Distribution of Young Women in Uttarakhand by Selected Background Characteristics

Background Characteristics	*Frequency*	*Percentage*
Age		
15-19	624	54.8
20-24	516	45.2
Place of Residence		
Urban	291	25.5
Rural	849	74.5
Education		
No education	171	15.0
Primary	144	12.6
Secondary & higher	825	72.4
Marital Status		
Never married	740	64.9
Married	398	34.9
Religion		
Hindu	964	84.6
Muslim	102	8.9
Others	74	6.5
Wealth Index		
Poorest	52	4.6
Poorer	175	15.4
Middle	233	20.5
Richer	277	24.3
Richest	402	35.3
Recent Sexual Activity		
Never had intercourse	742	65.1
Active in last four weeks	269	23.6
Not active in last four weeks—postpartum abstinence	29	2.5
Not active in last four weeks—not postpartum abstinence	100	8.8
Heard of STI		
No	260	22.8
Yes	878	77.0
Ever Heard of AIDS		
No	271	23.7
Yes	869	76.3
Total	1140	100.0

Note: The totals for 'marital status', 'wealth index' and 'heard of STI' may not add to 1140 due to missing cases.

Seven out of ten women had secondary or higher education whereas 15 per cent never attended school. The distribution by religion was more or less similar to the distribution of young men with about 85 per cent women being Hindus. Similar was the distribution by wealth index with richer and richest constituting about 60 per cent of the total women.

Knowledge about HIV Prevention

Except for 6.5 per cent, all men have heard about AIDS as well as STI. Three quarters of the young women have heard about both AIDS and sexually transmitted infections. Detailed below is the analysis by major means of prevention explored in NFHS-3:

Abstinence as Prevention against HIV

Overall 87 per cent men know that abstinence is a way to prevent HIV infection. More than four-fifths of men in the 15-19 age group know this. Nine out of ten men in the 20-24 age group are knowledgeable about the method of prevention. Near about 86 per cent of young men irrespective of the place of residence identifies abstinence as a mode of protection. Nine out of ten young men with secondary or higher educational attainment and 8 out of 10 primary educated are aware that abstinence from sex is a means of prevention against HIV infection. However, among the uneducated young men only half of them are aware about this. Approximately 95 per cent of the married recognises abstinence's potential as means of prevention. More than 90 per cent in the richer and richest groups, 85 per cent among the middle wealth group and 78 per cent among poorer wealth category know about abstinence. Among the poorest, 73 per cent knows about abstinence as a prevention method (Table 18.3).

Little above three quarters of women are aware that abstinence from sex is one of the prevention modes against HIV. Among both the age categories, a similar proportion of young women reported that they know that abstinence is one of the means of prevention against HIV infection. Four-fifths of the young women from urban Uttarakhand know that abstinence from sex prevents HIV whereas the proportion is 75 per cent in the case of rural young women. It was found that four-fifths of women with secondary or higher educational attainment understand abstinence

Table 18.3

Per cent Distribution of Young Men by Knowledge about HIV Prevention Method

Background Characteristics	*Abstinence from Sex*	*Limiting Sexual Intercourse with One Partner*	*Using Condoms*	*Comprehensive Knowledge#*
Age				
15-19	83.6	85.3***	81.8**	42.5***
20-24	91.8	95.1	92.7	57.8
Place of Residence				
Urban	88.1	94.1*	84.3	41.4*
Rural	86.4	86.9	87.3	52.6
Education				
No education	53.8***	76.9	69.2***	13.3***
Primary	78.9	84.2	73.7	20.8
Secondary & higher	89.1	90.3	88.0	52.8
Marital Status				
Never married	86.0	87.9*	85.2	47.2
Married	94.3	100.0	94.4	59.5
Religion				
Hindu	88.0*	89.1	87.5**	52.4***
Muslim	80.8	88.9	70.4	20.6
Others	80.0	93.3	93.3	43.8
Wealth Index				
Poorest	73.3*	93.3	92.9	35.3
Poorer	78.0	78.0	73.2	51.2
Middle	85.5	83.6	81.8	42.9
Richer	91.0	94.1	89.7	45.3
Richest	90.1	92.6	90.1	54.5
Total	87.0 (260)	89.3 (268)	86.3 (258)	48.6 (156)

Note: *** P < 0.001, ** P < 0.005, * P < 0.01.

Respondents with comprehensive knowledge say that use of condom for every act of sexual intercourse and having just one uninfected partner can reduce the chance of getting HIV/AIDS, say that a healthy-looking person can have HIV/AIDS, and rejects the two most common misconceptions in NFHS-3 about HIV/AIDS transmission or prevention.

as means of prevention of infection. Among the primary educated the proportion is 59 per cent and 73 per cent of women with no formal education also identifies this as a mode of prevention. Slightly above three quarters of married as well as unmarried women recognises that abstaining from sex will prevent HIV infection. More than 70 per cent of women from all major religious categories also recognises it. Near about two-third of young women from the poorest wealth index group and a similar proportion from the poorer wealth index group are aware about the prevention mode. Among the richest, 84 per cent know that abstinence is a way of prevention of HIV infection (Table 18.4).

Table 18.4

Per cent Distribution of Young Women by Knowledge about HIV Prevention Method

Background Characteristics	*Abstinence from Sex*	*Limiting Sexual Intercourse with One Partner*	*Using Condoms*	*Comprehensive Knowledge#*
Age				
15-19	75.3	82.6**	74.4*	31.9
20-24	78.9	89.2	80.5	35.1
Place of Residence				
Urban	80.6**	88.2	78.7	45.5***
Rural	75.3	84.2	76.4	29.2
Education				
No education	73.2***	83.1**	67.6***	7.0***
Primary	58.8	75.3	64.0	11.1
Secondary & higher	79.4	87.0	79.5	42.8
Marital Status				
Never married	76.6	84.6	76.7	38.8***
Married	77.6	87.5	78.0	23.4
Religion				
Hindu	77.3	85.9	78.4**	34.5**
Muslim	72.2	81.9	62.5	22.5
Others	78.3	85.0	78.0	32.9
Wealth Index				
Poorest	65.2***	91.7***	73.9	11.5***
Poorer	68.6	75.6	70.6	15.4
Middle	73.5	82.1	75.6	22.3
Richer	71.5	80.0	73.2	26.3
Richest	83.8	91.7	81.5	55.2
Total	76.9 (668)	85.5 (743)	77.1 (669)	33.4 (380)

Note: *** P < 0.001, ** P < 0.005, * P < 0.01.

Respondents with comprehensive knowledge say that use of condom for every act of sexual intercourse and having just one uninfected partner can reduce the chance of getting HIV/AIDS, say that a healthy-looking person can have HIV/AIDS, and rejects the two most common misconceptions in NFHS-3 about HIV/AIDS transmission or prevention.

Limiting Sexual Intercourse to One Partner

Among the young men, 90 per cent know that limiting sexual partners to one reduces the chance of HIV infection. Among the 20-24 age group, 95 per cent are aware about this and in the 15-19 age group, the proportion aware are less by 10 per cent points. Out of 10 secondary and above educated 9 know about the mode while 84 per cent of the primary educated were aware. Three quarters of young men who never attended school also know the scope of limiting partners to one in reducing HIV vulnerability. All the married and 88 per cent of unmarried men and near about 90 per cent men from major religions in Uttarakhand know about the method. The poorest, richer and richest wealth categories also have similar proportion of men having knowledge abut single partner relationship reducing HIV risk (Table 18.3).

Except for 15 per cent, all young women know that limiting to one sexual partner can reduce the risk of HIV infection of an individual. Nine out of 10 women in the 20-24 category and 83 per cent of women in the 15-19 category also are aware about the method. Roughly 85 per cent urban as well as rural youth and a similar proportion of unmarried as well as married women are aware that limiting partners reduce risk. Nearly four-fifths of the women in the uneducated and three quarters of primary educated as well as 87 per cent young women with secondary or above education were aware that single partner relationship can reduce the chances of getting infected. The proportion of women was nearly 85 per cent irrespective of the different religions also were aware. Three quarters of the poorer wealth index; about 80 per cent from the middle and richer categories, 92 per cent from poorest and richest categories knew single partner relationship would reduce the risk of getting HIV (Table 18.4).

Using Condoms

Overall 86 per cent men know that condom use prevents HIV. Among the 15-19 age group it was 82 per cent and 92 per cent in the case of 20-24 age group. Among both rural and urban young men, the proportion of men who know about the means of prevention was areound 85 per cent. Among men with no formal schooling roughly 70 per cent reported having knowledge about condom use as a method of AIDS prevention. The awareness about the method among the never married was 85 per cent and 95 per cent among the married men. Among Hindus, 87 per cent and 70 per cent of the Muslims and 93 per cent of men from other religious groups in Uttarakhand were knowledgeable about the means of HIV prevention. The proportion of men who know about condom use as a prevention means was highest in the poorest wealth index category (93 per cent), followed by the richest (90 per cent) and richer (89 per cent) (Table 18.3).

Little more than three quarters of all young women know that condoms prevent HIV infection. Three-fourths of women in the 15-19 age group and four-fifths from the 20-24 age group are aware about condom use. Slightly more than three-fourths of women from rural as well as urban areas also were aware about condom use as a mode of prevention of HIV infection. Two-thirds of the uneducated and a similar proportion of the primary educated as well as four-fifths of the women with secondary or higher education recognised condom as a means to prevent HIV infection during sexual intercourse. Three-fourths of the married as well as unmarried young women and Hindu women were also aware about condom use. Among Muslims, two-thirds knew about condom use as method to prevent infection. In all the wealth categories, more than 70 per cent of women were aware about the method, the richest having the highest proportion (81 per cent) (Table 18.4).

Comprehensive Knowledge about HIV

With the available data, a composite index was computed to understand the comprehensive knowledge of the youth about HIV infection. When the men report that using condoms for every act of sexual intercourse and having just one uninfected partner can reduce the chance of acquiring HIV infection and also aware of the fact that a healthy looking person can have HIV/AIDS and rejects the most common misconceptions among people about HIV/AIDS are termed as having comprehensive knowledge about HIV/AIDS.

Among the young men, near about half of them only have comprehensive knowledge about HIV prevention. Among the two age group categories, 42 per cent of the 15-19 age group and 58 per cent in the 20-24 age group have comprehensive knowledge. Half of the rural men and two-fifths of the urban young men have comprehensive knowledge. Half of the men with secondary and above education also have thorough knowledge. But only 13 per cent of the men who have never attended school and 21 per cent of the primary educated have comprehensive knowledge. Three-fifths of the married and half of the unmarried exhibited comprehensive knowledge. Half of the Hindus, one-fifth of the Muslims and two-fifths from the other religions were having sound knowledge about HIV/AIDS. Comprehensive knowledge among the poorest wealth category is only about one-third and slightly more than half in the case of poorer and richest categories. In the middle and richer categories it is 43 and 45 per cent respectively (Table 18.3).

Among the young women, one-third had comprehensive knowledge about HIV. Both the age categories had similar proportion of women with comprehensive knowledge. Thirty per cent of the rural and 45 per cent of the urban women demonstrated thorough knowledge about HIV. Two-fifths of the women with secondary or above educational qualifications, one-tenth of the primary educated and 7 per cent of the uneducated women had comprehensive knowledge. Among the married about a quarter and among the unmarried little above one-third had comprehensive information about HIV prevention. One-third of the Hindus, near one-fourth of the Muslims and a third of the other religious categories were correctly informed. More than half of the richest, a quarter of the richer, slightly less than a quarter of the middle, 15 per cent of the poorer and one-tenth of the poorest had comprehensive knowledge about HIV (Table 18.4).

Recent Sexual Activity

Table 18.5 shows the distribution of young men by their sexual activity. Out of the 320 young men, four-fifth never had a sexual intercourse. From among the rest 20 per cent, half of the youth were not sexually active in the past four weeks where the other half was active. Among the men in 15-19 categories, 9 out of 10 were not sexually active. Among the rest only 1.6 per cent was sexually active in the past four weeks. Among the married, hundred per cent were sexually active which is quite natural whereas among the never married men only 1 out of 10 were sexually active and sexual activity in the last four weeks was less than 1 per cent among the youth who have reported having sex ever. Both among the urban and rural young men, one-fifth reported ever having sexual activity. Half of the rural men who reported having sexual

Table 18.5

Per cent Distribution of Young Men by History of Sexual Activity

Background Characteristics	*Recent Sexual Activity*			*Total*
	Never had Intercourse	*Active in Last Four Weeks*	*Not Active in Last Four Weeks*	
*Age****				
15-19	92.2	1.6	6.2	193
20-24	61.4	21.3	17.3	127
*Marital Status****				
Never married	90.1	0.7	9.2	284
Married	0.0	77.8	22.2	36
Place of Residence				
Urban	80.2	8.1	11.7	111
Rural	79.9	10.0	10.0	209
Education				
No education	66.7	6.7	26.7	15
Primary	70.8	16.7	12.5	24
Secondary & higher	81.5	8.9	9.6	281
*Religion***				
Hindu	83.0	7.8	9.3	270
Muslim	67.6	14.7	17.6	34
Others	56.3	25.0	18.8	16
Wealth Index				
Poorest	70.6	11.8	17.6	17
Poorer	81.4	14.0	4.7	43
Middle	77.8	11.1	11.1	63
Richer	74.3	9.5	16.2	74
Richest	85.4	6.5	8.1	123
Respondent Currently Working				
No	93.7	1.3	5.1	158
Yes	66.5	17.4	16.1	161
Total	80.0 (256)	9.4 (30)	10.6 (34)	100.0 (320)

Note: *** $P < 0.001$, ** $P < 0.005$, * $P < 0.01$.

In some cases, the total may not add upto 320 due to missing cases.

activity ever were sexually active during the past 4 weeks whereas the proportion of ever sexually active being active in the previous 4 weeks of the survey was 8 per cent. Near about one-fifth of the young men having secondary education or more reported ever having sexual activity and out of them 9 per cent were active during the four weeks preceding the survey. Among the primary educated as well as the men with no formal schooling one-third were ever sexually active and the proportions active during the past four weeks were 16.7 and 6.7 per cent respectively. Among Hindus, 17 per cent were ever sexually active and near about 8 per cent were active during the past one month. One-third of the Muslims as well as the other religions reported ever having sexual intercourse. Nearly 30 per cent of the young men in the poorest wealth index category were sexually active and 1 out 10 such men were recently active. Among the poorer category, 19 per cent were sexually active and 14 per cent among them were recently active. More than one-fifth of the middle category of wealth index were sexually active and 11 per cent of them were active during the past four weeks of the survey. Among the richer and richest, 25 and 15 per cent respectively were active and the proportion among them who were active during the past one month was 9.5 and 6.5 respectively. One-third of the working men and 6 per cent of the not working group were sexually active. Out of the currently working men, near about one-fifth were recently active while only a negligible proportion (1.3 per cent) were active recently among the not working group.

Nearly two-thirds of the women never had a sexual intercourse and about a quarter were sexually active in the recent period (Table 18.6). Among the 15-19 age group, 11 per cent ever had sexual activity and 8 per cent were active in the last four weeks. In the 20-24 age group, two-thirds had intercourse ever and two-fifths were active in the previous one month. None of the never married women had sexual intercourse and almost all the married had sexual intercourse in which a quarter was sexually active in the recent past. Forty per cent of the rural women were sexually active and a quarter of the rural young women were sexually active in the last four weeks. About three-fourths of the uneducated, little less than half of the primary educated and a quarter of the young women with secondary and above education were ever sexually active. Half of the uneducated, a quarter of the primary educated and 17 per cent of the secondary and above educated were sexually active during the past one month of the survey. One-third of the Hindus, a quarter of the Muslims and one-third of women from

Table 18.6

Per cent Distribution of Young Women by History of Sexual Activity

Background Characteristics	*Recent Sexual Activity*				*Total*
	Never had Intercourse	*Active in Last Four Weeks*	*Not Active in Last Four Weeks-Postpartum Abst.*	*Not Active in Last Four weeks-Not Postpartum Abst.*	
*Age******					
15-19	89.3	7.9	0.2	2.7	624
20-24	35.9	42.6	5.4	16.1	516
*Marital Status******					
Never married	100.0	0.0	0.0	0.0	740
Married	0.5	67.6	7.0	24.9	398
*Place of Residence******					
Urban	79.7	15.8	1.0	3.4	291
Rural	60.1	26.3	3.1	10.6	849
*Education******					
No education	28.5	51.2	4.7	15.7	172
Primary	57.3	26.6	4.2	11.9	143
Secondary & higher	74.2	17.4	1.7	6.8	824
*Religion******					
Hindu	64.0	23.4	2.5	10.1	965
Muslim	74.5	19.6	3.9	2.0	102
Others	64.9	32.4	1.4	1.4	74
*Wealth Index******					
Poorest	51.9	32.7	0.0	15.4	52
Poorer	56.0	29.1	2.3	12.6	175
Middle	61.5	26.5	3.8	8.1	234
Richer	60.4	23.0	3.6	12.9	278
Richest	75.9	18.9	1.2	4.0	402
Respondent Currently Working					
No	65.4	24.9	2.4	7.3	714
Yes	64.4	21.7	2.6	11.2	419
Total	65.0 (742)	23.7 (270)	2.5 (28)	8.9 (100)	100.0 (1140)

Note: *** $P < 0.001$, ** $P < 0.005$, * $P < 0.01$.

other religions were sexually active in the recent past. Slightly less than half of the poorest and poorer group and little less than one-third of the middle and richer groups and a quarter of the richest ever had sexual intercourse. A quarter of the poorest, little less than that of the poorer, a quarter of the middle, little less than a quarter of the richer and less than 20 per cent of the richest were sexually active in the recent past. A little greater than a third from both working and non-working categories of women were sexually active and about a quarter each were sexually active in the past four weeks.

Last Intercourse Used Condoms

Table 18.7 shows the per cent distribution of youth who used condoms in last intercourse. Among the youth 30 per cent did not use condoms during the last intercourse. Among the 15-19 age group one-third did not use condoms whereas in the 20-24 category, a proportion slightly below one-third did not use condoms. Nearly half of the never married and one-fifth of the married also did not use condoms during the last intercourse. Irrespective of the place of residence, condom use was about 30 per cent among the rural and urban youth. While none of the primary educated used condoms during their last sexual intercourse, one-third each from the uneducated as well as the men with secondary education or more did not use condoms. None of the poorest, half of the poorer, nearly a quarter of the middle and richer group and two-fifths of the richest reported that they did not use condoms during the last sexual intercourse. Three out of ten working as well as four out of ten non-working young men did not use condom during their last intercourse.

In the last intercourse, 12.8 per cent of the young women used condoms. Among the 15-19 age group 9 per cent and in the 20-24 age group 13.5 per cent reported using condoms. Nearly 13 per cent of the married women used condoms in their last intercourse. 18.6 per cent urban women and 12 per cent rural women used condoms in their last intercourse. Among the women without schooling 9 per cent, primary educated 10.5 per cent and secondary and above educated 15.5 per cent used condoms during their last sexual activity. Condom use in the last intercourse was 11 per cent for Hindu women, 12 per cent for Muslim women and a third of women from other religions used condoms. Among the richest, 30 per cent used condoms while among the poorest it was 4 per cent. Among the currently working women 5.4 per cent and among the non-working 17 per cent used condoms during their last sexual intercouse (Table 18.7).

Table 18.7

Per cent Distribution of Youth who Used Condoms in Last Intercourse

Background Characteristics	*Last Intercourse Used Condoms*	
	Young Men	*Young Women*
Age		
15-19	33.3	9.0
20-24	30.2	13.5
*Marital Status***		
Never married	47.4	—
Married	22.2	12.8
Place of Residence		
Urban	31.6	18.6
Rural	30.6	11.7
Education		
No education	33.3	9.1
Primary	0.0	10.5
Secondary & higher	35.6	15.5
*Religion****		
Hindu	30.8	11.2
Muslim	0.0	11.5
Others	71.4	36.0
Wealth Index		
Poorest	0.0	4.3
Poorer	50.0	5.3
Middle	23.1	6.7
Richer	26.7	9.3
Richest	40.0	29.9
Respondent Currently Working		
No	42.9	17.2
Yes	29.2	5.4
Total	30.9 (17)	12.8 (50)

Note: *** $P < 0.001$, ** $P < 0.005$, * $P < 0.01$.

Relationship with Last Sexual Partner

While exploring the relationship with last sexual partner, it was found that near about two-thirds young men reported having sex with their spouse (Table 18.8). Another 24 per cent had sex with their girlfriends while the rest 11 per cent had sex with partners other than spouse or girlfriends. Among the 15-19 age group more than half had sex with girlfriends and another quarter had sex with their spouses. In the 20-24 age category, slightly more than three quarters had sex with their spouses and 14 with their girlfriends. The rest 9 per cent had sex with other partners. Among the married it was mostly with the spouses and among the unmarried more than two-thirds had sex with girlfriends. 5.3 per cent of the unmarried men had sex with their partners while more than a quarter of them reported having sex with partners other than spouse or girlfriend. Among the uneducated, one-third had sex with their spouses in their last intercourse while the rest two-thirds had with their girlfriends. Among the primary educated group, 57 per cent reported having sex with their spouses while 29 per cent had with their girlfriends. The rest 14 per cent of them had partners other than the above mentioned categories. Among the secondary and above educated group slightly above two-thirds had their last sex with spouses while one-fifths had sex with their girlfriends. 11 per cent of the category reported sex with partners other than girlfriends or spouse during their last sexual intercourse. Among Hindus, two-third had spouses as partners and a quarter had girlfriends as partners. Among Muslim men a similar two-thirds had sex with their wives while one-fifth had sex with their girlfriends. Among the other religious categories near about three out of five had sex with spouses and 29 per cent had partners other than spouses or girlfriends. Among the poorest wealth index category, three quarters had sex with their spouses and the rest with girlfriends. Among the poorer group three-fifths had sex with spouses while the rest had girlfriends during last sexual intercourse. In the middle wealth group seven out of ten had sex with spouses and 15.4 per cent each had sex with either girlfriends or other partners. Among the richer group a quarter had girlfriends as last partners and three-fifths had spouses. In the richest group, two-third had sex with their wives and another 20 per cent with their girlfriends.

Table 18.8

Per cent Distribution of Young Men by Relationship with Last Sex Partner

Background Characteristics	*Relationship with Last Sex Partner*			*Total*
	Spouse	*Girlfriend*	*Others*	
*Age******				
15-19	25.0	58.3	16.7	12
20-24	76.7	14.0	9.3	43
*Marital Status******				
Never married	5.3	68.4	26.3	19
Married	97.2	0.0	2.8	36
*Place of Residence****				
Urban	47.4	42.1	10.5	19
Rural	75.0	13.9	11.1	36
Education				
No education	33.3	66.7	0.0	3
Primary	57.1	28.6	14.3	7
Secondary & higher	68.9	20.0	11.1	45
Religion				
Hindu	66.7	25.6	7.7	39
Muslim	66.7	22.2	11.1	9
Others	57.1	14.3	28.6	7
Wealth Index				
Poorest	75.0	25.0	0.0	4
Poorer	62.5	37.5	0.0	8
Middle	69.2	15.4	15.4	13
Richer	60.0	26.7	13.3	15
Richest	66.7	20.0	13.3	15
Total	65.5 (36)	23.6 (13)	10.9 (6)	100.0 (55)

Note: *** $P < 0.001$, ** $P < 0.005$, * $P < 0.01$.

Among the women, only married women reported having sexual intercourse and in all the cases they reported that their last sexual intercourse was with their husband (Table 18.9).

Total Lifetime Sexual Partners

Table 18.10 shows the distribution of young men by total number of lifetime sexual partners. Except 20 per cent who had multiple

Table 18.9

Per cent Distribution of Young Women by Relationship with Last Sex Partner

Background Characteristics	*Relationship with Last Sex Partner*			*Total*
	Spouse	*Boyfriend*	*Others*	
Age		—	—	
15-19	100.0			67
20-24	100.0			325
Marital Status		—	—	
Never married	—			—
Married	100.0			392
Place of Residence		—	—	
Urban	100.0			59
Rural	100.0			333
Education		—	—	
No education	100.0			122
Primary	100.0			57
Secondary & higher	100.0			213
Religion		—	—	
Hindu	100.0			340
Muslim	100.0			26
Others	100.0			26
Wealth Index		—	—	
Poorest	100.0			23
Poorer	100.0			75
Middle	100.0			89
Richer	100.0			108
Richest	100.0			97
Total	100.0 (392)	000.0	000.0	100.0 (392)

partners, majority had only one lifetime partner. This trend was seen across the two age group categories. A quarter of the unmarried men and 17 per cent of married men had more than one lifetime partners. Near about one-third urban youth had multiple partners while only 14 per cent rural young men had multiple partners. One-fifth of the secondary and above educated as well as uneducated had multiple partners. Among the primary educated, 14.3 per cent had more than one sexual partner. Among the Hindus as well as Muslims, about one-fifth men reported

Table 18.10

Distribution of Young Men by Total Number of Lifetime Sexual Partners

Background Characteristics	*Total Number of Lifetime Sexual Partners*		*Total*
	Only One	*Two or More*	
Age			
15-19	80.0	20.0	15
20-24	79.6	20.4	49
Marital Status			
Never married	75.0	25.0	28
Married	83.3	16.7	36
*Place of Residence**			
Urban	68.2	31.8	22
Rural	85.7	14.3	42
Education			
No education	80.0	20.0	5
Primary	85.7	14.3	7
Secondary & higher	78.8	21.2	52
Religion			
Hindu	80.4	19.6	46
Muslim	81.8	18.2	11
Others	71.4	28.6	7
Wealth Index			
Poorest	100.0	0.0	5
Poorer	62.5	37.5	8
Middle	92.9	7.1	14
Richer	73.7	26.3	19
Richest	77.8	22.2	18
Total	79.7 (51)	20.3 (13)	100.0 (64)

Note: *** P < 0.001, ** P < 0.005, * P < 0.01.

multiple partners while in the other religious categories it was 28.6 per cent. All from the poorest wealth category had only one lifetime partner. Slightly above one-third of the poorer category had more than one partner. In the middle income category, 7.1 per cent had multiple sexual partners and about a quarter from the richer category reported having multiple partners. In the richest group, 22 per cent young men reported having more than one lifetime sexual partners.

Table 18.11

Distribution of Young Women by Total Number of Lifetime Sexual Partners

Background Characteristics	*Total Number of Lifetime Sexual Partners*		*Total*
	Only One	*Two or More*	
Age			
15-19	98.5	1.5	68
20-24	98.5	1.5	329
Marital Status			
Never married	98.5	1.5	395
Married	100.0	0.0	2
Place of Residence			
Urban	98.3	1.7	59
Rural	98.5	1.5	338
Education			
No education	97.6	2.4	123
Primary	98.4	1.6	62
Secondary & higher	99.1	0.9	213
Religion			
Hindu	98.6	1.4	345
Muslim	96.2	3.8	26
Others	100.0	0.0	26
Wealth Index			
Poorest	96.0	4.0	25
Poorer	100.0	0.0	77
Middle	97.7	2.3	88
Richer	97.3	2.7	110
Richest	100.0	0.0	97
Total	98.5 (391)	1.5 (6)	100.0 (397)

Note: *** $P < 0.001$, ** $P < 0.005$, * $P < 0.01$.

Among the women who reported having sexual intercourse, only 1.5 per cent reported having more than one lifetime sexual partners. Among both the age categories 1.5 per cent women had more than one partner. Among the married, all reported having single lifetime partner. Among the urban women 1.7 per cent and rural women 1.5 per cent reported having more than one partner. Among the uneducated 2.4 per cent and 1.6 per cent of the primary educated reported having more than one sexual partner. In the secondary and above educated group, 0.9 per cent women had multiple sex partners. None of the poorer and richest group reported having more than one partner while 4 per cent of poorest, 2.3 per cent of the middle and 2.7 per cent richer reported having multiple sex partners (Table 18.11).

Logistic Regression Analysis

Knowledge about HIV/AIDS

Abstinence as a Method of Prevention

Irrespective of age, place of residence, marital status, religion or economic status majority of young men identify abstinence from sex as a method to prevent HIV infection. However, in the case of men with no formal schooling only half of them have knowledge about the method. The older, the better educated and economically well-off are found to be more informed. More urbanites seem to be informed compared to the rural men about abstinence. However, the difference is statistically significant. Similar is the case of married and unmarried.

Women also show similar pattern except in the case of education where there is a zigzag pattern and the women with no education are found to be better informed compared to the primary educated. Here the difference is statistically significant also. Women across all the variables considered have lesser proportion informed about abstinence as means of prevention against HIV infection compared to young men with an overall difference of 10 per cent points. The differences were significant in the case of education, religion and economic status in the case of men whereas for women the proportions were significantly different in the case of place of residence, education and wealth index.

Limiting Sexual Partners

Men's knowledge about limiting sexual intercourse to one partner followed similar patterns as in the case of abstinence. Here, categories statistically different are significant for age, place of residence and marital status. For women the variables where the differences in proportions were significantly different are for age, education and wealth index.

Using Condoms

In the case of knowledge about condom use, majority know that it reduces the chances of HIV transmission during sexual intercourse both among men and women. Muslim men had a significantly lower proportion of men knowledgeable about this and fewer men with no formal education were informed compared to the educated. In the case of young women also, similar trends were seen.

Comprehensive Knowledge about HIV Prevention

Though in the case of individual preventive methods majority of youth knew about them, in the case of comprehensive knowledge it was relatively poor. Only about half of the young men and a third of the young women had comprehensive knowledge. Over age, with better education and improved economic status situations were slightly better for men. Only 13 per cent of the men with no formal education had comprehensive knowledge about HIV prevention. Also only one-fifth of the Muslim men had comprehensive knowledge whereas half of the Hindus were thoroughly informed. The rural men were found better compared to the urban counterparts and the married were better off when compared to the unmarried. For men, age, place of residence, education and religion showed significant differences in frequencies across various categories of the variable.

For women, the proportion with comprehensive knowledge varied significantly across categories in the case of place of residence, education, marital status, religion as well as economic status. On the contrary to young men's case, urban young women were far better informed compared to rural women. Also, the never married was better informed in comparison with the married. The proportion of women who had thorough knowledge was low for women with below secondary education. The poorer as well as the poorest segments of women also had very low proportion with comprehensive knowledge.

Table 18.12

Logistic Regression for Comprehensive Knowledge (Young Men)

Background Characteristics	*S.E.*	*Exp (B)*
Age		
15-19		
20-24	0.297	2.604***
Marital Status		
Never married		
Married	0.433	1.382
Place of Residence		
Urban		
Rural	0.306	1.504
Education		
No education		
Primary	0.987	1.497
Secondary & higher	0.841	6.928**
Religion		
Hindu		
Muslim	0.500	0.273***
Others	0.574	0.817
Wealth Index		
Poorest		
Poorer	0.668	1.775
Middle	0.639	0.947
Richer	0.628	0.965
Richest	0.629	1.550
Employment Status		
Not employed		
Employed	0.295	0.748
Constant	0.948	0.086

Note: *** $P < 0.001$, ** $P < 0.005$, * $P < 0.01$.

Logistic regression analysis shows that (Table 18.12) age, religion, place of residence and education were significant predictors of knowledge about HIV in the case of young men in Uttarakhand. Men with secondary or more education were seven times more likely to be knowledgeable compared to those who never attended school. Also men in the 20-24 age group were twice or more likely to have comprehensive knowledge about HIV compared to 15-19 aged. Hindus were more likely to have knowledge compared to Muslims and young urbanites were found less likely to be knowledgeable compared to rural men.

In the case of women, the regression release reveals that age, marital status, education, religion, economic status as well as employment status were significant predictors of knowledge. The

Table 18.13

Logistic Regression for Comprehensive Knowledge (Young Women)

Background Characteristics	*S.E.*	*Exp (B)*
Age		
15-19		
20-24	0.189	1.426*
Marital Status		
Never married		
Married	0.201	0.589***
Place of Residence		
Urban		
Rural	0.195	1.094
Education		
No education		
Primary	0.409	1.360
Secondary	0.329	4.668***
Higher	0.394	9.294***
Religion		
Hindu		
Muslim	0.298	0.595*
Others	0.289	1.110
Wealth Index		
Poorest		
Poorer	0.499	1.028
Middle	0.481	1.242
Richer	0.475	1.447
Richest	0.478	2.957**
Employment Status		
Not employed		
Employed	0.159	0.606***
Constant	0.552	0.086

Note: *** $P < 0.001$, ** $P < 0.005$, * $P < 0.01$.

unmarried as well as those in 15-19 age group were found less likely to have comprehensive knowledge compared to married and 20-24 age group. Women with education above secondary were found to be 9 times more likely to have knowledge compared to those who never attended school. Also it was found that secondary educated are 4 times more likely to have sound knowledge compared to the uneducated. Muslim women were found to be 40 per cent less likely to be knowledgeable compared to Hindus. Compared to the poorest, the richest were thrice more likely to be better informed about prevention of HIV. The analysis revealed that the odds of unemployed women having thorough knowledge is more compared to the employed young women (Table 18.13).

Multi-Partner Sexual Relationships

One-fifth of the men reported having more than one lifetime sexual partner whereas for women it was hardly 6 out of 397 women who were sexually active. Nearly 98 per cent of women across the categories of age, place of residence, religion and economic status reported having only one partner. Hundred per cent of the married women reported having single partner. More urban men and of poorer wealth index as well as never married reported having multiple partner compared to rural, wealthier and married categories. All women reported their last sexual intercourse was with spouse whereas a third of the men reported having partners other than spouse. Two-thirds of them had sex with their girlfriends in their last sexual intercourse. Younger men, never married, urbanites and men with no education were the ones who reported partners other than spouse. Age, marital status and place of residence categories were found to be significantly different in the case of men.

Conclusions

While acknowledging that youth in Uttarakhand are vulnerable to HIV, it is found that among the youth there are different vulnerable groups. Vulnerability of young men was different from that of young women and among men or women, various socio-cultural factors operate in addition to the biological factors in determining their vulnerabilities. Youth in Uttarakhand has a fairly high level of understanding that condoms prevent HIV infection; limiting partners to one reduces the chances of infection and abstinence is a means of safety measure against HIV infection. Having said this, the caution is that mere understanding about the modes does not provide a safety net over the youth from HIV vulnerability which is evident from the low level of comprehensive knowledge about HIV prevention. Half of the young men and two-thirds of the women still need to have a thorough understanding about preventing HIV infection. Age, religion, place of residence and education were significant predictors of knowledge of men whereas for women age, marital status, education, religion, economic status as well as employment status were significant predictors. Weeding out the myths and misconceptions and universalising education are not new recommendations of this research. However, we emphasise that this is yet to be achieved through state-wide programme. The other argument could be that knowledge does not always translate into behaviour. However, the vulnerability of the knowledgeable would be far less than the ignorant. In Uttarakhand, young men are found to be more vulnerable compared to women and irrespective of their level of knowledge, the vulnerability of majority of young women in Uttarakhand largely depend on the safe/risk behaviour of their husbands.

References

Goparaju (1993). "Unplanned unsafe: Male students sexual behaviour", Paper Presented at the workshop on *Sexual Aspects of AIDS/STDs Prevention in India*. Mumbai: Tata Institute of Social Sciences. November 23-27.

International Institute for Population Sciences and Macro International (2007). "National Family Health Survey (NFHS- 3), 2005-06", Ministry of Health and Family Welfare, Government of India.

Jejeebhoy, S.J. (1998). "Adolescent sexual and reproductive health behaviour—A review of the evidences from India", *Social Science and Medicines* 46(10): 1275-1290.

Khasakhala, Anne, A. and Akim J. Mturi (2008). "Factors associated with risky sexual behaviour among out-of-school youth in Kenya", *Journal of Biosocial Science*. Cambridge University Press.

National AIDS Control Organisation (NACO) (2007). "HIV sentinel surveillance and HIV estimation 2006", Ministry of Health & Family Welfare, Government of India, New Delhi.

————. (2004). "Facts & figures: Monthly updates on AIDS", Ministry of Health & Family Welfare, Government of India, New Delhi.

Pachauri, S. (1994). "Relationship between AIDS and family planning programmes: A rationale for developing integrated reproductive health services", *Health Transition Review* 4(l): 321-47.

Porter, S.B. (1993). "Public knowledge and attitudes about AIDS among adults in Calcutta, India", *AIDS Care* 5(2): 169-176.

Saidel, T.J. and Jarlais D. Des (2003). "Potential impact of HIV among IDUs on heterosexual transmission in Asian settings: Scenarios from the Asian epidemic model", *International Journal of Drug Policy* 14: 63-74.

Seidel, G. (1993). "The competing discourses of HIV/AIDS in sub-saharan Africa: Discourses of rights and empowerment versus discourses of control and exclusion", *Social Sciences and Medicine* 36(3): 175-194.

Sharma, A.K., A. Gupta and O.P. Aggarwal (2001). "HIV/AIDS related knowledge, risk perception, attitude and sexual behaviour of working women staying in hostels", *Indian Journal of Dermatology, Venereology and Leprology* 67(1): 21-24.

Singh, S.K., H. Lungdim, A. Chattopadhyay and T.K. Roy (2004). "Women's vulnerability to STI/HIV in India: Findings of the CHARCA baseline survey, Mumbai", Mumbai: International Institute for Population Sciences.

Tiwari, V.K. and Anil Kumar (2002). "The need of sex education among youths: Present perspectives and future prospects", *Demography India* 31(1): 129-159.

UNAIDS (2007). *AIDS Epidemic Update 2007*.

UNAIDS/WHO (2004). "India: Epidemiological Fact Sheets on HIV/AIDS and Sexually Transmitted Infections 2004", *Update*.

Winter, J.M. (1992). "War, family and fertility in twentieth-century Europe", in "The European Experience of Declining Fertility, 1850-1970", *Studies in Social Discontinuity*.

World Health Organization (2004). *Young People – A Window of Hope in the HIV/AIDS Pandemic*. WHO.

19

Study of HIV/AIDS Awareness among Teachers in Uttarakhand

A Mirror of Public Health Challenges

Narayan Prasad Uniyal and
Suyash Badola

Introduction

The 27th state of India, Uttarakhand, popularly known as *devbhoomi* gets its tourist intake in the state by several means. The most encouraging means are—the availability of natural beauty, four local shrines, one national shrine, one *jyotirlinga* out of 12 national ones, and several religious tourist places. Besides, Nepalese labourers called *dotiyal* also turn to this hilly state for earning their bread. Due to geographical difficulties, its youth is also bound to go outside the state as it has got very limited number of industrial establishments especially in hilly areas. Due to the youth going out and people coming to the state, HIV/AIDS's spread is on the increase here. The data indicates that the situation may become a problem in future as far as number of HIV/AIDS sufferers in the state is concerned. It is a point of serious concern that high profile areas like Mussoorie, Haridwar, Nainital and Udham Singh Nagar have come up as new centres of this deadly virus/ disease.

The youth of the state going out for livelihood has proved to be non-self-abstinent as far as sexual relation with unknowns are concerned, which has been one of the most sufficiently contributing factor in the increase of number of HIV/AIDS cases.

Here it is relevant to quote news published in one of the most circulated Hindi daily in the state, *Amar Ujala*, dated December 1,

2007. According to its news, 32 persons have died of AIDS till October, 2007. The number of AIDS cases is about to touch a figure of 200 in the state. In Uttarakhand, where the number of HIV+ cases was not even 100 in 2002, it has come up to cross a figure of 1200 in October 2007. Out of 13 districts, Rudraprayag is the only one, where there has been reported no case till October 2007 (refer Table 19.1). But in Pauri, Uttarkashi and Pithoragarh where there has been reported an increase in the intake of tourists, the virus/disease is also spreading with a faster rate. All the efforts made in this direction have been proved insufficient so far.

Table 19.1

District-wise Distribution of HIV+ Cases in Uttarakhand (till October 2007)

District	*Number*
Almora	25
Bageshwar	10
Chamoli	20
Champawat	15
Dehradun	671
Haridwar	64
Nainital	185
Pauri	78
Pithoragarh	49
Tehri Garhwal	16
U.S. Nagar	68
Uttarkashi	16
Rudraprayag	0

Source: Amar Ujala, Hindi daily of the state, dated December 1, 2007.

Newspaper also shows that the males are more prone than females to get this disease. Out of a total of 181, 142 are males while 39 are females. On the other hand, out of 32 deaths, only 6 were females.

There are certain myths or fallacies regarding the HIV infections/ AIDS which result in faulty knowledge of the subject. Besides, there are certain unhealthy attitudes and beliefs due to which people generally treat an HIV positive and AIDS patient with discrimination. All these false beliefs and unhealthy attitudes can be dealt with properly by providing AIDS awareness education to the teachers first so that they can influence their students in particular and the whole society in general. The execution and implementation of any such programme can be made a success only when it is all done after knowing the present level of their awareness regarding HIV/AIDS.

Table 19.2

A Picture of AIDS in State

Year	*Total Cases*	*Deaths*
2002	05	02
2003	06	02
2004	19	02
2005	48	09
2006	62	05
2007 (Till October)	41	12
Total	181	32

Source: Amar Ujala, Hindi daily of the state, dated December 1, 2007.

In a country like India, where poverty, illiteracy and poor health are rife, the spread of HIV present a daunting challenge to public health (*The Lancet*, 2003). India's first HIV case was reported in late 1986. Before it, concerns were raised about how India would cope once HIV/AIDS cases started to become widespread. This was all because India lacked the scientific laboratories, research facilities, equipment and medical personnel to deal with AIDS epidemic, unlike developed countries (Ghosh, 1986).

It is difficult to educate people about how they can avoid infections. AIDS outreach workers and peer educators have reported harassment (*Human Rights News*, 2002) and in schools, teachers sometimes face negative reactions from the parents of children whom they teach about AIDS (ActionAid, 2003).

A sample of 75 teachers (25 UG teachers, 25 PG teachers and 25 teachers who have research qualifications) was surveyed to measure and compare their attitudes towards AIDS education in these three categories of teachers. Analysis of data and the results of the study indicate that the teachers have positive attitude towards AIDS education. This study also demonstrates that there is no significant difference between the UG and PG teachers in respect of their attitudes towards AIDS education, but there is a significant difference between teachers who have research qualifications on the one hand and UG and PG teachers on the other, in respect of their attitude towards AIDS education. Teachers with research qualifications have scored higher than the other two categories. Attitude of teachers as a whole was found to be favourable towards AIDS education (Williams *et al.*, 2004).

On the basis of the teacher characteristics and the school characteristics associated with imparting HIV/AIDS education in schools, a survey was conducted to investigate the factors influencing whether high school teachers implemented HIV/AIDS education. Teacher characteristics were previous training, self-efficacy, student centredness, beliefs about controllability and the outcomes of HIV/AIDS education and their responsibility. The existence of a school HIV/AIDS policy, a climate of equity and fairness, and good school community relations were the school characteristics. Questionnaire was used as the tool of the study. Female teachers (74 per cent) were found to be more likely to have implemented HIV/AIDS education than males (58 per cent). These findings demonstrate the value of teacher training and school policy formulation. They also highlight the value and importance of interventions that go beyond a sexual health agenda, focusing on broader school development to improve school functioning and school climate.

A study was done to assess the awareness and attitude of senior secondary school teachers regarding HIV/AIDS and teaching of sex education in the schools. Although most of the teachers knew that AIDS is a deadly disease but the modes of transmission were known correctly to very few of them. The attitude towards sex education was found to be encouraging but only 70 per cent teachers had a positive attitude towards HIV positive person; 60 per cent of the teachers have ever discussed the issues of HIV/AIDS with their students. The female teachers had more positive attitude than their male counterparts (Badhan *et al.*, 2004).

Keeping all the above mentioned data and points in view, the researchers got inspired to prepare this paper. For the purpose, the basis has been the M.Ed. Dissertation of Suyash Badola on the levels of AIDS awareness among teachers. Teachers were taken as the population of the study, keeping in mind their vital role in the process of socialisation of a child. Any strategy to cope with this problem of the hour can be implemented successfully if the involvement of the teachers of the state is ensured. The involvement of teachers is important and sometimes seems to be compulsory in this regard as the education department of the state government is the largest department. It employs about 90,000 school teachers all over the state.

Objectives

The study has been carried out with the following objectives:

(i) To determine the level of knowledge of teachers regarding the general information, symptoms and effects of AIDS.

(ii) To determine the level of knowledge of teachers regarding the modes of transmission, prevention and treatment of AIDS.

(iii) To study the attitudes and beliefs of teachers towards the HIV/AIDS sufferers in the social scenario.

(iv) To draw the educational implications of the study such as regarding the implementation of the sex/AIDS education in schools.

Population

A total of 142 teachers from different primary or secondary schools in Garhwal region of Uttarakhand state were surveyed to assess their knowledge and compare their awareness, knowledge, attitudes and beliefs regarding HIV/AIDS.

Tool of the Study

For the study, AIDS awareness test (AAT) was prepared by the researcher, Suyash Badola during his M.Ed. Dissertation. It is a closed self-structured questionnaire. The original version of the AAT was framed in Hindi so that the teachers of Hindi medium background could also fill it easily. First two dimensions namely AIDS: General information, symptoms and effects (GISE) and AIDS: Modes of transmission, prevention and treatment (MTPT) are the ones which reflect the basic knowledge and factual information regarding HIV/AIDS. The last two dimensions AIDS: Social context (SC) and AIDS: Educational context (EC) mask attitudes and beliefs of the teachers in Uttarakhand regarding HIV/AIDS and its educational implications. Table 19.3 shows the distribution of items in the AAT.

Table 19.3

Dimension-wise Distribution of Items in 'AIDS Awareness Test' for School Teachers

S.No.	*Dimension*	*Total Items*
1.	GISE	15
2.	MTPT	19
3.	SC	12
4.	EC	15
	Total	61

Analysis and Interpretation of Data

Table 19.4 shows that the lowest percentage of correct responses in the dimension GISE was found for item no. 11 which deals with the knowledge of swollen lymphnodes as a symptom of AIDS. Only 36 per cent teachers had the correct knowledge of the fact. On the other hand, item no. 58 which deals with the fact that AIDS adversely affect the immune system of body was correctly responded by all the teachers. Rest of the items have got correct response rate of 84 per cent or more except item no. 2 which was responded correctly by 71 per cent teachers. Item no. 2 was related to the knowledge of "AIDS patient's life is life is different from normal".

In Table 19.5, all the items of MTPT except item no. 7 have got correct response rate of 82 per cent or more and even 99 per cent for item nos. 18, 49, and 51. Item no. 7 deals with the fact that the red light areas are source of spread of the epidemic of AIDS. For this item, correct responses were given by 78 per cent teachers.

Table 19.4

Question-wise Percentage of Correct Responses of School Teachers in GISE Dimension of AIDS Awareness Test

Item No.	*1*	*2*	*3*	*4*	*5*	*8*	*11*	*12*	*13*	*26*	*34*	*36*	*37*	*55*	*58*
% of correct responses	89	71	99	89	98	87	36	97	98	87	89	84	98	92	100

Table 19.5

Question-wise Percentage of Correct Responses of School Teachers in MTPT Dimension of AIDS Awareness Test

Item No.	*7*	*9*	*10*	*14*	*18*	*30*	*32*	*35*	*39*	*42*	*44*	*45*	*47*	*49*	*50*	*51*	*53*	*57*	*59*
% of correct responses	78	83	88	96	99	97	98	97	98	97	94	97	82	99	88	99	89	97	95

Both the above mentioned tables show that the level of knowledge about HIV/AIDS is sufficiently high in the teachers of Garhwal region of Uttrakhand.

Table 19.6 shows, that the teachers have more or less the same level of knowledge of dimensions GISE and MTPT as far as their bifurcations in the categories of sex, marital status, locality (urban/rural) and level of teaching (primary/secondary) is concerned. There is no significant difference in their level of knowledge at the 0.05 level of significance. But the primary teachers are less aware of the facts covered in the GISE dimension of the AAT than the teachers of secondary level. In MTPT, there is again no significant difference in this category too.

Item nos. 6, 16, 19, 38, 41 and 61 of the dimension SC in AAT support social boycott of the HIV/AIDS sufferer. Less percentage of yes in these items as shown in Table 19.7 indicates the positive attitudes of the teachers towards HIV/AIDS sufferers. Here item no. 24 was responded with 'yes' by 85 per cent teachers, which says that the friendship with an HIV+ female can be maintained. Higher percentage of 'yes' in item no. 48 signifies that 77 per cent teachers have opinion that adolescents are among the high risk groups.

Table 19.6

Mean and Significance of Difference in GISE and MTPT Dimensions of AAT among Teachers Working in Uttarakhand School Education with Respect to their Sex, Marital Status, Locality and Level of Teaching

Dimensions			*GISE*			*MTPT*		
Variables		*No. of Teachers*	*M*	*σ*	*"t"*	*M*	*σ*	*"t"*
Sex	Male	104	13.14	1.26	0.1373	17.61	1.52	1.0055
	Female	38	13.11	1.11		17.89	1.45	
Marital status	Married	75	13.01	1.32	1.2897	17.81	1.32	1.0577
	Unmarried	67	13.27	1.08		17.54	1.08	
Locality	Urban	46	13.17	1.10	0.8188	17.89	1.20	1.2765
	Rural	96	13.11	1.27		17.58	1.63	
Level of teaching	Primary	48	12.85	1.10	2.1091*	17.60	1.66	0.4281
	Secondary	94	13.28	1.24		17.72	1.41	

Note: * Significant at 0.05 level of significance.

Table 19.7

Item-wise Percentage of Responses of School Teachers in Social Context Dimension of AAT

Item No.	*6*	*16*	*19*	*20*	*21*	*24*	*29*	*38*	*41*	*46*	*48*	*61*
Yes %	5	1	7	44	49	85	34	11	8	17	77	9
No %	95	99	93	56	51	15	66	89	92	83	23	91

An examination of Table 19.8 reveals that the teachers are readily prepared to maintain a healthy and free environment in schools and are in favour of implementation of Sex and Adolescence education in the school curriculum. Item nos. 15, 22, 23, 25, 28, 33, 40, 43, 54 and 56 have got high percentage of 'yes' which indicates that the teachers support the idea of organising seminars, lectures, workshops of HIV/AIDS experts, introducing value-based education, spiritual education and compulsory sex education in schools. Lesser percentage of 'yes' in item nos. 17, 31, 52 and 60 shows that the teachers are not in favour of humiliating or discriminating the students because of their being HIV/AIDS affected. Item no. 60 has got 96 per cent 'no' which indicates that teachers do not think that it is immoral to provide sex education in schools.

Table 19.8

Item-wise Percentage of Responses of School Teachers in Educational Context Dimension of AAT

Item No.	*15*	*17*	*22*	*23*	*25*	*27*	*28*	*31*	*33*	*40*	*43*	*52*	*54*	*56*	*60*
Yes %	97	2	96	70	99	57	98	4	96	96	95	20	95	88	4
No %	3	98	4	30	1	43	2	96	4	4	5	80	5	12	96

Conclusions of the Study

1. No significant difference is found in the level of awareness of male and female teachers, married and unmarried teachers and rural and urban teachers of Garhwal region of Uttarakhand regarding general information, symptoms and effects, modes of transmission, prevention and treatment of HIV/AIDS.
2. Primary school teachers are found to be a little less aware of the subject than their secondary school counterparts regarding basic knowledge of AIDS.
3. Most of the teachers of Garhwal region do not believe in social boycott of the HIV+ or AIDS patients. They have shown acceptive attitudes towards the HIV/AIDS sufferers. The teachers have the opinion that there is no harm in having HIV+ male or female friends.
4. Most of the teachers have shown healthy attitudes towards HIV+ students and a very good deal of their approval to the open discussion of AIDS and related matters with the students in schools and outside.

5. Teachers also supported the introduction of sex education, value-based education and *yoga*/meditation etc., in schools to control this pandemic of AIDS.

Implications of the Study

1. Primary teachers are required to be trained for their better understanding of the HIV/AIDS related issues.
2. Teacher training programmes should be well-equipped with the knowledge of HIV/AIDS and related matters.
3. Regular seminars, lectures etc., should be organised in the schools by the experts.
4. Sex education should be implemented in schools but in a way that it may not be spoiling the adolescents.
5. *Yoga*/meditation/spiritual education should also be promoted in the schools so that the students may inculcate healthy values in them.
6. Orientation programmes/workshops for teachers should also be organised at regular intervals.
7. Programmes like School Adolescent Education Programme (SAEP) must be implemented in the schools of Uttarakhand.

Justification of the Present Study

The main aim of researchers has been to find out some concrete solutions to cope with the problem of HIV/AIDS. The school has always been the most effective means of bringing about any social change. If the HIV/AIDS awareness programmes are to be widespread among the residents of Uttarakhand, no other medium than schools can prove to be effective in this regard. In schools, this objective can be successfully achieved only by means of the involvement of the teachers. Therefore ultimately, first of all it is the teacher who needs to be well-equipped with the knowledge of HIV/AIDS related issues. That is why the researchers carried out this study to find out the level of knowledge of the subject among teachers.

References

ActionAid (2003). "The sound of silence: difficulties in communicating on HIV/AIDS in school", *Experiences from India and Kenya.*

Badhan, S.K., P. Lal and G.L. Kashyap (2004). "A Study of awareness and attitude regarding HIV/AIDS amongst school teachers of Delhi", Meeting Abstracts, International AIDS Conference, July, 11-16, MAM College and HKMC Trust New Delhi.

Badola, S. (2007). "A study of HIV/AIDS awareness among teachers undergoing B.Ed. training through distance mode", M.Ed. dissertation, H.N.B. Garhwal University, Srinagar, Uttarakhand, India.

Ghosh, T.K. (1986). "AIDS: A serious challenge to public health", *Journal of the Indian Medical Association* 84(1): 29-30.

Human Rights News (2002). "AIDS in India: Money won't solve crisis, Rising violence against AIDS affected people," November 13.

The Lancet (2003). "Spreading the word about HIV/AIDS in India", 361(3).

Williams, S. Sarah, B. Minnalkodi, S. Lilly Epsybai (2004). "Attitude of teachers towards AIDS education", *Experiments in Education* 32(9).

Appendix A-19.1

AIDS Awareness Test

Personal Profile

1. Name -
2. Age - __________Years
3. Sex - Female ( ) Male ( )
4. Marital status - Married ( ) Unmarried ( )
5. Edu. qual. -
6. Teacher training (undergone) -
7. Total teaching exp. - ___________Years
8. District of present school -
9. Locality of school - Urban ( ) Rural ( )
10. Status of school - Govt. ( ) Non-govt. ( )

Instructions

This test is being conducted only for a research work and your responses will be kept secret. So, be non-hesitant in giving responses. Mark the suitable choice out of Yes/No with (√) to which you agree.

	Yes	No
1. AIDS is a sex disease.		
2. AIDS patient's life is different from normal.		
3. India is free from AIDS.		
4. Eradication of AIDS requires spread of education.		
5. AIDS is caused by HIV.		
6. AIDS patient must be refrained from social contacts.		
7. Red light areas are sources of spread of AIDS.		
8. AIDS is a syndrome rather than an illness.		
9. DOTS is a treatment of AIDS.		
10. Having sexual relations with more than one partner invites AIDS.		

11. Swollen lymphnodes is a symptom of AIDS.
12. AIDS patient has reduced immunity.
13. AIDS is a fatal disease.
14. NACO is an AIDS related organisation.
15. AIDS related seminars, workshops etc., must be organised in schools.
16. AIDS patients must be boycotted from social programmes.
17. AIDS affected student must be kept apart from other students.
18. AIDS spreads by embracing.
19. AIDS patient is a neglected member of the society.
20. Females are more prone to get affected with AIDS.
21. AIDS treatment report must be kept secret.
22. Students must be allowed to put up sex-related queries.
23. Religious/spiritual education helps in AIDS control.
24. HIV+ females can be made friends.
25. Lectures of AIDS experts must be held in schools.
26. HIV+ is the state prior to revelation of symptoms of AIDS.
27. Meditation is helpful in AIDS control.
28. Teachers must provide AIDS knowledge to students.
29. Social progress of AIDS patient is adversely affected.
30. AIDS control system must be established at district level.
31. Admission of AIDS students must be prohibited in schools.
32. Preventive measures must be used during sexual intercourse.
33. School curriculum must include AIDS related information.
34. AIDS is completely curable.
35. *Nukkar* dramas improve level of AIDS awareness.
36. AIDS has become an epidemic.
37. AIDS patients recover quickly if affected with pneumonia.
38. AIDS patient must hide it from society.
39. Shaking hands with HIV+ is risky.

40. Teachers must undergo AIDS orientation programmes/workshops.
41. Friendship with HIV+ male is risky.
42. Infected blood can cause HIV infection.
43. Teacher must help HIV+ student for his/her medical test.
44. AIDS may spread by contaminated food/water.
45. Safe sex keeps away HIV infection.
46. HIV+ person may marry a normal person.
47. Antiretroviral treatment (ART) is related with AIDS.
48. Adolescence is high risk age for AIDS.
49. Prevention is the only cure of AIDS.
50. TV, radio etc., are ineffective in improving AIDS awareness.
51. Government should facilitate free HIV test and ART.
52. HIV+ student must be discussed in public.
53. Infection may spread by sharing food with HIV+.
54. Value-based education must be imparted to students.
55. AIDS patient shows gradual weight loss.
56. Sex education must be compulsory in schools.
57. Child may get infected by infected mother.
58. AIDS damages the resistance system of the body.
59. A syringe may be used by more than one person.
60. It is immoral to provide AIDS knowledge to students.
61. HIV+ person must be checked from working in hospitals etc.

F. Urbanisation and Migration

20 Spatial Pattern of Urbanisation and Urban Growth in Western Himalayan Region in India

Soumya Mohanty and R.B. Bhagat

Introduction

Urbanisation has been viewed as an important factor in the arena of economic change i.e., from traditional rural economies to modern industrial one, taking societies to a higher social formation. It refers to increasingly large number of people living in small places and basically engaged in non-agricultural activities, which depends on development of industrialisation, infrastructure within cities, towns and their neighbourhoods. Thus, urbanisation is considered as an index of modernisation (Roy, 1986; Singh, 1989). The economic system within a country generating migration opportunities to specific locations/regions is a refined input in urbanisation and urban growth as well. In ordinary language, 'urbanisation' has a dual meaning. Demographers, economists, statisticians and geographers see urbanisation with specific views, and tools in several ways. Demographers usually try to see urbanisation according to urban population, accretion of population in urban areas as 'per cent of total population'. Economists usually try to relate population growth, pattern of defined technology on the process of urbanisation. Statisticians try to relate production functions, growth rates of urban population (Roy, 1986). Geographers consider urbanisation in relation to distribution of urban spaces and see proportions and the growth of urban population at different spatial context. For present purposes, urbanisation has been defined as the proportion of total population living in designated urban areas whereas urban growth refers to the net growth of population in designated urban areas.

Over the last 50 years, there has been a worldwide shift from rural to urban living. Statistics show that at the beginning of the twentieth century, 10 per cent of people lived in cities. By 1960, this value had tripled to 34 per cent of the population and, if current trends continue, 60 per cent of the world's population will be urban dwellers by the year 2025 (Brown and Jackson, 1987; Folke *et al.*, 1997; Lowe, 1991). Nowhere is this trend more apparent than in the developing world where many cities are doubling every 10 to 15 years, accommodating nearly two-thirds of the developing world's population growth (Bartone, 1991; Lowe, 1991). Contrary to the developed countries, most cities in today's developing countries have failed to duplicate the path travelled by the cities of the developed countries. An excellent example of this is India which is a home to over a billion people. Although this population is still predominantly rural, with only about 28 per cent of individuals living in urban areas (Census of India, 2001), it is not immune to global urbanisation trends (Abram *et al.*, 1996; Gardner *et al.*, 1997; Kusey, 1996; Pandey *et al.*, 1998; United Nations, 1995). In the past two-three decades, the applicability of urban transition for India is being increasingly questioned as researchers have identified characteristics that are at variance with Western experiences. The peak in urban growth in India was observed during 1971-1981 when the decennial growth rate reached up to 46.1 per cent—the highest ever during the last century. After that, it has slowed down but never less than 30 per cent till 2001 Census. Studies also reveal that Indian cities grow by over 600,000 people each month and, as these urban areas swell, they threaten the sustainability of India's natural resources—despite the fact that the average Indian consumes much less than an inhabitant of a typical Western country (Abram *et al.*, 1996).

The growth of Indian cities is a strong indication that urban sustainability is fundamental to global sustainable development. The sheer number of people living in urban areas, however, is not the only rationale for adopting an urban focus to sustainability problems. At the urban level, the environmental impacts of human activities often emerge more quickly, more intensely and more acutely than elsewhere. Urban areas require large inputs of natural resources and usually hold major concentrations of polluting activities such as industrial development, automobile use and waste generation. As a result, these areas may act as early-warning indicators of more deep-seated, broader reaching sustainability crises (Wackernagel, 1998). In addition, urban areas generally house substantial economic and political power. Worldwide, cities are the largest contributor to gross world product and most economic and political decisions are made in cities (Wackernagel, 1998).

Hills and mountains located across the globe have not been an exception in this regard. Although development and urbanisation started relatively later in these part of landforms they, nevertheless, are in a critical situation as of today. Developmental works, growth of population both natural and through migration, unplanned tourism etc., across the urban settlements have both been upgradational and degradational in nature. In view of these circumstances, the need of planned and organised urbanisation has become a great concern as new urban areas have been added and proportion of urban population has been increasing. In this context, the present paper aims to study the emerging pattern of urbanisation and urban growth in the states of Western Himalayan Region with reference to India, and to discern and analyse different patterns of urbanisation and emergence of new towns/ cities across the districts of these states.

For this we have relied on secondary data sources. Census data published by the Registrar General of India for the period 1981-2001 have been used. Sample Registration System bulletins for the period 1981-2001 are also used. To study urbanisation, per cent urban and exponential growth of urban population is computed for the selected states. Urban-rural growth differential is also computed for selected states. The components of urban growth like natural increase in urban population, reclassification of towns, net rural-urban migration and population growth in urban areas due to jurisdictional change are also calculated to study the contribution of each component for the years 1991-2001. Mapping is carried out to locate the newly emerged towns in orientation to urban agglomerations.

Definition of Urban Areas

Before discussing the trend of urbanisation, it would be appropriate to provide a brief idea about the definition of urban areas as given by Census. There is no uniform definition of rural and urban areas throughout the world and differs from country to country due to various factors, such as, developmental level of economic, social, political and cultural situations prevailing in the country. Taking into consideration all these factors, and to ensure comparability of Census data with previous Censuses and to provide the basis for analysing trend of urbanisation, definition of urban unit of 1991 Census was retained as such. The following criteria were evolved for treating a place as urban at the 1991 Census which has been adopted as such for 2001 Census as well:

(a) all statutory towns i.e., all places with a municipality, corporation, municipal board, cantonment board or notified area council, etc.

(b) all other places which satisfy the following criteria:

   i. A minimum population of 5000;

   ii. At least 75 per cent of the male working population engaged in non-agricultural and allied activity; and

   iii. A density of population of at least 400 persons per sq. km. (or 1000 persons per sq. mile).

Besides, the directors of census operation in states/union territories were allowed to include in consultation with concerned state governments and union territory administration and the Census Commissioner of India, some places having distinct urban characteristic as urban even if such places did not strictly satisfy all the criteria mentioned in the category (b) above.

At the 1971 Census, the concept of urban agglomeration was introduced which has been in use since then. As per definition, an urban agglomeration is a continuous urban spread constituting a town and its adjoining urban out growths (OGs) or two or more physically continuous towns together and any adjoining urban OGs, of such towns. This definition was considered as an improvement on the Town

Group concept of 1961 under which 'urban spread' was not necessarily to be continuous.

The Western Himalayan Region

Since the main focus of this paper is to study the emerging pattern of urbanisation and urban growth in the states of western Himalayan region, it would be appropriate to have an idea about the physical setting of this region.

Figure 20.1

Indian Himalayan Region

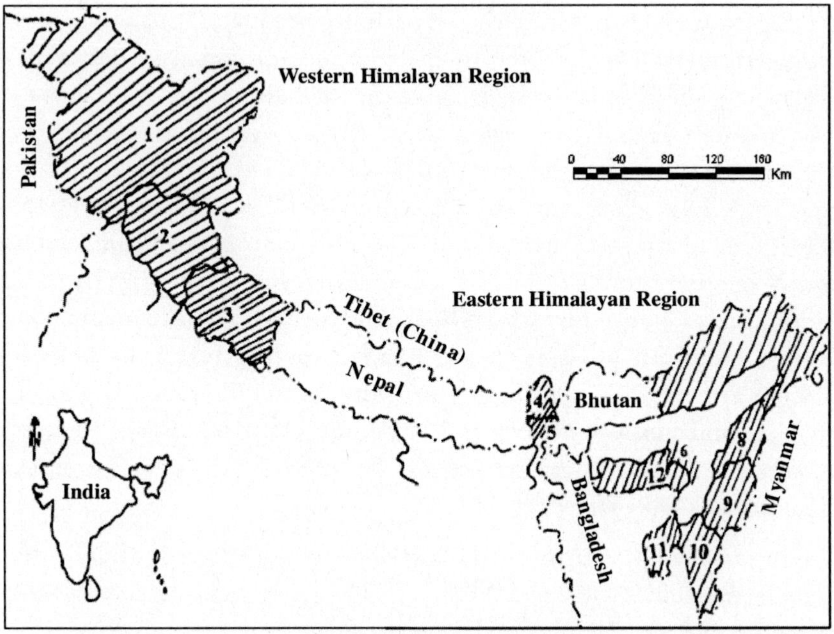

Note: 1.Jammu & Kashmir, 2.Himachal Pradesh, 3.Uttarakhand, 4.Sikkim, 5.West Bengal Hills, 6.Assam Hills, 7.Arunachal Pradesh, 8.Nagaland, 9.Manipur, 10.Mizoram, 11.Tripura, 12.Meghalaya.

The Indian Himalayan region (IHR) comprises 10 states and hill regions of two states of the Indian Republic (see Figure 20.1). Geographically, it is spread between 21°57'-37°5'N latitudes and 72°40'-97°25'E longitude covering an area about 5.3 lakh km.[2] The region occupies the strategic position of the entire northern boundary (north-west to north-east) of the nation and touches almost all the international borders (7 countries) with India. It contributes about 16.2 per cent of India's total geographical area, and most of the area is covered by snow-clad peaks, glaciers of higher Himalaya and dense forest cover of mid-Himalaya. The region shows a thin and dispersed human population as compared to the national figures due to its physiographic condition and poor infrastructure development but the growth rate is much higher than the national average. The percentage contribution of its population has gone up to 3.86 per cent in 2001 from 3.6 per cent in 1991 due to the higher decadel growth rate (about 25.43 per cent) as compared to the national average of 21.35 per cent during 1991-2001.

The Indian Himalayan region is bifurcated into the western and eastern Himalayan region due to the presence of Nepal in between. In this paper, we have mainly focused on the spatial pattern of urbanisation in the western Himalayan region. It covers an area of about 3.31 lakh km^2. Administratively, western Himalayan region is divided into Jammu & Kashmir, Himachal Pradesh and Uttarakhand. Contribution of these three states to the total population of the Indian Himalayan region is around 61 per cent which is important for planning from the developmental point of view. About 207 urban agglomeration/towns having 25 million population are located in this region as per 2001 Census. The region is rich in flora and fauna, natural and tourist ambience, and houses some of the most important pilgrimage centres of the country. The physical setting of the states in western Himalayan region is discussed below.

Jammu and Kashmir is the extreme most state of India and is situated between 32°15′ to 37°05′ latitude north and 72°53′ to 80°20′ longitude east. It is bounded by China in the north and east, by Afghanistan in the north-west and by Pakistan in the west. Punjab and Himachal Pradesh border it in the south. It has a geographical area of 2.22 lakh km^2 comprising 6.93 per cent of the total Indian territory which includes 0.78 lakh km^2 under illegal occupation of Pakistan, 0.05 km^2 illegally handed over by Pakistan to China and 0.37 km^2 under illegal occupation of China in Leh (Ladakh) district. Thus, in an area of 1.01

lakh km^2, 10.07 million people inhabit, which forms a density of 99 persons per sq. km. As per Census 2001, there are 14 districts in the state.

Himachal Pradesh is situated between $32^0 22'$ to $33^0 12'$ north and $75^0 45'$ to $79^0 04'$ east. It is bounded by Jammu and Kashmir in the north, China in the north-east, Punjab and Chandigarh in the south and Uttarakhand in the south-east. The entire region of Himachal Pradesh is characterised by hills and forests. It has a geographical area of 0.55 thousand km^2 comprising 1.69 per cent of the total geographical area of the country. As per Census 2001, it has 12 hilly districts having a population of 6.0 million with a density of 109 per km^2. Difficult communications inhibit development of all kinds in the state. In most of the district, industry has developed little beyond home-spun woolens.

Uttarakhand became the 27th state of the Republic of India on 9 November 2000 carved out of Uttar Pradesh and comprises 13 hilly districts. It is situated between $28^0 532$ to $31^0 272$ north and $77^0 342$ to $81^0 022$ east. It borders China, Nepal, Himachal Pradesh and Uttar Pradesh. It has a population of about 8.0 million at 94.4 per km^2. Out of its total area, 47,325 km^2 is covered by mountains, while 3,800 km^2 is Tarai plains. The total snow-covered area of this mountain region is 7,632 km^2 and is over 4,000 metres high.

Urbanisation and Urban Growth in the Western Himalayan Region

Urbanisation across the Western Himalayan Region has a long history that started before the advent of the British. The earliest urban characters were mainly the capital towns built by different rulers. They were essentially rural in character made up mainly of the palaces, high walls, temples, pavilions etc. With the advent of the British and subsequent colonisation of the Indian soil, centres for collection and other related activities started along with the development of administrative activities. Partition of India affected the towns by changing the population size and area of the towns. In the post-Independence era under the planned effort of development, decentralisation activities started and administrative units were reorganised and tempo of urbanisation accelerated in this region. The level and trend of urbanisation and the components of urban growth in the western Himalayan region comprising Jammu and Kashmir, Himachal Pradesh and Uttarakhand is discussed below in detail.

Table 20.1 shows the trend of urbanisation in India and the states of the western Himalayan region for the period 1981-2001. The urban population of India has increased from 109.11 million in 1971 to 286.12 million in 2001 resulting almost 9 per cent increase in the level of urbanisation during the period. The growth of urban population for the country as a whole was high with 3.79 per cent per annum during the period 1971-81. After 1981, this growth has come down to 2.76 per cent in 2001. A similar pattern is also found in the states of the western Himalayan region.

However, among all these three states the urban growth was highest for Uttarakhand during the period 1971-1981, which was even above the national average. During the period 1971-2001, the level of urbanisation in Uttarakhand has increased from 16.36 per cent to 25.59 per cent and is a sure sign of development in the region. Though Jammu and Kashmir is a politically disturbed state for quite a longer period of time but the level of urbanisation has always remained close to the national level during this period. Around 6 million population has been added to the urban areas of the Jammu and Kashmir in the last 30 years. Himachal Pradesh is the least urbanised state not only in this region but also among all other states of India with only 9.79 per cent of its population living in urban areas (Census, 2001b). Thus, majority of the population of Himachal Pradesh live in rural areas of the state. The table also reveals that the number of urban agglomeration or towns in India as well as in these selected states is slowly increasing.

Table 20.1

Trend of Urbanisation in India and in the States of Western Himalayan Region: 1981-2001

Census Year	Number of UAs/Towns	Total Population (in million)	Urban Population (in million)	Per cent Urban	Annual Exponential Growth Rate (%)
India					
1971	2,590	548.16	109.11	19.91	....
1981	3,378	683.33	159.46	23.34	3.79
1991	3,768	844.32	217.18	25.72	3.09
2001	4,378	1027.02	286.12	27.86	2.76
Jammu & Kashmir					
1971	45	4.62	0.86	18.59	....
1981	58	5.99	1.26	21.05	3.84
1991	N.A.	7.72	1.84	23.83	3.78
2001	75	10.07	2.51	24.88	3.09
Himachal Pradesh					
1971	35	3.46	0.24	6.99	....
1981	46	4.28	0.33	7.61	2.98
1991	55	5.17	0.45	8.69	3.21
2001	56	6.08	0.59	9.79	2.81
Uttarakhand					
1971	37	4.49	0.73	16.36	....
1981	61	5.73	1.15	20.07	4.47
1991	71	7.11	1.63	22.97	3.52
2001	76	8.48	2.17	25.59	2.84

Note: N.A.: Data not available.

Source: Rural-Urban Distribution, Paper-2, Census of India, 1991 and 2001.

Table 20.2 shows the urban-rural growth differential for India and the states of western Himalayan region. It is observed from the table that the growth rate of urban population has always remained faster than the rural population. This indicates that over the years, more urbanisation is taking place in the country and also in the western Himalayan region and the people from rural areas to urban areas are migrating for employment, education, trade, etc. However, the urban-rural growth differential has declined during 1981-1991 to 1991-2001.

The decline in this differential is more prominent for the states Jammu and Kashmir. It is mainly due to the increase in the growth of rural population in the state rather than major decline in the growth of urban population.

Table 20.2

Urban Rural Growth Differential (URGD) in India and in the States of Western Himalayan Region: 1981-1991 and 1991-2001

States	*1981-1991*			*1991-2001*		
	Urban	*Rural*	*Differential*	*Urban*	*Rural*	*Differential*
India	3.09	1.80	1.29	2.76	1.69	1.07
Jammu & Kashmir	3.78	2.18	1.60	3.13	2.60	0.53
Himachal Pradesh	3.11	1.65	1.45	2.92	1.61	1.31
Uttarakhand	3.52	1.80	1.72	2.84	1.41	1.43

Source: Census of India, 1991 and 2001.

Table 20.3 shows the growth of population in Class I cities of India and for the states of western Himalayan region. In India, there were 218 Class I cities in 1981 and it increased to 300 in 1991 and further to 394 in 2001. In Jammu and Kashmir, there were two Class I cities in 1981 namely, Jammu and Srinagar. There is no new addition of Class I cities in the last 20 years. No census had been conducted in the state in 1991. However, the Census of India has provided the interpolated figure of total urban population for the year 1991 as it is mentioned while interpreting earlier tables. It has been already discussed that Himachal Pradesh is one of the least urbanised state of India as it is also clear from Table 20.3.

There was no Class I city in Himachal Pradesh in 1981, but in 1991 only one Class I city was there i.e., Shimla and after that no Class I city has emerged in the state. Even during the period 1991 to 2001, only two new towns have emerged in the state. In case of Uttarakhand, there were 122 urban agglomeration/towns in 1981 and it increased to 152 in 2001. As per Census 2001, there are four Class I cities in Uttarakhand though in 1981, only two Class I cities were there. These four Class I cities are Dehradun, Haridwar, Haldwani-cum-Kathgodam and Roorkee. For further details about other classes of cities/towns in the states of western Himalayan region see Appendix A-20.1.

Table 20.3

Growth of Population in Class I Cities of India and in the States of Western Himalayan Region: 1981-2001

Size Class of UA/City/Town	Total Number of UAs/Towns			Number of UAs/Cities in Class I			Percentage of Population in Class I Cities		
	1981	1991	2001	1981	1991	2001	1981	1991	2001
India	3,378	3,768	4,378	218	300	394	60.42	65.20	68.67
Jammu & Kashmir*	112	N.A.	138	2	N.A.	2	65.80	N.A.	63.03
Himachal Pradesh	92	110	112	-	1	1	-	24.57	24.30
Uttarakhand	122	142	152	2	3	4	38.20	40.37	47.10

Note: * No. census has been conducted in the state in 1991.
Source: Census of India, 1991 and 2001.

Urban population growth is a very complex phenomenon. Factors influencing urban growth have changed considerably since early historical period. It is intended here to present a brief analysis on the three main components of urban population growth namely, natural increase, net rural-urban migration and area reclassification. Table 20.4 presents the birth and death rates and also the rate of natural increase in urban areas of India and the states of western Himalayan region.

Table 20.4

Birth Rate, Death Rate and Natural Increase in Urban Areas of India and the States of Western Himalayan Region: 1981-1990 to 1991-2000

India/States	1981-1990			1991-2000		
	Birth Rate	Death Rate	Rate of Natural Increase	Birth Rate	Death Rate	Rate of Natural Increase
India	27.11	7.59	19.52	22.26	6.54	15.72
Jammu & Kashmir	24.28	6.56	17.72	16.18	4.86	11.32
Himachal Pradesh	21.55	5.93	15.62	18.00	5.51	12.49
Uttarakhand*	N.A.	N.A.	N.A.	N.A.	N.A.	N.A.

Note: *Data is not available.
Source: Sample Registration System bulletins of various volumes published by the Office of the Registrar General, India.

It is clear from the table that the natural increase i.e., births minus deaths, has declined over the period of time in India. The rate of natural increase in urban areas was 19.52 per cent in 1981-1991 which declined to 15.71 per cent during the period 1991-2001. Similar trend is also found for the states of western Himalayan region. There may be some problem in the returns of birth and death rates for the states due to political disturbances. Since Uttarakhand is created after the year 2000, no data on birth and death rates is available separately for the period, for which it is not possible to estimate the contribution of natural increase in the total growth of urban population for the reference period. However, it can be revealed from the table that the rate of urban growth will probably continue to fall because of the declining urban birth rate.

Changes in urban frame resulting from the addition and deletion of new towns at the time of recent censuses are shown in Table 20.5. During 1991 to 2001, 1190 new towns were added up with the existing towns resulting around an increase of 153 lakh urban population and 537 towns were declassified during the same period. So, almost 8.45 lakh population was added up with the urban population due to the reclassification. Similarly, for the states of western Himalayan region, considerable number of population was added during the period. However, for Jammu and Kashmir the number of increase in urban population due to reclassification of towns cannot be computed since, no census has been conducted in the state in 1991. However, the Census 2001 provides information about the new towns which have come up after 1981 Census. Due to methodological issues, it will not be correct to consider this increase in population to know the contribution of reclassification for growth of urban population for the state. In case of Himachal Pradesh, only 23 thousand people were added with the existing urban population during the period 1991-2001. However, it is somewhat different for Uttarakhand. During 1991 to 2001, 15 new towns with 1.8 lakh population were added and only 5 towns with only 36 thousand population were declassified. So, it gained 1.4 lakh population due to reclassification of rural and urban areas. This is a healthy sign of development, as new towns are emerging in the state resulting increase in urban population.

Table 20.5

Number and Population of New and Declassified Towns in India and the States of Western Himalayan Region: 1991-2001

India/States	*New Towns*		*Declassified Towns*		*Net Reclassification*
	Number	*Population*	*Number*	*Population*	*Population*
India	1190	15346335	537	6894108	8452227
Jammu & Kashmir*	-	-	-	-	-
Himachal Pradesh	2	27832	2	4728	23104
Uttarakhand	15	180437	5	36687	143750

Note: * No census has been conducted in the state in 1991.

Source: Census of India, 2001.

Table 20.6 shows the contribution of the components for urban growth in India and selected states. However, it was difficult to estimate the contribution of each component in urban growth due to the non-availability of data. The contribution of natural increase for urban growth in India is around 57.6 per cent, 12.3 per cent due to net reclassification and almost 30 per cent due to migration and jurisdictional change. For Jammu and Kashmir, the contribution of natural increase in growth of urban population is only 33 per cent which is fairly below the national level. This may be due to the considerable decline in birth rate in the urban areas of this state. As it is discussed earlier, the contribution of net reclassification cannot be computed as no census was conducted in the state in 1991. In case of Himachal Pradesh, the contribution of natural increase in the growth of urban population during the period was around 41 per cent, for net reclassification it is 15.8 per cent and almost 43 per cent due to migration and jurisdictional change. Since Uttarakhand is a newly created state, no data on birth rate and death rate is available separately for the state as it was carved out from Uttar Pradesh. Thus, it is not possible to estimate the contribution of natural increase in urban population growth. However, the contribution of net reclassification is around 26.8 per cent in the total growth of urban population in the state during the period 1991 to 2001.

Table 20.6

Contribution of the Components for Urban Growth in India and the States of Western Himalayan Region: 1991-2001

India/States	*Components of Urban Growth (in percentage)*		
	Natural Increase	*Net Reclassification*	*Net Rural-Urban Migration & Jurisdictional Change**
India	57.6	12.3	30.00
Jammu & Kashmir	33.11	N.A.	-
Himachal Pradesh	41.02	15.86	43.12
Uttarakhand	N.A.	26.81	-

Note: * For details about the contribution of net rural to urban migration and jurisdictional changes, see Bhagat and Mohanty (2009).

Source: Census of India, 1991; 2001.

Spatial Pattern of Urbanisation and Emergence of New Towns

As the level and trend of urbanisation has already been discussed at the state level, it is also important to know about the current spatial pattern of urbanisation across the districts of these states of the western Himalayan region. For this, only one point data i.e., Census 2001 data have been used. Figure 20.2 shows the district-wise level of urbanisation for the states of western Himalayan region in 2001 (see Appendix A-20.2 also). The figure shows that in Himachal Pradesh, there are no urban areas in districts of Lahaul and Spiti and Kinnaur. Rudraparayag district of Uttarakhand is the least urbanised district in the Western Himalayan Region having only 1.2 per cent of its population living in urban areas followed by Bageshwar (3.13 per cent). Srinagar district of Jammu and Kashmir state is the most urbanised district in the region with 79 per cent of its population living in urban areas, followed by Dehradun district (53 per cent) of Uttarakhand. The figure clearly shows the regional concentration of urban population in these states. The frontier districts are more urbanised compared to the other districts of the region.

Table 20.7 shows the share of some of the largest Class I cities in the states of western Himalayan region. In Jammu and Kashmir, Srinagar

Figure 20.2

District-wise Level of Urbanisation in the States of Western Himalayan Region: 2001

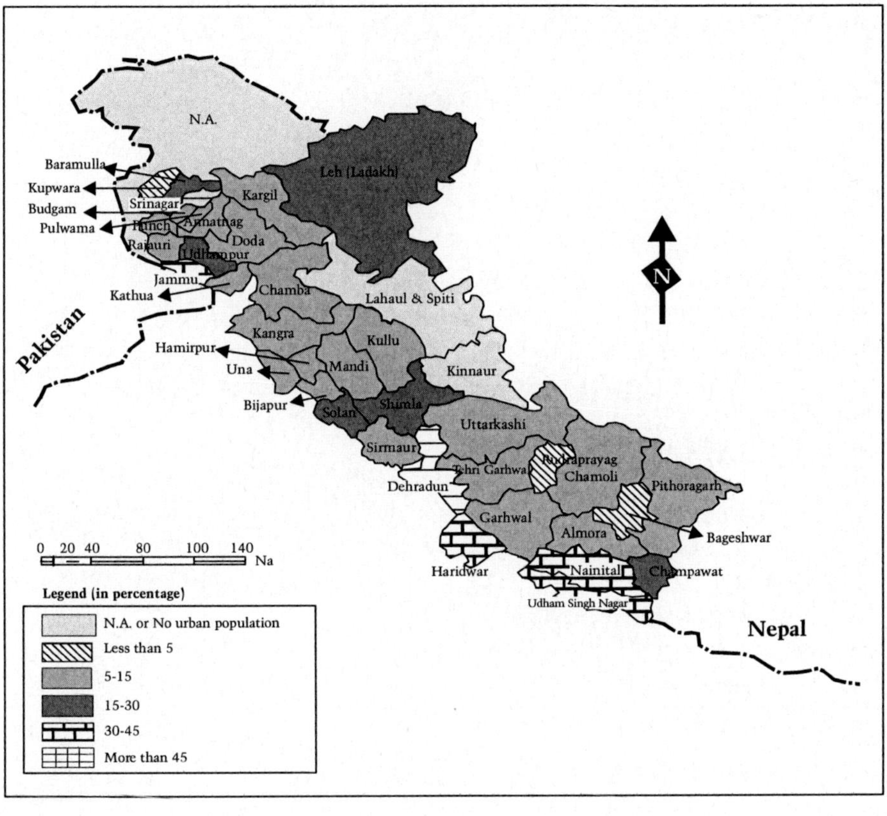

is the largest urban agglomeration in terms of population and it shares 38.7 per cent of the total population of the state, followed by Jammu which shares around 24.2 per cent of total urban population. In case of Himachal Pradesh, there is only one urban agglomeration in the state and it shares almost 24 per cent of total urban population of the state. As per 2001 Census, there are eight urban agglomerations in Uttarakhand. Dehradun is the largest urban agglomeration in the state sharing almost 24.3 per cent of total urban population of the state, followed by Haridwar.

Table 20.7

Share of Population of Selected Class I Cities in the States of Western Himalayan Region: 2001

Sl. No.	Urban Agglomeration	Population	Share in Total Urban Population
Jammu & Kashmir			
1	Srinagar	971,357	38.77
2	Sopore	60,063	2.40
3	Baramulla	72,014	2.87
4	Anantnag	97,610	3.90
5	Udhampur	88,491	3.53
6	Jammu	607,642	24.25
7	Kathua	50,092	2.00
Himachal Pradesh			
1	Shimla	144,578	24.30
Uttarakhand			
1	Dehradun	527,859	24.32
2	Mussoorie	29,319	1.35
3	Rishikesh	79,591	3.67
4	Almora	32,357	1.49
5	Nainital	39,840	1.84
6	Haldwani-cum-Kathgodam	159,020	7.33
7	Roorkee	114,811	5.29
8	Haridwar	220,433	10.16

Source: Census of India, 2001.

Figure 20.3 shows the location of urban agglomeration of the states of western Himalayan region and the location of new towns which have emerged in 2001. It is clear from the figure that all the urban agglomerations are located in the frontier districts of the western Himalayan region which is the lower Tarai plains. The new towns are mostly emerging around the existing urban agglomerations. No new towns have emerged along the northern districts of this region.

Conclusion

The scenario of urbanisation and urban growth indicates that the distribution of urban population in the western Himalayan region of the country is top heavy only in Jammu and Kashmir similar to all India.

Figure 20.3

Urban Agglomerations and New Towns in the States of Western Himalayan Region: 2001

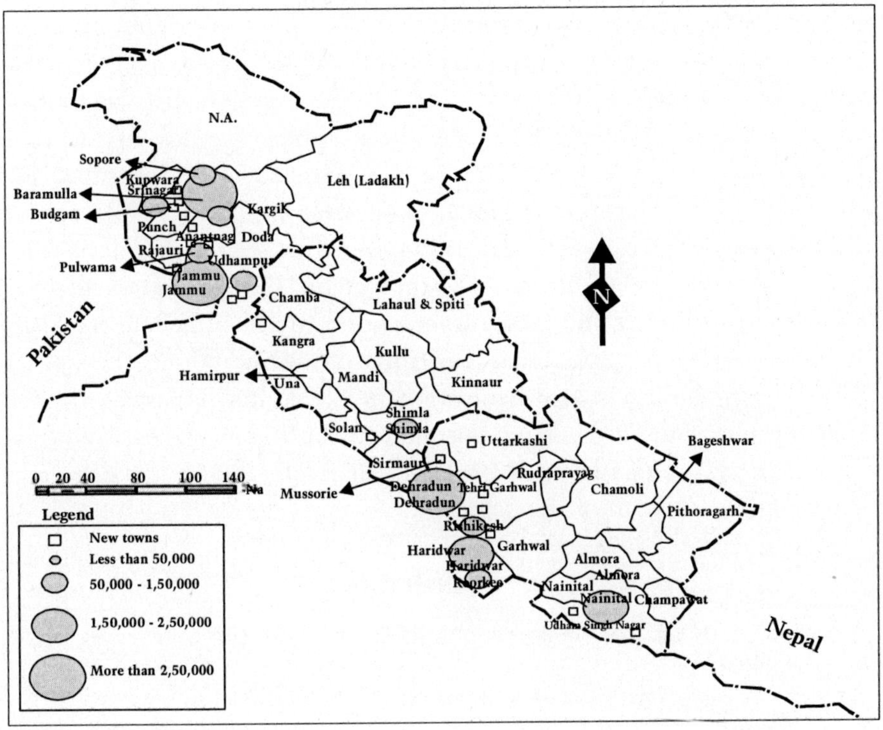

Uttarakhand is also progressing in a similar manner as the share of class I cities in total urban population has been increasing remarkably during the last two decades. However, in Himachal Pradesh there is only one class I city i.e., Shimla and its contribution to total urban population of the state has marginally turned down in 2001 compared to 1991. Analysis reveals that urban population in the hill towns are unevenly distributed among different size classes and are concentrated in few regions of these hilly states. The frontier districts of the western Himalayan region are more urbanised compared to other districts of the region. The study also reveals that the new towns are also emerging around the large urban centres, particularly the class I cities resulting further spatial disparity in urbanisation in the region.

Thus, there is a need for the policy makers and planners to revisit the urban situation across the western Himalayan region as the mountain areas have always posed enormous challenges for human habitation and developmental activities. The hilly terrain may not have the scope for lateral expansion of class I urban settlements as in the plain lands of India, keeping in view the physical set-up of the region. Moreover, cities in hills have not emerged as a result of planned intervention historically. They are the expanded version of the trade centres in the region. Hence, these centres need to be controlled and directed in a sustainable path. The medium and small towns, particularly the class towns are expanding with appreciable pace. They can be developed as major growth centres in the region through appropriate planning and policy intervention to accommodate the rising urban population. Such intervention may also reduce the spatial disparity in the levels of urbanisation in the region. However, the fact that the increasing level of urbanisation in the region will experience an increasingly urban future is probably in itself a good thing because urbanisation is a sign of development.

References

Abram, D., D. Den, H. Sharkey and G. Williams (1996). *India: The Rough Guide*. London: Penguin Books.

Bartone, C. (1991). "Environmental challenge in third world cities", *Journal of the American Planning Association* 57(4): 441-415.

Bhagat, R.B. and Soumya Mohanty (2009). "Emerging pattern of urbanisation and contribution of migration in urban growth in India", *Asian Population Studies* 5(1): 5-20.

Brown, L. and J. Jackson (1987). "The Future of Urbanization: Facing the ecological and economic constraints", *Worldwatch Paper* 77. Washington: Worldwatch Institute.

Census of India (1971). General Population Tables, Part II A-1971, Registrar General of India, New Delhi.

———. (1981). General Population Tables, Part II A-1981, Registrar General of India, New Delhi.

———. (1991). General Population Tables, Part II A-1991, Registrar General of India, New Delhi.

———. (2001a). Rural-Urban Distribution, Paper 2 of 2001, Jammu and Kashmir, Registrar General of India, New Delhi.

———. (2001b). Rural-Urban Distribution, Paper 2 of 2001, Himachal Pradesh, Registrar General of India, New Delhi.

———. (2001c). Rural-Urban Distribution, Paper 2 of 2001, Uttarakhand, Registrar General of India, New Delhi.

Folke, C., A. Jansson, J. Larsson and R. Costanza (1997). "Ecosystem appropriation by cities," *Ambio* 26(3): 167-172.

Gardner, J., R.B. Singh, J. Sinclair, Dr. Bahti and F. Berkes (1997). *Sustainability of mountain environments in India and Canada, Phase 2.* Project proposal. Winnipeg: Natural Resources Institute, University of Manitoba.

Kusey, F. (1996). *India.* 4th Edition. London: Cadogan Books.

Lowe, M. (1991). "Shaping cities: The environment and human dimensions", *Worldwatch Paper* 105. Washington: Worldwatch Institute.

Pandey, B.W., R.B. Singh and T. Singh (1998). "Population, urbanization and tourism in the Kullu district", in R.B. Singh (eds.), *Sustainable Development of Mountain Environment in India and Canada.* New Delhi: Oxford & IBH Publishing Co. Pvt. Ltd., pp. 153-171.

Roy, R. (1986). "Maritime surveillance of the Indian EEZ", *<http://www.idsa-india.org/an-apr8-4.html>*

Singh, T.V. (1989). *The Kullu Valley: Impact of Tourism Development in the Mountain Areas.* New Delhi: Himalayan Books.

United Nations (1995). *World Urbanization Prospects: The 1994 Revisions.* New York: United Nations.

Wackernagel, M. (1998). "The ecological footprint of Santiago de Chile", *Local Environment* 3(1): 7-25.

Appendix Table A-20.1

Growth of Urban Population by Size Class of Towns in States of Western Himalayan Region: 1981-2001

Size Class of UA/City/Town	Number of UAs/ Town			Population			Percentage of Population in Each Size Class			Percentage Decadal Growth Rate	
	1981	1991	2001	1981	1991	2001	1981	1991	2001	1981-1991	1991-2001
Jammu & Kashmir											
All classes	56	-	69	1,260,403	-	2,505,309	100.00	-	100.00	98.77*	
Class I	2	-	2	829,363	-	1,578,999	65.80	-	63.03	90.39	
Class II	-	-	5	—	-	368,270	—	-	14.70	-	
Class III	5	-	4	148,028	-	97,543	11.74	-	3.89	-34.11	
Class IV	6	-	18	76,593	-	251,032	6.08	-	10.02	222.75	
Class V	19	-	21	137,588	-	146,656	10.92	-	5.85	6.59	
Class VI	24	-	19	68,831	-	62,809	5.46	-	2.51	8.75	
Himachal Pradesh											
All Classes	46	55	56	325,971	449,196	594,881	100.00	100.00	100.00	37.80	32.43
Class I	-	1	1	—	110,360	144,578	-	24.57	24.30	51.17	31.01
Class II	1	-	-	73,004	-	-	22.40	-	-	-	-
Class III	2	4	6	40,869	87,228	153,912	12.54	19.42	25.87	113.43	76.45
Class IV	5	7	7	71,985	97,617	113,376	22.08	21.73	19.06	35.61	16.14
Class V	9	9	16	64,637	66,935	113,633	19.83	14.90	19.10	3.56	69.77
Class VI	29	34	26	75,476	87,056	69,382	23.15	19.38	11.66	15.34	20.30
Uttarakhand											
All Classes	61	71	76	1,149,136	1,634,084	2,170,245	100.00	100.00	100.00	42.20	32.81
Class I	2	3	4	438,956	659,640	1,022,123	38.20	40.37	47.10	50.27	54.95
Class II	3	4	3	208,149	293,993	261,289	18.11	17.99	12.04	41.24	-11.12
Class III	7	12	14	185,580	323,816	444,355	16.15	19.82	20.47	74.49	37.22
Class IV	11	14	13	155,307	193,972	205,263	13.52	11.87	9.46	24.9	5.82
Class V	12	14	26	96,617	92,067	193,428	8.41	5.63	8.91	-4.71	110.1
Class VI	26	24	16	64,527	70,596	43,787	5.62	4.32	2.02	9.41	-37.98

Note: * No census has been conducted in the year 1991 in Jammu and Kashmir. Thus, the decadal growth of population in each size class is computed for the period 1981-2001.

Source: Census of India, 1981, 1991, 2001.

Appendix Table A-20.2

District-level Socio-Economic Indicators in Urban Areas of States in Western Himalayan Region: 2001

Sl. No.	State/District	Per cent Urban	Sex Ratio (Females Per Thousand Males)	Per cent Scheduled Caste	Per cent Scheduled Tribe	Literacy Rate	Percentage of Non-Agricultural Workers
00	**Jammu & Kashmir**	**24.81**	**819**	**5.33**	**2.05**	**64.18**	**93.85**
01	Kupwara	3.92	688	0.05	2.90	54.25	80.28
02	Baramulla	16.78	859	0.04	0.41	52.52	86.60
03	Srinagar	78.69	835	0.11	0.13	58.92	96.48
04	Budgam	11.22	854	0.55	0.27	52.91	84.52
05	Pulwama	10.50	883	0.09	0.04	57.42	80.06
06	Anantnag	14.36	842	0.29	0.23	55.19	87.02
07	Leh (Ladakh)	24.43	611	1.50	64.83	74.19	95.83
08	Kargil	8.93	559	0.47	79.51	72.85	93.11
09	Doda	6.89	727	2.73	1.04	71.96	95.16
10	Udhampur	15.69	684	12.68	1.49	75.71	95.33
11	Punch	6.44	745	1.61	5.59	78.31	96.05
12	Rajauri	6.96	736	5.41	5.58	74.92	93.98
13	Jammu	44.14	828	13.61	2.10	74.14	96.49
14	Kathua	14.31	835	22.66	1.09	70.74	90.32
00	**Himachal Pradesh**	**9.79**	**795**	**16.64**	**1.26**	**79.61**	**95.66**
01	Chamba	7.49	866	17.98	5.41	79.97	97.48
02	Kangra	5.40	902	14.97	0.31	77.61	93.69
03	Lahaul & Spiti	0.00	0.00	0.00	0.00	0.00	0.00
04	Kullu	7.89	782	14.88	6.67	78.75	98.17
05	Mandi	6.77	894	19.83	0.68	81.58	93.85
06	Hamirpur	7.32	861	17.18	0.45	79.78	89.96
07	Una	8.79	895	18.92	0.07	71.96	85.73
08	Bilaspur	6.44	864	19.31	1.19	78.99	86.91
09	Solan	18.22	624	14.53	0.40	78.40	98.82
10	Sirmaur	10.39	859	19.08	0.35	77.37	97.26
11	Shimla	23.15	748	15.72	1.23	83.01	97.83
12	Kinnaur	0.00	0.00	0.00	0.00	0.00	0.00
00	**Uttarakhand**	**25.67**	**845**	**22.10**	**0.73**	**70.69**	**95.42**
01	Uttarkashi	7.77	726	24.99	1.03	76.25	91.19
02	Chamoli	13.69	716	28.85	5.43	77.49	85.29
03	Rudraprayag	1.20	444	15.64	1.06	73.61	99.86
04	Tehri Garhwal	9.90	628	14.36	0.70	75.97	99.23
05	Dehradun	52.94	863	22.35	0.65	76.17	98.33
06	Garhwal	12.89	821	20.13	0.27	77.30	97.79
07	Pithoragarh	12.94	824	25.55	7.26	79.05	94.86
08	Bageshwar	3.13	810	37.09	4.15	74.71	97.12
09	Almora	8.64	774	27.02	0.72	82.30	98.48
10	Champawat	15.04	849	24.79	0.49	67.93	92.30
11	Nainital	35.27	878	22.51	0.37	71.04	98.80
12	Udham Singh Nagar	32.62	876	20.35	0.35	59.28	87.52
13	Haridwar	30.84	844	22.11	0.04	66.95	96.19

Source: Census of India, 2001.

21 Migration and Workforce Participation in the Himalayan States

R. Lusome and R.B. Bhagat

Introduction

Since time immemorial, migration from one area to another in search of improved livelihood has been a key feature of human history. While some regions and sectors fall behind in their capacity to support populations, others move ahead and people migrate to access these emerging opportunities. Migration has become a universal phenomenon in modern times. Industrialisation widens the gap between rural and urban areas, including a shift of the workforce towards industrialising areas. In most countries, it has been observed that industrialisation and economic development has been accompanied by large-scale movements of people from villages to towns, from towns to other towns and from one country to another country.

There is extensive debate on the factors that causes populations to shift from those that emphasise individual rationality and household behaviour to those that cite the structural logic of capitalist development.

From the demographic point of view, migration is one of the three basic components of population growth of any area, the other being fertility and mortality. But whereas both fertility and mortality operate within the biological framework, migration does not. It influences size, composition and distribution of population. More importantly, migration influences the social, political and economic life of the people at the origin as well as at the destination.

The Indian Constitution provides basic freedom to an individual to move to any part of the country, right to reside and earn livelihood of their choice. Thus, migrants are not required to register either at the place of origin or at the place of destination. A number of economic, social, cultural and political factors play an important role in the decision to move.

Analysis of migration is important to understand the people's movement within the country as a response to changes in economic, political and cultural factors (Singh, 1998).

In India, permanent shifts of population and workforce co-exist with the circulatory movement of populations between lagging areas and developed regions and between rural and urban areas, mostly being absorbed in the unorganised sector of the economy.

Internal migration is now recognised as an important factor in influencing social and economic development, especially in developing countries. Indian censuses record that in 2001, 309 million persons were migrants based on place of last residence, which constitute about 30 per cent of the total population of the country. This is nearly double the number of internal migrants as recorded in the census of 1971 (159 million).

Migration is defined as a move from one migration defining area to another, usually crossing administrative boundaries made during a given migration interval and involving a change of residence (UN, 1993). The change in residence can take place either on permanent or semi-permanent or temporary basis (Premi, 1990).

A recent survey shows that census is the largest source of information on internal migration at the cross-country level. A study shows that 138 countries collected information on internal migration in their censuses compared to 35 through registers and 22 from surveys (Bell, 2003).

The paper uses data from Census 2001 to study the migration pattern in the four Himalayan states, Jammu and Kashmir, Himachal Pradesh, Uttarakhand and Sikkim. It attempts to gain insights on the association of workforce participation with migration status in the four Himalayan states. The initial part focuses on the migration pattern in these states, with emphasis on age and sex of the migrants, the duration and the reasons for migration. The later part of the paper discusses the workforce participation in these states amongst the different status group, i.e., total population, total migrants, intercensal migrants and non-migrants.

Results

In 2001, the four Himalayan states contributed about 2.5 per cent of the country's population. Table 21.1 gives the percentage of migrants to total population. The country's figures are also given for easy comparison. It is observed that migrants contribute a large share in the population of the respective states. Migrants constitute about 18 per cent of the population in Jammu and Kashmir, 35 per cent in Sikkim, 36 per cent in the states of Himachal Pradesh and Uttarakhand.

Table 21.1

Percentage of Migrants to Total Population: 2001

States/Country	*Total Population (in million)*	*Total Migrants (in million)*	*% of Migrants to Total Population*
India	1,028.6	314.5	30.6
JK	10.1	1.8	17.8
HP	6.1	2.2	36.1
SK	0.54	0.19	35.1
UTT	8.5	3.1	36.2

Further analysis has been based mainly on the intercensal migrants (0-9 years) as it is felt that studying of association of workforce participation and migration pattern would be better indicated by recent migrants.

Table 21.2 shows the percentage of intercensal migrants to total migrants by sex. The table indicates that the share of recent migrants among total migrants in Jammu and Kashmir is around 26 per cent, which is much lower than the corresponding share in the other states as well as the national figure (31 per cent). This indicates that the flow of recent migrants have been larger in Himachal Pradesh, Sikkim and Uttarakhand as compared to the state of Jammu and Kashmir. It is also seen from the table that the percentage of intercensal male migrants to total male migrants is larger than the percentage of female intercensal migrants to total female migrants in all states.

Table 21.2

Percentage of Intercensal Migrants with Duration 0-9 Years to Total Migrants

States/Country	Intercensal Migrants 0-9 Years	Males	Females
India	31.3	35.2	29.6
JK	25.7	26.3	25.3
HP	37.8	56.1	31.3
SK	34.5	41.3	31.2
UTT	42.6	44.2	41.1

Figure 21.1

Intercensal Migrants by Age Group (in %)

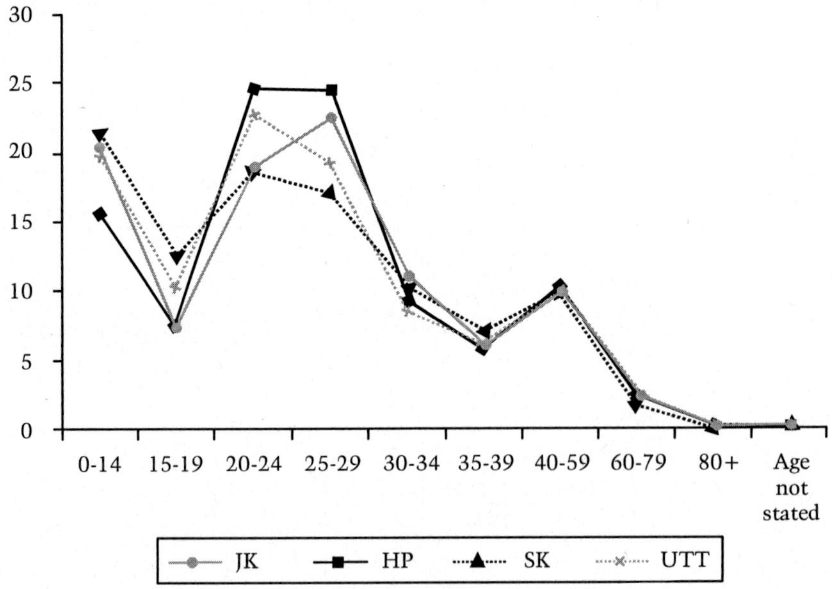

Figure 21.1 shows the age distribution of the intercensal migrants in the four states. It is seen from the figure that the intercensal migrants in the four states follow a similar pattern of age distribution.

More than three-fourth of the migrants are in the working age group (15-59 years) in all the four states. However, unlike the other states, the age distribution of intercensal migrants in Sikkim peaks at the age group 0-14 years with around 22 per cent of the migrants in the state belonging to this age group. It is also observed from the figure that the state of Himachal Pradesh has higher proportion of youth migrants as compared to the other three states.

Streams of Migration

Table 21.3 gives the percentage distribution of streams of intercensal migration in the four Himalayan states. Intra-district migration contributes the largest proportion to total migrants in all the states. However, around 61 per cent of the total migrants in Jammu and Kashmir are intra-district migrants as compared to 42 per cent in the state of Sikkim. The share of inter-state migrants in the states except Jammu and Kashmir is higher than the share of inter-district migrants to total migrants. This suggests that in the intercensal period of 1991-2001, there has been a considerable flow of inter-state migrants to the three states of Sikkim (28 per cent), Uttarakhand (33 per cent) and Himachal Pradesh (23 per cent). Regarding international migration, it is noted that the proportion of international migrants in Sikkim is quite high. There is a vast difference in the proportion of international migrants amongst the states, with the figures ranging from 0.6 per cent in Jammu and Kashmir to about 10 per cent in Sikkim.

Table 21.3

Percentage Distribution of the Streams of Intercensal Migration (0-9 Years)

Streams of Migration	*India*	*JK*	*HP*	*SK*	*UTT*
Intra-district	55.0	60.7	55.8	42.1	44.7
Inter-district	27.1	20.0	18.1	20.0	19.3
Inter-state	17.1	18.7	22.7	28.3	33.3
International	0.8	0.6	3.4	9.6	2.7

Table 21.4 provides sex ratio of the intercensal migrants by the streams of migration. Sex ratio has been calculated as the number of

female migrants per 100 male migrants. As in other studies of migration in India (Zachariah, 1964; Nair and Narain, 1985; Singh, 1998), female migrants dominate over male migrants in the short distance migration. But sex ratio of migrants in the state of Sikkim were similar to other states except inter-district migration. However, sex differential by streams of migration is quite low in Sikkim as compared to the other states. Among the inter-district migrants, sex ratio is favourable to female migrants only in the state of Sikkim (105 female per 100 male migrants). It is also interesting to note that the sex ratio of international migrants in the intercensal period for the state of Sikkim (80 female per 100 male migrants) is very high as compared to other states. This suggests that the state of Sikkim offer better opportunities for female migrants than the other states.

Table 21.4

Sex Ratio in Different Streams of Migration (0-9 Years)

Streams of Migration	*India*	*JK*	*HP*	*SK*	*UTT*
Intra-district	142	146	178	126	176
Inter-district	86	61	66	105	76
Inter-state	49	58	48	74	66
International	49	31	30	80	28

Note: Sex ratio = female/100 males.

Reasons for Migration

Table 21.5 provides the percentage distribution of reasons for intercensal migration in the four Himalayan states by sex. It is observed from the table that employment among males and marriage among females are the main reasons for migration. However, a vast difference is noted when the four states are considered.

Around 17 per cent of intercensal migrants in Jammu and Kashmir have migrated for work as compared to 24 per cent of migrants in Himachal Pradesh and 33 per cent in Sikkim. It is interesting to note here that Himachal Pradesh and Sikkim are in-migrating states. States having higher percentage of work-related migrants has correspondingly higher percentage of male and female migrating for work or business.

Though male migration in these states has been mainly work-related, there are vast differences among the states. Around 54 per cent of the male migrants in the states of Himachal Pradesh and Sikkim have moved for work-related reasons as compared to 38 per cent in Jammu and Kashmir and 46 per cent in Uttarakhand. About 3 per cent of female migrants in Uttarakhand have stated work as the reason for their move as compared to around 12 per cent of intercensal migrants in Sikkim.

Table 21.5

Percentage Distribution of Reasons for Migration by Sex for Duration (0-9 Years)

States		*Work*	*Education*	*Marriage*	*Family*	*Others*
India	Total	15.8	3.0	44.1	27.6	9.6
	Male	40.5	6.2	2.1	35.6	15.6
	Female	3.4	1.3	65.0	23.6	6.6
JK	Total	16.9	2.8	37.8	28.7	13.7
	Male	38.1	5.2	2.8	31.9	22.0
	Female	3.9	1.4	59.3	26.8	8.7
HP	Total	23.5	4.0	41.3	21.8	9.4
	Male	53.7	6.5	0.9	22.8	16.1
	Female	4.4	2.4	66.9	21.2	5.1
SK	Total	33.0	4.9	22.4	26.1	13.5
	Male	54.6	6.1	1.0	23.0	15.3
	Female	11.9	3.8	43.5	29.2	11.7
UTT	Total	19.9	4.3	35.4	31.5	8.9
	Male	45.7	7.9	0.6	32.3	13.5
	Female	3.2	2.0	58.0	30.9	5.9

Note: Work: Migrants giving work/employment and business as the reason for migration.
Family: Migrants moved after birth and moved with household as the reason.

Workforce Participation

The collection of data on economic activity has traditionally been a part of the population census of India. Census 2001 has recorded 313 million 'main workers', 89.2 million 'marginal workers' and 626.4 million 'non-workers' at the national level. The four Himalayan states recorded 7 million 'main workers', 3 million 'marginal workers' and 15 million 'non-workers' in 2001. Considering the working age (15-59) population, Census 2001 recorded 281 million 'main workers', 75 million 'marginal workers' and 227 million 'non-workers' at the national level and 6 million 'main workers', 2 million 'marginal workers' and 5 million 'non-workers' in the four Himalayan states.

Table 21.6

Distribution of Workers/Non-Workers in Working Age Group (15-59) among Migrants and Non-Migrants (in %)

State/Migration Status	*Main Workers*	*Marginal Workers*	*Non-Workers*	*Seeking Work*
India	48.1	13.0	38.9	10.9
Migrants 0-9 years	36.9	14.6	48.5	10.5
All migrants	38.7	15.9	45.4	8.9
Non-migrants	54.7	10.9	34.4	12.3
Jammu & Kashmir	40.1	16.3	43.6	14.2
Migrants 0-9 years	34.5	17.1	48.5	12.3
All migrants	33.5	17.8	48.7	11.8
Non-migrants	42.0	15.9	42.1	15.0
Himachal Pradesh	48.7	23.1	28.3	10.7
Migrants 0-9 years	48.5	23.2	28.3	10.5
All migrants	45.5	27.8	26.7	7.3
Non-migrants	51.5	18.9	29.6	13.7
Uttarakhand	44.2	14.4	41.4	11.2
Migrants 0-9 years	41.3	13.8	44.9	9.7
All migrants	43.2	15.6	41.2	7.9
Non-migrants	45.2	13.3	41.5	14.4
Sikkim	60.1	11.5	28.5	7.1
Migrants 0-9 years	61.0	10.4	28.6	7.5
All migrants	61.7	10.8	27.5	6.7
Non-migrants	58.8	12.0	29.2	7.4

Table 21.6 provides the percentage distribution of workforce participation among working age (15-59) by migration status. The table allows a comparison of workforce participation among the states. The national figure is also provided for easy comparison. The percentage seeking work includes marginal workers as well as non-workers. About 40 per cent of the population in Jammu and Kashmir is recorded as main workers as compared to 44 per cent in Uttarakhand, 48 per cent in Himachal Pradesh and 60 per cent in Sikkim. It is observed that a

significantly higher percentage of non-migrants is recorded as main workers as compared to migrants in all the states excepting the state of Sikkim. State-wise comparison of the percentage of workforce participation shows that the in-migrating states of Himachal Pradesh and Sikkim have higher percentage of main workers as compared to the out-migrating states of Uttarakhand and Jammu and Kashmir.

The percentage of seeking work shows that higher percentage of non-migrant population sought work as compared to the migrant population in all these states. Among the migrants, higher percentage of recent migrants sought work in comparison to the total migrants.

Table 21.7

Sex Ratio of Workforce in Working Age Group (15-59) among Migrants and Non-Migrants

State/Migration Status	*Main Workers*	*Marginal Workers*	*Non-Workers*	*Seeking Work*
India	33	176	311	98
Migrants 0-9 years	29	293	345	138
All migrants	33	284	323	98
Non-migrants	29	123	339	120
Jammu & Kashmir	20	188	269	109
Migrants 0-9 years	21	289	327	154
All migrants	22	245	292	99
Non-migrants	18	179	269	116
Himachal Pradesh	49	216	182	73
Migrants 0-9 years	41	449	255	163
All migrants	47	417	193	83
Non-migrants	36	153	244	103
Uttarakhand	43	133	220	54
Migrants 0-9 years	41	174	237	68
All migrants	46	197	232	50
Non-migrants	25	91	262	75
Sikkim	54	226	251	159
Migrants 0-9 years	50	294	348	224
All migrants	53	284	327	169
Non-migrants	53	208	224	160

Note: Sex ratio = female/100 males.

Table 21.7 gives the sex ratio for work participation among the working age (15-19) by migration status. A quick glance at the table indicates that sex differential is quite large in workforce participation at the national level as well as in the four Himalayan states. There is a clear dominance of males in the main workers category. It is observed that the sex ratio is very small, ranging from 20 females per 100 males in Jammu and Kashmir to 54 females per 100 males in Sikkim. But it is quite the opposite when marginal workers and non-workers categories are taken into consideration. In these categories, females outnumber the males to a very large extent. This indicates that males are more likely to be employed in better and more productive jobs as compared to females. A look at the sex ratio of those seeking work indicates that there is a clear difference between the states. Females seeking work outnumber males seeking work in the two states of Sikkim and Jammu and Kashmir. However, among recent migrants, females seeking work outnumber male migrants in all the states except the state of Uttarakhand. This seems to suggest that recent female migrants seek work more as compared to females belonging to other categories. There is large difference between the sex ratio of non-working or marginal workers and female seeking work, suggesting that a large proportion of non-working females are still not seeking work.

From Tables 21.6 and 21.7, it is seen that the state of Sikkim with higher workforce participation has larger representation of female main workers as compared to the other states. The percentage of main workers increases along with the increases in the sex ratio suggesting that the inclusion of female population in workforce increased the share of the total percentage of main workers.

Conclusion and Discussion

Though all these four states have similar topographical feature, the migration pattern has been diverse in these states. The contribution of intercensal migrants to total migrants has been greater for the in-migrating states of Himachal Pradesh and Sikkim. The flow of international migrants in the intercensal period 1991-2001 has been exceptionally high in the state of Sikkim where nearly 10 per cent of the total migrants have been international migrants. The age of the migrants in the four Himalayan states reinstate the finding that migrants mainly belong to the working age group. Analysis of the reasons for migration showed that work-related migrants have contributed higher percentage of migrants to the in-migrating states.

Results indicate that in-migrating states of Sikkim and Himachal Pradesh has higher work participation than the out-migrating states of Uttarakhand and Jammu and Kashmir. It is also found that there is higher female work participation in Sikkim and Himachal Pradesh. Results showed a positive relationship between female work participation and the overall work participation. It is found that large proportion of non-working females is not seeking work. The study also showed that among recent migrants seeking work, females outnumbered male migrants. A concerted effort to provide productive employment would not just uplift those seeking better work but also bring about faster growth and development of the states.

References

Bell, Martin (2003). "Comparing internal migration between countries: Measures, data sources and results", Paper Presented in Population Association of America, Minneapolis, May 1-3.

Bhagat, R.B. (2005). "Conceptual issues in measurement of internal migration in India", IUSSP XXVth International Conference, *Contributed Papers,* France, July 18-23.

Census of India (2001). Soft copy, India D-series, *Migration Tables.* Registrar General and Census Commissioner, India.

———. (2001). Soft copy, India B-series, *Economic Tables.* Registrar General and Census Commissioner, India.

Nair, P.S. and V. Narain (1985). "Internal migration in India: Demographic knowledge and policy issues", IUSSP Seminar on "Policy Formulation, Implementation and Evaluation: The case of East, South and South East Asia", *Contributed Papers,* Bombay, India, January 24-28.

Premi, M.K. (1990). "India", in Charles B. Nam, William J. Serow, and David F. Sly (eds.), *International Handbook on Internal Migration.* New York: Greenwood Press.

Singh, D.P. (1998). "Internal migration in India: 1961-1991", *Demography India* 27(1): 245-261.

United Nations (1993). *Readings in Population Research and Methodology.* New York: The United Nations Population Fund.

Zachariah, K.C. (1963). "Internal migration in India from the historical standpoint", Invited Paper, 34th Session. Ottawa, Canada: I.S.I.

———. (1964). "Historical study of internal migration in the Indian sub continent, 1901-1931", *Research Monograph* 1, Bombay: Demographic Training and Research Centre.

22 Urbanisation: New Challenges in Uttarakhand

Anup Badola

Introduction

The process of urbanisation, besides its own factors, has been impacted by the microeconomic factors at national level and global level. An analysis of secondary data from Census 2001 and National Sample Survey indicates that despite high rate of growth in economy, the pace of urbanisation and migration has increased in the last two decades. This is despite improvement in education, transportation and communication facilities, modernisation of norms and values etc. The states experiencing rapid demographic growth in urban areas were also those that reported heavy pressure on their urban infrastructure and basic amenities, suggesting presence of push factor behind rural-urban migration (Racine, 1997). Studies also established that areas who have higher levels of skills or economic assets, find it easier to establish linkages with urban economy through socio-cultural channels, put their foothold in the cities/towns and avail opportunity offered through migration. The census analysis also reveals that annual exponential growth of intercensal migrants in rural and urban areas work out to be 1.4 per cent and 2.5 per cent per anuam respectively. The population figures from census using simple identity, the incremental urban population during a decade can be classified into four components. These are: (a) natural increase, (b) new towns or less declassified towns (outside the agglomerations), (c) merging of towns and jurisdictional changes in agglomerations, and (d) rural-urban migration. The components where the changes in the share are substantial are (b), new (less declassified) towns and (c), merging of towns and areas with agglomerations (Kundu, 2003). The net increase in urban population due to additional declassification of towns in the terminal years, (N1-D1), can be estimated through subtraction of the increment in population of common towns from total increase in urban population over a decade. As per the Census 2001, the number of towns merged into neighbouring towns/cities was as many as 221 which are more than twice in number reported in 1991 (Census 2001). The expert committee for population projection for the Eighth Plan envisaged exponential growth rate of urban population at 4.4 per cent. The Approach paper to the Ninth Plan (Planning Commission, 1997) does not mention an exact figure but anticipated the rate of growth of urban population to be very high. Regional dimension has also played an important role in the growth in urban agglomerations. Neoclassical models of growth and labour mobility stipulated that spatial disparity in development would result in migration from backward to developed region which would help in bringing about optimality in the spatial distribution of labour and economic activities. The mobility pattern in India fits well in these models. The analysis of inter-state migrants, attempted on the basis of census as well as NSS data reveals that the less developed states report a high percentage of net out-migrants. The developed state on the other hand, turns out to be in-migration in character (Kundu, 2007). This paper would be dealing with the experience of Uttarakhand state and its areas after statehood and before statehood based on secondary data especially censuses and suggest the policy intervention that may be taken by the state to deal with new challenge.

Growing Urban Population and Changing Demography

On the eve of declaration of Uttarakhand state formation, the urban and rural population was 82.77 lakh. Dehradun, Haridwar, Udham Singh Nagar and Nainital account for most of the urban population. Looking back at the census figures of 1991, the total urban population in nine hill districts of Uttarakhand region were 16,34,084 accounting for 71 urban agglomerations. In 2001, proportion of urban population to the total population of Dehradun district was 53 per cent against 50 per cent in 1991, Haridwar district was 31 per cent against 30 per cent in 1991, U.S Nagar district was 33 per cent, Nainital district was 35 per cent against 32 per cent in 1991 (combined for Nainital and U.S. Nagar).

According to 2001 census, the urban population increased to 21,79,074 while towns/cities grew to 86 from 71 in 1991. However, due to rapid growth of the commercial as well as administrative activities in cities of Uttarakhand such as Dehradun, Haridwar, Rishikesh, Rudrapur, Bhimtal, Haldwani, Srinagar, Kotdwar etc., after formation of the state, there was an influx of migrant labourers in the state including unemployed youths from the villages of Uttarakhand. Taking into consideration the data of Census 2001 indicators, land use pattern analysis and other studies, the measuring points for delineation of urbanisation index on district and urban centres of size classes I to VI, the trend analysis of the projection of urban growth in the future is computed. The projected population change in urban agglomerations on the basis of 2001 census is given below.

Table 22.1

Urban Population Projection by 2021 in Uttarakhand (Based on 2001 Census)

Year	*Pop. Uttarakhand (in '000)*				
	Total	*Urban*	*Rural*	*% Age Change Urban*	*% Age Change Rural*
2001	8489	2179	6310	25.67	74.33
2002	8634	2239	6395	25.93	74.07
2003	8780	2300	6480	26.20	73.80
2004	8927	2362	6565	26.46	73.54
2005	9073	2425	6648	26.73	73.27
2006	9219	2488	6731	26.99	73.01
2007	9365	2553	6812	27.26	72.74
2008	9511	2619	6892	27.54	72.46
2009	9656	2685	6971	27.81	72.19
2010	9800	2752	7048	28.08	71.92
2011	9943	2820	7123	28.36	71.64
2012	10084	2888	7196	28.64	71.36
2013	10224	2956	7268	28.91	71.09
2014	10362	3026	7336	29.20	70.80
2015	10499	3095	7404	29.48	70.52
2016	10632	3165	7467	29.77	70.23
2017	10761	3234	7527	30.05	69.95
2018	10887	3303	7584	30.34	69.66
2019	11010	3373	7637	30.64	69.36
2020	11129	3441	7688	30.92	69.08
2021	11241	3509	7732	31.22	68.78

The population density of Uttarakhand state which was 133 per sq. km. in 1991 increased to 159 in 2001. In 1951, the density of Uttarakhand for all districts together was 53 per sq.km. By analysing the censuses held from 1951 to 2001, there has been about 30 per cent increase in 1961, 25 per cent in 1971, 4 per cent in 1981, 47 per cent in 1991 and 19 per cent in 2001 on urban population over a decade's period. In the hill district like Pithoragarh, Chamoli and Champawat too there has been 3-5 per cent increase in urban population between 1991 and 2001. At present the total urban population in the state accounts 25.66 per cent (Table 22.2).

Table 22.2

Percentage Share of Urban Population in the Districts of Uttarakhand during 1991 and 2001

District	*1991 Pop.*	*%age Share of Total Pop.*	*2001 Pop.*	*%age Share of Total Pop.*	*District*	*1991 Pop.*	*%age Share of Total Pop.*	*2001 Pop.*	*%age Share of Total Pop.*
Uttarkashi	17261	7%	22918	8%	Haridwar	348142	31%	446275	31%
Chamoli	40540	9%	50703	14%	Pithoragarh	42113	7%	59833	13%
Tehri Garhwal	32895	6%	59846	10%	Almora	53507	6%	54505	9%
Dehradun	515480	50%	678742	53%	Nainital	502964	33%	269050	35%
Pauri Garhwal	81182	12%	89875	13%	U.S. Nagar	-	-	403014	33%
Rudraprayag	-	-	2732	1%	Bageshwar	-	-	7803	3%
					Champawat	-	-	33748	15%
Uttarakhand						1634084	-	2179074	25.66%

Source: Census of India, 2001.

Changing and Growing Agglomeration

The smaller towns grew bigger and cities grew faster during the last two decades in Uttarakhand, thus increasing urban population rapidly. As estimated, the projected population of Uttarakhand by 2020 would be 34.21 lakh out of 111.24 lakh. Table 22.1 and Figure 22.1 clearly indicate that the growth pace in urban conglomeration will be rapid in comparison to rural population. The calculated projection of the urban population in Uttarakhand is estimated to 28.08 per cent increase by

2010 and about 31.22 per cent increase by 2021, which is about 6 per cent higher than the urban share in 2001.

As visible from Figure 22.2, due to emergence of more urban areas and expansion of present small towns, the shifting of the population in Uttarakhand would be towards urban areas, resulting in narrowing of the ratio between the share of population of urban and rural. In 2001, the ratio between urban and rural was 26:74 which is estimated to be 32:68 by 2020 as shown in the figure.

Figure 22.1

Urban Population Projection by 2020 in Uttarakhand

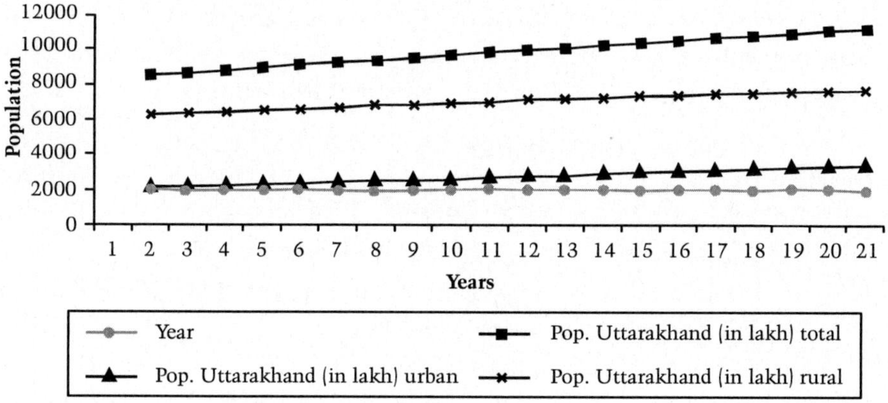

Figure 22.2

Percentage Change in Urban and Rural Population by 2020 in Uttarakhand

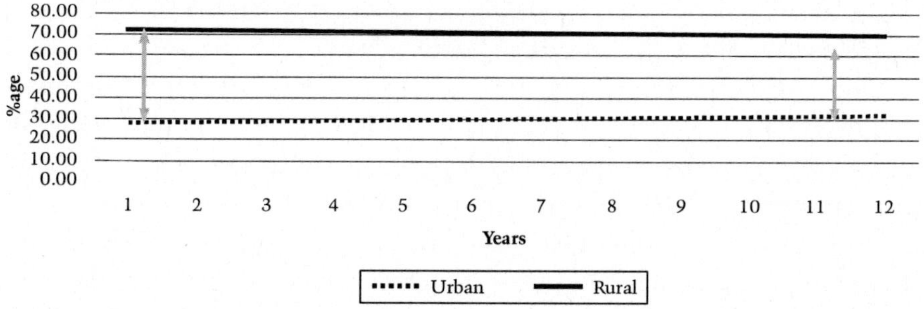

The objective of the above analysis was to envisage future challenges in Uttarakhand state and highlighting the possible policy interventions areas for the state government in its planning. The growing concerns that may need clear cut policy for the state in future are:

Policy for Growing Slums and for the Poor

Under the umbrella of the centrally sponsored Jawaharlal Nehru National Urban Renewal Mission (JNNURM), Dehradun, Nainital and Haridwar has been identified in Uttarakhand with the aim to provide access to basic urban services besides improvement in urban governance and civil services through Basic Services to the Urban Poor (BSUP) scheme. Though slums accommodate mostly migrant population from deeper hills, labourers from Bihar, Punjab and eastern UP (came way back for Tehri Dam construction and later on other dams as well as in commercial construction sites through their relatives).

According to the latest figures of rural development department, the final figure of the rural BPL families are 6,21,000. On the contrary, the state has issued only 3.39 lakh BPL, 1.48 lakh *antyodaya* and 0.08 lakh *annapurna* cards totalling 4.95 lakh BPL ration cards besides 17.77 lakh APL ration cards. Looking at the recent PDS problems in Uttarakhand and all over country, the Supreme Court on PIL of PUCL (People's Union for Civil Liberties) has suggested abolishing APL card looking at the misuse of quota to benefiting all the BPL families. As per the criteria suggested by Planning Commission of India, based on per capita consumer expenditure, if the per capita expenditure is less than Rs. 538 in urban location and is less than Rs. 356 in rural location, it will be treated below poverty line. In other words, if the family of 4 persons in urban setting spends Rs. 2142 per month and in rural settings Rs. 1424 per month, the family will be treated under BPL category. In this definition, a family of 4 persons having an annual income of Rs. 25,704 will come under BPL category in urban area and family of 4 persons having annual income of Rs. 17,088 will come under BPL in rural area while present limit of upper income for holding BPL card is Rs. 24000. In Uttarakhand, the BPL calculations are based on Central government directives for state-specific poverty line for year 2001-2002 through its D.O., suggests per capita monthly income for rural area of Rs. 433.00 and for urban area of Rs. 561.80. Taking this into consideration, the BPL must be in larger number in the state. In the recent survey figures of rural department, there are 6,21,000 BPL families in the villages of Uttarakhand while only 4.95 lakh BPL cards are made for BPL category, thus there is backlog of 1.26 lakh BPL cards to be issued in rural areas. However, as per GoI directives of calculating Uttarakhand population below poverty line on the basis of 47.42 per cent criteria, the BPL population in the urban area would be 10,33,316 on 2001 census i.e., taking the number of persons per family as 5, the number of families under poverty line would be about 2,06,663, of whom a negligible number of BPL cards have been issued as per departmental information.

Revisiting of PDS System

Since inception of Uttarakhand state, exact urban BPL families has not been determined, thus not enough BPL cards have been distributed in the cities and towns resulting no benefit of subsidised ration, no employment and self-employment scheme for these poor families. No health card facilities, as provided to the rural poor under health department, have been issued. Urban poorer are in dire state and their condition is worse than the rural poorer especially in Uttarakhand. Growing concern is about their health and education need.

Management and Planning Population due to Shrinking Cultivated Land

Due to rapid urbanisation, the cultivated land in and around cities and towns have been decreased. Of 7.9 lakh hectare cultivated land, about 57 per cent is in hilly area and 43 per cent in the plain area; on the other hand, only 10 per cent land in the hilly area and 44 per cent land of the plain area is under irrigation. In the last decade, much of the irrigated land has been converted into industrial belt, urban housing projects and other use. As per data available in 2003-04 for districts like Dehradun, Haridwar, U.S. Nagar, out of total 5.05 lakh hectare cultivable land only 3.25 lakh hectare was cultivated. Similarly in the hilly districts like Almora and Pauri Garhwal, out of total 2.63 lakh hectare cultivable land, only 1.67 lakh hectare was cultivated as shown in Table 22.3 and Figure 22.3.

Table 22.3

Total Cultivable Land and Actual Cultivable Land for the Districts of Uttarakhand

Districts	*Total Cultivable Land (in lakh ha) Statistical Figures: 2003-04*	*Actual Cultivated Land (in lakh ha) Statistical Figures: 2003-04*
Dehradun	0.78	0.53
Haridwar	1.81	1.22
U.S. Nagar	2.46	1.5
Plain districts	5.05	3.25
Pauri Garhwal	1.25	0.81
Almora	1.38	0.86
Hill districts	2.63	1.67

Figure 22.3

Cultivable Land in Use of Cultivation in 2001

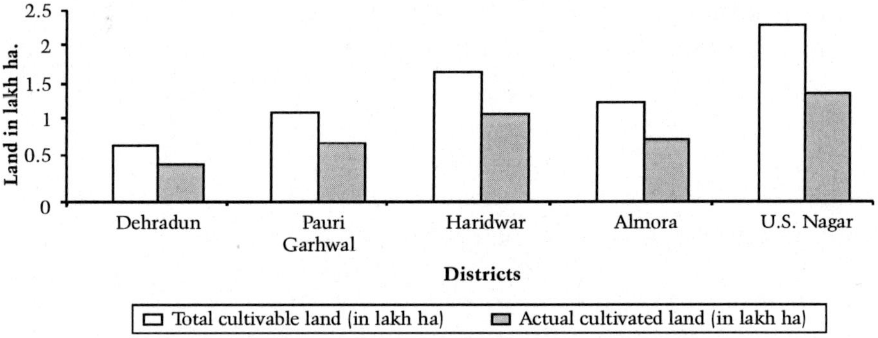

Increased Need of Urban Health Facilities

State urban health facilities are in dire state, having no specific fund allocation. The draft submitted by Urban Health Resource Centre, GoI, indicates that there is a worser situation in the urban setting than the rural setting of health. The Independent Commission on Health in India in its report of 1998 indicates that complete ANC in urban population is just 24.8 per cent against 30.4 per cent in rural; similarly, in urban area about 74.3 per cent deliveries are conducted at home and 57 per cent children of 0-3 year age are malnourished and about 60 per cent urban children are not immunised till they complete their one year. The state urban population especially those that are below poverty line do not have any specific facilities such as special health card as provided to rural BPL families, health insurance for unorganised sector is not in existence, industrial workplaces do not have required facilities nor are supported by state health services. The other growing concern is management of solid and bio-medical waste with more incinerators/deep burial facilities in the state and more space for landfill areas. Due to growing influx of private clinics and nursing homes in the cities and towns of Uttarakhand, the Clinical Regularity Act is warranted.

More Space for Education Population in Urban Settings

As per the study conducted by Pratham in 2005, a similar situation is there in the field of education as the state still have about 2 per cent children of 6-14 age group out of school. Similarly, of 98 per cent school going children of 6-14 age group 78 per cent goes to government school; rest are getting education in private schools. In primary section, pupil-teacher ratio in the state has been 1:32 and rooms availability in the primary schools for 50 to 225 enrolments are 3.2 to 3.3 rooms. But in the urban settings, it is not the same even in the worst state (State Education Statistical Report SSA, Uttarakhand, 2008).

The growing urban population and their requirement in future may warrant clear urban policy and projection of future demand of housing, water, schooling, health centres and overall population management in the Uttarakhand state.

References

Report: Census data (2001 & 1991). Census Book of India, GoI.

Racine, Jean Luc (1997). *Present Moorings: Village Ties and Mobility relations in South India.* New Delhi: Sage.

Kundu A. (2003) "Urbanization and urban governance: Search for a perspective beyond neo-liberalism", *Economic and Political Weekly* 38 (29).

———. (2007). "Mobility of population," in Kausik Basu (ed.) The Oxford Companion to Economics in India. Revised Edition. OUP. November.

Planning Commission (1997). Approach paper to the Ninth Plan.

Guidelines & Mission reports: Jawaharlal Nehru National Urban Renewal Mission (JNNURM)

Survey Report: *BPL list and findings of Rural development*. Department of Uttarakhand.

Report: Planning Commission of India report on suggesting criteria based on per capita consumer expenditure.

Source: Central government directives on BPL calculation for state specific poverty line for year 2001-02 issued by Ministry of Food & Supplies.

Statistical Annual Report "Statistical Figures 2003-04 of Uttarakhand" GoUK: Economic & Statistical Directorate.

Nagrajan, Rema (1998). On Draft report submitted by Urban Health resource centre, GoI and report of 1998 by Independent Commission on Health in India, GoI, TOI, January.

Study report: conducted by Pratham in 2005 for Uttarakhand.

Report: State Education statistics SSA Uttarakhand 2008.

G. Population and Development

23 Population and Development in Uttarakhand

Emerging Issues and Challenges

H.C. Srivastava

Introduction

The state of Uttarakhand separated from Uttar Pradesh in 2000, is one of the new and relatively less developed Indian states and as a result is classified as a special "category" state. It is located on the northern boundary of India and shares international borders with the People's Republic of China and Nepal. It has total land area of 53,483 square kms. Over 90 per cent of the state's terrain is hilly and 62 per cent is forested, limiting the availability of land for agriculture. The state's population as per the 2001 Census of India is 4.48 million. The literacy rate 72.3 per cent is much higher than the national average (65.4 per cent), while health indicators lag behind the national health indicators. Around 25 per cent (or 2.29 million) of the state's population live in 63 urban areas including its 13 districts (Asian Development Bank, 2008). After acquiring statehood, Uttarakhand is facing various challenges to fulfil the basic needs of the people. Due to its hilly terrains, sizeable area covered under forest and an isolated region, the state has its specific needs and priorities. There are several areas which still lack means of transportation and communication. The large segment of the society is deprived of basic amenities like drinking water, electricity, adequate facilities for public health and sanitation etc. Also another serious problem of the people of Uttarakhand is out-migration, particularly of the young males in search of employment due to lack of employment opportunities. There is also a need to generate resources in order to sustain development activities. This would require identification of potential areas, planning for their development and an effective implementation of these plans. Despite Uttarakhand's better demographic scenario as compared with many states of the country, still it lags behind some states of south India. Therefore, there is a need for development in different areas of the state for achieving the goals laid down in the Health and Population Policy of the state with regard to demographic situation and health and family welfare aspects. Apart from many other areas, improvement in the existing socio-economic condition of the people, public health system, transport and communication, women and child development etc., also deserves adequate attention of the programme personnel.

Agriculture continues to be the mainstay of the people of Uttarakhand and majority of the population of the state depends on agriculture for their livelihood. As Uttarakhand is predominantly rural with around 74 per cent of the population living in 16414 rural settlements of the total villages, more than four-fifth are small villages with population less than 500 persons. Another 10 per cent have population sizes ranging between 500 and 999 persons and the remaining 6 per cent are villages with over 1000 population. Small-sized scattered villages without road connectivity poses a major challenge to health service delivery. Hill districts are at a disadvantage compared with districts in the plain areas (Nautiyal, 2004).

For Uttarakhand, the barometer of development would be the development of villages, many of which are cut-off from the mainstream and deprived of the basic amenities. Some of the urgently required facilities for the remotely situated villages and their inhabitants are motorable roads, good link of communication, employment for the youth, drinking water, electricity, effective public health system, schools and good educational facilities etc. (Government of Uttarakhand, 2002).

Source of Data

The necessary data for the paper has been taken from the Census of India 2001, National Family Health Survey-3 (NFHS-3), District Level Household Survey (DLHS) and from other concerned sources.

Demographic Characteristics of the Population

Decadal Growth Rate

The selected demographic characteristics of the population of Uttarakhand, Jharkhand and Chhattisgarh as well as for India based on the 2001 Census figures are depicted in Table 23.1. It is evident from the table that population size of Uttaranchal, subsequently known as Uttarakhand as local people prefer to call the state by this name, was 8.5 million whereas population of the other two newly formed states Jharkhand was 26.9 million and for Chhattisgarh it was 20.8 million. Whereas for the country, the population was 1027 million. Looking at the population size of Uttarakhand, it is obvious that the state is relatively small in terms of its population size.

The decadal rate of growth during the period 1991-2001 in case of Uttarakhand was 19.20 per cent which is lesser than the rate of growth of the country's population (21.3 per cent). Among the three newly formed states, Jharkhand showed highest growth rate (23.2 per cent). On the contrary, Chhattisgarh showed the lowest figure (18.1 per cent).

Table 23.1

Selected Demographic Characteristics for India and Selected States: 2001

	India	*Uttarakhand*	*Jharkhand*	*Chhattisgarh*
Population (million)	1027	8.5	26.9	20.8
Decadal growth rate (%) (1991-2001)	21.3	19.2	23.2	18.1
Sex ratio (F/M*1000)	933	964	941	990
Child sex ratio (0-6)	927	906	966	975
Density of population (per square km)	324	159	338	154
Literacy rate (%)				
Total	65.4	72.3	54.1	65.2
Male	75.9	84.0	67.9	77.9
Female	52.4	60.3	49.4	52.4

Source: Census of India, 2001.

Sex Ratio

Sex ratio (females per 1000 males) in case of Uttarakhand, as per 2001 census was 964 against 933 for the country as a whole. The corresponding figures for Jharkhand and Chhattisgarh are 941 and 990 respectively. Among the districts, sex ratio varied from 868 for Haridwar to 1147 females per 1000 males for Almora (see Table 23.2). The hilly regions have higher sex ratio in favour of females, compared with the districts in the plains. It may be mainly because of heavy out-migration of males to the districts in plains within the state as well as outside the state in search of predominantly economic opportunities.

Child Sex Ratio (0–6)

The child sex ratio (0–6) showed lowest ratio for Uttarakhand (906) and highest for Chhattisgarh 975 females per thousand males. In case of India, the corresponding ratio as per the 2001 census was 927 girls per thousand boys. The phenomena clearly suggest deficiency of the females (0–6) in Uttarakhand. Probable reasons for the deficiency of female children (0–6) need to be examined and necessary measures should be adopted to improve the prevailing situation.

Density of Population

The density of population for Uttarakhand was 159 persons per square km whereas for Jharkhand and Chhattisgarh, the corresponding figures were 338 and 154 against 324 persons per square km for the country (Table 23.1). It is evident from the table that as compared with the density of population for the states under consideration as well as the corresponding figure for the country as a whole, the density of population in Uttarakhand is relatively low, mainly because of its difficult hilly terrain.

Selected Population Characteristics according to Districts of Uttarakhand

A comparison among the figures for the population growth of the districts revealed that there exist wide variations, as it ranges from 3.9 per cent for Garhwal district to 32.9 per cent for Nainital, followed by

27.8 per cent for Udham Singh Nagar district and 26.3 per cent for Haridwar (Table 23.2).

The table suggests wide variation in the sex ratio among the districts as the range has been observed between 868 for Haridwar to 1147 females per thousand males for Almora district. It is encouraging to observe that by and large each district within the state has shown higher literacy rate as compared with the corresponding figure for the nation with the exception of Haridwar. Interestingly, hilly districts have better literacy rate compared to the districts in the plains.

Table 23.2

Selected Population Characteristics according to Districts of Uttarakhand: 2001

Districts	*Population Growth (%)*	*Sex Ratio (F/M*1000)*	*Literacy Rate (%)*
Uttarkashi	22.7	941	66.6
Chamoli	13.5	1017	76.2
Pithoragarh	10.9	1031	76.5
Tehri Garhwal	16.2	1057	67.0
Bageshwar	9.2	1110	71.9
Rudraprayag	13.4	1117	74.2
Champawat	17.6	1024	71.1
Garhwal	3.9	1104	78.0
Almora	3.1	1147	74.5
Nainital	32.9	906	79.6
Dehradun	24.7	893	79.0
U.S. Nagar	27.8	902	65.8
Haridwar	26.3	868	64.6
Uttarakhand	19.2	964	72.3

Source: Census of India, 2001.

Registration of Births and Deaths

The vital statistics presented in Table 23.3 show that among the three states under consideration, the vital rates are lowest for Uttarakhand as compared to Chhattisgarh and Jharkhand. The crude birth rate (CBR) has been observed lowest (21 per thousand) for Uttarakhand and highest 26.9 for Chhattisgarh while for India as a whole, the corresponding figure was 23.5. Further CBR for the urban and rural areas were also observed lowest for Uttarakhand (17.3 and 22.0 respectively) as compared with the remaining two states as well as against the national average (18.8 for urban and 25.2 for the rural areas). While considering crude death rate (CDR) for Uttarakhand, the figures for the total, urban and rural areas were found lowest 6.7, 5.5 and 7.0 per thousand populations respectively. Whereas the corresponding figures for India are 7.5, 6.0 and 8.1 respectively.

The natural growth rate has also been found lowest in case of Uttarakhand as a whole, rural and urban areas (14.2, 14.9 and 11.7 percent) respectively. The corresponding figures for India are 16.0, 17.2 and 12.8 for the total, rural and urban areas respectively.

Further while considering the scenario of the infant mortality rates (IMR) in Uttarakhand, Chhattisgarh, Jharkhand and for the country as a whole, the state of Uttarakhand has shown the lowest figures 43, 54 and 22 infant deaths per thousand live birth for total, rural and urban areas respectively. The corresponding figures for the nation as a whole are 57, 62 and 39 for the total, rural and urban areas respectively.

Further, with regard to the total fertility rate (TFR) for the state of Uttarakhand, it was 2.55 children per woman for the state as whole (2.21 for urban and 2.67 for the rural areas) whereas for Jharkhand and Chhattisgarh, the corresponding figures were 3.31 and 2.68 children per woman. The figures for the total fertility rate for India were (2.68 for the total, 2.07 for urban and 2.98 for the rural areas). Though the crude birth rates, crude death rates, total fertility rates, natural growth rate and infant mortality rates were found lower than the corresponding values for the country but still these lagged behind as compared with the states of south India. Also, urban-rural differential in these rates are significant. Hence, there is a need for further reduction in these rates to attain demographic transition in the state as early as possible (Table 23.3).

Table 23.3

Vital Statistics and Total Fertility Rates of the Selected States and India

	CBR			*CDR*			*Natural Growth Rate*			*IMR*			*TFR**		
	T	*R*	*U*	*T*	*R*	*U*	*T*	*R*	*U*	*T*	*R*	*U*	*T*	*R*	*U*
India	23.5	25.2	18.8	7.5	8.1	6.0	16.0	17.2	12.8	57	62	39	2.68	2.98	2.07
Uttarakhand	21.0	22.0	17.3	6.7	7.0	5.5	14.2	14.9	11.7	43	54	22	2.55	2.67	2.21
Jharkhand	26.2	28.0	18.8	7.5	7.9	5.9	18.6	20.1	12.8	49	52	32	3.31	3.69	2.32
Chhattisgarh	26.9	28.5	19.9	8.1	8.5	6.3	18.8	20.0	13.6	61	62	50	2.68	2.98	2.07

Note: * International Institute for Population Sciences—NFHS-3 (2005-06).

Source: Office of the Registrar General and Census Commissioner of India—*SRS Bulletin* 42(1), October 2007.

Level of Registration of Births and Deaths

As per the Sample Registration System (SRS) of India, the states are classified by the level of registration of births and deaths. It is encouraging to note that as far the birth registration is concerned, the state of Uttarakhand falls in the category of those states where level of birth registration is between 60-80 per cent. In Chhattisgarh, it was between 40-60 per cent and Jharkhand in the category of below 40 per cent.

On the contrary while considering the level of death registration, Uttarakhand was placed in the category of the states where level of death registration was below 40 per cent. Jharkhand was also in the same category whereas Chhattisgarh was in the category of 60-80 per cent. This observation clearly suggests that in the state of Uttarakhand, there is a need to enhance the system of birth and death registration. Obviously, rigorous efforts are required to be made for the improvement in the death registration. It may be emphasised that for the improvement in the system of birth and death registration, more emphasis needs to be given to the rural and remotely located areas in the state.

Marriage and Family Planning Related Aspects

Some of the marriage and family planning, maternal and child health women empowerment related indicators available through the NFHS-3 survey are presented in Table 23.4 and description of the same is given below.

Marriage

The data available through NFHS-3 revealed that as far as the women aged 20-24 married by age 18 years is concerned, Uttarakhand had the lowest value (22.6 per cent); on the contrary the highest value (61.2 per cent) has been observed for Jharkhand. In case of the nation as a whole, the corresponding value was 44.5 per cent.

With regard to men aged 25-29 years married by age 21 years, the lowest percentage was for Uttarakhand (21.3 per cent) and highest for Jharkhand (47.1 per cent). The corresponding figure for India as a whole was 29.3 per cent (Table 23.4). It is evident from these figures that though the proportion of the women and men getting married by the prescribed age at marriage is relatively lower, however, in future further reduction may be brought in this area.

The proportion of males and females married below the prescribed age at marriage are relatively lower for Uttarakhand compared with the corresponding proportion for other states as well as for the country. Significant urban-rural differentials exist but still significantly high proportion of males and females get married before the legal age at marriage in Uttarakhand. Therefore, there is a need to educate and motivate the people to achieve the desired goals. In this regard, special programmes need to be developed for promoting family life education particularly to the adolescents. It would help them in knowing the advantages of getting married after the legally prescribed age and learning about reproductive health issues at an appropriate time.

Married Women with Two Living Children and Wanting No More

As far the married women with two living children and wanting no more is concerned, the findings of NFHS-3 suggest that in case of Uttarakhand, proportion of such women was 86.3 per cent whereas for Jharkhand and Chhattisgarh, the corresponding values were 64.3 and 75.3 respectively. Though it is encouraging to observe that the proportion of the married women with two living children and wanting no more is higher than the figure for the national average, however there is scope for improving the proportion of such women in Uttarakhand.

Family Planning

The analysis based on the data on current use of any method of family planning according to NFHS-3 suggests that among the three states, the highest percentage value 59.3 was observed for Uttarakhand and lowest for Jharkhand 35.7 per cent. With regard to current use of family planning methods is concerned, Uttarakhand has been found having better performance than that of the corresponding figure for the country (56.3 per cent). However, efforts to enhance such proportion need to be appreciated for the multi-sectoral development of the state.

Total Unmet Need for Family Planning

The proportion for unmet need for family planning was found lowest in case of Chhattisgarh (10.5 per cent), followed by Uttarakhand (11.3 per cent) and Jharkhand (23.7 per cent). Whereas for the country, the corresponding figure was 13.2 per cent (Table 23.4).

Maternal and Child Health

In view of the aspects related to maternal and child health, the area focused in the paper include birth attended by medical and paramedical personnel, institutional births and child immunisation and vitamin A supplementation and anaemia among children and adults.

With regard to mothers who had received at least three antenatal care visits at their last birth it was observed that around 51 per cent had received the care; in other words, 49 per cent did not receive such care in the country. As far as Uttarakhand is concerned, the mothers who did not receive at least three antenatal care visits, their proportion was more than 55 per cent. Further, corresponding percentage value for the rural areas of the state was significantly much higher (63 per cent). Obviously, this component of the maternal health care needs adequate attention and priority for the improvement.

The percentage for births assisted by a doctor/nurse/LHV/ANM/ other health personnel for Uttarakhand was 41.5 per cent for the entire state (for urban 64.6 and for rural 34.4 per cent), followed by Chhattisgarh (44.3 for total, 74.0 for urban and 38.5 per cent for the rural areas) and Jharkhand (28.7 for the total, 62.2 for urban and 20.8 for the rural areas). In case of the country as a whole, the figures were 48.3, 75.2 and 39.1 per cent for the total, urban and rural areas respectively (Table 23.4).

Institutional Births

Though Uttarakhand has shown relatively better picture with regard to institutional births as 36 per cent total births, 60 per cent births in urban and 28.6 per cent in rural areas are institutional which is relatively higher than the corresponding figures for the remaining two states. When we compare Uttarakhand's prevailing situation with the corresponding figures in case of the country as a whole, the percentage values were 40.7, 69.4, and 31.1 for the total, urban and rural areas respectively.

This clearly shows that though significantly high proportions of the births in Uttarakhand (nearly 59 per cent against around 52 per cent births in the country) are still delivered by untrained persons. Obviously, serious efforts are needed to improve this area by providing more facilities and changing people's attitude in this regard.

Anaemia among Children and Adults

The NFHS-3 collected data on children age a 6-35 months and adults who are anaemic and it is presented in Table 23.4. There were 61.5 per cent anaemic children in Uttarakhand which is lowest as compared to the corresponding values for Jharkhand (77.7 per cent) and Chhattisgarh (81.0 per cent). The figure for the country as a whole was 79.2 per cent.

In case of anaemic ever married women aged 15-49 in Uttarakhand is concerned, the percentage value was 47.6, which is lowest as compared with the corresponding figures for Jharkhand (70.4 per cent) and Chhattisgarh (57.6 per cent). The corresponding figure for India was 56.2 per cent. Likewise percentage for the ever married men aged 15-49 who are anaemic for Uttarakhand was 26.1 whereas for India as a whole it was 24.3 per cent. The scenario of anaemic children and adults suggests that efforts need to be made for improving iron deficiency among the people of Uttarakhand, particularly among the children and women in order to improve general health condition of the masses in the state specially in rural areas.

Women Empowerment

To examine aspects of women empowerment, attempts have been made in the NFHS-3 and the findings based on the following two indicators are presented in Table 23.4.

The percentage of currently married women who usually participate in household decisions in the three states showed lowest values in

Uttarakhand (47.9 for the total, 60.4 for urban and 43.4 per cent for the rural areas) as compared with the corresponding value for Jharkhand (59.0 per cent) and Chhattisgarh (51.3 per cent). While comparing the situation of Uttarakhand with percentage values for the country as a whole, one may notice that the situation of the country in this regard is better than Uttarakhand as the percentage values for the country as a whole, urban and rural areas were 52.5, 61.4 and 48.5 per cent respectively. This clearly suggests that more than 52 per cent women in Uttarakhand do not participate in household decisions. For improving women empowerment, this aspect needs to be improved by bringing about behavioural change in the society in general and among the men in particular.

Another indicator for assessing women empowerment used here is percentage of ever married women who have ever experienced spousal violence. It is evident from Table 23.4 that Uttarakhand showed lowest percentage value 27.9 for the states as a whole as compared with Jharkhand (37.0 per cent) and Chhattisgarh (30.0 per cent). Whereas the corresponding values for the country as a whole was 37.2 per cent. It is encouraging to observe that incidence of spousal violence are lowest in the present context. However, for women development efforts are required to be taken for the reduction of such social evil.

Infrastructural Facilities as Indicator of Development

Some of the facilities available in the household which indicate level of development of the members of the household namely, source of drinking water, source of electricity/lighting, availability of latrine, *pucca* house and television, have been discussed here with the assumption that higher the percentage value for the same, higher would be the level of development.

Household with Selected Amenities

In addition to the above mentioned variables, the NFHS-3 also provides information on households with selected amenities and some amongst them are presented in Table 23.5.

Table 23.4

Per cent Distribution of the Selected Key Indicators, NFHS–3 (2005-06)

	India			*Uttarakhand*			*Jharkhand*			*Chhattisgarh*		
	T	*R*	*U*	*T*	*R*	*U*	*T*	*R*	*U*	*T*	*R*	*U*
(A) Marriage												
1. Women aged 20-24 married by age 18	44.5	52.5	28.1	22.6	24.7	16.3	61.2	71.0	33.6	51.8	60.3	25.4
2. Men aged 25-29 married by age 21	29.3	36.5	16.7	21.3	30.0	7.1	47.1	54.7	26.8	44.8	51.9	17.5
3. Married women with two living children wanting no more children	83.2	79.9	88.9	86.3	85.7	87.5	64.3	55.6	82.7	75.3	71.2	87.2
(B) Family Planning												
1. Currently use any method	56.3	53.0	64.0	59.3	57.2	65.3	35.7	28.2	60.0	53.2	49.9	65.4
2. Total unmet need	13.2	14.6	10.0	11.3	11.7	10.3	23.7	27.0	13.4	10.5	10.8	9.3
(C) Maternal and Child Health												
1. Birth assisted by a doctor/nurse/LHV/ANM/other health personnel	48.3	39.1	75.2	41.5	34.4	64.6	28.7	20.8	62.2	44.3	38.5	74.0
2. Mothers who had at least three antenatal care visit for their last birth (%)	50.7	42.8	73.8	44.8	36.2	71.5	36.1	28.8	67.1	54.7	49.2	82.3
3. Institutional births	40.7	31.1	69.4	36.0	28.6	59.9	19.2	11.0	54.1	15.7	7.5	58.0

contd...

...*contd*...

	T	R	U	T	R	U	T	R	U	T	R	U
(D) Anaemia among Children and Adults												
1. Children age 6-35 months who are anaemic	79.2	81.2	72.7	61.5	62.0	60.2	77.7	80.5	65.9	81.0	82.1	75.6
2. Ever married women aged 15-49 who are anaemic	56.2	51.5	58.2	47.6	48.8	44.3	70.4	73.4	59.4	57.6	59.4	50.3
3. Ever married men aged 15-49 who are anaemic	24.3	27.7	17.2	26.1	28.8	20.1	37.4	41.8	23.1	26.4	28.7	17.9
(E) Women Empowerment												
1. Currently married women who usually participate in household decisions	52.5	48.5	61.4	47.9	43.4	60.4	59.0	58.0	62.1	51.3	49.3	58.3
2. Ever married women who have ever experienced spousal violence	37.2	40.2	30.4	27.9	29.8	22.8	37.0	40.8	24.6	30.0	30.5	28.1

Source of Drinking Water

Table 23.5 presents per cent distribution of the households by source of drinking water in India and in three states under study. Since tap is the main source of drinking water and data pertaining to the same is available from three sources—Census, DLHS and NFHS-3 all the three have been considered here.

While considering Uttarakhand, all the three sources showed that the percentage for tap water varies from 65.9 (for census) to 66.7 per cent (for DLHS). In case of India as a whole, the percentage value for tap as a source of drinking water varies between 36.7 (for census) to 49.0 per cent (for DLHS). Further it is evident from the table that availability of tap is lesser in rural areas as compared with the urban areas, suggesting a need for providing more taps in the rural areas. Next to tap, hand pump was found as a source of drinking water as nearly 20 per cent households in Uttarakhand against around 34 per cent in India depend on it. The corresponding percentages for Jharkhand and Chhattisgarh were 27 and 53.3 respectively.

Availability of Latrine in the Household

It is noticed from the table that around 43 per cent household in Uttarakhand does not have the facilities of latrine according to NFHS-3 data whereas as per census 2001, 45 per cent household fall in that category. The situation in Jharkhand and Chhattisgarh is still worse in this regard. While considering as a whole, nearly 64 per cent as per the Census and 56 per cent according to NFHS-3 lack availability of latrine in the household. Though Uttarakhand has shown a better picture but much more needs to be done in this regard specially in the rural areas.

Living in Pucca House

Further the table depicts that as far as *pucca* houses are concerned, in case of the country as a whole the percentage value was 41.4 (25.5 per cent in rural and 74.1 per cent in urban areas). While considering Uttarakhand, around 49 per cent household live in *pucca* houses; in other words, more than 50 per cent of the houses in the state were *kachha*. Further it is disappointing to note that around 65 per cent of the households in the rural areas were *kachha* houses and one can understand the plight of those living in such houses. Situation of Jharkhand and Chhattisgarh is still worse in this regard. Obviously, this needs urgent attention of the policy makers and programme managers.

Households Having Televisions

The NFHS-3 data shows that in India, around 44 per cent households have television (30 per cent in rural and 73.2 per cent in urban areas). In case of Uttarakhand, 61 per cent households had TV (53 per cent rural and 81.3 per cent urban) while in case of Jharkhand and Chhattisgarh, only 27.1 per cent and 33.4 per cent households were found having TV. Though Uttarakhand showed relatively better picture in this regard but still a large number of the households in the rural areas (around 47 per cent) do not have television (Table 23.5).

Table 23.5

Per cent Distribution of the Household by Selected Amenities

	Tap[1]	*Tap*[2]	*Tap*[3]	*Hand Pump*[3]	*Tube Well*[3]	*Well*[3]	**Other*[3]	*Latrine*[3]	*Latrine*[2]	*Live in Pucca House*[3]	*Have a TV*[2]
India											
Total	49.0	42.0	36.7	33.7	5.6	18.2	3.9	36.4	44.5	41.4	44.2
Rural	-	27.9	24.3	43.2	5.7	22.2	3.5	21.9	25.9	25.5	30.1
Urban	-	71.0	68.7	16.2	5.1	7.7	2.2	73.7	83.1	74.1	73.2
Uttarakhand											
Total	66.7	66.3	65.9	19.8	1.0	1.2	13.3	45.1	56.7	48.8	61.0
Rural	-	58.7	60.5	21.4	1.1	1.6	15.5	31.6	42.2	35.3	53.0
Urban	-	85.5	82.3	14.9	0.6	0.2	2.0	86.8	93.7	83.1	81.3
Jharkhand											
Total	28.0	11.3	12.6	27.0	3.1	51.8	5.6	19.7	22.6	28.1	27.1
Rural	-	0.0	2.7	29.9	2.9	58.2	6.3	6.5	5.0	10.4	11.3
Urban	-	44.4	48.0	16.4	3.8	28.7	3.1	66.6	73.7	79.6	73.1
Chhattisgarh											
Total	33.9	16.8	15.5	53.3	1.7	24.6	4.8	14.2	18.7	17.2	33.4
Rural	-	6.0	5.0	59.9	1.2	28.1	5.8	5.2	5.6	5.7	22.2
Urban	-	55.5	60.0	25.2	3.6	9.7	1.5	52.6	65.5	58.4	73.5

Note: * Other includes tank, pond, lake, river, canal, spring and any other.

1. DLHS, Phase-II, 2003.
2. International Institute for Population Sciences–NFHS-3 (2005-06).
3. Office of the Registrar General and Census Commissioner of India, Census of India 2001, Series-1.

Household with Source of Lighting

The availability of electricity in the household is usually considered as a sign of development. Keeping in view the same, Table 23.6 provides the distribution of households by source of lighting. As per the census of 2001, nearly 56 per cent households in the country reported having electricity. Residence-wise break-up suggests that while 87.6 per cent households in the urban areas have electricity, the corresponding figure for the rural areas is only 43.8 per cent. Next to electricity the source of lighting is kerosene (43.3 per cent) for the country as a whole. While considering the three states, availability of electricity in the households has been found highest for Uttarakhand (80 per cent according to the NFHS-3 and 60 per cent for the Census 2001). Though relatively more households have electricity in rural Uttarakhand but there is much scope for improvement as nearly 50 per cent households in the rural areas does not have electricity in the state.

Table 23.6

Per cent Distribution of the Household by Source of Lighting

	Electricity[1]	*Electricity*[2]	*Kerosene*[2]	**Other*[2]	*No Light*[2]
India					
Total	67.9	55.8	43.3	0.6	0.3
Rural	55.7	43.8	55.6	0.6	0.3
Urban	93.1	87.6	11.6	0.4	0.4
Uttarakhand					
Total	80.0	60.3	37.3	2.2	0.3
Rural	74.1	50.3	46.7	2.2	0.3
Urban	95.0	90.9	8.4	2.7	0.3
Jharkhand					
Total	40.2	2.4	75.3	0.4	0.1
Rural	22.8	10.0	89.6	0.3	Negligible
Urban	90.8	75.6	23.8	0.5	0.1
Chhattisgarh					
Total	71.4	53.1	46.0	0.6	0.4
Rural	65.5	46.1	52.9	0.6	0.4
Urban	92.2	82.9	16.5	0.3	0.3

Note: * Other includes solar energy, other oil and other sources.

Source: 1. International Institute for Population Sciences—NFHS-3 (2005-06).

2. Office of the Registrar General and Census Commissioner of India-Census of India 2001, Series-1.

Conclusion, Issues and Strategies for Development

While concluding the present paper, it may be emphasised that the following issues and strategies have emerged for implementation in the state of Uttarakhand to provide multi-dimensional development and improving quality of life of the people of Uttarakhand.

(1) In view of the foregoing discussion, it may be argued that as there are significant inter-district as well as urban-rural differentials in the socio-economic, demographic, health and family welfare indicators within the state of Uttarakhand, efforts should be made for narrowing down such differentials.

(2) There is a need for pursuing sustainable model of development plan for the state. Some of the strategies to be adopted include strengthening infrastructure facilities particularly in the rural areas like availability of drinking water, electricity, transport and communication, adequate facilities to the PHCs/CHCs etc., for providing better health care to the masses.

(3) As at present the state faces challenges of combating communal diseases like tuberculosis (TB), malaria, leprosy and HIV/AIDS as well as non-communicable diseases, special and specific programmes should be implemented to eradicate the diseases and for reducing risk of HIV/AIDS in the state. For this purpose, besides adopting different strategies special attention should be given to the risk-prone segments of the population.

(4) In addition, the emerging lifestyle diseases need to be identified and accorded proper attention in terms of facilities and programmes.

(5) Due to recent decline in fertility, the problem of elderly people has been increasing. The joint and extended family structure which used to provide necessary social and economic support to the elderly is undergoing significant changes posing serious consequences for the welfare of the aged persons. In view of the same, special programmes catering to the need of the aged persons should be implemented.

(6) Though the demographic and family welfare related indicators for the population of Uttarakhand are relatively better than many states in the country but still they lag behind when compared with states in south India. Therefore, there is a need for further reduction in these indicators to attain demographic transition in the state as early as possible.

(7) As health status of the women and children in the state is far from satisfactory, there is a need for betterment particularly by improving nutrition and maternal and health care for the women and children. For this purpose, besides several necessary measures, transport and communication facilities must also be improved. Availability of well-connected motorable roads with the isolated and remotely located areas should be given top priority.

(8) With regard to the system of registration of births and deaths in Uttarakhand is concerned, on the one hand birth registration has been placed in the category of those states which have a level of registration 60-80 per cent, this needs to be enhanced to make it 100 per cent as early as possible. On the other hand, surprisingly the level of registration of deaths in the state has been placed in the category of those states where it is below 40 per cent. First of all, there is a need to examine reasons for such poor reporting of registration of death and necessary measures need to be evolved for the complete registration of the deaths in the state.

(9) For the development in economic sector, the prevailing unemployment problem may be improved with the creation of more employment and income opportunities for the people and for this purpose, utilisation and augmentation of the available resources in the state need to be explored.

(10) The other high priority areas for the development in Uttarakhand are horticulture, diversification of agriculture, tourism, animal husbandry, soil conservation, local resource-based industries etc.

Uttarakhand has immense potential for becoming a leading state in the country. The need of the hour is to explore and utilise its resources including human resource by cultivating new ideas and strategies for providing sustainable development and improving the quality of life of the people of Uttarakhand.

References

Asian Development Bank (2008). Report and Recommendations of the President to the Board of Directors, Proposed Multi trench facility—"India: Uttarakhand Urban Sector Development Investment Programme", Project No. 38272, January.

Bose, Ashish and Vhai Team (2002). *Health and Development Challenges of Chhattisgarh, Jharkhand and Uttaranchal*. New Delhi: Voluntary Association of India.

Census of India (2001). Series-1, "Tables on Houses, Household Amenities and Assets for General Population", New Delhi, 2003.

———. Series-1, "General Population Tables"—India, States and Union Territories (Table A-4), Part–II, New Delhi, 2007.

———. Sample Registration System, Statistical Report of 2006.

Draft Five Year Plan (1995-96). c.f. Mehta G.S. (1978-1983) *Uttarakhand and Prospects of Development*. New Delhi: Indus publication Co.

Government of Uttarakhand (2002). "Health and Population Policy of Uttaranchal", Department of Medical, Health and Family Welfare, December.

International Institute for Population Sciences (2007). National Family Health Survey-3, Ministry of Health and Family Welfare, Govt. of India, September.

———. and Government of India (2002-2005). Ministry of Health and Family Welfare, Reproductive and Child Health District Level Household Survey (DLHS-2), New Delhi.

Nautiyal, Aparna (2004). "Uttaranchal Tomorrow", in B.C. Upreti (ed.), *Uttaranchal Issues and Challenges of Development and Change*. Delhi: kalinga Publication.

Office of the Registrar General and Census Commissioner India.

Sati, Vishambhar Prasad and Kamlesh Kumar (2002). *Uttaranchal Dilemma of Plenty and Scarcities*. New Delhi: Mittal Publications.

Upreti, B.C. (e.d.) (2004). *Uttaranchal Issues and Challenges of Development and Change*. Delhi: Kalinga Publications.

The author is thankful to Shri Santosh Kumar Singh, research officer, International Institute for Population Sciences, Mumbai for typing out the draft of the paper.

24 Population Growth and Land Use in Uttarakhand

Dewaram A. Nagdeve

Introduction

The present paper is an attempt to study the population growth and its impacts on land use in Uttarakhand. The district-wise data from various secondary sources have been analysed by computing ratio, percentage and index from 1981 to 2001. The analysis reveals that the total population of Uttarakhand has increased more than double and wide inter-district variation in population growth observed from 1981 to 2001. The land utilisation pattern shows variation in land use. An inconsistent relationship between the growth rate of population and cropping intensity was observed in most of the districts of the state. The increase in total cropped area lagged far behind the population growth in half of the districts in the state during 1991-2001. Therefore, more efforts are required for intensification and extensification of land use for satisfying the needs of growing population and to cater the future need of the state.

Increasing population pressure and short supply of arable land have been the main areas of concern for planners and policy makers in the country. The large size of population has a negative impact as it reduces the capacity to make additional investment and size of land for cultivation. Uttarakhand is the 27th state of the Republic of India and Dehradun is the capital city. It was formed on 9 November 2000 and was carved out of Uttar Pradesh after a long struggle of the Uttaranchali people. Earlier there were only 8 districts in Uttarakhand but after becoming a state, Uttarakhand consists of 13 districts. Uttarakhand lies in the northern part of India amidst the magnificent Himalayas and dense forests. The state is bordering Himachal Pradesh in the north-west and Uttar Pradesh in the south and has international borders with Nepal and China. The state today with 13 districts can be grouped into three distinct geographical regions, the high mountain region, the mid-mountain region and the Terai region. The population of the state is around 7 million. The land area is about 55,845 sq km. The region is mostly hilly (approximately 88 per cent) and the remaining 12 per cent falls in the plains. The state is very rich in natural resources especially water and forests as it has many glaciers, rivers, forests and mountain peaks.

After being carved out of Uttar Pradesh, Uttarakhand has been richer in terms of wildlife and forest area. The thick forests and mountains house a variety of wildlife and plant species. The state of Uttarakhand has tremendous potential of developing tourism industry due to the beautiful landscape, religious places, trekking trails, national parks, mountain peaks and historical and archeological sites. Apart from tourism, the rural population is engaged in agriculture. Doon Valley, Nainital district, Udham Singh Nagar and Haridwar districts produce large quantities of food grains. The state has immense potential for the development of horticulture crops—apple, orange, malta, pear, grapes, peach, plum, appricot, litchi, mango, guava etc., are widely produced fruits. The region also holds good promises for developing herbal pharmaceutical industry owing to abundant medicinal plants. Due to its water resources, the state has the capacity to generate many mega watts of power. Presently, it is producing 500 MW of power. There are 17 hydroelectric projects already producing electricity and many ambitious power projects including Tehri Dam are under construction. The industrial sector of the state is insignificant. It is hoped that by development and proper exploitation of its natural resources, Uttarakhand can overcome its economic backwardness.

The report of a workshop on population and land use in developing countries concluded that, in the long run, population growth almost certainly affects land use pattern. The effects of population growth occur mainly through the extensification and intensification of agricultural production (Preston, 1993). In the paper entitled "Population, land use and environment-A long history", the author has found that there is a strong relation between population size and land use pattern (Wolman, 1993). The author in his study found that, the land use pattern changes with the changing need of the population (Stamp, 1948).

Rapidly increasing population increases the demand for the products of land, yet the area of land is limited. Land is the important resource to improve the economic, social status and needs of human beings. At the same time, land is a scarce resource, therefore its efficient use is necessary to satisfy the human wants and to obtain the maximum economic returns. The most important features of land use in Uttarakhand are fallow and other cultivated land excluding fallow land, which can be extensified under cultivation. The main emphasis, therefore, should be laid on intensification and extensification of arable land to satisfy the wants of rapidly increasing population in Uttarakhand. Any piece of land has a definite capacity to sustain a definite number of population (individuals) although it varies according to the extent of technical advancement of the area concerned. The land is utilised for various uses and the pattern of land utilisation changes according to the capacity of man who efficiently and economically uses it i.e., land-man ratio, prior needs of the population, technological development, government policies, changes in production techniques, national and international markets. Therefore, the changes in land use and the pressure of population on it are necessary prerequisites to study the population growth and land use in Uttarakhand state.

Objectives of the Study

The present paper is an attempt to study population growth and land use in Uttarakhand. However, specific objectives of the present study are as follows:

1. To examine the pattern of population growth at the district level.
2. To analyse the district-wise pattern of land use and variation in availability of land at the district level.
3. To examine the inter-relationships between population growth and agricultural land use in different districts.

Sources of Data

Population data are obtained from the *Uttarakhand Update* and census and agricultural data on land utilisation, cropping intensity and irrigated area are obtained from *Uttarakhand Update* and land use statistics at a glance from 1981 to 2002.

Methodology

The present study follows a district-wise analysis approach to explore the nature and magnitude of land use change in response to population. The old five-fold land use classification is used in the present study. District-wise analysis has been done by computing ratio, percentage and average decadal growth rates of population. In the second stage, index is used to find out the cropping intensity and the volume of land use change. Bivariate relationship between population growth and cropping intensity has been used to examine the inter-relationship between population growth and agricultural land usc.

Analysis and Findings

Population Growth in the Districts of Uttarakhand

The selected demographic characteristics of the population in the districts of Uttarakhand from 1981 to 2001 are presented in Table 24.1. The population of Uttarakhand increased more than 1.7 times from 4836 thousand in 1981 to 8480 thousand in 2001. It is seen from table that the total population has been increasing continuously from 1981 to 2001. The decadal growth rate of population has declined from 24.2 per cent during 1981-1991 to 19.2 per cent during 1991-2001.

It is observed from the table that decade 1981-1991 witnessed a net increase in the population of Uttarakhand state at an average decadal rate of 24.2 per cent in 1981-1991. A higher growth rate was experienced in six districts namely Uttarkashi, Dehradun, Champawat, Nainital, Udham Singh Nagar and Haridwar as compared to the state average. Districts like Udham Singh Nagar, Dehradun and Nainital witnessed an even greater increase in population by an average decadal growth rate of 44.4, 34.7 and 29.9 per cent respectively.

Table 24.1

Selected Demographic Characteristics of the Population in the Districts of Uttarakhand: 1981-2001

State/Districts	Population in Thousand			Decadal Growth Rate of Population		Population Density in Per sq. km	
	1981	1991	2001*	1981-1991	1991-2001*	1991*	2001*
Uttarakhand	4835.7	5926.1	8479.6	24.2	19.2	133	159
Uttarkashi	190.9	239.7	295.0	25.5	22.7	30	37
Chamoli	364.3	454.9	319.7	21.9	13.5	43	48
Rudraprayag*	-	-	227.4	17.4	13.4	106	120
Tehri Garhwal	497.7	580.2	604.7	16.6	16.2	128	148
Dehradun	761.7	1025.7	1282.1	34.7	24.7	332	414
Garhwal	637.9	682.5	697.1	9.1	3.9	124	129
Pithoragarh	1136.5	1540.2	462.3	14.1	10.9	59	65
Champawat*	-	-	224.5	26.4	17.6	107	126
Almora	757.4	836.6	630.6	9.4	3.1	198	205
Bageshwar*	-	-	249.5	15.5	9.2	99	108
Nainital	489.3	566.4	762.9	29.9	32.9	149	198
Udham Singh Nagar*	-	-	1235.6	44.4	27.8	332	424
Haridwar*	-	-	1447.2	28.4	26.3	485	612

Note: * Census of India, Uttaranchal, Provisional Population Totals, 2001.
Source: Uttarakhand Update: A Statistical Profile for Development Planning, 1999.

The decade 1991-2001 experienced a decrease in the decadal growth rate of population from 24.2 per cent in 1981-1991 to 19.2 per cent in 1991-2001. A higher growth rate was experienced in five districts namely Uttarkashi, Dehradun, Nainital, Udham Singh Nagar and Haridwar as compared to the state averagc. Districts like Nainital, Udham Singh Nagar and Haridwar witnessed an even greater increase in population by an average decadal growth rate of 32.9, 27.8 and 26.3 per cent respectively. The inter-district variations in the average decadal growth rates of population can be explained by uneven spread of the practice of contraception, differential fertility, mortality and migration.

The density of population per square kilometre in Uttarakhand has been increased from 133 in 1991 to 159 in 2001. Five districts namely Dehradun, Almora, Nainital, Udham Singh Nagar and Haridwar are having higher population density as compared to the state's average whereas other districts are having lower population density in 1991 and

2001. The highest population density of 485 and 612 persons per square kilometre was found in Haridwar and lowest population density of 30 and 37 persons per square kilometer was found in Uttarkashi in 1991 and 2001 respectively.

Land Utilisation Pattern in Uttarakhand

A change in land utilisation pattern implies an increase or decrease in the proportion of area under different land uses at a point in two or more time periods. Table 24.2 describes the land utilisation pattern in Uttarakhand from 1981 to 2002. Despite past expansion of the area under cultivation, less agricultural land is available to feed each person in Uttarakhand. The land utilisation pattern shows variations in land use and a narrow range of fluctuations in the proportion of net sown area to total land in the state since 1981 to 2002. The total reporting area of Uttarakhand is 5567 thousand hectare in 2002. The area under forest has been increased from 3443 thousand hectare in 1981 to 3466 thousand hectare in 2002. The land not available for cultivation has been increased from 408 thousand hectare in 1981 to 462 thousand hectare in 2002. The land part to non-agricultural uses has been increased from 118 thousand hectare in 1981 to 167 thousand hectare in 2002. More than 295 thousand hectare are barren and uncultivable land in 2002. Similarly, other uncultivated land excluding fallow land has been increased from 719 thousand hectare in 1981 to 764 thousand hectare in 2002. The fallow land increased from 53 thousand hectare in 1981 to 82 thousand hectare in 2002. The net sown area increased by 12.64 per cent from 704 thousand hectare in 1981 to 793 thousand hectare in 2002. The area sown more than once increased by 31 thousand hectare from 444 thousand hectare in 1981 to 475 thousand hectare in 2002. The gross cropped area has been increased from 1148 thousand hectare in 1981 to 1268 thousand hectare in 2002. The cropping intensity has been decreased from 163 in 1981 to 159 in 2002.

Land Use Patterns in the Districts of Uttarakhand

A change in land utilisation pattern implies an increase or decrease in the proportion of area under different land uses at a point in two or more time periods. Proper understanding of the land use pattern

Table 24.2

Land Utilisation Pattern in Uttarakhand: 1981-2002

(Thousand hectare)

Classification	*1980-81*	*1985-86*	*1990-91*	*1992-93*	*1993-94*	*2001-02@*
I. Reporting area for land utilisation purposes	5327	5392	5359	5359	5369	5567
1. Forest	3443	3438	3425	3426	3435	3466
2. Not available for cultivation (a+b)	408	423	432	434	433	462
(a) Land part to non-agricultural uses	118	124	136	137	136	167
(b) Barren and unculturable land	290	299	296	297	297	295
3. Other uncultivated land (excluding fallow land) (a+b+c)	719	799	761	763	762	764
(a) Permanent pasture and other grazing land	217	272	227	227	228	223
(b) Area under miscellaneous shrubs, grooves etc.	186	208	217	220	218	218
(c) Culturable waste	316	319	317	316	316	323
4. Fallow land (a+b)	53	626	71	72	72	82
(a) Current fallow	21	11	8	8	8	14
(b) Other fallow	32	615	63	64	64	68
5. Net area sown	704	675	669	663	667	793
6. Area sown more than once	444	428	430	437	424	475
7. Gross cropped area	1148	1103	1099	1100	1091	1268
8. Cropping intensity*	163.00	163.30	164.29	165.90	163.50	159.90

Note: @= *Land Use Statistics at a Glance* 2001-02—2002-03.

Source: Uttarakhand Update: A Statistical Profile for Development Planning, 1999.

prevalent in the state involves an evaluation of land utilisation. It is evident that there is an imbalance in land utilisation in various districts of the state. The land utilisation pattern in the districts of Uttarakhand from 1981 to 1999 is given in Table 24.3. It shows the district-wise variations in land use and a narrow range of fluctuations in the proportion of net sown area to total land in the state since 1981 to 1999. Forest category includes all areas actually under forests whether state owned or private and administered as forests under any legal enactment dealing with forests. It is evident from the table that the percentage of forest area in the state declined from 64.6 per cent in 1981 to 63.9 per cent in 1991 and again it declined to 62.6 per cent in 1999 in

Table 24.3

Land Utilisation Pattern in the Districts of Uttarakhand: 1981-1999

(In percentage)

State/Districts	*Forest*			*Not Available for Cultivation**			*Other Uncultivated Land (Excluding Fallow Land)***			*Fallow Land****			*Net Area Sown*		
	1980-81	*1990-91*	*1998-99*	*1980-81*	*1990-91*	*1998-99*	*1980-81*	*1990-91*	*1998-99*	*1980-81*	*1990-91*	*1998-99*	*1980-81*	*1990-91*	*1998-99*
Uttarakhand	64.6	63.9	62.6	7.7	8.1	8.2	13.5	14.2	13.8	1.0	1.3	1.4	13.2	12.5	14.0
Uttarkashi	88.4	88.6	88.8	1.3	3.4	3.2	5.9	3.9	3.7	0.3	0.5	0.5	4.2	3.6	3.8
Chamoli	61.2	62.6	68.2	22.8	21.9	17.8	10.3	9.6	8.8	0.2	0.2	0.2	5.5	5.6	5.1
Rudraprayag*	-	-	43.1	-	-	31.8	-	-	15.7	-	-	0.3	-	-	9.1
Tehri Garhwal	69.1	69.1	69.1	2.8	4.0	4.3	13.9	12.9	13.9	1.0	1.4	1.6	13.2	12.5	11.1
Dehradun	70.0	69.7	68.0	5.5	6.1	7.2	5.1	6.0	5.6	1.9	2.3	2.5	17.5	15.9	16.7
Garhwal	63.2	59.3	59.0	5.4	6.8	6.6	15.7	19.5	19.0	1.4	2.4	2.3	14.2	12.0	13.1
Pithoragarh	53.4	51.8	55.8	6.7	6.6	6.3	26.8	28.7	27.6	1.7	2.2	2.1	11.4	10.7	8.3
Champawat*	-	-	43.8	-	-	8.0	-	-	35.0	-	-	2.7	-	-	10.5
Almora	54.3	53.9	55.3	7.0	6.9	6.7	22.0	23.4	22.6	1.0	1.2	1.1	15.6	14.6	14.3
Bageshwar*	-	-	47.5	-	-	7.9	-	-	26.6	-	-	1.3	-	-	16.8
Nainital	57.5	57.5	55.8	5.2	5.3	6.3	6.8	6.6	27.6	1.2	1.4	2.1	29.3	29.3	8.3
Udham Singh Nagar*	-	-	33.4	-	-	9.3	-	-	1.7	-	-	1.8	-	-	53.8
Haridwar*	-	-	31.0	-	-	12.1	-	-	1.0	-	-	2.5	-	-	53.3

Note: *Not available for cultivation= barren and unculturable land + land part to non-agricultural uses.

**Other uncultivated land (excluding fallow land)=culturable waste +permanent pasture and gazing land +area under miscellaneous shrubs groves etc.

***Fallow land=current fallow + other fallow.

Source: Uttarakhand Update: A Statistical Profile for Development Planning, 1999.

Uttarakhand and in the districts of Dehradun, Garhwal and Nainital whereas it increased in other districts of Uttarakhand. The highest percentage of forest area was found to be 88.8 per cent in Uttarkashi district and lowest 31 per cent in Haridwar district in 1999. This decrease in forest area might be due to deforestation, forest area coming under cultivation and due to the demand for wood and forest products to satisfy the human wants such as fuel, wooden implements, timber and for other purposes. The increase in forest area in some districts might be due to the forest and social forestry programmes and private cultivation of forest by cultivators.

The area under not available for cultivation category includes land put to non-agricultural uses like rivers, railways, roads etc., and barren and uncultivable land like mountains, deserts etc. In other words, it includes land which cannot be brought under cultivation unless at a very heavy cost. The percentage of area under not available for cultivation increased from 7.7 per cent in 1981 to 8.2 per cent in 1999 in the state. The percentage of area under not available for cultivation increased in the districts of Uttarkashi, Tehri Garhwal, Dehradun, Garhwal and Nainital whereas it decreased in Almora, Pithoragarh and Chamoli districts of Uttarakhand.

Other uncultivated land (excluding fallows) consists of: 1) permanent pasture and other grazing land means all grazing lands whether they are permanent pastures and meadows or village common grazing land; 2) miscellaneous tree crops and groves not included in the net area sown. Actually these are the lands for very limited agricultural use but whose areal extent is not included in the net sown area category; and 3) culturable waste means cultivated once but not cultivated during the year and last five years i.e., lands under casuarina trees, thatching grasses, bamboo bushes, other groves for fuels which are not included under orchard. The percentage of area under other uncultivable land excluding fallow land in the state was 13.5 per cent in 1981 which increased to 14.2 per cent in 1991 and decreased to 13.8 per cent in 1999. It increased in the districts of Dehradun, Garhwal, Pithoragarh, Almora and Nainital districts whereas it decreased in Uttarkashi and Chamoli districts of Uttarakhand. The highest percentage of uncultivable land might be due to the lack of rain, irrigation facilities, poverty, finance, agricultural technology, production techniques, land uneconomical to cultivate and land under miscellaneous tree crops and groves. The reasons vary from district to district and vice-versa for the lowest percentage of uncultivable land excluding the current fallow.

Fallow land means land which is not available for cultivation during one year. Current fallow means during the current agricultural year and other fallow means fallow not less than one year and not more than 5 years. Land used for arable purposes can be identified by examining the percentage of fallow land and percentage of net area sown. The percentage of fallow land slightly increased from 1 per cent in 1981 to 1.4 per cent in 1999 in the state as a whole. The percentage of fallow land increased in seven districts namely Uttarkashi, Tehri Garhwal, Dehradun, Garhwal, Pithoragarh, Almora and Nainital. The high percentage of fallow land might be due to the lack of rain, topography and shortage of irrigation facilities, inadequate supply of water, poor land, lack of agricultural inputs, agricultural land uneconomical for cultivation, silting of canals and rivers, malarial climate, water logging and poverty, improper management of land. Fallow land provides the availability of land for areal extension of agriculture.

The percentage of total net area sown in Uttarakhand was 13.2 per cent of total reporting area for land utilisation purposes in 1981 which decreased to 12.5 per cent in 1991 and increased to 14 per cent in 1999. The percentage of net area sown decreased in all the districts of Uttarakhand during 1981 to 1999. The highest percentage of net sown area was 53.8 per cent in Udham Singh Nagar district and lowest 3.8 per cent in Uttarkashi district. The percentage of net sown area varies from district to district. Extensification and intensification of agriculture through reclamation of wasteland, bunding to store the water are important for developing agriculture although modernisation, intensification and extensification of agriculture are of paramount significance. The rapidly growing population, decreasing land-man ratio and competition for agricultural land among the rural agricultural population together call for cultivation of fallow land and horizontal expansion of agriculture. Thus the study has indicated that, there is a scope to increase net sown area by cultivating fallow land.

Cultivated Land in Uttarakhand

The net area sown, area sown more than once and gross cropped area in the districts of Uttarakhand from 1981 to 1999 is presented in Table 24.4. The total net area sown in Uttarakhand decreased from 704 thousand hectare in 1981 to 669 thousand hectare in 1991 and increased to 784 thousand hectare in 1999. The area sown more than once declined from 444 thousand hectare in 1981 to 430 hectare in 1991 but increased to 475 thousand hectare in 1999. Similarly, almost all districts experienced decline in area sown more than once except Pithoragarh district from 1981 to 1991. The gross cropped area in Uttarakhand declined from 1148 thousand hectare in 1981 to 1099 thousand hectare in 1991 and increased to 1259 thousand hectare in 1999. But almost all the districts registered decline in net area sown and gross cropped area from 1981 to 1991 and again in 1999. The increase in net area sown, area sown more than once and gross cropped area in 1999 might be due to the restructuring and formation of new districts. The lowest net area sown might be due to less availability of productive land, lack of sufficient rain, lack of irrigation facilities, lack of transportation and communication facilities, agricultural infrastructures, fertilisers, finance and low economic returns. This varies from district to district for different reasons.

Association between Population and Agriculture

The efficient use of land depends upon the relationship between land and population. It also changes according to population growth and distribution in the districts. The increase in population alters the land use changes.

Land-Man Ratio

Land-man ratio shows the per capita share of land in the districts of Uttarakhand. It is a fact that rural economy of Uttarakhand is based on the agricultural income. Therefore, agricultural economy can be understood by studying land-man ratio. The per capita land in the districts of Uttarakhand from 1981 to 1999 is given in Table 24.5. The per capita land in Uttarakhand has been increased from 0.63 hectare in 1981 and 1991 to 0.66 hectare in 1999. Per capita reported land was

Table 24.4

Net Area Sown, Area Sown More Than Once and Gross Cropped Area in the Districts of Uttarakhand: 1981-1999

(Per thousand hectare)

State/Districts	Net Area Sown			Area Sown More Than Once			Gross Cropped Area		
	1980-81	1990-91	1998-99	1980-81	1990-91	1998-99	1980-81	1990-91	1998-99
Uttarakhand	704.2	669.1	784.1	443.5	430.2	475.3	1147.7	1099.3	1259.4
Uttarkashi	33.6	29.1	31.0	19.5	16.2	17.8	72.4	45.2	48.8
Chamoli	47.0	46.4	32.9	25.4	26.1	17.3	53.1	72.5	50.2
Rudraprayag*	**	**	18.5	**	**	11.4	**	**	30.0
Tehri Garhwal	75.6	72.1	63.8	48.0	46.7	39.7	123.6	118.8	103.5
Dehradun	56.4	50.1	51.0	32.2	35.5	27.1	88.5	85.6	78.1
Garhwal	102.4	91.1	98.8	50.3	46.6	52.2	152.6	137.7	151.0
Pithoragarh	70.6	68.4	39.7	23.2	54.3	32.4	123.8	122.7	72.1
Champawat*	**	**	17.7	**	**	12.6	**	**	30.3
Almora	113.6	105.9	83.5	75.3	69.3	50.4	189.0	175.2	134.0
Bageshwar*	**	**	23.3	**	**	18.8	**	**	42.1
Nainital	205.0	206.0	39.7	139.6	135.7	32.4	344.6	341.6	72.1
Udham Singh Nagar*	**	**	150.0	**	**	107.2	**	**	257.3
Haridwar*	**	**	124.5	**	**	55.3	**	**	179.8

Note: *: Newly created district, 2000.

**: Data is not available.

Source: Uttarakhand Update: A Statistical Profile for Development Planning, 1999.

Table 24.5

Per Capita Land in the Districts of Uttarakhand: 1981-1999

State/Districts	Total Land			Arable Land			Net Area Sown			Gross Cropped Area		
	1980-81	1990-91	1998-99	1980-81	1990-91	1998-99	1980-81	1990-91	1998-99	1980-81	1990-91	1998-99
Uttarakhand	0.63	0.63	0.66	0.09	0.09	0.10	0.08	0.08	0.09	0.14	0.13	0.15
Uttarkashi	2.73	2.72	2.78	0.12	0.11	0.12	0.11	0.10	0.11	0.25	0.15	0.17
Chamoli	2.33	2.25	1.75	0.13	0.13	0.09	0.13	0.13	0.09	0.14	0.20	0.14
Rudraprayag*	-	-	0.89	-	-	0.08	-	-	0.08	-	-	0.13
Tehri Garhwal	0.95	0.95	0.95	0.13	0.13	0.12	0.13	0.12	0.11	0.20	0.20	0.17
Dehradun	0.25	0.25	0.24	0.05	0.04	0.05	0.04	0.04	0.04	0.07	0.07	0.06
Garhwal	1.03	1.09	1.08	0.16	0.16	0.17	0.15	0.13	0.14	0.22	0.20	0.22
Pithoragarh	1.34	1.38	1.04	0.18	0.18	0.11	0.15	0.15	0.09	0.27	0.27	0.16
Champawat*	-	-	0.75	-	-	0.10	-	-	0.08	-	-	0.13
Almora	1.15	1.15	0.93	0.19	0.18	0.14	0.18	0.17	0.13	0.30	0.28	0.21
Bageshwar*	0.00	0.00	0.56	0.00	0.00	0.10	0.00	0.00	0.09	0.00	0.00	0.17
Nainital	0.92	0.92	0.63	0.28	0.28	0.07	0.27	0.27	0.05	0.45	0.45	0.09
Udham Singh Nagar*	-	-	0.23	-	-	0.13	-	-	0.12	-	-	0.21
Haridwar*	-	-	0.16	-	-	0.09	-	-	0.09	-	-	0.12

Note: *: Newly created district, 2000.

- : Data is not available.

Source: *Uttarakhand Update: A Statistical Profile for Development Planning*, 1999.

found to be highest 2.78 hectare in Uttarkashi district and lowest 0.16 hectare in Haridwar district in 1999. Out of 13 districts, 9 districts namely Rudraprayag, Tehri Garhwal, Dehradun, Champawat, Almora, Bageshwar, Nainital, Udham Singh Nagar and Haridwar were having less than one hectare per capita land. It is a fact that, per capita land gives only idea of per capita availability of land. Therefore, the general standard of living and agricultural efficiency of people will depend upon their per capita share in net and gross cropped land.

Agricultural land means net sown area and fallow land that can be used for agricultural use. The per capita share of net sown area gives only the condition of people in any given year. The share of agricultural land shows the real land-man ratio for any agricultural year and the pressure of population on land. The per capita share of agricultural land in Uttarakhand was 0.09 hectare in 1981 and 1991, slightly increased to 0.10 hectare in 1999. Among the different districts, Uttarkashi, Rudraprayag, Garhwal, Pithoragarh, Champawat and Udham Singh Nagar were found to have higher per capita agricultural land whereas other districts were having lower per capita agricultural land as compared to the state average in 1999.

The per capita net area sown in Uttarakhand was 0.08 hectare in 1981 and 1991, slightly increased to 0.09 hectare in 1999. The highest per capita net sown area was 0.13 hectare reported in Almora district and lowest 0.04 hectare reported in Dehradun district during 1999. The per capita net sown area varies from district to district. Five districts registered higher per capita net sown area as compared to the state average whereas other districts were having either similar or lower net sown area as compared to the state average. The higher per capita net sown area might be due to the more area under cultivation, irrigation facilities and agricultural infrastructural facilities whereas the lower per capita net sown area might be due to the less area under cultivation due to the area under rivers, hills and inaccessible folds of mountains and more area under non-agricultural uses.

The per capita gross cropped area means net sown area and area sown more than once. The per capita gross cropped area increased from 0.14 hectare in 1981 to 0.15 hectare in 1999. The per capita gross cropped area was found to be highest 0.22 hectare in Garhwal district and lowest 0.06 in Dehradun district. Seven districts reported higher per capita gross cropped area as compared to state average whereas other districts were having either similar or lower gross cropped area as compared to state average.

Agricultural Population and Gross Cropped Area

Since cultivable area is an important limiting factor in agricultural development, the status of agricultural population is often defined in terms of the land-man ratio. Where the land-man ratio is unfavourable, the population is considered to be suffering from population pressure. The static measure of population pressure outlines the balance between population and resources in an agricultural population at a point of time. The area already under cultivation may be taken as a rough measure of the existing production possibilities for an agricultural population. The gross cropped area per cultivator and agricultural labour in the districts of Uttarakhand from 1981 to 2001 is presented in Table 24.6. It is generally expected that there is a negative association between the gross cropped area per cultivator and agricultural labour and the proportion of arable land that remains to be brought under cultivation. The gross cropped area per cultivator and agricultural labour increased from 1981 to 2001. This might be due to the restructuring of districts and more and more land was brought under cultivation in each successive decade in Uttarakhand. The changes taking place in gross cropped area per cultivator and agricultural labour from 1981 to 2001 is presented in the table. This will be followed by an examination of relationship between these variables. It is found that the gross cropped area per cultivator was 0.97 hectare in 1981 that increased to 1.14 hectare in 1991 and again it increased to 1.24 hectare in 2001. The gross cropped area per cultivator was found to be highest at 2.55 hectare in Rudraprayag district and lowest 0.45 hectare in Udham Singh Nagar district. Nine districts were having higher gross cropped area per cultivator whereas other districts were having lower gross cropped area per cultivator as compared to the state average in 2001.

Table 24.6

Gross Cropped Area Per Cultivator and Agricultural Labour in Districts of Uttarakhand: 1981-2001

State/Districts	Gross Cropped Area Per Cultivator			Gross Cropped Area Per Agricultural Labour		
	1981	1991	2001	1981	1991	2001
Uttarakhand	0.97	1.14	1.24	0.08	0.13	0.21
Uttarkashi	1.08	1.97	2.09	0.01	0.00	0.05
Chamoli	2.48	1.94	2.05	0.01	0.02	0.04
Rudraprayag*	-	-	2.55	-	-	0.02
Tehri Garhwal	1.53	1.51	1.79	0.01	0.02	0.03
Dehradun	0.78	0.87	0.96	0.22	0.37	0.36
Garhwal	1.08	0.99	1.20	0.01	0.03	0.03
Pithoragarh	1.18	1.39	1.86	0.01	0.01	0.03
Champawat*	-	-	2.08	-	-	0.06
Almora	9.21	1.47	1.64	0.02	0.02	0.03
Bageshwar*	-	-	2.11	-	-	0.09
Nainital	0.47	0.60	1.63	0.20	0.27	0.33
Udham Singh Nagar*	-	-	0.45	-	-	0.39
Haridwar*	-	-	0.54	-	-	0.45

Note: *: Newly created district, 2000.

Source: Calculated from Census, *Uttarakhand Update: A Statistical Profile for Development Planning*, 1999 and *Land Use Statistics at a Glance* 2001-02—2002-03.

The gross cropped area per agricultural labour was 0.08 hectare in 1981, increased to 0.13 hectare in 1991 and again it increased to 0.21 hectare in 2001. The gross cropped area per agricultural labour was found to be highest at 0.45 hectare in Haridwar district and lowest 0.02 hectare in Rudraprayag district. Four districts namely Dehradun, Nainital, Udham Singh Nagar and Haridwar were having higher gross cropped area per agricultural labour as compared to the state average in 2001. The lower gross cropped area per agricultural labour was found in Uttarkashi, Chamoli, Rudraprayag, Tehri Garhwal, Garhwal, Pithoragarh, Champawat, Almora and Bageshwar districts. Overall, gross cropped area per agricultural labour has increased in Uttarakhand during 1981 to 2001.

Changes in Irrigated Area

Irrigation plays an important role in expansion of cropped area through intensification and extensification of arable land as well as raising crop production. It is therefore, reasonable to expect the expansion of irrigated area with increasing population. The irrigated land and its percentage share in each district from 1981 to 1999 are shown in Table 24.7. In 1981, net irrigated area was 28.6 per cent of the net cropped area; it increased to 43.3 per cent of the net cropped area in 1999 and recorded an increase of 14.7 per cent over 1981. Percentage of net irrigated land to net cultivated land varies from 7.7 per cent in Chamoli district to 94.5 per cent in Udham Singh Nagar district. The percentages of net irrigated land to net cultivated land were higher than the state average in 4 out of 13 districts whereas other districts were having lower percentages of net irrigated land to net cultivated land.

Table 24.7

Net Irrigated Area as Percentage of Net Cultivated Area in the Districts of Uttarakhand: 1981-1999

(Per thousand hectare)

State/Districts	*Net Irrigated Area*			*Percentage of Net Irrigated Area to Net Cultivated Area*		
	1980-81	*1990-91*	*1998-99*	*1980-81*	*1990-91*	*1998-99*
Uttarakhand	201.5	233.6	339.8	28.6	34.9	43.3
Uttarkashi	5.0	4.4	5.2	14.9	15.3	16.9
Chamoli	2.5	2.5	2.5	5.4	5.4	7.7
Rudraprayag*	**	**	**	**	**	**
Tehri Garhwal	10.8	10.0	9.3	14.3	13.9	14.5
Dehradun	23.7	22.4	24.0	42.0	44.8	47.0
Garhwal	8.6	8.1	8.0	8.4	8.9	8.1
Pithoragarh	6.2	5.5	6.4	8.8	8.1	16.2
Champawat*	**	**	**	**	**	**
Almora	10.9	12.9	10.9	9.6	12.2	13.1
Bageshwar*	**	**	**	**	**	**
Nainital	133.	167.7	30.3	65.3	81.4	76.3
Udham Singh Nagar*	**	**	141.8	**	**	94.5
Haridwar*	**	**	101.3	**	**	81.4

Note: *: Newly created district, 2000.
**: Data is not available.

Source: Uttarakhand Update: A Statistical Profile for Development Planning, 1999.

The gross irrigated area as a percentage of gross cultivated area in the districts of Uttarakhand from 1981 to 1999 is shown in Table 24.8. The gross irrigated area to gross cropped area increased from 28 per cent in 1981 to 34 per cent in 1991. The inter-district variations in percentage of gross irrigated area to gross cropped area were found in districts of Uttarakhand. Out of eight districts only two districts namely Dehradun (44 per cent) and Nainital (74.2 per cent) were having higher percentage of gross irrigated area to gross cropped area and other districts were having lower percentage of gross irrigated area to gross cropped area in 1991. The lower percentages of gross irrigated area to gross cropped area were registered in Chamoli (17.7 per cent), Pithoragarh (7.9 per cent), Garhwal (10.5 per cent), Almora (14.6 per cent), Tehri Garhwal (16.4 per cent) and Uttarkashi (17.7 per cent) districts.

Table 24.8

Gross Irrigated Area as a Percentage of Gross Cultivated Area in the Districts of Uttarakhand: 1981-1999

(Per thousand hectare)

State/Districts	*Gross Irrigated Area*			*Percentage of Gross Irrigated Area to Gross Cultivated Area*		
	1980-81	*1990-91*	*1998- 99*	*1980-81*	*1990-91*	*1998-99*
Uttarakhand	317.7	373.3	**	27.7	34.0	**
Uttarkashi	9.0	8.0	**	12.4	17.7	**
Chamoli	4.3	4.8	**	12.4	17.7	**
Rudraprayag*	**	**	**	**	**	**
Tehri Garhwal	21.0	19.5	**	17.0	16.4	**
Dehradun	36.0	37.7	**	40.6	44.0	**
Garhwal	14.1	14.5	**	9.2	10.5	**
Pithoragarh	10.4	9.7	**	8.4	7.9	**
Champawat*	**	**	**	**	**	**
Almora	21.2	25.6	**	11.2	14.6	**
Bageshwar*	**	**	**	**	**	**
Nainital	201.7	253.7	**	58.5	74.2	**
Udham Singh Nagar*	**	**	**	**	**	**
Haridwar*	**	**	**	**	**	**

Note: *: Newly created district, 2000.

**: Data is not available.

Source: Uttarakhand Update: A Statistical Profile for Development Planning, 1999.

Cropping Intensity

Land under agricultural crops can be increased by providing irrigation facilities, fertilisers, agricultural modern technology, finance, high yielded improved certified seeds and production techniques etc. All these inputs will maximise the crop yield and can be measured in terms of intensity of cropping (IC). It is the index of multiple cropping and implies the degree of cropping i.e., double or triple cropping in the same field during one agricultural year.

The intensity of cropping is calculated as:

intensity of cropping (IC) = gross cropped area/net sown area * 100

In the above index, intensity of Cropping increases more than 100 as the area sown more than once increases. This index of intensity of Cropping is calculated for the districts of Uttarakhand during 1981, 1991 and 1999. For convenience of analysis, the intensity of cropping has been classified as follows:

I. High intensity index: 166 and above.

II. Medium intensity index: 150-165.

III. Low intensity index: 135-149.

By using the above criteria, districts of Uttarakhand according to the intensity of cropping has been classified from 1981 to 1999 and presented in Table 24.9. It is found that, intensity of cropping has been changed during 1981 to 1991. Uttarakhand's cropping intensity index has been unchanged and remains in medium category during 1981, 1991 and 1999. The districts such as Chamoli (113) and Garhwal (149) which were in low intensity of cropping index in 1981 have gone upto medium intensity of cropping category during the study period 1991 and 1999. Dehradun district which was in medium intensity of cropping category reached to high intensity of cropping category in 1991 and 1999 whereas Tehri Garhwal remained in medium intensity of cropping category during the study period. Districts such as Nainital and Pithoragarh were found to have high intensity of cropping category during the study period 1981, 1991 and 1999. Almora and Uttarkashi districts which were in high intensity of cropping category in 1981 reached to medium intensity of cropping category during 1991 and 1999.

Table 24.9

Districts of Uttarakhand according to the Intensity of Cropping (IC) Index: 1981-1999

Intensity/Index	*Districts according to Cropping Intensity*		
	1980-81	*1990-91*	*1998-99*
Uttarakhand	162	164	161
High (166 & above)	Almora (166) Nainital (168) Pithoragarh (175) Uttarkashi (215)	Nainital (166) Dehradun (171) Pithoragarh (179)	Udham Singh Nagar*(171) Champawat*(172) Bageshwar*(181) Nainital (182) Pithoragarh(182)
Medium (150-165)	Dehradun (157) Tehri Garhwal (164)	Garhwal (151) Uttarkashi (156) Chamoli (156) Tehri Garhwal (165) Almora (165)	Chamoli (152) Uttarkashi(153) Garhwal (153) Dehradun (153) Almora(160) Rudraprayag*(161) Tehri Garhwal (162)
Low (Less than 150)	Chamoli (113) Garhwal (149)		Haridwar*(144)

Note: * Newly created district, 2000.

Source: Calculated from *Uttarakhand Update: A Statistical Profile for Development Planning*, 1999.

Relationship between the Growth of Population and Cropping Intensity

The bivariate relationship between the growth of population and cropping intensity in the districts of Uttarakhand from 1981 to 2001 is presented in Table 24.10. One would expect a positive association between cropping intensity and growth of population. The bivariate distribution showed a close association between the growth of population and cropping intensity during the study period. However, there are inter-district variations in relationships between these variables. In the decade 1971-1981, only Nainital district recorded both high growth of population and cropping intensity, while two districts namely Chamoli and Garhwal had low cropping intensity and population growth. Uttarkashi and Dehradun districts had high growth rates of population and low rates of cropping intensity. In contrast, Tehri Garhwal, Pithoragarh and Almora districts had low growth rates of population and high cropping intensity. An inconsistent relationship between the growth rate of population and cropping intensity was observed in most of the districts of the state. An almost similar pattern was observed during 1981-1991 except Dehradun district which was having high cropping intensity during 1981-1991 as it was low during 1971-1981. During 1991-2001, two districts namely Nainital and Udham Singh Nagar were having both high growth rates of population and cropping intensity. Three districts namely Chamoli, Garhwal and Almora were having both low growth rate of population and cropping intensity. The high growth rates of population and low cropping intensity is found in Uttarkashi, Dehradun and Haridwar districts. In contrast, the low growth rate of population and high cropping intensity was observed in 4 districts out of 13 districts namely Tehri Garhwal, Pithoragarh, Champawat and Bageshwar.

Table 24.10

Bivariate Relationship between Decadal Population Growth Rate and Cropping Intensity in the Districts of Uttarakhand: 1981-2001

State/Districts	*Districts during Years*		
	1971-1981	*1981-1991*	*1991-2001**
Uttarkashi	HL	HL	HL
Chamoli	LL	LL	LL
Rudraprayag*	L**	L**	LS
Tehri Garhwal	LH	LH	LH
Dehradun	HL	HH	HL
Garhwal	LL	LL	LL
Pithoragarh	LH	LH	LH
Champawat*	L**	H**	LH
Almora	LH	LH	LL
Bageshwar*	L**	L**	LH
Nainital	HH	HH	HH
Udham Singh Nagar*	H**	H**	HH
Haridwar*	H**	H**	HL

Note: S = Similar state and district growth rate.
HH = High growth of population and high cropping intensity.
HL = High growth of population and low cropping intensity.
LH = Low growth of population and high cropping intensity.
LL = Low growth of population and low cropping intensity.
*: Newly created district, 2000.
**: Data is not available.
The average state figures of the corresponding variables are considered here as the crossing point of H and L cropped area.

Source: Calculated from Census, *Uttarakhand Update: A Statistical Profile for Development Planning*, 1999, *Land Use Statistics at a Glance* 2001-02–2002-03.

Summary and Conclusions

The population of Uttarakhand increased nearly double and very wide inter-district variation in population growth was observed during 1981 to 2001. The land utilisation pattern shows inter-district variations in land use pattern in Uttarakhand. The net sown area increased and forest land declined but it varies from district to district during the study period. The percentage of land not available for cultivation, other uncultivated land excluding fallow land and fallow land increased during the study period. The percentage of fallow land increased in seven districts during 1981 to 1999. The per capita land, gross cropped area per cultivator and agricultural labour increased in the state from 1981 to 1999. The net irrigated area to net cultivated area increased from 29 per cent in 1981 to 43 per cent in 1999 and the gross irrigated area to gross cropped area increased from 28 per cent in 1981 to 34 per cent in 1991. The cropping intensity index has been unchanged and remains in medium category throughout the study period in Uttarakhand. An inconsistent relationship between the growth rate of population and cropping intensity was observed in most of the districts of the state. The increase in total cropped area lagged far behind the population growth in half of the districts in the state during 1991-2001. There is a close association between the growth of population and cropping intensity in Nainital and Udham Singh Nagar districts. To conclude, the population in the state has been doubled but the state could not efficiently intensify and extensify land use to satisfy the needs of population and to obtain maximum economic returns. Therefore, more efforts are required for intensification and extensification of land use for satisfying the needs of growing population and to cater the future need of the state.

References

Director of Census Operations (2001). "Census of India, Uttaranchal", *Provisional Population Totals*, Paper-1 of 2001, Lucknow.

Directorate of Economics and Statistics (2005). "Land use statistics at a glance", Ministry of Agriculture, Department of Agriculture and Cooperation, New Delhi.

Joshi, A., P.S. Garia and I. Hasnain (1999). *Uttarakhand Update: A Statistical Profile for Development Planning*. New Delhi: Kanishka Publishers & Distributors.

Preston, Samuel (1993). "Summary", in C.L. Jolly and B.B. Torrey (eds.), *Population and Land Use in Developing Countries.* Washington: National Academy Press, pp. 9-10.

Stamp, L.D. (1948). *The Land of Britain and How it is Used*. London: Longman.

Wolman, M.G. (1993). "Population, land use and environment: A long history", in C.L. Jolly and B.B. Torrey (eds.), *Population and Land Use in Developing Countries.* Washington: National Academy Press. pp. 17-22.

25 Tribes of Uttarakhand

A Comparative Study

Ravendra K. Sharma, D.C. Jain
and Manju Rani

Introduction

The United Nations declared 1993 as the international year of the indigenous people, that is, the aborigines as the original inhabitants of the land. With this, the year 1993 became the landmark in the struggle for human rights by indigenous people all over the world (Patil, 1999). According to Goodland, a tribe is a group comprising families, alone, or generations, having its own customs, occupying a specific geographical territory, and being independent of, or having little contact with the dominant national society of the country in which they live (Goodland, 1982). The tribes are the most underprivileged section of our society, which have been subjected to economic exploitation and social discrimination for ages. The age-old exploitation and repression of the tribals have cut them from the mainstream of the socio-economic development. This sorry state has been largely responsible for their abject poverty, illiteracy and overall backwardness. Due to geographical isolation, they have been alienated from the rest of the community as a result of which they have been forced to lead a life of economic and social subjugation. The Constitution of India, in its Articles 14(4), 46, 244(i) and 339 promises special care for the educational and economic interest of the scheduled tribes and protection from social injustice and economic exploitation, special provisions meant for the administration and control of scheduled areas and tribal terrains (Verghese, 1983). Based on these constitutional provisions, specific policy enunciations for tribal development have been incorporated in the strategy of economic development in our Five Year Plans (Maurya, 1975).

Eradication of poverty and raising the standard of living of weaker sections (scheduled castes and schedules tribes) have been the most important objectives of the country's economic planning. In the initial years of planning, it was presumed that economic growth by itself, would ensure that benefits reach the poorer sections of the population which is commonly known as the 'trickling down' or percolation theory. However, this could not actually happen and planners realised that unless specific plans/programmes/schemes were formulated in respect of the poorer sections of the society, especially STs, the objective of eradication of poverty through economic planning would not be achieved (Government of India, 1994). Different tribal groups are living in different geographical regions and in different degree of economic and social backwardness. They are scattered along the length and breadth of the country, from the Himalayas to the Indian Ocean and from the Arabian Sea to the eastern frontiers. They live generally in inhospitable terrain where productivity of the land is low and their hamlets are found in the interior forest areas along with the hill streams. There are no communication facilities between the different isolated tribal groups, as well as between the tribal and the world at large (Nadu, 1999). Some of these communities, particularly in the north-eastern states are far ahead of the general educational level in the country, but on the other end, there are communities which are still at a pre-literate level (Sharma, 1982).

Areas inhabited by tribal population constitute a major part of the backward areas of the country. It is estimated that predominated tribal areas comprise about 15 per cent of total geographical area of the country (Government of India, 1985). An idea of the enormity of the problems facing scheduled tribes (ST) can be gathered from the demographic profile which indicates that India has the largest tribal population in the world. According to the Census 2001, tribal groups constitute 8.2 per cent (84.3 million) of total population of the country, i.e., one tribal man for every 13 Indians (Census of India, 2001). The tribal population in India is more than the population of France or United Kingdom and is about four times that of Australia (Patil, 1999). Further, the census data also revealed that ST children between the ages of 0-6 years constituted about 20 per cent of total ST population. This means that about one-fifth of their population belongs to most vulnerable and formative age groups. This needs a larger investment in the areas of education, nutrition, health, etc.

This paper discusses the social, economic and demographic aspects of tribes of Uttarakhand state—a totally hilly state in northern India. The variations between different tribes are investigated to study the existing disparity among different tribes of a small state. Most of the statistics discussed in the paper are taken from Census 2001 publications and the terms tribes and scheduled tribes are used as interchangeable throughout the paper.

Uttarakhand: A Profile

The hilly region of Uttar Pradesh state as carved out on 9 November 2000 as the new state of Uttarakhand. The state is heavily forested and extremely hilly in the central Himalayan zone. It is located between latitudes 28°43′N-31°27′N and longitudes 77°34′E-81°02E covering a geographical area of 53,483 km^2 (Government of Uttarakhand, 2009). The Tons river separates the region from Himachal Pradesh in the north-west, while the Kali river separates it from Nepal in the east. Starting from the foothills in the south, the region extends up to the snow-clad peaks of the Himadri, marking the Indo-Tibetan boundary (Rao and Nandy, 2001). The region being situated centrally in the long sweep of the Himalaya forms a transitional zone between the perhumid eastern and the dry to subhumid western Himalaya. The region comprises two administrative units *viz.*, Garhwal (north-west portion) and Kumaon (south-east portion).

Agriculture sector plays an important role in the economy of Uttarakhand in terms of production and supply of off-season vegetables, temperate fruits, forest products and several other resources including manpower resources. Many pilgrimage places *viz.*, Kedarnath, Badrinath, Gangotri and Yamunotri have immense potential for adventure tourism and makes this region a great potential area for tourism-based industry. Uttarakhand with its vast natural resource base, large forest cover and enormous power potential holds the potential of being one of the most prosperous states in the country. The state gross domestic product at current prices was around Rs. 29,7093 million during 2006-07 with a per annum growth rate of 10.4 per cent during 2006-07 (Government of Uttarakhand, 2009). The high level of literacy and existence of large number of good quality educational institutions, research and training institutes and institutes of excellence indicate the abundant availability of quality human resource base (IBEF, 2004).

Scheduled Tribe Population in India

Total Indian population has increased from 439.24 million in 1961 to 1027.02 million in 2001. The ST population has increased from 29.88 million to 84.33 million during the same period. The proportion of ST population to total population has increased from 6.8 per cent in 1961 to 8.2 per cent in year 2001. This reflects that the tribal population over the period has increased at a higher rate as compared to total population (Figure 25.1).

Figure 25.1

Decadal Growth of Tribal Population in India: 1961-2001

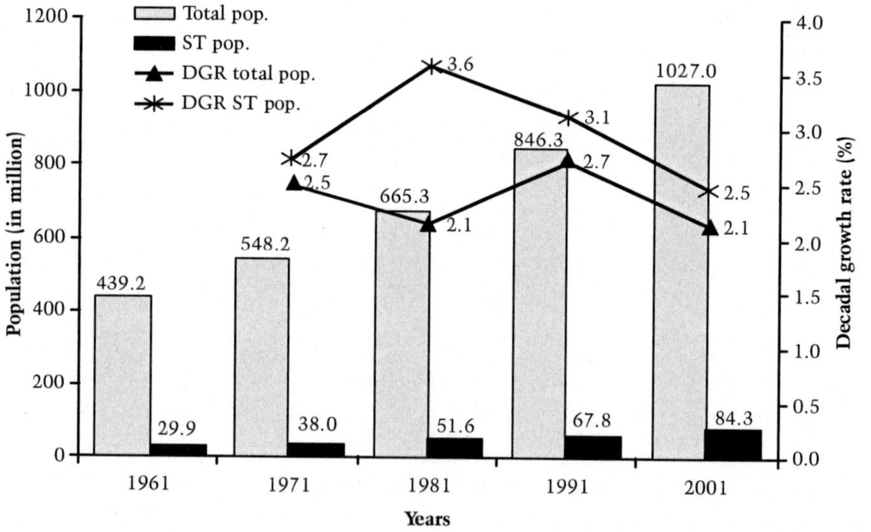

Source: Census of India, 2001; Census of India, 1991.

About one-fourth (24.4 per cent) of total Indian population reside in the eight northern states/union territories. These states comprise about 32 per cent of total Indian SC and 2 per cent of total ST population. There is no specified tribe in states/UTs like Chandigarh, Delhi, Punjab and Haryana. Overall, less than one per cent (0.7 per cent) of 250.74 million inhabitants residing in northern states was classified as tribal population in Census 2001. About 11 per cent, 4 per cent and 3 per cent of total population of Jammu & Kashmir, Himachal Pradesh and Uttarakhand respectively was classified as tribal population in 2001 census (Table 25.1).

Table 25.1

Scheduled Caste and Scheduled Tribe Population in North Indian States: 2001

Indian State/ Union Territory	Total Population	Scheduled Caste Population	Scheduled Caste %	Scheduled Tribe Population	Scheduled Tribe %
India	1,027,015,247	166,635,700	16.2	84,326,240	8.2
Chandigarh	900,914	157,597	17.5	—	—
Delhi	13,782,976	2,343,255	17.0	—	—
Haryana	21,082,989	4,091,110	19.4	—	—
Himachal Pradesh	6,077,248	1,502,170	24.7	2,44,587	4.0
Jammu & Kashmir	10,069,917	770,155	7.6	11,05,979	11.0
Punjab	24,289,296	7,028,723	28.9	—	—
Uttar Pradesh	166,052,859	35,148,377	21.2	1,07,963	0.1
Uttarakhand	8,479,562	1,517,186	17.9	2,56,129	3.0
Northern India	250,735,761	52,558,573	21.0	1,714,658	0.7
% of Indian pop.	24.4	31.5		2.0	

Note: Compiled and computed from Census of India, 2001a.

Scheduled Tribes and their Regional Distribution in Uttarakhand

Uttarakhand state is divided into two geographical administrative regions, *viz.*, Kumaon and Garhwal. As per Census 2001, out of 8.49 million state population, 3.56 million (42 per cent) was recorded in Kumaon region and 4.92 million (58 per cent) in Garhwal region. The overall sex ratio was higher (980) in Kumaon region compared to the Garhwal region (950). One-fourth of state population lives in urban areas. But Garhwal region (27.4 per cent) was relatively more urbanised compared to Kumaon region (23.2 per cent). Nainital (35.3 per cent) and Udham Singh Nagar (32.6 per cent) were the most urbanised districts of Kumaon region, while Dehradun (52.9 per cent) and Haridwar (30.8 per cent) of Garhwal region were more urbanised districts. More than half of the Dehradun district population is living in urban areas, whereas only 1.2 per cent population of Rudraprayag district reside in urban areas (Table 25.2). The decadal growth rate also indicates the regional disparities in the population growth, the population of Nainital district has grown by 33 per cent during 1991-2001, followed by district Udham Singh Nagar (27.8 per cent), Haridwar (26.3 per cent), Dehradun (24.7 per cent) and Uttarkashi (22.7 per cent). Whereas it was far lesser as compared to state average (20.6 per cent) in districts Almora (3.1 per cent) and Garhwal (3.9 per cent). About 37 per cent of total population was classified as workers in 2001 census and the proportion of workers was comparatively higher in Kumaon region (38.5 per cent) than that in Garhwal region (35.8 per cent).

Table 25.2

Regional Distribution of Uttarakhand Population and its Basic Characteristics

Districts	*Total Population*	*Sex Ratio*	*Decadal Growth Rate (%)*	*Urbanisation (%)*	*Total Workers (%)*
Kumaon Region	35,65,383	980	—	23.2	38.5
Almora	6,30,567	1146	3.1	8.6	46.3
Bageshwar	2,49,462	1105	17.6	3.1	47.6
Udham Singh Nagar	12,35,614	902	27.8	32.6	31.7
Nainital	7,62,909	906	32.9	35.3	36.6
Pithoragarh	4,62,289	1031	10.9	12.9	43.0
Champawat	2,24,542	1021	9.2	15.0	40.2
Garhwal Region	49,23,966	950	—	27.4	35.8
Chamoli	3,70,359	1016	13.5	13.7	44.5
Dehradun	12,82,143	887	24.7	52.9	31.2
Garhwal	6,97,078	1106	3.9	12.9	38.7
Haridwar	14,47,187	865	26.3	30.8	29.4
Rudraprayag	2,27,439	1115	13.4	1.2	44.9
Tehri Garhwal	6,04,747	1049	16.2	9.9	43.8
Uttarkashi	2,95,013	941	22.7	7.8	46.1
Uttarakhand	84,89,349	962	20.6	25.7	36.9

Note: Compiled and computed from Census of India, 2001b.

About two-third population (64 per cent) of the state was residing in five districts only, *viz.*, Haridwar (17.0 per cent), Dehradun (15.1 per cent), Udham Singh Nagar (14.6 per cent), Nainital (9.0 per cent) and Garhwal (8.2 per cent). The tribal population was not uniformly distributed within the state and it was more concentrated in few districts. About 9 per cent of Udham Singh Nagar population was classified as scheduled tribes, followed by districts Dehradun (7.8 per cent) and Pithoragarh (4.2 per cent). However, about 82 per cent of total tribal population was residing in Udham Singh Nagar (43 per cent) and Dehradun (39 per cent) districts only (Table 25.3). The proportion of tribal population to total population was even less than one per cent in Almora, Bageshwar, Champawat, Garhwal, Rudraprayag and Tehri Garhwal districts.

Table 25.3

Scheduled Tribe Population and its Distribution in Uttarakhand State: 2001

Districts	*Total Population*	*% of Dist. Pop. in State Pop.*	*Scheduled Tribe Pop.*	*% ST Pop. in Dist. Pop.*	*% Dist. ST Pop. in Total ST Pop.*
Almora	6,30,567	7.4	878	0.1	0.3
Bageshwar	2,49,462	2.9	1,943	0.8	0.8
Chamoli	3,70,359	4.4	10,484	2.8	4.1
Champawat	2,24,542	2.6	740	0.3	0.3
Dehradun	12,82,143	15.1	99,329	7.8	38.8
Garhwal	6,97,078	8.2	1,594	0.2	0.6
Haridwar	14,47,187	17.0	3,139	0.2	1.2
Nainital	7,62,909	9.0	4,961	0.6	1.9
Pithoragarh	4,62,289	5.4	19,279	4.2	7.5
Rudraprayag	2,27,439	2.7	186	0.1	0.1
Tehri Garhwal	6,04,747	7.1	691	0.1	0.3
Udham Singh Nagar	12,35,614	14.6	110,220	8.9	43.0
Uttarkashi	2,95,013	3.5	2,685	0.9	1.0
Uttarakhand	84,89,349	100.0	256,129	3.0	100.0

Note: Computed from Census of India, 2001b.

Five different population groups are notified as scheduled tribes in Uttarakhand state and all of them were enumerated in Census 2001. A brief ethnographical description about these tribes is given in Appendix

A-25.1. Out of these five notified scheduled tribes in Uttarakhand, Buksas and Rajis are classified as primitive tribes. The primitive tribes are the most backward tribes having a declining or stagnant population, low level of literacy, pre-agricultural level of technology and are economically backward. They are the most vulnerable sections among the scheduled tribes and priority is required to be accorded for their protection, checking the declining trend of their population and their development (Government of India, 2007).

Most of the tribal population of the state belongs to Tharu and Jannsari tribal groups and are residing in Udham Singh Nagar and Dehradun districts. The district-wise distribution of tribes shows that Bhotias are the predominant tribal group in Almora, Bageshwar, Chamoli, Pithoragarh, Rudraprayag and Uttarkashi districts. Tharus are predominant in Champawat, Tehri Garhwal and Udham Singh Nagar districts. Similarly Buksa is a leading tribe in the districts of Garhwal, Haridwar and Nainital. The Jannsari is the important tribal group of Dehradun district (Table 25.4).

Table 25.4

Distribution of Important Tribes in Districts of Uttarakhand

Districts	*ST Pop.*	*Major Tribe(s)*
Almora	878	Bhotia (89.9)
Bageshwar	1,943	Bhotia (98.5)
Chamoli	10,484	Bhotia (97.2)
Champawat	740	Tharu (57.7), Bhotia (27.7)
Dehradun	99,329	Jannsari (82.7)
Garhwal	1,594	Buksa (75.4)
Haridwar	3,139	Buksa (92.1)
Nainital	4,961	Buksa (59.4), Bhotia (24.3)
Pithoragarh	19,279	Bhotia (96.7)
Rudraprayag	186	Bhotia (54.3), Tharu (17.0)
Tehri Garhwal	691	Tharu (39.7), Jannsari (31.3)
Udham Singh Nagar	110,220	Tharu (76.7), Buksa (31.3)
Uttarkashi	2,685	Bhotia (66.4), Jannsari (25.5)
Uttarakhand	256,129	Tharu (33.5), Jannsari (32.5)

Note: Compiled and computed from Census of India, 2001b.

Socio-Demographic Characteristics of Tribes of Uttarakhand

Age distributions differ among different communities of any region mainly because of differences in the levels and trends of fertility. A population with persistently high fertility, for instance, has a large proportion of children and a small proportion of aged persons. Age-sex distribution of tribal population—an important demographic indicator is shown in Table 25.5. Age distribution of tribal population in Uttarakhand shows that concentration of population in younger age groups (less than 15 years) was higher among tribes as compared to non-tribal population. Overall about 11 per cent of total population was in 0-4 years age group and relative figures for non-tribal and tribal population was 10.5 per cent and 12.6 per cent respectively. Similarly, the proportion of population in age groups 5-9 and 10-14 was higher among tribal as compared to non-tribal communities. On the other hand, the proportion of elderly population (60+ years) was higher among non-tribal communities (8.0 per cent) in comparison to tribal population (6.3 per cent).

The Tharu (33.4 per cent) and Jannsari (32.5 per cent) are the two most populated tribal groups of the state. Another 18.3 per cent and 14.2 per cent tribal population was classified as Buksa and Bhotia tribe respectively. In Census 2001, only 517 persons were classified as Rajis. Sex ratio among tribes (950 females per 1000 males) of the state was relatively poor as compared to the state's overall sex ratio (962). The sex ratio was favourable to females in Bhotia tribe (1049) and it was much appalling in Raji tribe (833). The child sex ratio (0-6 years) of 955 among tribal population of state was little bit better than the overall tribal sex ratio (950). Though the Raji tribe had the highest proportion (23.8 per cent) of child (0-6 years) population but it has the worst child sex ratio (757). On the other hand, Bhotia tribe who has least child population (12.8 per cent), and highest overall sex ratio (1049), has poor child sex ratio (939). This poor sex ratio in some tribes, particular in small tribes like Raji is a matter of serious concern and the government should interfere immediately with appropriate policy and programme to stop further descend in the sex ratio. Most of the tribal communities reside in rural and hilly terrain, but about 6 per cent of their population was residing in urban areas. Bhotia tribe was the most urbanised tribe of Uttarakhand—one-fourth of the Bhotia population resides in the urban areas. About 9 per cent of Rajis and 4 per cent of Jannsaris were living in urban areas (Table 25.6).

Table 25.5

Age Distribution of Scheduled Tribe and Non-Scheduled Tribe Population in Uttarakhand

	Proportion of Population of		
Age Groups	*Total (%)*	*Non-ST (%)*	*ST (%)*
0-4	10.9	10.5	12.6
5-9	12.6	12.2	14.3
10-14	12.9	12.7	13.6
15-19	11.0	11.0	10.8
20-24	8.7	8.9	8.2
25-29	7.4	7.4	7.2
30-34	6.4	6.5	6.2
35-39	6.2	6.2	6.1
40-44	5.1	5.2	4.8
45-49	4.4	4.5	4.1
50-54	3.6	3.7	3.3
55-59	2.8	2.9	2.5
60+	7.7	8.0	6.3
Age not stated	0.2	0.2	0.1
All ages	100	100.0	100
Total population	922085	731239	190846

Note: Computed from Census of India, 2001b.

Table 25.6

Socio-Demographic Characteristics of Tribes of Uttarakhand

Tribes	*Total Population*	*% ST Pop.*	*Overall Sex Ratio*	*Sex Ratio (0-6 yrs.)*	*% Urban*	*% (0-6 yrs.) Pop.*
Bhotia	3,64,38	14.2	1049	939	25.8	12.8
Buksa	46,771	18.3	928	958	0.8	19.1
Jannsari	83,262	32.5	918	962	3.8	18.1
Raji	517	0.2	833	757	8.9	23.8
Tharu	85,667	33.4	963	958	1.9	15.6
All STs	2,56,129	100.0	950	955	6.2	16.7

Note: Computed from Census of India, 2001a.

Education among Tribes

Uttarakhand has the historical advantage in the education field. The state is known for its good schooling and have many national and international reputed schools, college, universities and research centres. The government has made various efforts through its five year plans to make the education available for all sections of communities. During 2002-03, the state of Uttarakhand was amongst the few states with 100 per cent trained teachers in all the levels of education. A key factor going in Uttarakhand's favour in attracting services and industrial investments is its significantly high level of literacy. The overall rate of literacy in the state jumped up to 72.3 per cent in 2001 from 57.7 per cent in 1991 (IBEF, 2004).

Both male and female literacy rates were higher in the state as compared to the country's average. Overall, about 63.2 per cent scheduled tribe population was literate as compared to 71.9 per cent non-tribal population (Census of India, 2001a). The gap between tribal and non-tribal literacy rates was greater among older age groups, whereas no such differences was observed in children aged 7-14 years (Figure 25.2). According to 2001 Census, about 14.2, 12.2 and 10.4 per cent of non-ST population respectively in age groups 20-29, 30-39 and 40-49 were graduates or above educated as compared to 7.6, 5.4 and 3.0 per cent ST population respectively in these age groups. Overall, 6.6 per cent non-ST population was graduate or higher educated compared to 2.7 per cent tribal population. Unfortunately, this gap remains prevalent even in younger age groups (Figure 25.3).

The overall literacy rates may not provide the whole picture of education status in the state, thus the proportion of population attending schools were computed which shows the recent scenario and trend in education. Figure 25.4 shows the proportion of tribal and non-tribal children aged 6-24 years attending the schools/institutions in year 2001. Almost equal proportion of tribal and non-tribal children aged 6-14 years were attending schools. But about 55 per cent of tribal children aged 15-19 years were attending schools in comparison to 61 per cent non-tribal children.

Figure 25.2

Percentage of Literate Population by Age Group

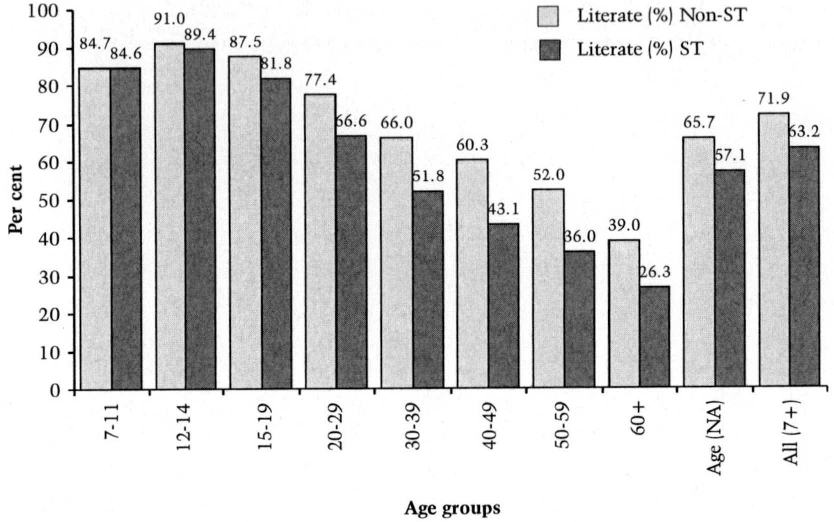

Figure 25.3

Proportion of Graduate and Above Educated Population by Age Groups

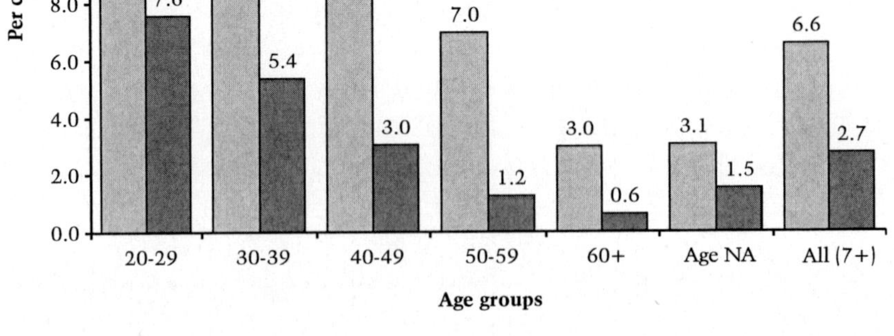

Figure 25.4

Proportion of Children (6-24 Years) Attending School

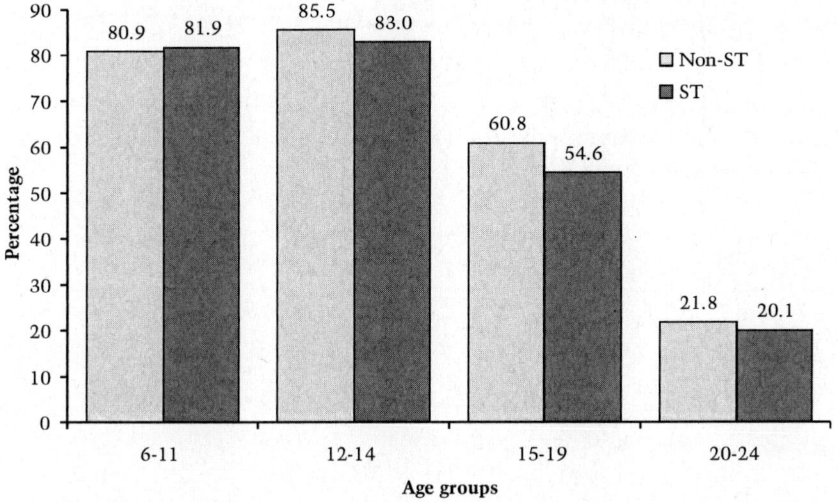

Among scheduled tribes of the state, 63.2 per cent of the tribal population was literate, which was well above the national average of literacy rate for scheduled tribes (47.1 per cent). However, the literacy rates among the scheduled tribes of the state were lower as compared to overall state literacy rates. Nevertheless, male and female literacy rates of 76.0 per cent and 49.4 per cent respectively suggest the existence of wider gender gap within tribal population. The Bhotias with 79.9 per cent literacy rate were well ahead of the other tribes. Literacy rates were relatively lower for Buksa and Raji tribes; Rajis were the most educationally deprived tribe of Uttarakhand (Table 25.7). But the gap between male and female literacy rates was highest among Buksas (33.6 per cent), followed by Tharus (27.3 per cent) and Jannsaris (26.9 per cent) whereas Bhotias have the lowest gender gap in literacy rates (22.4 per cent).

Work Participation Rates among Tribal Population

Uttarakhand is pre-dominantly a rural state with population usually concentrated in the valleys and mountain slopes. Given the terrain of the state and favourable climatic conditions, agriculture continues to be the major source of income for more than three-fourths of the state's population (IBEF, 2004). However, inadequate production in the agricultural fields, increase in population, increasing demand on natural resources and lack of alternative employment opportunities within Uttarakhand together were responsible for out-migration of the menfolk from the villages to cities within the state and outside the state. In the absence of men, customarily the entire burden of managing the household comes on the ladies of the house (USSP, 2006).

Table 25.7

Literacy among Tribes of Uttarakhand

	Literacy (7+ Years)		
Tribes	*Male*	*Female*	*Persons*
Bhotia	91.5	69.1	79.9
Buksa	66.0	32.4	49.9
Jannsari	71.7	44.8	58.9
Raji	47.2	22.5	35.8
Tharu	80.4	53.1	67.0
All STs	76.0	49.4	63.2
Uttarakhand	84.0	60.0	72.0

Note: Computed from Census of India, 2001b.

In 2001 Census, 41.1 per cent of the STs were recorded as workers, which was lower than the 49.1 per cent aggregated national level for STs. Among these 41.1 per cent workers, 30 per cent were main workers and 11.1 per cent were marginal workers. The work participation rate was higher for males in comparison to females. While about half of ST males were counted as workers, only 32 per cent females were recorded as workers. Most of the males worked as main workers, whereas more and more females were reported as marginal workers. Among tribal groups, Bhotia had highest work participation rates and it was lowest for Buksa. Raji had the highest proportion of marginal workers among total workers (Table 25.8).

Among the main workers, about 68 per cent tribal workers were recoded as cultivators. It postulates that more than three-fourth tribal workers (67.9 per cent cultivators + 7.7 per cent agricultural labourers) were engaged in agriculture and most of them were cultivators i.e., had own agriculture land. About 5 per cent workers were engaged in household industries and 19.2 per cent were classified as 'other workers'. This demonstrates that a relatively good number of Uttarakhand's tribal population is engaged in other works, i.e., salaried/ waged jobs. The Jannsaris and Tharus are predominantly cultivators.

Table 25.8

Tribe-wise Workers, Main and Marginal Workers in Uttarakhand: 2001

Tribes	*% Total Workers*			*% Main Workers*			*% Marginal Workers*		
	P	*M*	*F*	*P*	*M*	*F*	*P*	*M*	*F*
Bhotia	43.1	44.9	41.5	30.5	35.9	25.4	12.6	9.0	16.0
Buksa	34.9	51.2	17.2	24.3	40.8	6.6	10.6	10.5	10.7
Jannsari	42.6	50.0	34.6	35.3	45.4	24.2	7.4	4.6	10.4
Raji	41.6	46.1	36.2	16.1	21.6	9.4	25.5	24.5	26.8
Tharu	42.2	51.0	33.1	28.0	43.0	12.4	14.2	7.9	20.6
All STs	41.1	49.9	31.9	30.0	42.3	17.1	11.1	7.5	14.8

Note: Computed from Census of India, 2001b.

Among total main workers, 80.6 per cent Jannsari and 78.5 per cent Tharu workers were recorded as cultivators. The proportion of agricultural labourer was highest (28.3 per cent) among Buksa, followed by Raji (10.8 per cent). Thus, it is important to note that about 30 per cent of Bhotia workers were engaged in primary sector and about 29 per cent and 42 per cent of them were engaged in household industries and other salaried jobs respectively (Table 25.9). This explored the vivid differences in the economic conditions of different tribes in the state. Bhotias have definitely advantages over other tribes of the state.

Table 25.9

Occupational Distribution of Main Workers: 2001

Tribes	*Total Main Workers*	*% Distribution of Main Workers*			
		Cultivators	*Ag. Labourer*	*Household Industries*	*Others*
Bhotia	11,128	28.8	0.7	28.9	41.7
Buksa	11,372	54.1	28.3	1.5	16.1
Jannsari	29,352	80.6	1.8	1.3	16.3
Raji	83	67.5	10.8	0.0	21.7
Tharu	24,005	78.5	8.5	0.8	12.2
All STs	76,961	67.9	7.7	5.2	19.2

Note: Computed from Census of India, 2001b.

Conclusion

The above analyses explored that tribal population are not uniformly distributed in Uttarakhand state; most of the tribal population is concentrated in Udham Singh Nagar and Dehradun districts only. Bhotias are mostly scattered throughout the state, while Rajis and Jannsaris are concentrated in few pockets. As expected, the proportion of younger cohorts is higher among tribal population as compared to that of total state population. However, Bhotias have the lowest proportion of younger population among tribes. Though the overall sex ratio among tribes is low, but it was favourable for females among Bhotias (1049) and was worst among Rajis. Moreover, the Rajis who have 25 per cent of its population in age group 0-6 years have meagre child sex ratio (757). Though there is no major difference in literacy rates between tribal and non-tribal population, but within tribal communities a vast gap exists. Similarly, a considerable gender gap prevails in education among different tribes. Literacy both for males and females was relatively much higher among Bhotias and it was higher even than the overall state average. However, literacy rates were relatively very poor for primitive tribes, i.e., Buksa and Rajis. Buksas have had highest work participation rate (WPR) for males but had least WPR for females. The Jannsaris and Tharus are two major landholding tribes in the state, but Bhotias—another landholding tribe, have had highest participation in non-agricultural sectors. Conclusively, Bhotias are socially, economically and demographically more advantageous among the five different tribal groups of the state. But overall, poor sex ratio among tribal population, especially child sex ratio is a matter of serious concern and needs immediate interventions. Vast differences among tribes in respect to literacy, WPR and occupational distribution show the need of tribe specific development plan strategies, such as establishment of tribe specific development authorities.

References

Census of India (1991). Paper 2 of 1992- *Final Population Totals: Brief Analysis of Primary Census Abstract*. New Delhi: Registrar General and Commissioner of India.

———. (2001a). *Total Population of Uttaranchal*. New Delhi: Registrar General and Commissioner of India.

———. (2001b). *Uttaranchal: Data Highlights: The Scheduled Tribes* (downloaded from *www. censusindia.gov.in*). New Delhi: Registrar General and Commissioner of India.

Crooke, W. (1896). *The Tribes and Castes of the Northern-Western India*. Calcutta: Government Printing Press (Reprinted in 1975, Cosmo Publication, Delhi), Vol. IV.

Das, J.C. (1983). *The Raji of the Himalaya: An Anthropological Study*. Calcutta: Anthropological Survey of India.

Goodland, Robert (1982). *Tribal People and Economic Development*. New York: World Bank.

Government of India (1985). "Tribal development – A statistical profile", *Backward paper* on Tribal Development No. 12. Ministry of Home Affairs, New Delhi.

———. (1994). *Report of National Commission for Scheduled Castes and Scheduled Tribes*. Ministry of Human Resources Development, New Delhi. (downloaded from *http:// education.nic.in/cd50years/g/S/I6/0SI60401.htm*).

———. (2007). *Scheme of Development of Primitive Tribal Groups* (PTGs) (Government Order No. F.No.22040/58/2007-NGO). Ministry of Tribal Welfare, New Delhi. (downloaded from *http://tribal.nic.in/writereaddata/mainlinkFile/File1082.pdf*)

Government of Uttarakhand (2009). *Uttarakhand at a Glance 2008-09*. Directorate of Economics and Statistics, Dehradun. (download from *http://gov.ua.nic.in/uaglance/*)

IBEF (2004). *Indian States—Economy and Business: Uttranchal*. Gurgaon: Indian Brand Equity Foundation (downloaded from *www.ibef.org*)

Kumar, Satinder (2000a). *Encyclopaedia of South-Asian Tribes*, Vol. 1. Delhi: Anmol Publication Pvt. Ltd.

———. (2000b). *Encyclopaedia of South-Asian Tribes*, Vol. 4. Delhi: Anmol Publication Pvt. Ltd.

———. (2000c). *Encyclopaedia of South-Asian Tribes*, Vol. 9. Delhi: Anmol Publication Pvt. Ltd.

———. (2000d). *Encyclopaedia of South-Asian Tribes*, Vol. 10. Delhi: Anmol Publication Pvt. Ltd.

Majumdar, D.N. (1962). *Himalayan Polyandry Structure, Functioning and Culture Change—A Field Study of Jaunsar Bawar*. Calcutta: Asia Publishing House.

Maurya, B.P. (1975). "Development of the tribals", *Co-operative New Digest* XXIV, January.

Mohanty, P.K. (2004a). *Encyclopaedia of Primitive Tribes of India*, Vol. 1. Delhi: Kalpaz Publication.

———. (2004b). *Encyclopaedia of Primitive Tribes of India*, Vol. 2. Delhi: Kalpaz Publication.

Nadu, T.S. (1999). "The Preamble", in T.S. Nadu (ed.), *Strategic Planning for the Future Development of the Tribes in India*. Pondicherry: Centre for Future Studies, Pondicherry University.

Nag, N.G. and B.K. Roy Burman (1974). "A Scheduled tribe in Uttar Pradesh", Part V-B (IV), Vol. 1, *Census of India. 1971*. Delhi: Manager of Publication.

Patil, V.T. (1999). "Foreword", in T.S. Nadu (ed.) *Strategic Planning for the Future Development of the Tribes in India*. Pondicherry: Centre for Future Studies, Pondicherry University.

Rao, K.S. and S.N. Nandy (2001). "Land use pattern and population pressure in Uttaranchal", *ENVIS Bulletin: Himalayan Ecology & Development* 9 (1).

Sharma, B.D. (1982). "Administration for tribal development", *Occasional Paper* on Tribal Development – 20. Government of India, Ministry of Home Affairs, New Delhi.

USSP (2006). *Uttarakhand – State Plan 2007-08. Dehradun: Uttranchal Sabi Ke Liya Shiksha Parishad (USSP)*. Sarva Shiksha Abhiyaan, State Project Office, Dehradun. (downloaded from *www.gov/ua.nic.in/ssaua/*)

Verghese, Alexander V. (1983). "Tribals and sub-plans seminar", in T.S. Nadu (ed.), *Strategic Planning for the Future Development of the Tribes in India*. Pondicherry: Centre for Future Studies, Pondicherry University. February.

Appendix A-25.1

Brief Ethnography of the Tribes of Uttarakhand

1. Buksa/Bhoksa: Buksa tribe is classified as a primitive tribe in Uttarakhand and Uttar Pradesh states. Buksas are also known as Mehre or Mehra in Uttarakhand and Uttar Pradesh states. Buksas are Mongoloid (Mohanty, 2004a). The common surnames are Singh and Chowhan. According to a legend, Buksas came from *dakhin* (Crooke, 1896), while others have specifically stated that they migrated from Delhi (Kumar, 2000a). Nag and Roy Burman (1974) trace the etymology of the word "Bhoksa" to the legend of their conquering the *bhakshi* (cannibals) in the terai; they become Bhoksa—the killers of *bhakshi*. A section of Bhoksa also claims descent from the royal family of Raja Jagatdeo, a famous warrior of Rajasthan. Others believe that their ancestor was Udaijit, a Panwar Rajput. Many of them consider themselves to be Kushvanshi Rajputs (Kumar, 2000a).

They are mainly found in Nainital, Dehradun and Garhwal districts of Uttarakhand and Bijnore district of Uttar Pradesh. They speak Hindi language and use Devanagri script for writing. They are non-vegetarian and they are fond of rice, dal and fish and they use liquor beverages. The Buksas are mainly agriculturists but most of them are marginal farmers. They sow crops like wheat, rice, gram, barely etc. Animal husbandry is their subsidiary occupation which they adopted recently (Mohanty, 2004a; Kumar, 2000a).

The Buksas are divided in many exogamous clans (got) and intra-clan marriage is prohibited. Adult marriage is common and most of the marriages are arranged through negotiation, but marriage by elopement and service are also reported. Junior sororate and junior levirate marriages are allowed. The post-marital residence is patrilocal. Bride price is customary and they are monogamous. Divorce and re-marriages are allowed. Both nuclear and extended families exist in the community. The vermilion mark, toe-rings and a nose stud are symbols of married women (Mohanty, 2004a). They mainly follow the Hindu religion and worship several gods and goddesses as well as their deities like *Bhumiya*, the village and regional deities. They have their traditional community council known as the *biradari panchayat*. This council, however, has been relegated to a secondary position after the introduction of the statutory village council (Mohanty, 2004a).

2. Bhotia: A generic term for several groups of people inhabiting the ranges in the snowy peaks of the Himalayas. They are also known as Shauka, Monpa, Rankas and Rongpa and Rang. Bhotias are popularly believed to have originated from the term *bhot* or more correctly *bod* which means Tibet. Ancient Sanskrit literature referred to the region where they lived as *Bhotantik*, that is, the area touching the border of *bhot*.

Those who reside in Uttarakhand believe that the name *Bhoti* is derived from the word *bhot*, wrongly elucidated area, now inhabited by the community. Historical accounts state that they are the descendants of the Bhil Kirat or the Mon Khmer who entered India from the eastern direction (Kumar, 2000a).

In Uttrakhand, the Bhotias are one of the earliest inhabitants of the Kumaon and Garhwal hill. They speak various dialects of the Bhotia language which belong to the Tibeto-Burman family of languages. They are conversant with Indo-Aryan languages such as Hindi, Nepali, Kumaoni and Garhwali. They use the Devanagari script. Bhotias are a landholding community. They are non-vegetarians and eat meat, their staple food include rice, wheat, pulse, vegetables, fruits and roots. Both men and women smoke tobacco or *beedis* and consume alcoholic beverages. They have traditional occupation of trading and play major role in export of musk, borax, tails of yaks, herbs and hides. Weaving, agriculture and goat rearing are their secondary occupations. Many of them are now in salaried jobs (Kumar, 2000a).

They are divided into eight subgroups on the basis of religion, territory, occupation and dialect. These subgroups are again divided into several clans and lineages. They practice endogamy at territorial level and exogamy at the clan/lineage level. Marriages are mainly arranged through negotiation and they are monogamous. Some of them practice cross-cousin marriage, while sororate and junior levirate are practiced by all. Most of the groups follow the practice of bride price, in term of both cash and kind. The vermilion mark, a necklace and a nose ring (*nath*) made of gold are the marriage symbols among some of the Bhotia subgroups. Most of them profess Hinduism. In 1981, 89.26 per cent of them followed Hindu religion. The Nanda Devi is their main deity along with clan/village deities (Kumar, 2000a).

3. *Jannsari:* The word "Jannsari" is from the region Jaunsar Bawar in Uttar Pradesh. Thus, Jannsari is a blanket term which embraces various groups, namely the people enjoying a high social status like the Brahman and Rajput or Khasa and the lowly placed castes comprising various occupational groups, who share the appellation Kolta. The communities like Kolta and Bajgi represent the non-Aryan stock of the hills (Majumdar, 1962; Kumar 2000b).

They are mainly found in Dehradun district of Uttarakhand and speak in Jannsari which belongs to the Pahari group of Indo-Aryan stock of the hills. They use Devanagari script. They are primarily dependent on agriculture and partially on animal husbandry. The Jannsari manufacture woolen blankets (*pankhi*), woolen rugs (*numda*), snow-shoes (*khurshay*) and such items of wool procured from domestic sheep.

The Jannsari society is primarily divided along caste lines and is stratified. The most important social unit which regulates marriage is lineage. The earlier practice of child marriage is largely replaced by adult marriage. The traditional form of marriage was fraternal polyandry, where brothers used to share one wife, which has declined in favour of monogamy. Cases of polygynandry were also common. The symbol of a married woman is a nose-ring. The systems of bride price as well as dowry are prevalent, dowry being a recent practice in the community. Both joint and nuclear families exist. They are followers of Hinduism; according to 1981 Census, 99.99 per cent of them were Hindu. Their main deity is Mahsu and other deities are Kali, Nag, Parsuram and Kaplaveer. They have a traditional socio-political institution, the *sayanachari*, which is responsible for social control at the village level. There is a higher office of the *sadrsayna*, who perform the task of solving conflicts and disputes unresolved at the village council level (Kumar, 2000b).

4. Raji/Raji: Raji is another primitive tribe of Uttarakhand state. They are also described as Ban Rawat, Ban Raji or Ban Manush, and until recently they were a community of nomadic hunters and gatherers (Kumar, 2000c). They mainly use Singh as their surname (Mohanty, 2004b). They are also found in the contiguous areas of Nepal across the river Kali. They claim themselves as Rajput and trace their descent from the federal royalty of Askot and call them as Raji, meaning royal people (Das, 1983). Crooke (1896) stated that the Raji or Rawat were found in Askot, and in small numbers along the lower Himalayan ranges of Kumaon. He was also of the opinion that they were servants of the King of Katpur, who expelled them from his kingdom.

They are mainly found in Pithoragarh, Almora and Chamoli districts of Uttarakhand. They speak Jangali language, which belong to Tibet-Burman family of languages. They speak Indo-Aryan language, Kumaoni, with others and use Devanagari script. They are non-vegetarian and eat meat, fish and eggs. Their staple food comprises wheat, maize and rice, supplemented with roots and tubers. Smoking tobacco is a common habit among them. Land and forests are the primary economic resources of the Raji, and all families own some amount of land. Most of them are engaged in agriculture, animal husbandry, tailoring and some other occupations. Earlier they were dependent on *dahya* cultivation and the making of vessels out of wood for their livelihood. Their traditional occupation of hunting and gathering is now their secondary occupation (Kumar, 2000c; Mohanty, 2004b).

The Rajis are divided in number of exogamous patrilineages called *rath*. Different ways of acquiring spouses are negotiation, elopement, exchange and intrusion. Monogamy is a norm, however levirate, sororate and cross-cousin marriages are practiced. Divorce and re-marriage are permitted. Post-marital residence is patrilocal. Pendulous nose-ring (*bulaki*) is used by married women as a symbol of marriage (Kumar, 2000c). Men mostly wear loin cloth. Nuclear family predominates, followed by the extended type. The important rites observed are related to the naming of a baby, marriage and death. The Raji religion is a mixture of their traditional faith and local forms of Hinduism. More than 99 per cent are Hindus and their deities are of three types, some are for the entire community, some are of lineage and others of village levels. The traditional council of elders (*sayana panchayat*) is headed by the *pradhan*, and the council helps to resolve their disputes (Mohanty, 2004b).

5. *Tharu:* Tharus live close to the Nepal border and are widely dispersed in the districts of Uttar Pradesh and Uttarakhand. Crooke (1896) has written that Tharus trace their origin to Rajput forefathers, who fled from the great battle described in the epic *Mahabharata*. They derived their name from *thithurna*, meaning 'quake'. While others claim them to be migrants from the Thar desert in Rajasthan, some say that these are descendants of the children that were born out of the liaisons between the Rajput women and their servants who fled the Muslim invades (Kumar, 2000d).

In Uttarakhand, they are mainly found in Udham Singh Nagar and Tehri Garhwal districts. The mother tongue of Tharus belongs to the central group of the Indo-Aryan family of languages. They use Hindi for inter-group communication and use Devanagari script for writing. The Tharus are non-vegetarians and eat pork. Their staple food consists of wheat, rice and pulses. Mustard oil is used as the cooking medium. Some alcoholic drinks are also popular among them. The Tharus are a landholding community with individual proprietorship of land. They did hunting and gathering in the past, but presently they depend on settled cultivation. They made baskets of different sizes and shapes for their use and their women make their own dresses. Agricultural labour, government and private services and animal husbandry are the other means of their livelihood (Kumar, 2000d).

They are divided into three endogamous groups, namely Rana, Katheria and Dangura, which are further subdivided into a number of exogamous lineages. Marriages are generally fixed through negotiation and bride price is paid in cash. Earlier they practiced child marriage, but now they follow adult marriages. Monogamy is the rule but divorce and re-marriage are also permissible. Junior sororate and junior levirate marriages are also permissible among them. Tharu is a patrilocal society. Bangles and toe-rings are the marriage symbols of the marriage. They prefer to live in nuclear families. These people worship the Hindu deities but more often worship Hanuman. They have traditional community council to maintain social control. The head of this council is elected by a voice vote (Kumar, 2000d).

26

Availability and Quality of Drinking Water in Uttarakhand at Habitation and Household Level

U.V. Somayajulu and Tilak Mukherji

Introduction

Human development and population growth exert many and diverse pressures on the quantity as well as quality of water resources and on access to them. Infectious, water-related diseases are a major cause of morbidity and mortality worldwide.

The Millennium Development Goals (MDGs) agreed by the international community in 2000 comprise 8 goals, 18 targets and 48 indicators. Water is interconnected with all the eight MDGs and basic sanitation was added to the list at the 2002 World Summit on Sustainable Development in Johannesburg. Halving by 2015 the proportion of people without sustainable access to safe drinking water and basic sanitation is one of the quantified and time-bound targets defined for the MDGs.

Objectives and Data Sources

The specific objective of this paper is to understand the situation in rural Uttarakhand in terms of:

- Categorisation of habitations in to not covered, partially covered and fully covered at the habitation level.
- Sources of drinking water, quantity as well as quality of drinking water.
- Management and maintenance systems of public assets for drinking water etc., at the household level.

This paper is based on the data from the Random Sample Survey of Habitations, commissioned by the Government of India (2003 and 2006). The survey covered all the Indian states but the present paper is based on the data collected in Uttarakhand. For the sake of comparison, national average is presented besides the state figure. The 2006 survey covered 730 habitations with 21,161 households and 164,684 household survey respondents in Uttarakhand and 16,769 habitations with 31,85,129 households and 1,64,684 household survey respondents across the 26 states. The survey provides information elicited using questionnaires on habitation, household and water supply.

Coverage of Habitations with Rural Water Supply Programmes

Coverage

The coverage of habitations with rural water supply programmes is presented in Table 26.1 for all-India and Uttarakhand state. As per the Random Sample Survey of 2006, one-fifth of the habitations in India and one-tenth in Uttarakhand are either not covered or partially covered. Four-fifth of the habitations in India and most of the habitations in Uttarakhand (91 per cent) are fully covered. Since 2003, the coverage status improved significantly in Uttarakhand.

Table 26.1

Distribution of Habitations by Coverage Status

(Per cent)

	Habitation Survey (HS) 2003		*Reassessment of HS 2003*		*Random Sample Survey 2006*	
	Uttarakhand	*India*	*Uttarakhand*	*India*	*Uttarakhand*	*India*
Not covered	12	17	8	12	6	9
Partially covered	36	26	6	12	3	12
Fully covered	52	57	86	77	91	79
No. of habitations	39142	1598719	39142	1598719	39142	1598719

Reasons for Slippage

The reasons for slippage in status of coverage since 2003 habitation survey can be understood from Table 26.2. Decrease in water table, permanent defunct status of water supply source, and increase in population/number of habitations emerge as the major reasons leading to slippage of habitations in terms of coverage of rural drinking water supply programmes.

Table 26.2

Distribution of Habitations by Reasons for Slippage from HS 2003 to RSS 2006

(Per cent)

Reason	*Uttarakhand*	*India*
Decrease in water table	36	56
Permanently defunct water supply source	16	14
Increase in population	22	10
Increase in no. of habitations	9	6
Contaminated water	0	3
Others	17	11
No. of habitations with slippage	64	6834

Quality Issues

Water Quality at Village Level

Table 26.3 gives the findings on water quality at village level. It is encouraging to note that almost all the villages in Uttarakhand are free from quality-related problems. More than one-tenth of the villages across the country do not have any of the quality-related problems listed.

Water Quality at Habitation Level

Table 26.4 gives the rating of water quality at the habitation level as perceived by the habitation survey respondents. Water quality seems to be not an issue in Uttarakhand as more than three-fourth of the respondents rated it as good while only 6 per cent of the respondents rated it as poor. For the country as a whole, almost one-fifth of the respondents rated the quality of water as poor or very poor.

Table 26.3

Distribution of Villages by Water Quality-related Problems

(Per cent)

	Uttarakhand		*India*	
Problems	*2003*	*2006*	*2003*	*2006*
Arsenic	0	0	0.5	0.6
Fluoride	0	0	2.1	2.0
Salinity	0	0	4.3	4.4
Iron	0	0	8.4	8.1
Nitrate	0	0	0.2	0.2
Others	0.1	0.1	1.0	1.1
No problem	99.9	99.9	83.5	83.6
No. of villages	39142	39142	1598719	1598719

Table 26.4

Distribution of Habitations by Rating of Quality of Water Available at Habitation Level

(Per cent)

Quality	*Uttarakhand*	*India*
Very good	0.8	5.3
Good	77.5	42.7
Average	15.3	32.4
Poor	5.9	15.8
Very poor	0.4	3.9
No. of habitations	730	16769

Perceptions about Taste, Colour and Smell

The household survey respondents were asked about their perceptions in terms of colour, taste and smell of water. In Uttarakhand, majority of the household survey respondents reported the water to be colourless and odourless with good taste. Thus, taste of water seems to be not an issue in Uttarakhand. About one-tenth of the respondents reported about some issues relating to these three aspects such as reddish and muddy, slightly brackish and slightly pungent.

Table 26.5

Distribution of Respondents by Perceptions about Colour, Taste and Odour

(Per cent)

Description	*Uttarakhand*	*India*
Colour		
Colourless	91	86
Reddish	6	9
Muddy	3	4
Taste		
Good	90	83
Slightly brackish	9	15
Brackish	<1	2
Smell		
Odourless	91	87
Slightly pungent	8	12
Pungent	1	1
No. of HH survey respondents	8527	228286

Quantity Issues

Perception about Quantity and Adequacy of Water

Table 26.6 gives the rating of water quantity available at habitation level and adequacy of the same at the household level as perceived by the habitation survey and household survey respondents.

Quantity of water seems to be not a major issue in Uttarakhand, as it is rated as good in about three-fourth of habitations with poor rating in less than one-tenth of the habitations. However, in one-fourth of the habitations, water quantity is rated as average or poor. On the other hand, almost one-fifth of the habitations at the national level got rating of poor or very poor in terms of water quantity.

At the household level, two-third of the respondents reported about adequacy of the water while one third mentioned about inadequacy of the same in Uttarakhand as well as India. Thus, adequacy of water is an issue at the household level in the state of Uttarakhand and the magnitude seems to be same with that of the national level.

Table 26.6

Distribution of Habitations/Respondents by Rating of Quantity of Water and Adequacy

(Per cent)

Description	*Uttarakhand*	*India*
Quantity		
Very good	0.3	6.2
Good	73.6	36.0
Average	18.5	39.1
Poor	7.4	16.2
Very poor	0.3	2.5
No. of habitations	730	16769
Adequacy		
Sufficient	67	66
Insufficient	33	34
No. of HH survey respondents	8527	228286

Scarcity of Water

Intensity of water scarcity by season at the habitation level can be understood from Tablc 26.7. Almost three-fifth of the habitations in Uttarakhand have no scarcity of water at all with the national figure being one-third of the habitations. One-tenth of the habitations have water scarcity throughout the year, while one-fifth reported so in summer. These findings are in line with the findings discussed above and thus indicate the need to address the same.

Table 26.7

Distribution of Habitations by Period of Scarcity of Water

(Per cent)

Period of Scarcity	*Uttarakhand*	*India*
Whole year	12	11
Summer (April-July)	23	34
Winter (August-March)	<1	6
Few months a year	7	15
No scarcity	58	34
No. of habitations	730	16769

Quantity of Water Consumed

Table 26.8 gives the quantity of water consumed the previous day by the households. Quantity of water consumed seems to be low in

Uttarakhand, compared to the country as a whole, as two-third of the households consumed 50-200 litres. Only one-tenth of the households consumed 200+ litres in Uttarakhand, while one-third reported so at the national level.

Table 26.8

Distribution of HHs by Consumption of Water on Previous Day

(Per cent)

Quantity Consumed (litres)	*Uttarakhand*	*India*
<50	22	14
50-100	44	23
101-200	21	29
201-300	10	19
301-500	1	11
500+	2	4
Total no. of HH survey respondents	8527	228467

Source of Water Supply

Source

As Table 26.9 indicates, public standpost with surface water followed by spring source is the major source of drinking water in Uttarakhand. On the other hand, for the country as a whole, the major sources reported include hand pump, dug well, public standpost with surface water and underground water.

Table 26.9

Distribution of Households by Water Supply Source

(Per cent)

Source	*Uttarakhand*	*India*
Hand pump (pvt./govt.)	4.3	35.9
Public standpost (surface water)	55.2	11.4
Public standpost (underground water)	1.0	9.4
Spring sources	34.2	7.7
Dug well	0.7	16.5
Others	4.6	19.1
No. of HHs	8527	228286

Location of Source

Availability of drinking water source within the dwelling/yard/plot is not so common in Uttarakhand as only 4 per cent of the households have this facility. Majority of the households have the source within the habitation, while one-fifth of the households have the source outside the habitation. At the national level, more than one-fourth of the households have the source within dwelling/plot/yard, while three-fifth have the same within the habitation.

One-fourth each of the households with the drinking water source outside the dwelling/plot/yard cover 101-400, 401-700 and 101+metres respectively to reach the source of drinking water in Uttarakhand.

Table 26.10

Distribution of Respondents by Location of Source and Distance from HH

(Per cent)

	Uttarakhand	*India*
Location		
Within dwelling/yard/plot	3.5	27.0
Within habitation	73.0	61.9
Outside habitation	23.5	11.1
No. of HH survey respondents	8527	228286
Distance (metres)		
<100	22	
101-400	27	
410-700	25	
701-1000	9	
1000+	17	
No. of HHs without source in dwelling	8495	

Maintenance of Water Assets

Department/People Responsible

Maintenance of water assets seems to be taken care by the water supply department in majority of the cases, while the role of *panchayat* was reported in about one-fourth of the habitations. Role of user group or community was reported in about one-tenth of the habitations in Uttarakhand.

Table 26.11

Distribution of Habitations by Maintenance of Public Water Assets

(Per cent)

	Uttarakhand	*India*
Water supply dept.	61	42
Gram panchayat	24	38
User group	7	13
Community	5	3
Others	2	5
Total no. of habitations	730	17042

Mobilisation of Resources

As regards mobilisation of resources for maintenance, collection of water charges from users, followed by use of *gram panchayat* fund emerges as the major approach in Uttarakhand.

Table 26.12

Distribution of Habitations by Efforts to Mobilise Resources for Maintenance

	Uttarakhand	*India*
Utilise GP fund	34	55
Water charges from users	58	31
Others	9	14
No. of habitations	270	9375

Concluding Remarks

The analysis indicates several areas that need intervention which are listed below.

Water scarcity is a problem in Uttarakhand as two-fifth (42 per cent) of the habitations face this problem (against the national average of 66 per cent). One-tenth of the habitations face water scarcity throughout the year while two-fifth of the habitations have water scarcity at some or other point of time.

People also raised concerns about adequacy and quality of water available. One-tenth of the respondents mentioned about issues relating to colour, smell and taste of the water, which need to be addressed. Efforts are needed to make quality water available in required quantity across the state as quality-related issues also emerge from the study.

Non-availability of the drinking water source within the habitation was reported by a sizeable proportion of households and this needs attention so as to increase the accessibility.

At the habitation level, more than one-fourth of the habitations are either partially covered or not covered by rural drinking water supply programme. Thus, coverage of habitations with rural drinking water supply programme is an area that needs attention.

Involvement of community and user groups in maintenance of public water assets seems to be very limited and this perhaps can be enhanced as this has its own advantages.

There is also need for in-depth research studies to understand the linkages between quality of water and the health status of people in general and children in particular.

References

Government of India (GoI) (2006). *Random Sample Survey of Habitations—2006*, Ministry of Rural Development, Department of Drinking Water Supply.

———. (2003). *Random Habitation Survey—2003*, Ministry of Rural Development, Department of Drinking Water Supply.

27

Population Ageing in Uttarakhand

Salient Demographic and Spatial Characteristics and Policy Implications

Hemkhothang Lhungdim

Introduction

Uttarakhand became the 27th state of India on November 9, 2000 and according to 2001 Census it has a population of 8.5 million. The state was carved out of Uttar Pradesh to fulfil the aspirations of the people of the 'hilly' region (*paharis*). Till 2006, the state was known as Uttaranchal with 13 districts and the capital at Dehradun, from the original 9 districts of northern Uttar Pradesh. Geographically, the state is divisible into: (1) Garhwal division, consisting of 6 districts, and (2) Kumaon division, with 7 districts. Over the years, Uttarakhand has been a popular religious and tourist destination. By March 2008, Uttarakhand's population has reached 9.5 million, with an annual growth rate of 1.6 per cent. A study of the demographic behaviours of the state indicates interesting pattern of the demographic parameters. For instance, falling fertility, birth rate and mortality levels, lower infant mortality than the more developed neighbouring states, improving life expectancy, intra-migration to more developed districts, uneven population distribution by age, residence, and across the state (RGI/SRS, 2007; IIPS and Macro International, 2007; Census 2001). Besides, although a newly formed state, there is evidence of population ageing being underway in the state. In 2001, the elderly persons (age 60 or more) account for nearly 8 per cent of the total population, and in 9 of the 13 districts the proportion is more than 9 per cent. Another source indicates further increase in older population to 8.8 per cent in Uttarakhand; 9.4 per cent in rural and 7.2 in urban areas (IIPS and Macro International, 2007). The bulging as well as concentration of the elderly population shows an interesting pattern. Three districts already have very high proportion of aged persons (10 per cent or more), comparable to districts in Kerala and Punjab (Census 2001).

Population or demographic ageing refers to the process by which older individuals (age 60 or 65 and over) become a proportionally larger share of the total population. Population ageing has become a global phenomenon, which is effected primarily by falling fertility levels over the years and also by improvement in health or mortality and, to a certain extent by migration. As observed in the developed countries, "Fertility declines and mortality improvements affect not only the proportion of the elderly in the total population at the macro level but also the elderly's way of life at the micro level. As a result of lowered fertility, each elderly person has fewer children on whom he or she can rely for old-age security. Owing to the extension of life expectancy, people may need to increase their savings and modify their retirement plans" (Ogawa, 2001). However, every country's experience of population ageing differ hugely by its pace and characteristics. The global demographic transition model indicates that the developed countries were the first to exhibit fall in mortality and fertility levels in the last two centuries while in most developing countries, the experience has been quite recent. The United Nations has described ageing of population as "...one of the most distinctive demographic events of the twentieth century" (UN, 2002). Essentially, population ageing illustrates the success of human efforts through modern technology to improve health. Today, people in both developed and developing countries live longer and major communicable diseases have been eradicated and compressed in older ages as life improves. In a developed country like Japan, life expectancy for men in 2005 has reached 78.56 years and 85.52 years for women.

Similarly, in India also fertility and mortality indicators show gradual improvement over the years. For instance, fertility rate has come down substantially to 2.7 children per woman in 2006 (IIPS and Macro International, 2007) from 5.4 children in 1970. Health situation has also improved as indicated by life expectancy at birth, which shows an increase from a lowly 41.2 years (1951-1960) to 49 years in 1970 and to 62.5 years by 2000 (Sample Registration Survey, 1998-2002). The life expectation for India is projected to reach 65.63 years for males and

67.22 years for females by 2008 (Sample Registration Survey, 2006-2011). However, within India the effects of improvement in demographic parameters have not been felt equally across the state. States such as Kerala, Punjab, Himachal Pradesh, Tamil Nadu and Maharashtra have shown transition to a higher stage much earlier than other states. These states also experienced the bulging of elderly population (above 6 per cent) in the 1970s, prior to Census 1981. By 2001, the proportion of elderly persons had crossed the 10 per cent mark in Kerala (10.5 per cent) and followed closely by Punjab and Himachal Pradesh (over 9 per cent).

In Uttarakhand, the process of population ageing appears to have started way back in the 1960s. By 2001 most of the districts have very high elderly population (above 9 per cent), with varying differentials. The aged population is found to grow at a much faster rate than the overall population, indicating that the older persons will double their size in 24 years or so. Taking into account the recent demographic scenario in the state, this paper on population ageing in Uttarakhand has three objectives:

- To illustrate the process of ageing in the state through measures such as proportion of 60+, median age, ageing index, dependent ratios such as old age dependency and potential support ratio (PSR),
- To bring out the socio-demographic and spatial characteristics as indicated by the ageing indices, and
- To impress the urgency and need to address ageing and in particular, the welfare of older persons from policy perspective.

Few important reasons necessitate the study or to focus on population ageing in a state like Uttarakhand. As mentioned earlier, Uttarakhand is a very young state (created in 2000) but its demographic behaviours suggest inching towards higher demographic transition stage with falling fertility and mortality and improvement in socio-economic and health aspects as well. As a new state created to fulfil the aspirations of the long neglected 'hilly' population, the state priorities pertain to overall socio-economic developments rather on issues related to population ageing or the aged persons. In terms of absolute size, the elderly persons are yet to make their presence felt or more visible in most of the districts. Despite its smaller size, the elderly population is growing at a faster pace than the overall population. For instance, the population grows at a rate less than 2 per cent but the elderly persons at 3 per cent annually. While the overall population doubles in 43 years or so, the older population will take less time of 24 years to double its size. Besides, since larger parts of the state is rural and lie in the mountainous areas, the issues of ageing become more depressing than actually imagined. Urbanisation is another growing concern in the state, which is often associated with changes in the social structure and familial relationships. Lastly, it may be pointed out that the problems of population ageing affect all age groups and not only confined to the senior citizens. Population growth affects age structure, implying increase in potential dependents or 'economic burden' on the working population. Therefore, as observed in most developing countries, population ageing usually 'takes place before the social and economic conditions that facilitate and secure transfer of wealth towards the elderly have a chance to emerge, develop or consolidate' (Palloni, 2001).

Data and Methods

Along with the various secondary data, the Census reports of 1981, 1991 and 2001 pertaining to Uttar Pradesh and Uttarakhand are the primary data source of the analysis. In some cases, NFHS-3 data is also used and mentioned to highlight the health and demographics of the older persons.

Among the many important measures of ageing, three indices (proportion of 60+ and 80+, median age and dependency ratios) are used to highlight the demographic and economic trends and levels of population ageing. Analysis of the ageing trend is shown from 1981 (at the state level) by taking the original 9 districts in erstwhile Uttar Pradesh. The computed ageing measures/indices are mapped using Geographic Information System (GIS) (Mapinfo) to show the spatial pattern of the different aspects of population ageing in the state.

Comparative Level and Trends of Ageing: Uttarakhand and Selected States

According to 2001 Census, proportion of elderly persons (age 60+) in Uttarakhand is 7.7 per cent, indicating an increase of one per cent point since 1981 (Table 27.1). Comparing with the all-India level and that of Kerala and other neighbouring states, Uttarakhand has about the same proportion of 60+ as in Haryana and the country but much lower than that of Kerala (10.5 per cent), Punjab and Himachal Pradesh (9 per cent). The levels in Uttar Pradesh, Jammu & Kashmir and Rajasthan (7 per cent or less) are lower than that of Uttarakhand. Along with Uttarakhand, Punjab and Himachal Pradesh have a fairly high proportion of 60+ persons.

The one interesting ageing characteristic in Uttarakhand observed when compared to other neighbouring states and also Kerala is that the state recorded a much higher increase as well as the fastest pace of growth of the elderly population. Since 1981, Uttarakhand shows nearly 100 per cent increase with an annual growth rate of 5 per cent (or a lower 2.9 per cent in 1991-2001). Uttarakhand experiences a growth rate of its elderly population higher or faster than even that of Kerala, a state known for ageing with an increase of 75 per cent and less than 4 per cent annual growth rate since 1981. However, the annual rate of growth for 1991-2001 indicates a lower speed than that of the country, Punjab and Rajasthan (Table 27.1).

Table 27.1

Proportion and Growth of Elderly Persons in Uttarakhand and Selected States: 1981-2001

Sl. No.	*State*	*Per cent 60+, 2001*	*Per cent 60+, 1981*	*Per cent Increase 1981–2001*	*Annual Growth Rate (%), 1981-2001*	*Annual Growth Rate (%), 1991-2001*
1	India	7.5	6.5	77.5	3.9	3.01
2	Jammu & Kashmir	6.7	5.8	96.0	4.8	-
3	Himachal Pradesh	9.0	7.5	70.5	3.5	2.65
4	Punjab	9.0	7.8	67.4	3.4	3.21
5	Uttarakhand	7.7	6.8	99.6	5.0	2.9
6	Haryana	7.5	6.3	93.4	4.7	2.23
7	Rajasthan	6.8	6.0	84.5	4.2	3.2
8	Uttar Pradesh	7.0	6.8	60.6	3.0	-
9	Kerala	10.5	7.5	74.7	3.7	2.62

Note: Growth rate/per cent change calculated by author.

Source: Census of India, 1981 and 2001.

Growth and Demographic Characteristics of Elderly Population

In 1981, the elderly persons in Uttarakhand (as in the 9 districts of erstwhile Uttar Pradesh, prior to 2001 Census) account for 6.8 per cent of the total population. They number about 3.2 lakh, with an increase by nearly 100 per cent to 6.5 lakh in 2001 (Table 27.2). The growth of elderly population over the years shows important demographic features. Since 1981, the female elderly persons experience higher growth than males. Female elderly population increases by 116 per cent from 1981 nearly doubling by 2001 or grew by nearly 4 per cent annually between 1991 and 2001. However, the overall growth of 60+ persons shows a lower rate between 1991 and 2001. The male elderly persons are more in number but experience lower growth than the females. Between 1981 and 2001, males show a lower increase of 86 per cent. In the last decade, the males have increased by 26 per cent with a growth rate of 2.3 per cent.

Table 27.2

Levels, Trend and Growth of Elderly Population in Uttarakhand: 1981-2001

State/ Characteristics	*Sex/ Residence*	*Persons 60+, 2001*	*Persons 60+, 1991*	*Persons 60+, 1981*	*Per cent Change and Growth 1991-2001*	*Per cent Change 1981-2001*
Uttarakhand	Persons	654356	488608	327849	33.9 (2.9%)	99.6
Persons	Male	326715	260199	176026	25.6 (2.3%)	85.6
	Female	327641	228409	151823	43.4 (3.6%)	115.8
Residence	Urban	131299	82634	44736	58.9 (4.6%)	193.5
	Rural	523057	405974	283114	28.8 (2.5%)	84.8

Note: Growth rate/per cent change calculated by author.
Source: Census reports.

The elderly population is densely concentrated in the rural areas, amounting to 5.2 lakh (nearly 80 per cent) compared to 1.3 lakh in the urban areas. In the past decade, it grew by 2.5 per cent or increased annually by 29 per cent. Despite larger proportion of elderly persons in the rural areas, the increase and growth is not very substantial when compared to the urban areas. The concern for elderly population is that their growth is faster in the urban areas. As presented in Table 27.2, urban areas show an increase by 194 per cent since 1981 (59 per cent in the last one decade). In the urban areas, the aged population is growing at nearly 5 per cent every year and as seen in 2001, their number has nearly tripled.

As indicated in Table 27.2, clearly one area of concern regarding elderly population in Uttarakhand pertains to increasing female elderly persons and higher growth in the urban areas.

Distribution, Change and Spatial Patterning of Elderly Population

The proportion of elderly persons is not evenly distributed across the 13 districts nor between the two geographical regions in Uttarakhand. The proportion of 60+ ranges from 5.9 per cent in Udham Singh Nagar to 10.5 in Garhwal (Table 27.3). Of the 13 districts, 6 districts have a fairly high level of the elderly population (9 per cent or more) and in 3 districts (namely Haridwar, Nainital and Udham Singh Nagar), their population is comparatively lower (below 7 per cent).

Among the districts, the decadal increase in elderly population (per cent change) is highest in Dehradun district (50 per cent), which also is the state capital and the most urbanised. The increase in the aged population is also fairly high in the districts of Garhwal and Haridwar (28 per cent) and Uttarkashi (26 per cent). Barring the four newly formed districts, four districts show a negative growth in the past one decade; highest in Nainital (-42.5 per cent), followed by Almora (-9 per cent), Chamoli (-1.7) and Pithoragarh (-1.6). Incidentally, the districts showing negative growth are in fact those districts most affected by changes in administrative units or boundaries in 2000 when the state was formed.

The spatial distribution, as illustrated by Figure 27.1, indicates higher concentration of the elderly population in the Garhwal division. Garhwal division, which comprises seven districts, has 59

Table 27.3

Distribution (and Per cent Change) of Elderly Population by District in Uttarakhand: 1991-2001

Sl. No.	State	Per cent 60+	% Change (1991-2001)
1	Almora	10.2	-9.3
2	Bageshwar	9.5	-
3	Chamoli	8.3	-1.7
4	Champawat	7.4	-
5	Dehradun	7.2	49.6
6	Garhwal	10.5	28.1
7	Haridwar	6.5	27.9
8	Nainital	6.6	-42.5
9	Pithoragarh	9.1	-1.6
10	Rudraprayag	9.2	-
11	Tehri Garhwal	8.7	11.9
12	Udham Singh Nagar	5.9	-
13	Uttarkashi	7.2	25.9
	Uttarakhand	7.7	33.9

Figure 27.1

Spatial Distribution of the Elderly Population (Age 60+) in Uttarakhand: 2001

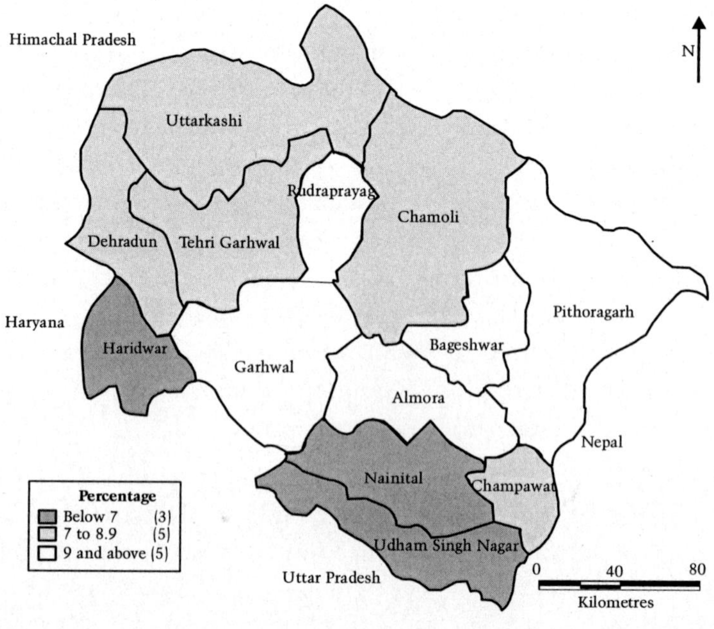

per cent of the elderly population. In the Garhwal division, only one district has less than 7 per cent of the elderly population. In contrast, the Kumaon division has two districts, namely Nainital and Udham Singh Nagar, with aged population less than 7 per cent, but the division has more districts (three districts, namely Almora, Bageshwar and Pithoragarh) with very high proportion of aged persons (9 per cent or more), compared to two in Kumaon division (Pauri/ Garhwal and Rudraprayag).

The figure clearly indicates that in Uttarakhand, the elderly population is concentrated more densely in the mountainous parts of the state in both the divisions.

Ageing of the Older Population: Increasing 80+ ("the Oldest Old")

Another very important feature of ageing population, also observed in Uttarakhand, is the ageing of the ageing population, i.e., the increase in the 'oldest old' (age 80+) over the years. The ageing phenomenon reflected by simultaneous increase of age 80+ in an ageing population is a natural outcome. An ageing population is further associated by "...the progressive demographic ageing of the older population itself. For most nations, regardless of their geographic location or developmental stage, the 80 or over age group is growing faster than any younger segment of the older population" (UN, 2002).

In Uttarakhand, the 'oldest old' constitutes about 0.5 per cent of the population and is growing at the rate of 2.54 per cent. This segment of the population is projected to cross one per cent in the next census of 2011 (RGI, Census 2006), and already constitutes 11 per cent of the elderly population. The oldest old population (age 80+) is more than one per cent of the population in four districts, namely Almora, Bageshwar, Pithoragarh (Kumaon division) and Garhwal (Garhwal division). The oldest elderly persons are concentrated more in the Kumaon division.

Figure 27.2

Spatial Distribution of the 'Oldest Old' Persons (Age 80+) in Uttarakhand: 2001

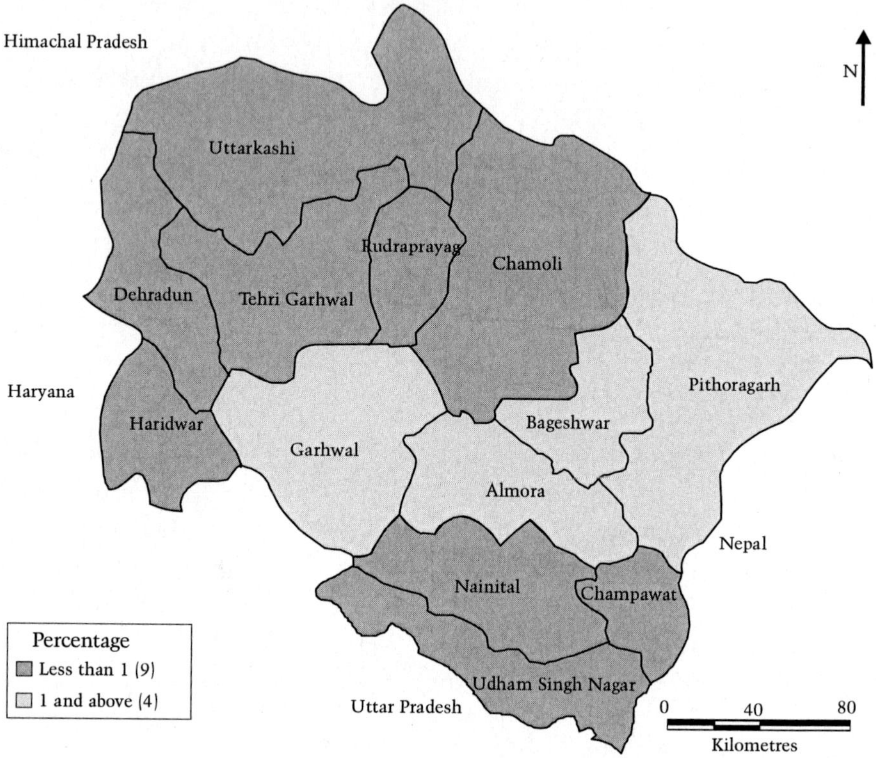

Median Age: Defining Population Ageing

The progress and impact of population ageing is best illustrated by the median age of the population. Median age divides the age distribution of an area into two equal parts: one-half of the population falling below the median value and one-half above the median value. In the case of the country, it is 23 years and 21.5 years in Uttarakhand (in 2001). The median age increases to by nearly one year from 20.7 years in 1991, clearly illustrating the ageing process. The median age also clearly indicates that India and Uttarakhand has a population which is no longer 'young' demographically. Population ageing has made the median age in Uttarakhand to cross 20 years, which indicates a recent transition to a mature population.

As presented in Table 27.4 and Figure 27.3, the median age varies substantially by sex and across the districts and does not always necessarily reflect correlation with high proportion of age 60+ in an area. For instance, the proportion of age 60+ is much lower in Nainital, Haridwar and Udham Singh Nagar (less than 7 per cent) but the median age in Nainital is much higher than some of the districts with higher proportion of age 60+. Overall, the median age is higher for females by over one year (22.1 years) compared to males (20.9 years) in Uttarakhand. Similarly, the median age show higher variation across the districts, ranging from 19.8 years in Udham Singh Nagar to 23.5 years in Dehradun.

Table 27.4

Median Age by Sex across the Districts in Uttarakhand: 2001

Sl.No.	*State/District*	*Persons*		
		Total	*Male*	*Female*
1	Uttarkashi	21.2	21.1	21.4
2	Chamoli	21.5	20.7	22.1
3	Rudraprayag	21.2	19.6	22.6
4	Tehri Garhwal	21.1	20.0	22.0
5	Dehradun	23.5	23.5	23.5
6	Garhwal	22.3	20.5	23.7
7	Pithoragarh	22.5	21.1	23.7
8	Bageshwar	22.1	20.2	23.4
9	Almora	21.6	19.6	23.2
10	Champawat	20.6	19.6	21.5
11	Nainital	22.2	22.1	22.3
12	Udham Singh Nagar	19.8	19.7	19.9
13	Haridwar	20.1	20.0	20.3
14	Uttarakhand	21.5	20.9	22.1

Source: Census 2001.

Figure 27.3

Patterning of Median Age across the Districts in Uttarakhand: 2001

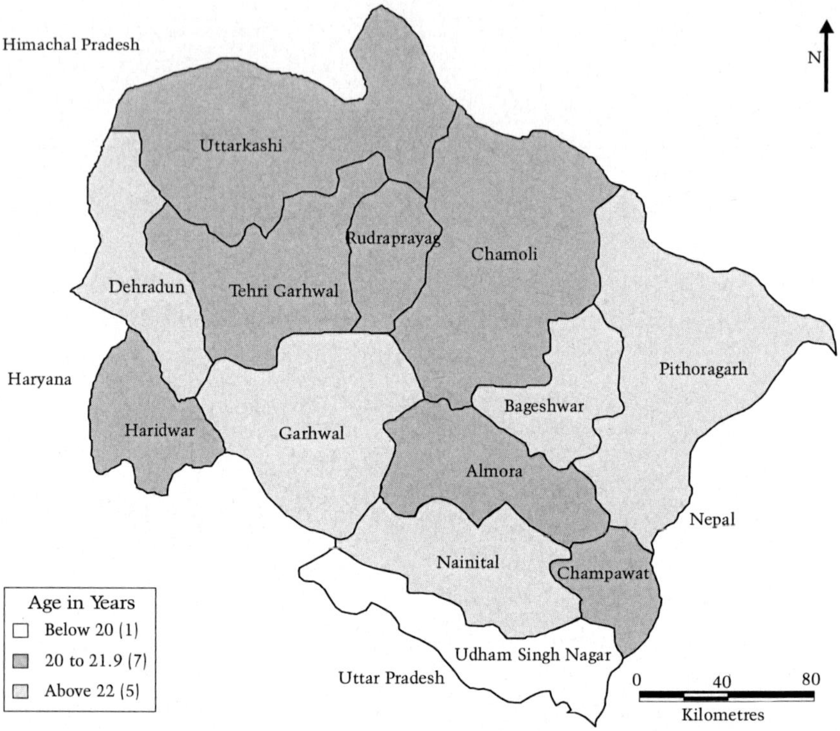

As shown in Table 27.4, in seven districts the median age is between 20-22 years, mostly in the Garhwal division, and in five districts the level is over 22 years, more in the Kumaon division (Figure 27.3). The variation in median age is best illustrated by sex in the state. In the case of males, median age is 20 years or less in six districts and highest in Dehradun with 23.5 years. But for females, it ranges from 19.9 years in Udham Singh Nagar to nearly 24 years in two districts (Garhwal and Pithoragarh). So in nine districts, the median age for females in Uttarakhand is over 22 years.

Differentials in median age in the state become more pronounced and depict interesting pattern when analysed by sex and residence. The rural areas show lower median age (20.7 years) than the urban areas

(23.3 years), a level below the state average (21.5 years). The median age is higher by nearly 3 years in the urban areas than in the rural areas. Among the rural areas, median age is the lowest in Haridwar (18.7 years) and highest in Pithoragarh (22.4 years), which indicates an age gap of 3.7 years between the lowest and highest level in rural areas. In the case of urban areas, the lowest median age is 20.2 years in Udham Singh Nagar and highest with 26.7 years in Rudraprayag district. The difference in the age gap between the highest urban and rural median age is over 4 years. In four districts, namely Rudraprayag, Almora, Dehradun and Tehri Garhwal, the median age in the urban areas is 25 years or over (Table 27.5).

Table 27.5

Median Age by Sex and Residence in Uttarakhand: 2001

State/District	*Persons*	*Rural*			*Urban*		
	Total	*Total*	*Male*	*Female*	*Total*	*Male*	*Female*
Uttarkashi	21.2	21.1	20.8	21.3	23.1	23.4	22.6
Chamoli	21.5	21.0	19.8	22.1	23.6	24.4	22.4
Rudraprayag	21.2	21.1	19.4	22.6	26.7	28.3	22.8
Tehri Garhwal	21.1	20.5	19.1	22.0	24.6	25.5	22.8
Dehradun	23.5	21.7	21.7	21.7	24.9	24.8	25.1
Garhwal	22.3	22.0	19.8	23.7	23.4	23.2	23.7
Pithoragarh	22.5	22.4	20.7	23.7	23.2	22.9	23.7
Bageshwar	22.1	22.0	20.0	23.4	23.7	23.6	23.7
Almora	21.6	21.0	18.9	23.0	25.2	25.1	25.4
Champawat	20.6	20.4	19.2	21.5	21.7	21.7	21.7
Nainital	22.2	21.9	21.9	21.9	22.7	22.5	22.9
Udham Singh Nagar	19.8	19.6	19.5	19.7	20.2	20.2	20.2
Haridwar	20.1	18.7	18.6	18.9	23.1	22.9	23.3
Uttarakhand	21.5	20.7	19.7	21.6	23.3	23.2	23.3

Source: Census 2001; Calculations by author.

The median age is found to reach the highest level and also reflects the widest gap among the areas when considering sex differential by residence. As mentioned earlier, males and rural areas show lower median age compared to the females and urban areas. However, the pattern and fluctuation in median age is most uneven among urban males. The highest median age in Uttarakhand is observed among males in the urban areas of Rudraprayag with 28.3 years; 8 years higher than the lowest median age for males in urban areas in Udham Singh Nagar (20.2 years). In the case of females, the lowest-highest median age gap is 5.2 years among the urban residents; highest with 25.4 years in Almora and lowest with 20.2 in Udham Singh Nagar.

Ageing and Burden of Economic Dependency

One of the important reasons for studying population ageing has been to understand the socio-economic impact, usually measured by 'dependency ratios'. The two widely used indices are the overall dependency ratio (ODR) and old age dependency ratio (OADR). Besides, in recent years one other measure has been widely used to capture the likely support or dependency level in the form of potential support ratio (PSR). The PSR is the inverse of dependency ratio, which indicates the number of working adults (age 15-59) for every elderly person.

In India, estimates related to dependency levels are also provided by the National Sample Survey (NSS). According to NSS (52nd Round, July 1996-June 1996), 53 per cent of elderly persons are fully dependent; higher among women (61 per cent) than men (45 per cent), and in the urban areas (55 per cent) than rural areas (51 per cent). However, based on 2001 Census, for every elderly person in Uttarakhand there are 7.2 working persons or 720 for every 100 aged persons; a decline from 7.8 persons (780/100) in 1991 (Table 27.6). All the districts have experienced fall in PSR for older persons. The PSR is lowest in Garhwal and Almora with 5.3 working persons. The ratio is the highest in Udham Singh Nagar and Nainital with 9.2 and 8.8 working persons per elderly person respectively. Other dependency ratios (TDR, OADR) also indicate increasing burden of dependency in the state.

The decline in PSR values suggest rising burden of dependency in the state on the working population. The elderly females and those living in the urban areas experience larger fall in the support ratio than others (Table 27.7). The urban areas show a fall in support ratio by 13 per cent (from 1170 to 1020 per 100 aged persons) and among females by 11 per cent (from 810 to 720 per 100 female aged persons). The decline in PSR is the least among the males, from 760 in 1991 to 730 per 100 aged persons in 2001.

Table 27.6

Burden of Dependency by District in Uttarakhand: 2001

Sl.No.	*District*	*PSR per 100*	*TDR*	*OADR*	*PSR/100 (1991)*
1	Uttarkashi	770	79.9	12.9	780
2	Chamoli	670	78.8	14.9	790
3	Rudraprayag	600	83.0	16.7	-
4	Tehri Garhwal	630	84.2	16.0	650
5	Dehradun	840	65.0	11.8	980
6	Garhwal	530	80.4	19.0	640
7	Pithoragarh	610	80.0	16.4	680
8	Bageshwar	570	85.1	17.6	-
9	Almora	530	86.9	19.0	620
10	Champawat	720	87.0	13.9	-
11	Nainital	880	71.0	11.3	940
12	Udham Singh Nagar	920	83.8	10.8	-
13	Haridwar	830	84.3	12.1	810
14	Uttarakhand	720	79.1	13.8	780

Note: PSR: Potential support ratio; TDR: Total dependency ratio; OADR: Old age dependency ratio.
Source: Census reports, ratios calculated by author.

Table 27.7

Trend and Differential in Potential Support Ratio (PSR) by Sex and Residence in Uttarakhand: 1981-2001

State/ Characteristics	*Sex/ Residence*	*PSR 2001*	*PSR 1991*	*Per cent Change (1991-2001)*	*PSR 1981*
Uttarakhand	Persons	720	780	-7.70	780
Persons	Male	730	760	-3.95	740
	Female	720	810	-11.11	840
Residence	Urban	1020	1170	-12.82	1180
	Rural	650	700	-7.14	720

Source: Census 2001; ratios and changes calculated by author.

Figure 27.4

Spatial Patterning of Potential Support Ratio (PSR) in Uttarakhand: 2001

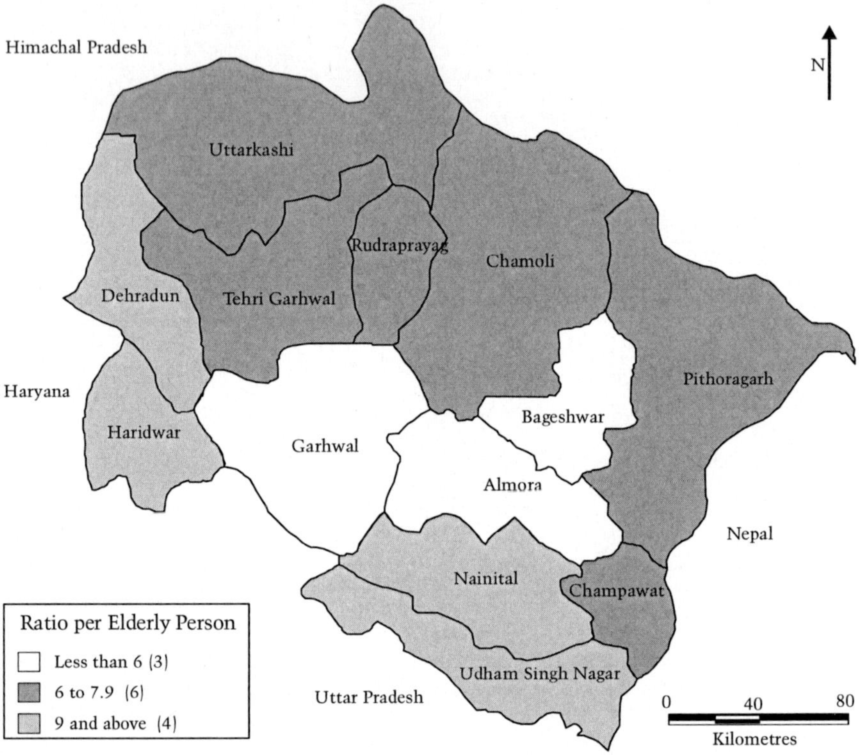

Figure 27.4 presents the spatial patterning of potential support ratio (PSR) in the state, which clearly indicates that barring two districts in the north-west (Haridwar and Dehradun) and two districts in the south-west (Nainital and Udham Singh Nagar), the PSR in the state is eight or less working persons per aged person. The four districts with higher PSR values (9 and above) are also the more developed ones (two in Kumaon division and two in Garhwal division).

Salient Socio-Economic Characteristics of the Elderly Persons

This section describes in brief the socio-demographic and health status of older persons in the state so as to gauge and identify areas of concern. The urgency to address as well as direct policies and implement programmes for the elderly persons hinges on the understanding of their education, marital status, health and work status. Census 2001 indicates that not every household has an elderly person in Uttarakhand. Sixty-eight per cent of the households have no elderly person and only in 23 per cent of the households there is one aged person, and in 6 per cent of the households there are 2 elderly persons (Census 2001).

An indication of the economic well-being of the older persons in the state can be inferred from NFHS-3 data. About one-fifth of the older population of Uttarakhand is within the poor wealth quintile and another one-third in the highest wealth quintile (IIPS and Macro International, 2007).

Education

Majority of elderly persons are not highly educated or with technical skills; only 3 per cent have completed graduation and above and very few have technical diploma. As presented in Table 27.8, the proportion of educated decreases as age increases. About 12 per cent of elderly persons have education up to primary level and another 6 per cent upto middle level. Less than 5 per cent have studied up to 10th standard or secondary level. Over three-fifths (61 per cent) of older persons have no formal education or are illiterate (Census and NFHS-3), accounting for 17 per cent of the illiterates in the state and about 10 per cent have completed 12 years or more of education.

The overall education levels suggest that most of the aged persons in Uttarakhand will not have old age security and need economic support.

Marital Status

Overall 63 per cent of the elderly persons are married, but the proportion of married decreases as age increases. The proportion of married declines to 41 per cent among the 'oldest old' (age 80+). Nearly

Table 27.8

Educational Level of Elderly Persons by Age Group in Uttarakhand: 1981-2001

Age Groups	*Total Population*	*Literate Without Edu. Level*	*Below Primary*	*Primary*	*Middle*	*Matric Secondary*	*Higher Secondary*	*Graduate and Above*	*Technical Diploma*
60-64	229,519	4,662	15,409	30,505	15,544	12,995	6,659	8,283	666
65-69	166,863	3,466	13,297	20,601	10,444	8,579	3,937	5,350	338
70-74	127,320	2,794	12,181	14,363	6,218	5,237	2,105	2,891	184
75-79	60,470	1,337	6,576	7,158	3,085	2,432	922	1,335	65
80+	70,184	1,580	6,743	7,106	2,924	2,218	958	1,277	88
Total	654,356	13,839 (2.1%)	54,206 (8.3%)	79,733 (12.2%)	38,215 (5.8%)	31,461 (4.8%)	14,581 (2.2%)	19,136 (2.9%)	1,341 (0.2%)

Source: Census 2001.

Table 27.9

Marital Status of Elderly Persons by Age Group in Uttarakhand: 2001

Age Groups	*Total Population*	*Never Married*	*Married*	*Widowed*	*Divorced/Separated*
60-64	229,519	3,728	165,654 (72.2%)	59,396 (25.9%)	741
65-69	166,863	3,112	111,414 (66.8%)	51,876 (31.1%)	461
70-74	127,320	2,414	72,420 (56.9%)	52,187 (41.0%)	299
75-79	60,470	1,215	32,582 (55.1%)	26,445 (43.7%)	128
80+	70,184	3,123	28,827 (41.1%)	38,124 (54.3%)	110
Total	654,356	13,592 (2.0%)	410,997 (62.8%)	228,028 (34.9%)	1739 (0.3%)

Source: Census 2001.

one-third of aged persons (35 per cent) are widowed, 2 per cent are never married and 0.3 per cent divorced/separated. The proportion widowed is highest among age 80+ (54 per cent). Clearly, as the proportion of married persons declines over the years, the proportion of widowed increases, which indicates survival of singles without their spouses. Majority of the elderly persons are already living alone and need more specific support and care (Table 27.9).

Work Status

Less than half (43 per cent) of the elderly persons are working, of which 72 per cent (a little over 2 lakh) are main workers. The proportion working is higher in the rural areas (47 per cent) than in urban areas (26 per cent). More male elderly persons are working compared to the females; three times higher. Also, among those working, majority are main workers (69 per cent in rural areas and 90 per cent in urban areas). The number of female elderly workers is very small in the urban areas (less than 3000 persons compared to over 49,000 males).

Table 27.10

Proportion of Workers among Aged Persons by Residence and Sex in Uttarakhand: 2001

State	*TRU (60+)*	*Total Workers*	*Main Workers*	*Males*	*Females*
Uttarakhand	Total (654356)	283,157 (43.3%)	202,629 (71.6%)	151,152	51,477
(Main workers)	Rural (523057)	249,633 (47.7%)	172,473 (69.1%)	123,970	48,503
	Urban (131299)	33,524 (25.5%)	30,156 (89.9%)	27,182	2,974

Note: TRU: Total Rural Urban.
Source: Census 2001.

Health Status

Improvement in health over the years has contributed to a longer life and gradual ageing of the population. Life expectancy at birth in India has crossed 60 years (62.1 years for men and 63.7 years for women; 68.3 years in urban areas). According to the estimates by the RGI

(2006), the life expectation for elderly persons in the age group 60-64 years is 18.6 years and 12.2 years for age 70 and above. Despite increase in life expectancy, the improvement has not translated into complete health for some elderly persons in the state.

According to NFHS-3, about one per cent of the older persons suffer from tuberculosis (TB) in Uttarakhand. The older persons who suffer from TB accounts for 27 per cent of the total persons with TB in the state (IIPS and Macro International, 2007).

Table 27.11(a)

Distribution of Disabled Persons by Age Group among the Elderly Persons in Uttarakhand: 2001

Age Groups	*Population*	*Disabled Persons*		
		Total	*Males*	*Females*
60-69	3,96,382	18,837 (4.8%)	10,053	8,784
70-79	1,87,790	12,784 (6.8%)	6,831	5,953
80-89	70,184	5,172	2,710	2,462
90+	(9.4%)	1,394	629	765
Uttarakhand	654,356	38,187 (5.8%)	20,223 (53%)	17,964 (47%)

Source: Census 2001.

Nearly 6 per cent of elderly persons in Uttarakhand (2001) are reported as disabled (Table 27.11a). The proportion of disabled is highest among the "oldest old" group (over 9 per cent), followed by those in their 70s (7 per cent). More than half of male (53 per cent) and 47 per cent of female elderly persons are disabled. Most elderly persons suffer from problems related to vision and mobility. The aged persons account for 38 per cent of hearing and 23 per cent of vision problems in the state (Table 27.11b). The aged persons are also prone to other problems such as difficulty in movement (17 per cent), speech (9 per cent) and in mental health (7 per cent).

Table 27.11(b)

Types of Disability by Age Group among the Elderly Persons in Uttarakhand: 2001

Age Groups	*In Seeing*	*In Speech*	*In Hearing*	*In Movement*	*Mental Health*
60-69	9,297	891	2,573	5,218	858
70-79	6,627	410	2,211	3,168	368
80-89	2,725	119	938	1,266	124
90+	714	32	295	307	46
Elderly persons account for	22.6%	8.7%	37.6%	17.6	7.0%
Uttarakhand	85,668	16,749	15,990	56,474	19,888

Source: Census 2001; Calculations by author.

Discussion, Conclusions and Policy Implications

Despite being a newly formed state, the population of Uttarakhand has shown evidences of ageing. In 2001, the proportion of age 60 and over is nearly 8 per cent, an increase from 6.8 per cent in 1981. The NFHS-3 has indicated that the older population in the state has reached 9 per cent. The aged population grows faster than the overall population with nearly 3 per cent annually compared to less than 2 per cent for the overall population. The growth rate of the aged persons is even higher than that of Kerala or Punjab. The aged persons increase by nearly 50 per cent compared to 17 per cent for the overall population between 1991 and 2001. In 10 districts, the elderly persons are more than 7 per cent of the district population and 10 or more per cent in two districts, namely Garhwal and Almora. Growth of the aged persons is highest in Dehradun (4 per cent annually).

There is also evidence of 'ageing' of the aged population. Over the years, the 'oldest old' group age 80 and above has been increasing and growing at 2.54 per cent annually. As of 2001, the 80+ persons constitute about 0.5 per cent of the population (11 per cent of the elderly population). By 2011, they will constitute about one per cent of the population. In four districts, namely Garhwal, Almora, Bageshwar and Pithoragarh, their share is already 1 per cent or more.

In terms of growth, ageing is more pronounced in the urban areas (although lesser in absolute number) and among the females. Ageing has increased the median age of the population to 21.5 years from 20.7 years in 1991. Among the districts the median age is highest at 23.5 years in Dehradun, but found to be much higher when considering sex and residence. In four districts, the median age of the urban areas is 25 or more years, reaching 28.3 years among the males in Rudraprayag, followed by 25.5 years among males in Tehri Garhwal. In the case of females also, urban areas depict higher median age with the highest of 25.4 years in Almora and 25.1 years in Dehradun.

Another salient feature of population ageing in Uttarakhand is the gradual increase in the burden of dependency. In terms of potential support ratio (PSR) to aged persons, the number has declined to 7.2 from 7.8 working persons per an elderly person (or 720 per 100). All the districts show decline in the PSR over the years; lowest in Garhwal and Almora with 5.3 per elderly person. The total dependency ratio (TDR) is also high at 79.1 and the old age dependency ratio (OADR) at 14 per 100 working persons.

The ageing scenario also highlights the increasingly inclement socio-demographic impact on the elderly person. As age increases, the number of unmarried/singles or widowed among the older population also increases in the state. More than one-third (35 per cent) of elderly persons are widowed and it increases to 55 per cent among the 'oldest old' group.

Majority of the older population is not well-educated (5 per cent with secondary level and 3 per cent are graduate and above), and most of them are not economically active (43 per cent workers), particularly in the urban areas (only 26 per cent workers). About 6 per cent of aged persons are disabled, of which 53 per cent are males. Their main disabilities are vision and mobility. In the overall population with disability, the aged persons account for 37 per cent of those with hearing problems, 22 per cent of vision problems and 17 per cent of movement problems in the state. As indicated by NFHS-3, the prevalence of TB is also high among aged persons (accounts for 27 per cent of those suffering).

Evidently, population ageing is underway in Uttarakhand and the present demographic and health status of the older population clearly implies urgency in addressing them, keeping in mind the geography and socio-ecology of the state. Policy must address the social, economic, cultural and health aspects of the elderly persons, but more importantly on issues related to social security and health care, including insurance, pension and homes or living arrangements.

References

Alam, M. (2006). *Ageing in India: Socio-economic and Health Dimensions.* New Delhi: Academic Foundation.

Bongaarts, J. and G. Feeney (2002). "How long do we live?", *Population and Development Review* 24: 271-291.

Bose, A. and Mala K. Shankardass (2004). *Growing Old in India: Voices Reveals, Statistics Speak.* Delhi: B.R. Publishing Corporation.

Chakraborti, R. Dhar (2004). *Greying of India: Population Ageing in the Context of Asia.* New Delhi: Sage.

Dhoundiyal, D.C., V.R Dhoundiyal and S.K. Sharma (eds.) (1993). *The Separate Hill State.* Almora: Shri Almora Book Depot.

Gavrilov, L.A. and P. Heuveline (2003). "Aging of population", in P. Demeny and Geoffrey McNicoll (eds.), *The Encyclopedia of Population.* New York: Macmillan Reference.

International Institute for Population Sciences (IIPS) and Macro International (2007). *National Family Health Survey (NFHS-3), 2005-06: India: Volume 1.* Mumbai: IIPS.

Joshi, P.C. (1995). *Uttarakhand: Issues and Challenges.* New Delhi: Har-Anand Publications.

Mari Bhat, P.N. (1992). "Changing demography of elderly in India", *Current Science* 63(8): 440-48.

Mawdsley, E.E. (1996). "The Uttarakhand agitation and the other backward classes", *Economic and Political Weekly* 27(1): 205-210.

———. (1999). "A new Himalayan state in India: Popular perceptions of regionalism, politics, and development", *Mountain Research and Development* 19(2): 101-12.

Mehta, G.S. (1996). *Uttarakhand, Prospects for Development.* New Delhi: Indus Publications.

Mishra, U.S., R.S. Irudaya and P.S. Sarma (1999). *India's Elderly: Burden or Challenge?.* New Delhi: Sage.

Ogawa, N. (2001). "Ageing trends and policy responses in the ESCAP region", Paper prepared for the Fifth Asian and Pacific Population Conference, 11-17 December 2002, Bangkok. Economic and Social Commission for Asia and the Pacific and United Nations Population Fund.

Palloni, A. (2001). "Living arrangements of older persons", *Population Bulletin*, Special Issue, Department of Economic and Social Affairs, Population Division. New York:United Nations.

Preston, S.H., C. Himes and M. Eggers (1989). "Demographic conditions responsible for population aging", *Demography* 26: 691-704.

Radha Devi, D., T.K. Roy, S. Santhosh and A. Asharaf (1999). "Aged in a Changing Society: A Case Study of Kerala", *Research Report* No. 24-2000. Mumbai: IIPS.

Rawat, A.S. (1989). *History of Garhwal 1358-1947: An Erstwhile Kingdom in the Himalayas.* New Delhi: Indus Publishing Company.

Registrar General of India (2006). *Population Project for India and States 2001-2026*, Report of the Technical Group on Population Projections, National Commission on Population, New Delhi.

———. (2007). *SRS Bulletin, Sample Registration System* 42(1). New Delhi: RGI.

Riley, J.C. (2001). *Rising Life Expectancy: A Global History.* New York: Cambridge University Press.

United Nations (1992). *Economic and Social Aspects of Population Ageing in Kerala, India.* Department of Economic and Social Affairs. New York: UN.

———. (2002). *World Population Ageing 1950-2050.* Department of Economic and Social Affairs. New York: UN.